W9-ALN-379

Disaggregating International Regimes

Earth System Governance: A Core Research Project of the International Human Dimensions Programme on Global Environmental Change
Frank Biermann and Oran R. Young, series editors

Oran R. Young, *Institutional Dynamics: Emergent Patterns in International Environmental Governance*

Frank Biermann and Philipp Pattberg, eds., *Global Environmental Governance Reconsidered*

Olav Schram Stokke, *Disaggregating International Regimes: A New Approach to Evaluation and Comparison*

Disaggregating International Regimes

A New Approach to Evaluation and Comparison

Olav Schram Stokke

The MIT Press
Cambridge, Massachusetts
London, England

© 2012 Massachusetts Institute of Technology

All rights reserved. No part of this book may be reproduced in any form by any electronic or mechanical means (including photocopying, recording, or information storage and retrieval) without permission in writing from the publisher.

MIT Press books may be purchased at special quantity discounts for business or sales promotional use. For information, please email special_sales@mitpress.mit.edu or write to Special Sales Department, The MIT Press, 55 Hayward Street, Cambridge, MA 02142.

This book was set in Sabon by Toppan Best-set Premedia Limited, Hong Kong. Printed on recycled paper and bound in the United States of America.

Library of Congress Cataloging-in-Publication Data

Stokke, Olav Schram, 1961–
Disaggregating international regimes : a new approach to evaluation and comparison / Olav Schram Stokke.
    p.   cm.—(Earth system governance: a core research project of the international human dimensions programme on global environmental change)
Includes bibliographical references and index.
ISBN 978-0-262-01801-2 (hc : alk. paper)—ISBN 978-0-262-51784-3 (pbk. : alk. paper)
1. Fishery law and legislation. 2. Fishery law and legislation—Barents Sea. 3. Economic zones (law of the sea)—Barents Sea. 4. Barents Sea I. Title.
K3895.S76   2012
343.07'692—dc23
2012004937

10 9 8 7 6 5 4 3 2 1

Contents

Series Foreword

Humans now influence all biological and physical systems of the planet. Almost no species, no land area, and no part of the oceans has remained unaffected by the expansion of the human species. Recent scientific findings suggest that the entire earth system now operates outside the normal state exhibited over the past 500,000 years. Yet at the same time, it is apparent that the institutions, organizations, and mechanisms by which humans govern their relationship with the natural environment and global biogeochemical systems are utterly insufficient—and poorly understood. More fundamental and applied research is needed.

Yet such research is no easy undertaking. It must span the entire globe because only integrated global solutions can ensure a sustainable coevolution of natural and socioeconomic systems. But it must also draw on local experiences and insights. Research on earth system governance must be about places in all their diversity, yet seek to integrate place-based research within a global understanding of the myriad human interactions with the earth system. Eventually, the task is to develop integrated systems of governance, from the local to the global level, that ensure the sustainable development of the coupled socioecological system that the Earth has become.

The series Earth System Governance is designed to address this research challenge. Books in this series will pursue this challenge from a variety of disciplinary perspectives, at different levels of governance, and with a plurality of methods. Yet all will further one common aim: analyzing current systems of earth system governance with a view to increased understanding and possible improvements and reform. Books in this series will be of interest to the academic community but will also inform practitioners and at times contribute to policy debates.

This series is related to the long-term international research effort, the Earth System Governance Project, a core project of the International Human Dimensions Programme on Global Environmental Change.

Frank Biermann, *Vrije Universiteit Amsterdam*
Oran R. Young, *University of California, Santa Barbara*
Earth System Governance Series Editors

Preface

This book on international regime effectiveness has been written with a wide audience in mind—scholars, students, and practitioners interested in environmental governance, the management of living resources, or cooperative problem solving in strategically contested regions.

Those seeking to understand environmental governance will find new tools for evaluating the performance of international institutions—notably, a disaggregate approach to effectiveness that makes cross-comparison possible by breaking down the problem addressed by the regime and the relevant empirical evidence to make the analytical operations tractable yet broadly applicable. A technique for formalized comparative analysis based on set theory helps bring out contingent relationships—how the effects of regime features or regime-based activities often depend on factors beyond the reach of regime participants. Readers interested in the international management of marine living resources will learn how the Barents Sea fisheries regime has dealt with challenges that are highly topical worldwide, such as transshipment at sea and extensive illegal, unreported, or unregulated fishing, in part by mobilizing other, broader regimes that are better placed to implement the relevant port-state control measures. Readers interested in international cooperation in conflict-ridden regions will see how members of competing military alliances—Norway, the Soviet Union and later Russia, and a range of EU states—have succeeded in building and adapting an international institution that has helped insulate collaborative management practices from fluctuations in broader interstate relations.

Those who deserve warm thanks for their help during the preparation of the study are indeed many. First of all, my wife, Helene Aarseth, and our children, Jakob and Line—not for spending late nights and early mornings intensely debating the drivers and impediments of institutional effectiveness (we didn't) or for lovingly accepting utter neglect on my part of the delights and responsibilities of family life while working on this study (little neglect, and acceptance unlikely), but for everything else.

Next in line are the two people who have had the greatest influence on my thinking on international institutions and how these can help states deal with difficult challenges, Arild Underdal and Oran Young. Their candid criticism, firm encouragement, and keen eye for the larger picture have been important for this work, as always. Both have for many years been central to a transnational network of scholars that has been important for this study, also through the Institutional Dimensions of Global Environmental Change (1998–2007) project under the International Human Dimensions Programme on Global Environmental Change, as well as its successor, the Earth System Governance project (2009–). Of the team of experts surrounding this study, four others also stand out for carefully reading and commenting on every part of it: Steinar Andresen, a veteran in the study of international regime effectiveness, who shared extensive insights in his usual, amiable way; Alf Håkon Hoel, who combines a deep understanding of the politics of the Barents Sea fisheries with sophisticated institutional argument; Jon Hovi, who highlighted ways of trimming the argument to illuminate my general propositions more sharply; and Helge Hveem, who helpfully pointed out how to make the argument richer by drawing on a broader range of general propositions. Clay Morgan of the MIT Press involved three exceptionally insightful and constructive anonymous reviewers, whose attention to the work greatly influenced its structure and the clarity of the argument. As with the persons mentioned below, none of these should be assumed to agree with any of the decisions I myself have made.

Warm thanks are due to the following for reading and commenting so constructively on individual chapters: Regine Andersen, Thomas Bernauer, Bjarte Bogstad, Anatoly Filin, Lars Gulbrandsen, Peter Gullestad, Bjørn Hersoug, Geir Hønneland, Anne-Kristin Jørgensen, Arild Moe, Charles Ragin, Kristin Rosendal, Peter Johan Schei, Jon Birger Skjærseth, Davor Vidas, and Jørgen Wettestad. As always, I have received excellent administrative assistance from the core team comprising Rigmor Hiorth, who maintains order where chaos would otherwise rule; Susan Høivik, who has improved not only the language but also the reasoning; Ola Just Haugbo, who has met all computer challenges with calm effectiveness and also drew several of the figures; Kari Lorentzen, for locating and quickly obtaining whatever documents I needed; Claes Lykke Ragner, who drew the map; and Maryanne Rygg, who carefully formatted my text, tables, and figures.

I am grateful to the Fridtjof Nansen Institute for directly financing part of this work, but most of all for providing a generous, stimulating, and extremely supportive working environment. Part of the study has been financed by the Research Council of Norway through its RAMBU/ Miljø2015 program.

My final thanks go to you, the reader, for your interest in this study: I hope you will enjoy it.

Olav Schram Stokke
Oslo, Spring 2012

List of Abbreviations

ACFM Advisory Committee on Fisheries Management (ICES); in 2008 it merged with other committees to become the Advisory Committee (ACOM)

EC   European Community

EEZ   exclusive economic zone

FAO   (United Nations) Food and Agriculture Organization

FSB   Federal Security Service (Russia)

ICES International Council for the Exploration of the Sea

IDGEC Institutional Dimensions of Global Environmental Change (of the IHDP)

IHDP International Human Dimensions Programme on Global Environmental Change

IMO   International Maritime Organization

IMR   Institute of Marine Research (Norway)

JCF   Joint Commission on Fisheries; when officially referred to in English, its full name is given variably as the Joint Norwegian-Russian Fisheries Commission, the Joint Russian-Norwegian Commission on Fisheries, the Mixed Norwegian-Russian Fisheries Commission, and the Mixed Russian-Norwegian Fisheries Commission (prior to 1992, "Soviet" was used, and not "Russian")

MF   Ministry of Fisheries and Coastal Affairs (Norway); up to 2003 the Ministry of Fisheries

NEAFC North-East Atlantic Fisheries Commission

OAG   Office of the Auditor General (Norway)

PCME Permanent Committee for Management and Enforcement (under the JFC)

PINRO (Knipovich) Polar Marine Research Institute of Marine Fisheries and Oceanography (Murmansk, Russia)

SN   Statistics Norway
ST   Stortinget (the Storting, or Norwegian Parliament)
St.f.   Stortingsforhandlinger (deliberations in the Storting, Norway)
St.meld.   Stortingsmelding (report to the Storting, or white paper, Norway)
TAC   total allowable catch (of a species)
VNIRO   Russian Federal Research Institute of Fishery and Oceanography (Moscow)
WTO   World Trade Organization

1

Introduction: A Disaggregate Approach

Do international regimes actually work? How can we measure the effectiveness of a regime, or the difference it makes to the problem it is meant to address? What conditions promote or impede effectiveness? This book develops a new approach to analyzing international regime effectiveness and applies it to the regional regime for managing fisheries in the Barents Sea.[1] The approach is disaggregate in three respects. It decomposes the problem addressed by the regime in a way that applies to all or most international institutions. It splits into three parts the difficult counterfactual analysis of what the outcome would have been had there been no regime. And it decomposes the empirical evidence to maximize the number of observations. This disaggregate approach responds to the need for a bridge between the intensive case study analyses that have dominated empirical studies of regime performance and the increasingly ambitious recent efforts to devise quantitative methods for examining the causal impacts of institutions.

Decomposing the specific problem dealt with by an international regime into its cognitional, regulatory, and behavioral components is a key characteristic of the disaggregate approach. The cognitional component entails building a shared and well-founded understanding of what measures available to regime members will best achieve the social purpose of the regime. When the social purpose is the management of living resources, this means clarifying how various levels of harvesting pressure will affect the state of the stocks and their long-term ability to support employment, yield incomes, and provide food. The regulatory component has to do with translating this shared understanding of means–end relationships into normative commitments. The behavioral problem, finally, is to ensure that those normative commitments shape the performance of target groups. Those components are different enough to invite distinctive causal modeling—the factors influencing success or failure are not necessarily the same—yet general enough to allow comparison with other regimes, which may be beyond the realm of environmental governance.

Disaggregating the problem makes the causal analysis more valid and determinate. The key tasks of evaluating regime effectiveness, such as defining what constitutes full problem solving, measuring actual problem solving, and explaining variation in outcomes, are far more tractable when the phenomenon under study is sharply defined and closely related to concrete and observable regime activities such as research, regulation, and compliance control.

A second main characteristic of the disaggregate approach is to decompose the counterfactual analysis that forms the backbone of all regime-effectiveness research: one must substantiate what the state of affairs would be in a *counterfactual* situation in which the regime did not exist. I decompose this analysis by first building and empirically validating a causal model that accounts well for *actual* variation in problem solving, then go on to examine how the regime affects modeled factor properties, and finally use the results from the causal analysis to narrow the plausible range of counterfactual outcomes. This decomposition of the counterfactual analysis minimizes those aspects of an effectiveness assessment that cannot be firmly linked to observation of actual cases.

The third characteristic of the disaggregate approach is that it decomposes the empirical evidence by segmenting the timeline into distinct phases and, where appropriate, by measuring causal factors and outcome diversity at unit levels that maximize the number of relevant observations. Such a decomposition of the evidence allows the use of a wider range of comparative or statistical techniques to substantiate any causal connections between the international regime and the state of the problem the regime is intended to address.

The transparency and analytical rigor inherent in the disaggregate approach are reinforced by qualitative comparative analysis (QCA), a set theory–based tool that complements statistical techniques and narrative comparison. The QCA tool, here in the fuzzy set version appropriate for multichotomous or continuous variables, is especially relevant for examining complex causal relationships with intermediate numbers of observations, which is often a predicament in empirical research on regime effectiveness. This book shows how this technique can help identify evidence-based paths to success and failure in the various aspects of problem solving, and the joint ability of the different aspects to achieve the social purpose. Such paths, or combinations of causal conditions that reliably deliver either high or low performance, help answer the counterfactual question of what problem solving would be like if the regime did not exist. They also facilitate the formulation of conditional policy implications as to designing international regimes and the substantive focus of work under them.

I apply the disaggregate approach to a specific case, the international regime for managing shared stocks in the Barents Sea, a part of the Northeast Atlantic that stretches from the Svalbard archipelago to Novaya Zemlya. These waters are home to the greatest cod stock in the world, which migrates south and west into neighboring seas. In medieval times, the Hanseatic trading network linked these cod fisheries to a Europe-wide market for dried and salted fish; today the same stock feeds harvesting, processing, and distribution networks around the globe. Norway and Russia are the leading states in this international regime, but also noncoastal states—states not littoral on the Barents Sea—participate: trawlers flying numerous European flags engage in harvesting operations according to regime rules and procedures. This regional regime has experienced dramatic ups and downs in performance but today is acclaimed as one of the most successful of its kind in the world. Important considerations here include the healthy state of the ecosystem, the valuable commercial stocks, and the fact that the regime members have otherwise been involved in competing military-strategic blocs and have disagreed for forty years on how to divide the maritime areas in question. Findings from our analysis here can shed light on more general questions of the design and operation of effective international institutions in earth system governance.

Thus, the disaggregate approach to regime effectiveness developed in this book ensures explicit attention to widely applicable core aspects of international governance, firm empirical leverage on the counterfactual problem, and explanatory precision. This introductory chapter elaborates on the central questions of regime effectiveness and notes where my approach differs from that of other regime scholars. I first relate the notion of international regimes to the broader concept of governance. Then I define effectiveness in terms of its substantive contribution to problem solving and contrast it with usage in other fields of study. The subsequent section elaborates on the cognitional, regulatory, and behavioral aspects of the problem and shows the wide applicability of that trichotomy. Next, I explain in greater detail the disaggregate research design—the operations that serve to substantiate regime effectiveness—and show how this study differs from earlier regime-effectiveness analyses, as well as previous assessments of the Barents Sea fisheries regime. The final section summarizes the chapter and outlines the organization of the book.

International Regimes and Governance

Examining the development and implementation of policy through the lens of regime analysis gives pride of place to states and formal institutions within a specific area, but it can also be sensitive to non-state actors, practice-based norms, and influences from other issue areas. The more general term *governance* derives ultimately from the Greek *kybernetes,* with etymological links to navigation and helmsmen. A typical definition refers to "the various means used to shape society to a desired end."[2] At the international level, however, such hierarchic connotations can be misleading, since a post-Westphalian government with recognized control over its territory enjoys considerable autonomy in regulating conduct within that territory.[3] In principle, governance is horizontal between states and vertical within them, but in practice, the contrast is less sharp. As a result of differences in power among and between states, some international rules do not emerge from horizontal negotiations but are imposed on states (Young 1982, 284; Snidal 1985). Some states, like the members of today's European Union, have accepted very deep intrusions into their regulatory competence. Within states, moreover, governance is not always hierarchical, since many states lack an effective government capable of enforcing rules or willing to do so. Seeking to balance these horizontal and vertical connotations, Oran Young (1994, 15) has defined governance as the "establishment and operation of . . . rules of the game that serve to define practices, assign roles and guide interaction" in order to grapple with collective problems.

A distinctive feature of international governance is that the primary actors responsible for establishing and operating such "rules of the game" are also the ones to be governed—states jealously guarding their sovereignty. *International regimes* is a label applied since the mid-1970s to an important subset of such rules of the game, or governance systems (Ruggie 1975; Young 1980; Krasner 1983; Stokke 1997). This section delineates that phenomenon at a general level and dismisses the view that two key features, issue specificity and state centrism, may unduly constrain our analysis of the specific regime in question.

Regime Definitions, Thick and Thin

The concept of international regimes has been subject to intense debate, and international law provides means for clarifying various different positions and combining their merits. A widely accepted starting point is Stephen Krasner's (1982, 186) definition of regimes as "sets of implicit or explicit principles, norms, rules, and decision-making procedures around which actors' expectations converge in a given area of international relations." In terms of precision, however, this definition leaves much to be desired, especially as regards the blurred boundaries between its first three components. After all, few would argue that substantive principles and rules are not also norms. Krasner's (1982, 186) clarification that "rule" is the most specific of the three runs counter to common usage in international law, where the term primarily denotes bindingness and applies no less to procedural than to substantive injunctions.[4]

In fact, this "consensus definition" is broad enough to permit specification in two widely different directions. One is favored by "thinliners," who warn against making the regime concept too inclusive and give priority to operational clarity.[5] The most prominent thinliner, Robert Keohane, has defined international regimes as "institutions with explicit rules, agreed upon by governments, that pertain to particular sets of issues in international relations" (1989, 4); he sees institutions as "persistent and connected sets of rules (formal and informal) that prescribe behavioral roles, constrain activity, and shape expectations" (1989, 3). Others, by contrast, have argued that this specification ignores the intersubjective and communicative nature of regimes inherent in the consensus definition, especially the part pertaining to the convergence of expectations. Such critics favor a thicker concept that includes state practices, notably those concerning the interpretation of rules, the justification of behavior, and refutation of the same (Kratochwil and Ruggie 1986).[6] Right from the outset, therefore, the regime concept has been used by scholars subscribing to a range of different epistemologies, which in turn has nourished a healthy conceptual and methodological debate (Stokke 1997).

Elaborating on the distinction between thinliners and thickliners, Keohane (1993, 27) has argued that they differ mainly on "whether regimes are to be identified on the basis of *explicit rules and procedures*, or on the basis of *observed behavior*, from which rules, norms, principles, and procedures can be inferred" (italics in original). This formulation downplays the epistemological issues involved in inference from behavior to regime. According to Kratochwil and Ruggie (1986, 766), the inter-subjective nature of international regimes makes an interpretive method-ology inevitable: valid regime analysis must start from how actors give meaning to their behavior. Reporting from a "regimes summit" of direc-tors of several large-scale, multiyear projects on the effects of interna-tional regimes, Young (1991, 2–3) introduced a sliding scale that seeks to reconcile thinliner and thickliner concerns. On this scale, all interna-tional regimes involve explicit norms, whether legally binding or not; some have also achieved prescriptive status, in that actors regularly refer to them when describing or evaluating behavior; and some of these norms even give rise to rule-consistent behavior.

In practice, Young's scale adopts a thin definition of regimes while recognizing that thickness is important. Thus, substantiation of prescrip-tive status is not necessary for pinpointing a regime: figuring saliently in participants' interpretations or deliberations on behavior is a contingent rather than a constitutive feature. With respect to the third step of the scale, broad agreement exists that the ability to shape behavior is not a constitutive feature, but reasons differ tellingly. Thinliners argue from a methodological standpoint: requiring of a regime that it actually shape behavior would severely complicate the operations needed to identify the regime (Keohane 1993, 28). In contrast, thickliners argue from a con-ceptual point of view: noncompliance with a norm does not invalidate it (Kratochwil and Ruggie 1986, 768; see also Hasenclever, Mayer, and Rittberger 1997, 16). Thus, different conceptualizations of international regimes invite different methodologies for describing and analyzing them.

This study takes an intermediate position in the debate between thin-liners and thickliners, a position that leans heavily on international law. The description of regime components starts with the language of inter-national treaties and then branches out to include several other sources. Salient among the unwritten sources for describing international regimes is international customary law, which arises from general state practice that has become accepted as law. Customary rules have an edge over treaty rules in that they may legally bind all states, not only those that have signed or acceded to a given treaty (Wolfke 1993). For instance, a basic feature of the Barents Sea fisheries regime is the spatial extent of coastal state jurisdiction over harvesting, and the corresponding rights and duties of other states, within and outside 200-mile exclusive eco-nomic zones (EEZs). This concept emerged as international customary law several years before the UN Law of the Sea Convention codified it in 1982, and well before that treaty entered into force (see chapter 3).

The multitude of relevant sources when delineating an international regime is highlighted in the Vienna Convention on the Law of Treaties, which states that treaties are to be interpreted with due regard for the context and circumstances of their adoption, other relevant agreements among the parties, as well as subsequent state practice (Articles 31–32). Thus, some important principles in regional resource management regimes are not articulated explicitly in any instrument but have emerged from practice and thereby gained prescriptive status among regime participants. One example of such implicit "rules in use" (Ostrom et al. 1999) is the recurrent practice of allocating quotas of shared stocks according to certain fixed, historically derived division keys (Stokke 2000). Proving that an informal or implicit norm forms part of a regime is certainly more demanding than for explicitly spelled-out norms, but some guideline criteria do exist (Wolfke 1993). What is seen as relevant evidence includes the conjunction of behavioral regularity and participant statements describing, justifying, or denouncing behavior on the basis of the norm.

International law, in short, offers means for delineating international regimes in a manner that heeds thinliner concerns for scholarly discipline and operational clarity while taking seriously the thickliner insight that international norms may also emerge through state practice.

State Centrism and Issue Specificity

Thinliners and thickliners alike place states centrally in the analysis of international regimes and address governance within specific issue areas (Potter 1980). The combination of state centrism and issue specificity distinguishes regime analysis from several other influential strands in the study of international relations, such as neo-functional integration theory and structural realism, but does not unduly constrain this study of international resource management. On the contrary, as Biermann (2008, 282) argues, understanding the processes of issue-specific regimes and their interaction is crucial for the broader study of institutional architecture in earth system governance.

Regime analysis emerged as an offshoot of the literature on interdependence (Ruggie 1975; Keohane and Nye 1977; Young 1980), which in turn was a response to the failure of integration theories to explain the slowdown in European integration during the early 1970s (Keohane and Nye 1975, 365). The concept of interdependence gave greater prominence to the structure of the state system—notably, national interests and relative actor capabilities—while still paying attention to international institutions (Nye 1970; Keohane and Nye 1987, 730). It is this basis in a strand of analysis that highlights patterns of actor interest and power that sets regime analysis apart from those theories of integration that are vague on agency, especially when emphasizing "incrementalism" (Haas 1964), "transaction volumes" (Puchala 1970), or "functional spillover" (Haas 1970). In regime analysis, states are the central actors (Baldwin 1993, 9; Keohane and Martin 2003), although the term "complex inter-dependence" (Keohane and Nye 1977, 25–26) signals that other actors may also be relevant. Most regime analysts have embraced the agency and system assumptions of structural realism (Waltz 1979; see Keohane 1986; Young 1994): states are seen as the key players in world politics, and within broad issue areas they can usefully be modeled as unitary, boundedly rational actors within an international system marked by anarchy, or the absence of centralized authority.

This state centrism also distinguishes regime analysis from contributions by scholars working within the conceptual framework of "global governance" and seeking to capture what many perceive as the rising significance of various non-state actors in the making of behavioral norms (Stokke 1997, 28). Thus, Rosenau (1995, 16–19) and others have argued that authority in a broad sense is in the process of being relocated from the level of state interaction—international governance, the main concern of regime analysts—to arenas where subnational, transnational, and even supranational actors are salient (see Biermann 2008). In the study of EU politics, the concept of "multilevel governance" illustrates this tendency and has gained some popularity as an alternative to the predominant intergovernmental approach (Marks, Hooghe, and Blank 1996).

Another strand of global governance analysis is what Cutler, Haufler, and Porter (1999) term "private governance," or governance centered on institutions in which states play no or only peripheral roles. Some private governance institutions, such as the World Business Council for Sustainable Development, are created by industry associations and encourage various means of self-regulation, including structures for demonstrating and guiding corporate social and environmental responsibility (Stokke and Thommessen 2003, 327–328). Others are partnerships involving a range of stakeholders aligned around certain areas of production, especially environmental certification and labeling arrangements of the type pioneered by the Forest Stewardship Council in the forestry sector. A common characteristic of these various types of private governance is the leading role of civil-society or business organizations in the formulation and monitoring of standards, which tend to be voluntary and dependent on markets to stimulate compliance (Cashore, Auld, and Newsom 2004).

International regime analysis differs from these global governance approaches primarily by maintaining a focus on states as the salient actors in the making and enforcement of norms that shape behavior. Choosing a regime-analysis approach rather than a global governance approach to Barents Sea fisheries management does not constrain this study in ways that would reduce its more general relevance. As yet, private governance has played a far more modest role in world fisheries than in forestry, despite the recent success of the Marine Stewardship Council in attracting applications for certification and label access from fisheries associations in some major fisheries (Gulbrandsen 2009). One reason why private governance has not made as much headway in fisheries as in forestry is the much higher level of governmental involvement in the fisheries sector, which leaves less room for new actors in norm building. The fact that neither of the Barents Sea coastal states is an EU member or delegates jurisdiction over EEZ resources to authorities at lower territorial levels has also served to keep the governance system relatively simple and devoid of supranational actors. Moreover, as the next section explains, a state-centric approach does not preclude careful attention to various target groups and other societal organizations when examining the consequences of international regimes for the challenges that states face in world affairs. The emphasis in regime analysis on states as the salient actors in making and implementing norms seems appropriate for the case at hand, as well as allowing sensitivity to differences in interests and competence among non-state and sub-state actors.

Another distinctive feature of regime analysis is issue specificity. Where theories of integration typically deal with institutions within the context of broader regional processes involving many sectors of the societies in question, regime analysis narrows in on international institutions with clearly delimited functional and spatial boundaries (Krasner 1982). In part, such issue specificity reflects the historical setting in which regime analysis emerged. The building of a European Community, the most prominent case of regional integration in modern times, appeared to lose momentum during the 1970s over disagreement on monetary collaboration, while political controversy mixed with institutional dynamism marked issue-specific institutions in areas such as trade and finance (Spero 1990). At the same time, states were actively negotiating a series of new global and regional regimes in the environmental field, where international rules had been scarce (Haas 2002). In short, issue-specific institutional analysis was in high demand, and policy relevance has always been a priority in regime analysis (Rochester 1986, 803; Keohane, Haas, and Levy 1993, 18). Targeting institutional analysis at the level of specific issues also gives a sharper focus to the analysis, rendering causal assessment more tractable. Policy relevance as well as methodological considerations can justify sustained attention to certain sectors or limited spatial areas.

The flip side of the coin is that issue specificity confirms and reproduces conventional ways of delineating clusters of actors and problems, and therefore may reduce researcher sensitivity to processes that cut across such clusters. Kratochwil (1993, 82) points out that the functional and spatial circumscription of regime rules reflects a political domain consensus that regime analysis should thematize. To illustrate, for many years the operators of international fisheries regimes successfully argued that resource management differs sufficiently from environmental protection as a way of justifying lower levels of transparency and openness to, for instance, environmental organizations than those emerging in international environmental diplomacy. Then the 1992 UN Conference on Environment and Development triggered a process whereby governance principles that had emerged within environmental regimes, such as precaution and transparency, were adopted in global and regional fisheries management regimes as well (Stokke 2000).

During the past decade, such institutional interplay, in which one regime significantly affects the content, operation, or effectiveness of another, has been subjected to systematic conceptual and empirical analysis (see Oberthür and Stokke 2011).[7] Interplay was one of the three analytical themes of the 1998–2007 Institutional Dimensions of Global Environmental Change project of the International Human Dimensions Programme on Global Environmental Change (IHDP) (see Young, King, and Schroeder 2008). With respect to the operation and effectiveness of regimes, many scholars have pointed to the tension between, on the one hand, certain trade-related measures aimed at improving participation in or compliance with international environmental regimes and, on the other hand, global or regional rules of free trade (e.g., Schoenbaum 1997). Several U.S. trade measures intended to discourage foreign bycatch-intensive methods in fisheries for tuna and shrimp, justified in part by international conservation agreements, have been challenged under the World Trade Organization (WTO) or its predecessor (Joyner and Tyler 2000). The fact that no similar complaints have been put forward over trade measures explicitly deriving from provisions under multilateral environmental regimes indicates that states have been able to adapt those measures to the "environmental window" of the global trade regime, thereby reducing the potential for conflict (Stokke 2004b, 2009; Gehring 2011). The recent spate of studies examining the interplay of international regimes shows that taking issue-specific institutions as points of departure can support analyses of broader governance systems (Biermann 2008, 288).

Accordingly, neither state centrism nor issue specificity has prevented regime scholars from studying the roles of civil-society groups or industry organizations in the creation and operation of regime norms and structures, or problems and challenges that cut across issue boundaries. In this study, the domestic institutions and non-state actors examined in chapter 3 influence the causal modeling of regime effectiveness elaborated in chapters 4 to 7. Regime interplay underlies both the emergence of a precautionary approach to fisheries research and regulation and the adoption of trade measures to improve behavioral adherence to the rules of the Barents Sea fisheries regime.

Defining Regime Effectiveness

The concept of effectiveness that predominates in international regime analysis highlights substantive problem solving and differs significantly from usage in some adjacent fields of inquiry. Whereas political science may trace its preoccupation with the consequences of institutional arrangements at least to Plato's *Republic*, the subject arrived relatively late on the agenda of international regime studies.[8] In fact, many scholars have criticized regime analysts for expending too much energy on questions related to regime formation and change while remaining vague on whether those regimes actually make a significant difference in world affairs (see Young 1986, 115; Mearsheimer 1995).

Such criticism was only partly appropriate when it was initially put forward, since even early regime analyses identified ways in which international institutions enable states to coordinate their behavior in mutually beneficial ways (Young 1980; Krasner 1982; Keohane 1984), thus in effect theorizing also to regime consequences. Moreover, beginning in the early 1990s, several large-scale, empirical inquiries have been launched regarding the consequences of international regimes. Causal impact and institutional performance were two of the three research foci of the Institutional Dimensions of Global Environmental Change project (see

Young, King, and Schroeder 2008). They underlie several of the core analytical themes taken up by its successor project on earth system governance, especially that of architecture (Biermann 2008). This section contrasts the concept of effectiveness as applied in regime analysis to its usage in other fields of inquiry.

Problem Solving and Causality

When students of international regimes began to speak of *effectiveness*, they soon converged on the definition offered by Levy, Osherenko, and Young (1991):[9] effective regimes contribute significantly to reducing or solving the issue-specific problem they address. This emphasis on substantive problem solving echoes notions that political scientists have used when evaluating institutions at the national level: Seymour Lipset (1983, 65), for instance, defines such effectiveness as the "extent to which the system satisfies the basic functions of government." The rapid spread of the problem-solving definition of effectiveness is evident in the work reported by Keohane, Haas, and Levy (1993, 7), Bernauer (1995, 364), and Stokke and Vidas (1996a, 17), all of whom cite Levy, Osherenko, and Young (1991). Whereas Arild Underdal (2002a, 11) terms this definition the "common sense notion of effectiveness," it differs from other conceptions in use among many legal scholars, evaluation researchers, and economists.

Defining effectiveness as substantive problem solving avoids the formalism inherent in some legal notions of effectiveness and in early attempts at evaluating international institutions on the basis of formal organization or decisions. One understanding of "effective" in international law is that it applies when a rule has entered into force and is legally binding on states. That meaning differs sharply from the concept that underlies this study. In fact, a significant body of literature examines whether progress in specific international problem solving, or regime effectiveness, is best served by reliance on binding international treaties or by various soft law arrangements, which states can usually negotiate more rapidly and which operate more flexibly (Sand 1991; Abbott and Snidal 2000; Skjærseth, Stokke, and Wettestad 2006).

Also differing from my understanding of regime effectiveness is the concept underlying early evaluations of international regimes, such as those reported by Kay and Jacobson (1983), which focused on such aspects of formal organization as the establishment of committees, the adoption of declarations, and the conduct of research. Case studies reported by Brown Weiss and Jacobson (1998) took this output orientation one step closer to substantive problem solving by also examining how regime commitments "engage states" by encouraging legislative amendments or program development at the national level. Few effectiveness studies would try to omit scrutiny of governmental measures, but, while such measures may promote substantive problem solving, they do not constitute problem solving. In the broader context of policy evaluation, Guba and Lincoln (1989, 22) similarly criticize what they perceive as short-sightedness in many early evaluation studies that failed to trace the causal relevance of institutional outputs for the furtherance of institutional purposes. In contrast, the effectiveness concept underlying this study joins the mainstream of regime-effectiveness analysis by stressing the causal impact on behavior that enhances, upholds, or mitigates the problems that states seek to solve.

The notions of effectiveness used by many economists—that the benefits of a policy exceed the costs (cost-effectiveness) or are achieved at the lowest possible cost (cost efficiency)—also differ from the concept as employed in this study. The economic understanding of effectiveness permeated much early research on evaluation of public policy (Guba and Lincoln 1989). For those who create, operate, or analyze international institutions, cost efficiency is an increasingly important dimension of a regime's performance. The flexibility mechanisms in the global climate regime, aimed at exploiting cost differentials among projects that will reduce greenhouse gas emissions, provide clear evidence of such rising saliency (Stokke, Hovi, and Ulfstein 2005). A corresponding flexibility mechanism exists in the Barents Sea fisheries regime (see chapter 5). While important, however, regime efficiency should be kept distinct from regime effectiveness, since a regime that leads to substantial improvements in the state of the problem that motivated its creation can be termed "effective" even if this result might otherwise have been obtained at lower cost.

In speaking about effectiveness, therefore, regime analysts have in mind a causal relationship between the regime and the state of the problem that motivated its creation. Substantiating such causality requires examining regime outputs, such as knowledge building and regulation, but also, and more important, the *behavior* that connects the regime and the state of the problem.

Impact on Behavior and Problem

The problem addressed by a regime may be conceived of in behavioral terms or by reference to state goals, whether in the political, or socioeconomic, or biophysical domains. David Easton's (1965) distinctions between regime output (decisions, norms, and programs), outcome (actor behavior), and impact (in the problem domain) as possible objects of analysis in assessing public policy are useful when elaborating the concept of regime effectiveness. The approach to regime effectiveness advanced here uses all three references, but sequentially.

To avoid formalism, regime effectiveness must imply at least a causal link between regime outputs and the behavior in question (Keohane, Haas, and Levy 1993, 7; Stokke and Vidas 1996a, 15; Jacobson and Brown Weiss 1998a, 1–2; Young and Levy 1999, 5–6; Underdal 2002a, 6–7). Exactly which actors are of interest in such behavioral assessment will depend on the problem addressed. For instance, if knowledge about the state of a fish stock is inadequate for estimating whether ongoing levels of harvesting will jeopardize replenishment, regime effects on researcher activities can clearly be relevant to problem solving (Andresen et al. 2000). Always relevant are target groups—those actors involved in the activity that generates the socioeconomic or biophysical problem the regime is intended to mitigate or solve. Ronald Mitchell (1994), for example, has examined whether the operators of tanker vessels adapt their behavior in response to various types of international regulation of intentional oil pollution. Outcome-oriented effectiveness research focuses on whether a regime makes a significant difference to behavior, be it discharges by vessel operators, the shooting of elephants, or the harvesting pressure that fishing fleets exert on a stock.

The behavioral and the problem-domain notions of effectiveness are closely related yet clearly distinct. Both refer ultimately to the state of the problem to be dealt with by the regime, but the causal chains are longer in problem-domain analysis. Indeed, demonstrating impacts on behavior can be ambitious enough. International regimes typically address complex social systems, and the regime is only one of many factors that may shape decision making and target-group behavior. Consider, for instance, the introduction of a more stringent minimum mesh-size rule for the protection of young fish. The rule itself may influence the actual use of such gear, but other changing factors may also be relevant, such as whether the new gear will constrain total catches significantly (which may discourage its use) or the existence of great price differentials between large and small fish (which may encourage it). Evaluating such alternative explanations of any behavioral adaptation and distinguishing the contribution made by the regime is a considerable challenge. Various means for doing so are examined in chapter 2.

The causal complexity is even greater when the impact focus shifts from fisher behavior to the state of biophysical systems and their ability to sustain resource use over time, which is the ultimate problem in fisheries management. For example, even if the agreed-on mesh-size rule does alleviate the harvesting pressure on juveniles, mortality among the young fish may nevertheless rise owing to other factors, such as water temperature, salinity, or a greater abundance of predator species. Such nonregime factors often change over time in ways that can be difficult to track. The chain of causal links between a regime and the ultimate problem—here, combining good catches with good replenishment—is longer and sometimes considerably more fragile than the causal chain connecting the regime and relevant behavior.

The greater causal complexity inherent in the ultimate-problem notion of effectiveness poses a dilemma of analytical tractability versus conceptual validity. After all, states do not create regimes in order to adapt actor behavior; that is merely a means to improve the state of affairs in domains they consider important. In fact, there is no necessary relationship between regime-driven behavioral adaptation and desirable impacts on the ultimate problem. If regime participants have an inadequate understanding of the complex processes at play in an issue area, such adaptation could in theory work against the purpose that motivated the formation of the regime in the first place (Weale 1992). To illustrate, in the early 1980s Soviet scientists argued that adherence to the request by the Barents Sea regime's scientific advisory body for larger mesh size in the trawls would undermine recovery of the regional cod stock by stepping up the pressure on older, more fertile fish (Stokke, Anderson, and Mirovitskaya 1999).

The difficulty of substantiating the social or biophysical impacts of a regime may vary from one issue area to another, which is one reason for choosing a flexible approach in trying to balance analytical tractability and closeness to the conceptual core of regime effectiveness. How deeply into the problem domain the analyst should pursue the causal inquiry depends on the causal complexity of the given case. The closer to the ultimate problem an analyst can take the causal analysis validly, the better, but the validity proviso is decisive. Sound causal substantiation of behavioral impact clearly relevant to the problem domain, such as reduced harvesting pressure on a threatened stock, is certainly a better basis for judging a regime effective than is an assessment that also attempts to cover impacts on the state of the stock and on the fishing industries, with no solid evidence for each causal link. One purpose of the disaggregate approach to regime effectiveness is to reduce or remove the dilemma of analytical tractability versus closeness to the concept by ensuring that the causal analysis more readily attends to each link.

To summarize, this study starts from the problem-solving definition of effectiveness that predominates in regime analysis but requires a measurement tool that can capture both behavioral and problem-domain impacts. Generating outputs such as stringent regulations and capacity-enhancing programs does not constitute effectiveness, although dynamism in this respect could be a driving factor behind effectiveness. For a regime to qualify as effective, such outputs must affect behavior in a way that improves the state of affairs in the problem domain addressed by the regime. Ideally, the analyst should specify the strength of those causal connections that link outputs, behavior, and problem-domain impacts; however, causal complexity may justify the more limited aspiration of substantiating that the behavior serves to move the state of affairs in the right direction.

As the next section shows, the disaggregate approach to international regime effectiveness makes the causal analysis more tractable by decomposing the problem. This allows separate attention to each of the links that connect the regime with the state of affairs of interest in the problem domain.

Disaggregating the Problem

Splitting the basic problem addressed by an international regime into its cognitional, regulatory, and behavioral aspects facilitates the causal analysis essential to effectiveness analysis and helps make findings from one study comparable to those from another. This section defines each aspect, shows its significance for the basic problem addressed under international regimes in various issue areas, and specifies it in the area in focus here, resource management.

The Cognitional Aspect

The cognitional part of problem solving entails building a shared, well-founded understanding of how best to achieve the social purpose that motivated states to create the regime. Such activities may take place inside or outside formal institutions and can also be important for achieving progress on the regulatory and behavioral aspects of the problem.

Cognitional problem solving is an ongoing practice in most international regimes that deal with issues of resource management or the protection of the human environment. Most international fisheries treaties acknowledge the need for scientific input into management decisions and encourage the parties to cooperate on research. Coordinating the compilation and analysis of biological and other data by harmonizing methods has obvious efficiency benefits and can also make scientific input more persuasive. In other areas of environmental governance as well, broad international involvement in cognitional problem solving tends to enhance the perceived legitimacy of scientific input among industries and governments (see Mitchell et al. 2006; see also chapter 2 in this book). International environmental regimes often create separate scientific advisory bodies, as with the several assessment panels of the Montreal Protocol on Substances that Deplete the Ozone Layer and the Intergovernmental Panel on Climate Change.

In other issue areas, too, such as maritime shipping and international trade, cognitional problem solving is important in helping tackle the larger problem in focus. The Assembly of the International Maritime Organization (IMO), responsible for improving safety at sea, adopts binding or voluntary instruments based on input from several committees and subcommittees, including the Maritime Safety Committee. These committees are open to representatives from all member states, typically drawn from maritime agencies and jointly mobilizing considerable technical expertise. Around sixty maritime industry associations and civil-society groups, including the four major transnational environmental organizations, enjoy consultative status in the IMO and are allowed (and indeed expected) to submit documents and oral presentations on member-state proposals (de La Fayette 2001, 166). Similarly, the WTO, which operates a range of multilateral treaties with the overarching aim of liberalizing world trade, has set up several specialized bodies, such as the Committee on Trade and Environment, to elucidate controversial issues in upcoming or ongoing negotiations and to explore ways of dealing with them (Schoenbaum 1997).

The basic problem motivating those who negotiated the Barents Sea fisheries regime was the international management of shared marine living resources. Generally speaking, resource management involves the making and implementation of decisions concerning use and conservation.[10] "Use" refers to exploitation, whereas "conservation" is about ensuring future availability. Even when resources are renewable, as fish stocks are, those objectives will usually compete in the short term, since balancing utilization and conservation means forgoing some use today to enable future use. The cognitional part of this problem, examined in chapter 4, involves specifying that relationship, or ensuring that regime members understand the consequences that various levels of harvesting pressure will have on the future availability of the resource.

In general, then, cognitional success is evident when regime members have shared, well-based knowledge on how regulatory and other measures under consideration can help achieve the agreed-upon social purpose of the regime.

The Regulatory Aspect

The regulatory problem in focus for international regimes is to establish a set of behavioral rules that reflects the best available knowledge on how to achieve the social purpose. Impediments to regulatory problem solving may arise from various conditions that are wholly or partly external to the regime, including differing perceptions of the need for costly action and the distributive impacts of the measures recommended. External impediments are often reinforced by a feature common to most international institutions: decisions are taken unanimously, or states are allowed to reserve assent and opt out of any contentious obligation (see Breitmeier, Young, and Zürn 2006, 187). Such procedures may have certain merits, such as encouraging states to accommodate each other's interests and to explore opportunities for bridging gaps between initial positions, but the net effect is often to slow down the adoption of joint rules reflecting the best available knowledge or to reduce participants' level of ambition (Underdal 2002a).

Differing perceptions of the need for costly regulatory action mark many fisheries management regimes, including the one under study here. Since the early 2000s, Russian fisher organizations, supported by some scientists, have argued that the main commercial stock in the Barents Sea ecosystem has in fact been in better shape than indicated by the scientific advisory body (Aasjord and Hønneland 2008), and, at least in some years, that appears to have influenced Russia's positions on quota levels (see chapter 5). The distributive impacts of the proposed measures for preventing dangerous interference with the climate system explain to a great extent why regulatory progress has been so modest after the 1997 Kyoto Protocol. Reducing emissions of greenhouse gases entails substantial costs that differ among those committed by the protocol—and the protocol does not commit all of the world's large economies to control their emissions. Regulatory slowness marks the IMO, whose membership flags as much 98 percent of the world's tonnage. This organization has provided the venue for negotiating some fifty legally binding treaties and protocols, but the inclusive and consensus-oriented processes involved are widely perceived as time-consuming (de La Fayette 2008, 565) and as yielding results that lack the stringency necessary for protecting seafarers and the environment (Devanney 2006).

In resource management, this regulatory aspect of problem solving involves inducing all states whose vessels engage in the fisheries to adopt and implement regulations that reflect the best available knowledge on how use will affect stock replenishment. Here too, the distributive effects of measures that might otherwise improve the balance between present and future use can be a stumbling block. After World War II, for instance, the United Kingdom proposed a freeze on total harvesting capacity in the Northeast Atlantic, but opponents argued convincingly that such a measure would favor those states, especially the UK, that already possessed modern and efficient fishing fleets (Sen 1997).

The relationship between cognitional and regulatory problem solving has been the focus of numerous studies of whether "epistemic communities"—networks of experts well placed in national decision-making systems and largely agreeing on what must be done to tackle a problem—can account for the adoption of shared, more ambitious rules in areas such nuclear arms control, trade and finance, and environmental protection (Adler and Haas 1992). This is one of several theory traditions that underlie the modeling of regulatory problem solving as presented in chapter 5 (see also chapter 2).

The Behavioral Aspect

The behavioral problem in focus for international regimes is to ensure that international rules really do influence the actions of the target groups—those that engage in the activities regulated by the regime. International regulations are not worth much if governments fail to implement them or if target groups do not comply, yet the behavioral aspect has generally been a weak spot in international governance. Recent trends, however, indicate greater prominence given to this aspect among international regimes.

Several impediments to behavioral problem solving exist under international regimes, most fundamentally that participants may have weighty incentives for not heeding their obligations. Such incentives are often quite strong when the social purpose of the regime is to overcome a public good problem, as in international resource management. In the fisheries sector, the common property nature of most stocks means that fishers often face individual incentives that can be collectively disruptive.

After all, each fisher enjoys the full benefit from the catch hauled on board, whereas any cost of that activity in terms of reduced availability of fish will be shared by many—including, in the worst of cases, future generations. More generally, some of the costs disappear from the actor's cost–benefit calculations because they affect others, and such "externalities" typically generate more of the activity in question than is collectively desirable (Underdal 1987; see chapter 2). An individual fisher may find it profitable to violate conservation rules as long as the violation can go undiscovered and does not serve to reduce the compliance of others. Should such free riding on the compliance of others (Olson 1971) become pervasive, however, the total pressure may jeopardize stock replenishment. This situation is what Hardin (1968) described as the "tragedy of the commons," whereby the sum of individually rational behaviors brings ruin to all.

International regimes concerning highly salient issues, such as nuclear arms control and international trade, have often been the most advanced in terms of building structures intended to prevent behavioral failure. The nuclear Non-Proliferation Agreement of 1970, for instance, requires recipients of nuclear technology to accept certain safeguards, including intrusive inspection of nuclear facilities by the International Atomic Energy Agency (Smith 1987). The U.S.-Soviet strategic arms limitation agreement of 1979, never in force but complied with by both states, obliged the parties to refrain from actions that might impede "national technical means" for verification, such as satellite surveillance and telemetric information; and the subsequent Strategic Arms Reduction Treaties include extensive rights of inspection. Similarly, an important way in which the global trade regime was strengthened by the establishment of the WTO in 1994 was the addition of a compulsory and binding dispute settlement system empowered to authorize bilateral trade sanctions if a state is found to have violated the nondiscrimination rules of the global trade regime.

Such strong measures for behavioral problem solving have been lacking in most other areas of international governance. In fisheries, systems of mutual inspection were established in some regional commissions by the late 1960s, but legal prosecution of violators remained the prerogative of the flag state, and the effect was minimal (Sen 1997). Early international environmental agreements typically based their evaluation of behavioral adherence entirely on self-reporting by the member states, which frequently failed even to file such reports (Andresen 1992). Gradually, somewhat stronger procedures for verifying information and reviewing its adequacy emerged in the more advanced global regimes, like that based on the Montreal Protocol (Wettestad 2005). A prominent instance is the Marrakesh Accords under the Kyoto Protocol, which established a compliance committee with a facilitative branch and an enforcement branch. The enforcement branch shall determine whether a party is in noncompliance with its greenhouse gas emissions target and reporting requirements, whether it satisfies the eligibility requirements for participation in the flexibility mechanisms, and whether any violation would warrant "consequences" in the next commitment period, should agreement on new commitments be achieved (Stokke, Hovi, and Ulfstein 2005).

Behavioral problem solving is also pursued with greater vigor in areas other than security, trade, and the environment. Under the global shipping regime, stubborn resistance among many flag states to mandatory review procedures has constrained activities within the IMO, but an external compliance component has emerged, triggered by frustration at the highly varying levels of adherence to existing commitments, especially among flag-of-convenience states (Tan 2006, 90). The 1982 Paris Memorandum of Understanding on port-state controls, now with twenty-seven parties, commits states to use their jurisdiction over vessels voluntarily in their ports to collectively raise the frequency and quality of vessel inspection and response action toward substandard vessels (Molenaar 2007). This external compliance mechanism has set an example for other maritime regions: today, a total of nine such regional agreements cover all of the world's oceans.

Like the cognitional and the regulatory aspects, the behavioral problem (studied in chapter 6) of aligning target-group action to regime rules is addressed by a wide range of international institutions, and the institutional means for doing so are becoming more powerful.

Merits and Challenge of Disaggregation

Splitting the general problem in focus for an international regime into its cognitional, regulatory, and behavioral components offers several advantages, as well as one challenge.

Among the advantages is substantive scope: such disaggregation ensures that an effectiveness analysis attends, in operational detail, to the three main activities that participants and sub-bodies in international regimes actually engage in—generating knowledge, building norms, and taking measures to enhance compliance. Second, it permits a more nuanced assessment of effectiveness, one that is sensitive to advances on part of a problem even when overall performance is low. Third, since we cannot assume that the factors that best explain success or failure in one aspect of problem solving are also decisive for the others, a separate analysis of each aspect means that any lessons drawn about the conditions for problem solving will be more precise than would otherwise be the case.

Yet another advantage of decomposing the problem is dynamism, in the sense of incorporating some of the changes that occur over time in how states define the social purpose of the regime. With the Barents Sea fisheries regime, the introduction in the late 1990s of a precautionary approach to scientific advice and management implied a new balance between the competing concerns of short-term use and conservation. The disaggregation used here allows for the fact that the problems that states address through international regimes are to some extent moving targets. As the next section shows, a final important merit is to make the analytical operations inherent in regime-effectiveness analysis more manageable and more transparent.

The challenge that arises from disaggregating resource management concerns the need to aggregate the components subsequently. Yin (2003, 45) points out that among the pitfalls to be avoided in embedded studies, which examine the components of a phenomenon, is failure to return to the larger phenomenon itself. In chapter 7 I return to the aggregation, examining how cognitional, regulatory, and behavioral problem solving interact in helping achieve the social purpose of the Barents Sea fisheries regime.

Designing the Study

Any empirical study of regime effectiveness, understood as a significant contribution to the level of problem solving, must establish whether the regime makes an impact on the problem and, if so, evaluate its adequacy. The causality task is, as Young (2001, 100) puts it, to "separate the signal of regime effects from the noise arising from the impacts of a wide range of other forces that operate simultaneously." The adequacy task involves assessing such regime effects against an appropriate standard (Underdal 1992, 230–234).

Scholars of regime effectiveness have paid more attention to the causal dimension of effectiveness than to the adequacy dimension, and have differed substantially in their approaches. My disaggregate approach proceeds as follows. In chapters 4 to 6, each dealing with an aspect of the larger problem, I first measure the variation across observations in success and failure. Then I identify major regime and nonregime factors that might account for such variation and confront the hypotheses inherent in the model with empirical data. The explanation of success and failure thereby obtained is important for estimating what level of problem solving would most plausibly pertain in a counterfactual situation in which the regime did *not* exist. That estimate allows me to assess the regime impact, using a yardstick that takes account of the amount of improvement on the hypothetical no-regime situation, as well as how far the problem is from being fully solved. The final step is to aggregate the results, in chapter 7, by examining how various combinations of success and failure with respect to the aspects of problem solving influence the level of ultimate success: a good balance between utilization and conservation.

The yardstick of effectiveness, the role of counterfactual analysis, and the methods for substantiating causal impact are explained in detail in chapter 2. Here I outline each step only briefly, showing first why an embedded case study like the one reported here retains the strengths and counters the limitations of an intensive analytical strategy.

Embedding the Case Study

This study combines features of an intensive case study with comparative techniques for teasing out patterns in the empirical evidence; it also employs statistical analysis.[11] Among the merits of focusing on one or a few instances of a phenomenon is the ability to examine it in depth from different angles, using various types of evidence, in order to gain a solid understanding of the workings of the factors identified as relevant (Yin 2003, 13–15). According to Miles and Huberman (1994, 148), such intensive analysis is the best way to pinpoint causal mechanisms, evaluate the quality of data, sort out chronologies of events, and move back and forth between concepts, hypotheses, and observations. Having a large number of observations, they argue, usually implies superficial knowledge of each, and thus risks misinterpreting data and ignoring important nonmodeled factors.

To this argument, proponents of more extensive analysis counter that causal accounts based on a small number of cases are prone to be overdetermined, leaving the researcher unable to choose among various plausible explanations (King, Keohane, and Verba 1994, 208–210). Such inability is frequently termed a degree-of-freedom, or limited-diversity, challenge. It concerns the internal validity of the study: the analyst has too few observations to determine the relative significance of the explanatory candidates, or indeed whether any one of them is a cause at all. Another criticism concerns external validity. Case studies frequently incorporate too many case-specific features to support propositions whose generalizability, or "traveling capacity" (Sartori 1991), can be examined in other contexts. A small number of observations allows compilation and use of broader and more diverse information about each case but offers fewer means for evaluating competing explanations and the external validity of findings.

The case study reported in this book is *embedded* by the systematic compilation of evidence on parts of the phenomenon in focus—here, regime effectiveness—in order to draw inferences about the whole phenomenon (Yin 2003, 43–45). It is functionally embedded through separate examination of each of the regime structures set up to generate scientific knowledge in support of management, produce agreed-upon regulations, and enhance behavioral adherence to regime rules among target groups. Yet it is the temporal embeddedness of the study that permits the use of several comparative and statistical techniques. Drawing on general propositions in the literature on regime effectiveness, chapters 4 to 6 examine efforts to solve the subproblems of resource management on a year-by-year basis and identify changes in explanatory factors that can account for patterns of success and failure. This embedded case study thus combines the strengths of the case study approach with the greater ability of extensive analysis to impose controls on explanatory candidates.

Measuring Problem Solving

Problem solving under the Barents Sea fisheries regime is measured along three dimensions applicable to a broad set of regimes—knowledge building, regulation, and target-group behavior, with four values distinguished for each dimension. Measuring the degree of problem solving is necessary because effectiveness refers to impact on problem solving. The measurement needed becomes more manageable, the more precisely the problem is defined.

Ideally, any yardstick of problem solving should balance validity, generality, and determinacy. A valid yardstick is one that can capture the substantive essence of the problem that states try to solve—which is decisive, because regime impacts on the margins of a problem are irrelevant to effectiveness. A general yardstick is one that makes sense in several empirical contexts, a characteristic that is highly useful because many pertinent questions about regime effectiveness require comparison across regimes or time periods (Mitchell 2002, 61). A determinate yardstick, finally, differentiates straightforwardly among observations. Determinacy is important because a yardstick that offered the analyst leeway in allocating cases to categories would be unreliable and could allow opportunistic coding, or the categorization of cases in such a way as to confirm the analyst's favorite propositions. Validity, generality, and determinacy need balancing because they sometimes compete, and they are no less relevant when the researcher is elaborating a yardstick for measuring regime effectiveness.

The decomposition of the problem under scrutiny here creates a good balance among the three yardstick criteria. Validity is high because separate yardsticks are devised for three core aspects of the problem that motivated the creation of the regime in focus, resource management. Validity might have been even higher had the problem definition included certain other objectives that states also pursued when negotiating this regime, such as "good-neighborly relations" and the protection of competing sovereignty claims.[12] However, such higher validity is achievable only by ceding on determinacy and generality. Determinacy would drop because different analysts might weigh the additional dimensions differently against those of the larger problem under scrutiny. Generality would drop because not all international regimes, whether dealing with resource management or other problems, have to grapple with tense interstate relations or unresolved boundary disputes. By measuring problem solving on dimensions that make good sense for other international regimes as well, our findings here should be comparable with those from other studies.

Moreover, the determinacy of each yardstick gains by splitting the larger problem into parts. In the empirical chapters, I develop yardsticks for each aspect by means of explicit "qualitative anchors" (Ragin 2000, 317), complemented by procedures to prevent category boundaries that are insensitive to distributional clusters or separate cases with very similar scores on an underlying quantitative dimension. To illustrate, the annual recommendation by the scientific advisory body of the Barents Sea fisheries regime provides a qualitative anchor for measuring regulatory problem solving (see chapter 5). Cases where managers set quotas fully in line with this recommendation receive a full score on this aspect of resource management, whereas a quantitative procedure ensures that thresholds for lower scores do not differentiate among cases with similar distance (measured in percent) from the recommendation. Thus, I place the thresholds on steep parts of the curve that plots all values from the lowest to the highest, paying particular attention to whether the observations cluster around a small number of values that could provide a basis for categorization. A secondary distributional criterion, used only if the qualitative or clustering criteria do not allocate cases determinately, is that the four categories should capture roughly the same number of observations.

Finally, one comment on the choice of a four-value scale of problem solving: the number of values on a yardstick should reflect the analyst's ability to differentiate determinately and validly among cases with respect to the operational parameters. Such ability depends on conceptual maturity and the amount and reliability of data available (Ragin 2000, 167–168). The understanding of regime effectiveness as contributing significantly to substantive problem solving is relatively new, and the study of factors that influence success and failure in these terms remains at an early stage, so the scale should not be too fine-grained. Using four values permits a somewhat nuanced differentiation without requiring very precise measurement. These considerations explain why chapters 4 to 6 specify thresholds for distinguishing among full, substantial, modest, and insignificant levels of problem solving along the cognitional, regulatory, and behavioral dimensions.

Building Causal Models

The next step is to develop, for each dimension of the problem, a causal model that may account for variation in success and failure. Without a good model of problem solving, the analyst cannot answer the central question in effectiveness analysis: would problem solving have fared significantly worse had there been no regime?

Because the tasks of building knowledge, adopting regulations, and shaping target-group behavior differ in nature, we cannot assume that the sets of factors driving or impeding success on those tasks will be the same. Accordingly, in chapters 4 to 6 I develop separate explanatory models to account for the diversity of outcomes concerning each aspect. Certain common features of those models are nevertheless worth mentioning here. First, they all draw on findings from twenty years of research on regime effectiveness. Having such a grounding in earlier investigations of the same phenomenon is especially important for case-oriented analysis, with its limited ability to impose controls on plausible causal factors (Eckstein 1975; King, Keohane, and Verba 1995, 477; see also Ragin 2000, 68). Second, the models of cognitional, regulatory, and behavioral problem solving all build on certain causal mechanisms that may mediate between the regime and the outcome of interest. Certain general mechanisms cover most of the specific versions in use by regime-effectiveness scholars and highlight cognitional, normative, or utilitarian processes (Stokke 2001b, 2007a; see also chapter 2). Regimes affect relevant behavior by cognitional means when they influence actors' awareness about certain problems or the pros and cons of various options for solving them, by normative means when they shape actors' perceptions about what is right and proper conduct within an issue area, and by utilitarian means when they alter their incentives for pursuing various options.

Thus, each of the explanatory models of cognitional, regulatory, and behavioral problem solving developed here concerns a more sharply defined object than the larger problem under scrutiny, resource management. Each model is derived from findings in earlier effectiveness research, from consideration of general causal mechanisms, and from the specific experience of Barents Sea fisheries management.

Explaining Success and Failure

A causal model of a phenomenon is an important part of an explanation, but the explanation also requires a confrontation with empirical evidence that can show which factors or combinations of factors may produce the outcome of interest. In this study, two outcomes of particular interest are success and failure, because an effectiveness study must substantiate whether an actual success would have been less successful, or would even have failed altogether, had there been no regime.

The number of observations derived from examining problem solving on a year-by-year basis over roughly thirty years of the Barents Sea fisheries regime remains at the low end of what statistical analysis requires and at the high end of what a narratively structured case comparison can handle. Therefore, my study relies heavily on a set-theoretic comparative technique that Charles Ragin (1987, 2000, 2008) has developed on the basis of John Stuart Mill's ([1853] 1904) classical methods of comparison. This technique, qualitative comparative analysis (QCA), occupies a middle position between case-oriented analysis and quantitative approaches and offers a formalization of Mill's logical operations that improves their applicability. The QCA procedure is a powerful tool for analyzing regime effectiveness because it can help clarify, even with a moderate number of observations, whether a certain causal condition—a particular score on a variable, or a combination of scores on several variables—consistently correlates with high or low levels of problem solving in an empirical data set and thus may indicate a reliable path to success or to failure (Stokke 2004a, 2007c).

Estimating the No-Regime Counterfactual

An important feature of the disaggregate approach is its use of such empirical findings about reliable paths to success or to failure among actual cases to estimate what level of problem solving would have been achieved if the regime had not existed. To illustrate the reasoning: if a condition much influenced by an international regime—for instance, a high degree of transparency concerning target-group behavior—proves to be a factor that distinguishes among reliable successes and reliable failures, that finding may help substantiate the problem solving that would mark a no-regime situation. Conversely, a reliable success combination that does *not* include regime-driven factors, or a failure combination that includes them, can prevent the analyst from drawing hasty conclusions about the regime's significance. In chapter 2 I systematize such *counterfactual path analysis*, which uses findings about actual cases to substantiate the counterfactual estimate required in effectiveness analysis: the most plausible estimate of the level of problem solving that would pertain without the regime.

Assessing Regime Impacts

The counterfactual problem-solving estimates thus derived are then used to assess the impacts of the regime, but two other points of reference are also important: actual problem solving and full problem solving (Underdal 1992; Hovi, Sprinz, and Underdal 2003).

Measuring effectiveness as the distance between the actual level of problem solving and the most plausible no-regime situation is perhaps the most intuitive approach to measuring regime effectiveness, and marks many early studies (e.g., Haas, Keohane, and Levy 1993; Stokke and Vidas 1996c; Young 1999b; Mitchell 2002): the wider the difference, the greater the effectiveness. As Underdal (1992, 231) has pointed out, however, the no-regime counterfactual is merely one of several reasonable starting points for assessing effectiveness. Equally relevant is whether the regime achieves everything that can be accomplished, or meets the requirements of an optimal solution in light of the state of knowledge at the time. Both points of reference are meaningful and may readily yield different evaluations of the same regime. A regime's causal weight can be substantial even if the state of affairs is far from the collective optimum, and being close to a collective optimum says nothing about causal impact, since problem solving might stem from nonregime factors (Underdal 1992, 231). Sprinz and Helm (1999) combine those two references in a single compact formula: they measure regime effectiveness as the ratio of actual improvement on the no-regime situation to potential improvement, the latter denoting the difference between an optimal solution and the no-regime counterfactual.

In chapter 2 I examine the validity, generality, and determinacy of various versions of this "Oslo-Potsdam solution" to measuring regime effectiveness (Hovi, Sprinz, and Underdal 2003). By adapting that formula for use in a qualitative analysis employing the QCA tool, my study is in line with the tendency among regime scholars to give greater attention to the question of adequacy, which concerns the distance from full problem solving, when measuring regime effectiveness.

Aggregating the Evidence

The final step in this assessment of international regime effectiveness is to aggregate the evidence of regime impacts on each dimension of problem solving and examine how they interact in influencing developments in the domain that motivated states to create the regime. Such aggregation ensures that the embedded study returns to the larger phenomenon under scrutiny (Yin 2003, 45), which is the overall ability of states to balance utilization and conservation.

The three aspects of resource management have complementary roles in the assessment of states' ability to balance present against future use. Scientific advice and regulatory measures are outputs that may indicate regime dynamism and contribute to regime effectiveness, but only if they shape behavior in a way conducive to the problem domain. Accordingly, while significant behavioral effectiveness is a necessary condition for aggregate effectiveness, cognitional and regulatory effectiveness scores can help substantiate any causal connection between the regime and such behavior—and between behavioral effectiveness and developments in the problem domain.

Throughout the existence of the Barents Sea regime, scientists and managers have recognized certain biological reference points concerning the size of the spawning stock as appropriate standards for evaluating the state of the stock (see chapter 4). Such reference points now form the basis for the *precautionary* approach to fisheries, as defined in international law (Stokke 2001c). Chapter 7 assesses the aggregate effectiveness of the Barents Sea fisheries regime in the period under study by relating changes in the catches derived from the fisheries and in the state of the stock, as measured by those reference points, to the behavioral, regulatory, and cognitional regime impacts substantiated in chapters 4 to 6.

Sources of Information

This study draws on documents published by international organizations, government agencies, legislative assemblies, and nongovernmental organizations, as well as news media and a wide range of secondary analyses. Using different kinds of sources to illuminate several aspects of a phenomenon and to cross-check the information contained in each is a defining characteristic of a case study (Miles and Huberman 1994, 148).

The main types of primary sources in this study are official documents that governments and international organizations publish, either in print or electronically.[13] With respect to cognitional problem solving, especially useful are the annual reports of the regime's scientific body, the Advisory Committee on Fisheries Management of the International Council for the Exploration of the Sea (ICES), as well as the scientific collaboration appendix to the annual protocol of the regime's political body, the Joint Commission on Fisheries (see chapter 3).[14] The annual report of the ICES Advisory Committee presents the most authoritative assessment of the stock and the ecosystem. It usually includes consensual recommendations on what the scientific community considers appropriate measures with respect to certain aspects of management, especially the total allowable catch. All Advisory Committee reports from 1978 to 2010 were included in the basis for this study. Regarding regulatory and behavioral problem solving, primary source documents of special relevance are the protocols from the sessions of the Joint Commission on Fisheries, which provide the only official accounts of the formal negotiations and detail the regulations, and various governmental white papers that sketch national positions. All Joint Commission protocols from the period studied were included in the basis for this study.

Among documents published by governments, important Norwegian sources are the annual reports to the Storting (the Norwegian Parliament) by the Ministry of Fisheries and Coastal Affairs concerning fisheries agreements with foreign states, as well as records of debates in the Storting.[15] Also highly relevant are the reports from a parallel evaluation of the management system for the Barents Sea fisheries conducted by the Office of the Auditor General (OAG) of Norway and a similar office in Russia (Norway OAG 2007; Russia 2007). The Russian report provides both current and historical information on that state's institutional structures in the fisheries sector, including legal acts and regulations pertaining to fisheries in the Barents Sea, and assessments of the management process. Information on actual harvesting pressure derives in part from ICES data, especially its annual publication reporting on advice from its Advisory Committee, and in part from national sources. Beyond these various primary sources, the study draws on newspaper accounts and the extensive secondary literature on the regional fisheries collaboration and High Northern affairs more broadly.[16]

Since the author is a Norwegian without a command of the Russian language, this study inevitably draws more on information on Norway's research, regulatory, compliance control, and harvesting behavior than on similar information on Russia. Until around 1990, even well-connected Russian researchers would have had access to relatively little data on Soviet fisheries–related activities in the Barents Sea beyond the information published in connection with the international regime (Stokke, Anderson, and Mirovitskaya 1999, 92). Such regime publications include Joint Commission on Fisheries protocols, ICES statistics, and data from a series of Soviet-Norwegian scientific symposia carried out under the auspices of the Joint Commission. Maritime operations in the region were seen as having strategic and even military importance, and dissemination of data was strictly limited. With the transition from the Soviet Union to the Russian Federation, information on fisheries employment, capital investment, and the composition of fishing fleets became more readily available, also from regional sources. However, public information on such matters as Russian compliance control activities and the extent of rule violation they expose remains sparse even today.

Three conditions serve to reduce the implications of this asymmetry in the information base for the reliability of this study. First, documents from the regime's scientific and political bodies are approved by both parties, and in the case of ICES reports, by experts from other states as well. Second, most of the Northeast Arctic cod catches occur in waters under Norwegian jurisdiction, where the database is richer. In the period from 1978 to 2005, Norwegian vessels took more than half of the total cod catches while Russia took slightly more than a third.[17] Moreover, a substantial share of the Russian catches of cod occurs in Norway's EEZ or its Fisheries Protection Zone at Svalbard. Third, this study compensates for the asymmetry in the information base in several ways. Paragraphs describing or analyzing Russian behavior have been reviewed by Russian-speaking experts on Northwest Russia's fisheries sector as a quality control on facts and evaluations.[18] Whenever Norwegian and Russian official views have differed significantly on matters relating to the evaluation of problem solving and effectiveness, as for instance the level of Russian overfishing in the 2000s, such divergence is explicitly mentioned in the text.

Thus, numerous sources of information have been used in this study. The overwhelming part of the data used in the comparative analyses underlying the effectiveness assessments in chapters 4 to 7 comes from publications by regime agencies that both Norway and the Soviet Union/ Russia, or scientific representatives of both states, have contributed to and approved.

Distinctiveness

The features that most clearly set the disaggregate approach apart from earlier studies of regime effectiveness are the decomposition of the larger problem addressed by the regime and the explicit and transparent way this approach deals with causal substantiation, including the counterfactual analysis.

Disaggregating the resource management problem has not been usual in regime-effectiveness analysis; most previous studies either based their assessments primarily on one aspect or failed to explain the aggregation over several aspects. Whereas some early projects focused on regulatory problem solving (e.g., Kay and Jacobson 1983), the more usual approach has been to consider the behavioral aspect as well, with some account of problem-domain developments (see the case studies reported in Haas, Keohane, and Levy 1993; Stokke and Vidas 1996c; Young 1999a; and Miles et al. 2002). Exactly which of these various criteria weigh the most is frequently unclear or varies across cases in comparative works.

One of many merits of an effectiveness study by Miles and associates (2002) is the high transparency concerning the assessments of effectiveness as well as the scores on explanatory factors. Another is a conception of the problem to be solved that is general enough to fit the many regimes they consider. To some extent, that generality competes with transparency, since the reader must rely largely on the authors' overall judgments of what aspects of problem solving are the most important. Some of the underlying case studies base their assessments mostly on changes in behavioral problem solving, such as changes in the amounts of various materials dumped annually into world oceans (see Skjærseth 2002; Miles 2002a). Others highlight a distributive aspect of regulatory problem solving, for instance the effects of the Forum Fisheries Agency in helping South Pacific states acquire a greater share of the benefits from regional tuna fisheries without undermining sustainability (Miles 2002b). Yet others, such as Wettestad's (2002b) study of long-range transboundary air pollution, explicitly base their evaluation on progress in all three aspects of problem solving, without providing separate scores or explaining how they aggregate such scores into singular ones.

In another ambitious comparative study of international regimes, Breitmeier, Young, and Zürn (2006) do provide separate scores on outcomes that are close to what I have termed cognitional, regulatory, and behavioral problem solving but do not offer any substantive criteria for assigning them. Instead, the authors devise a procedure that leaves such assignment to selected experts on each regime. They assemble those scores in an International Regime Database that also contains the experts' assessments of numerous factors of potential relevance to the formation, change, and effectiveness of international regimes.

These various studies rely ultimately on specialists' judgments, whose aggregation across reasonable criteria remains undefined. By contrast, I specify in chapters 4 to 6 substantive yardsticks for measuring problem solving and effectiveness regarding each of the three aspects of resource management, and use the subsequent measurements to analyze aggregate effectiveness in chapter 7.

My decomposition of the problem also sets this book apart from earlier studies of the Barents Sea fisheries regime, as does the more explicit examination of causal contributions and their adequacy. Earlier studies have typically narrowed in on one particular aspect of resource management, or even parts of one aspect, and have rarely dealt with the questions of causality and adequacy. For instance, Nakken (1998) examined cognitional problem solving in a way that has inspired parts of chapter 4, by using the annual updates by the regime's scientific advisory body to evaluate the quality of the first stock assessment. However, Nakken did not measure forecasting accuracy, or seek to explain variation over time in assessment quality. Churchill and Ulfstein assessed the legal basis for regulatory and enforcement activities in various jurisdictional zones in the Barents Sea but without evaluating cognitional, regulatory, or behavioral problem solving except in very general terms (Churchill and Ulfstein 1992, 123–125). Hønneland has examined causes of behavioral problem solving (Hønneland 2000) and more recently also the regulatory dynamics of interstate bargaining over rules and compliance arrangements (Hønneland 2006, 2012), but substantiation of causal connections and assessment of the adequacy of regime contributions are not what these studies are after. Substantively broader and explicitly focusing on causal impact is a study by Stokke, Anderson, and Mirovits-kaya (1999) that traces regime impacts on coastal state scientific, regulatory, and enforcement activities, as well as effects on fisher behavior and stock sustainability. However, that study does not specify clear criteria for measuring success on each dimension and indicates no procedures for aggregating across them.

While most regime-effectiveness scholars acknowledge the counterfactual statement inherent in an effectiveness claim (e.g., Underdal 1992, 231; 2002b; Keohane, Haas, and Levy 1993, 18–19; Mitchell 1994, 23; Stokke and Vidas 1996a, 17; Young and Levy 1999, 18–19), they rarely expend much energy on substantiating this empirically (Young 2001, 104). Counterexamples include Levy's (1993) early analysis of the Convention on Long-Range Transboundary Air Pollution and Mitchell and associates' (1999) examination of the global regime on vessel-source oil pollution. Far more common, however, is either not to address the counterfactual levels of problem solving (e.g., Peterson 1993), or else explicate them in a general way or consider only parts of the problem at hand. For instance, counterfactuals appear in a general way in most of the effectiveness studies reported by Miles and associates (2002), in the form of aggregate evaluations based on the evidence presented as to whether the state of affairs would have been either worse or roughly the same without the regime. Counterfactual analysis restricted to parts of the problem characterizes, for instance, Stokke, Anderson, and Mirovitskaya's (1999) assessment of the Barents Sea fisheries regime, which uses explicit counterfactuals in evaluating the impacts on sovereignty protection but not on other aspects of problem solving.

In contrast, the present study uses causal analysis of actual cases to estimate for each year and for each aspect of the problem the level of success most plausible had there been no regime. For each aspect, I derive those estimates by combining empirical findings about what conditions drive or impede success with specification of how the regime has influenced those conditions. As chapter 2 explains in greater detail, this sequential partition of the counterfactual analysis makes it more manageable and helps minimize that part of an effectiveness assessment that cannot be firmly linked to observation of actual cases.

Summary and Implications

This chapter has located the regime-effectiveness question within the larger study of governance: It has clarified some core concepts and pinpointed distinctive features of the new approach advanced in this book. An effective international regime is one that contributes significantly to solving the problem that motivated states to create the regime in the first place.

Several features of the disaggregate approach to regime effectiveness distinguish this book from earlier contributions. First, it decomposes the larger problems addressed by international regimes into their cognitional, regulatory, and behavioral components. Second, the approach makes counterfactual analysis central, using empirical findings about drivers of and impediments to problem solving to estimate the levels most plausible had the regime not existed. Prominent here is counterfactual path analysis, which helps narrow the range of plausible counterfactual estimates by comparing the counterfactual causal conditions to the reliable paths to success and failure. A third feature, explicit attention to whether regime impacts are adequate, sets my study apart from early contributions in this field of research but not from some more recent ones. The disaggregate approach also splits the regime operation into several phases to allow some control on competing explanatory factors in the causal analysis of each aspect of resource management. In sum, the approach advanced in this book ensures not only broad substantive coverage and nuanced assessment of problem solving but also explanatory precision: the conditions for regime effectiveness clarified in this study concern a more sharply defined set of outcomes than usual in the field.

Among the five central analytical themes addressed within the Earth System Governance project of the IHDP (see Biermann 2008, 286–298), this study deals especially with architecture, adaptation, and allocation. It deals with institutional architecture by showing how the Barents Sea fisheries regime is nested within broader institutions and how its effectiveness has depended on conducive interplay with other regimes, especially with respect to the cognitional and the behavioral aspects of problem solving. It looks into the problem of adaptation by examining factors internal or external to the regime that have influenced its capacity to induce institutional and behavioral change. And it examines the problem of allocation by demonstrating how certain decision rules and flexibility mechanisms have mitigated the risk of regime members sidestepping distribution issues by ignoring conservation matters.

In chapter 2 we delve more deeply into the theories and methods of regime-effectiveness analysis, exploring each of the analytical operations needed for substantiating and evaluating regime impacts on the problem in focus. Chapter 3 prepares the ground for applying the disaggregate approach empirically by reviewing the complex of national and international institutions involved in the management of shared fish stocks in the Barents Sea region and examining their interaction with broader regimes. The core of the application is found in chapters 4 to 6, which examine cognitional, regulatory, and behavioral effectiveness. They proceed in a parallel manner by first specifying the relevant aspect of resource management and then developing a yardstick for measuring variation over time and applying it to each year of problem-solving effort. Thereafter these chapters substantiate estimates of the most plausible no-regime levels of problem solving, based on empirically validated models derived from earlier studies. Finally, they use my adapted version of the Oslo-Potsdam formula to derive annual effectiveness scores. Chapter 7 aggregates the empirical findings by employing these partial effectiveness analyses to assess the regime's impact on the ultimate parameters of interest here, the catches derived from the fisheries and the state of the stock. In the concluding chapter 8, I summarize the theoretical and methodological findings of the study and relate them to earlier contributions in the field, and then go on to examine the wider implications for the design and operation of international institutions in earth system governance.

2

Effectiveness Theories and Methods

At the core of regime-effectiveness studies are two questions: would problem solving be significantly lower if the regime had not existed, and how far is the problem from being fully solved? As this chapter shows, answering the first, counterfactual question requires a good explanation of why the actual level of problem solving varies. The approach taken here is to identify the main drivers of and impediments to problem solving and then examine whether those factors have been influenced by the regime. Answering the second question, on the adequacy of any regime effects, requires clear specification of what would constitute full problem solving.

The first section examines how regime effectiveness can be measured in a way that is valid and determinate, and yet general enough to allow comparison across regimes and issue areas. My yardstick is an adapted version of the Oslo-Potsdam formula, which takes account of the causal effect of the regime on the problem, as well as the adequacy of that effect. Especially important here is the level of problem solving that would pertain if there were no regime. Accordingly, the subsequent section considers some objections to the use of counterfactual analysis in causal assessment and identifies general standards for doing it persuasively. Substantiating the most plausible no-regime level of problem solving requires clarifying the role of the regime within a broader set of factors that may influence problem solving. That is why I then turn to causal modeling and consider how the "mechanism approach" common in analyses of regime effectiveness can be a useful first step in identifying drivers and impediments. Among the factors that come into focus are malignancy, or tension between individual and collective interests, and collaboration, the state of knowledge, obligation, and behavioral transparency.

Theoretical models must be empirically validated. In the subsequent section we will see how various techniques such as process tracing and comparative or statistical analysis can be applied and sometimes combined for this purpose. Among them, fuzzy set qualitative comparative analysis (QCA) is especially helpful when causality is complex and the number of observations is intermediate, as is often the case in studies of international regime effectiveness. The final substantive section explains how QCA-based analysis can help to identify causal paths—that is, certain combinations of scores on a set of causal factors—that reliably yield either high or low levels of problem solving. Whenever the regime can be shown to influence the scores on the causal factors involved, such paths to success or failure can help determine the most plausible no-regime level of problem solving, allowing us to measure how effective that regime is.

Measuring Effectiveness: Causality and Adequacy

What kind of yardstick is best suited for measuring regime effectiveness? Like the tools for measuring problem solving, such a yardstick should differentiate cases validly and determinately but also with high generality, because with many important questions, effectiveness has to be differentiated over time or across cases. For instance, examining the significance of certain regime properties—such as access to information, qualified majority procedures, or intrusive compliance mechanisms—for problem-solving effectiveness usually requires comparison among different regimes.

The scant attention that early effectiveness studies paid to measuring effectiveness explains in part why they typically pitched comparative analysis at a high level of generality. While those studies frequently offer rich and compelling accounts of causal relationships between a regime and certain aspects of problem solving, they report few findings about the relative effectiveness of regimes or about specific conditions that will promote regime effectiveness (see Levy, Keohane, and Haas 1993; Stokke and Vidas 1996b; Young 1999b). By showing how the regimes studied make a difference to problem solving, they highlight the causality dimension of effectiveness, but they have little to say about the adequacy dimension, which concerns how far the problem still is from being fully solved. The yardstick specified below incorporates both dimensions, thereby providing a more valid, yet still general and determinate, basis for measuring regime effectiveness.

Making a Difference? Measurement on the Causal Dimension
During the 1990s, most attempts to measure degrees of effectiveness focused on the difference between the observable level of problem solving

and some account of the no-regime situation. The instruments used for measuring that difference have ranged from qualitative expert aggregation to statistically derived coefficients.

Early case study–based projects on regime effectiveness gave primacy to validity within the cases under study—and paid a price in the form of low determinacy and low generality. Jacobson and Kay (1983a, 18–19), for instance, used an extremely heterogeneous yardstick consisting of more than twenty generally phrased questions within five substantive clusters, including problem-domain impact. In summarizing findings from eleven case studies, they noted that the study "did not readily yield highly comparable units of analysis . . . [and was] greatly hindered by the failure of international programs to include specific statements of objectives or progress indicators to facilitate such comparison" (Jacobson and Kay 1983b, 319). The broadness of their approach to measurement may have been justified by the pioneering and exploratory nature of the project, but it severely impeded any effort to assess determinately the overall level of problem solving in each case, let alone compare such problem solving across cases (see also Bernauer 1995, 357).

Later comparative case studies highlighting the causality dimension of effectiveness have achieved higher generality by grading achievements in abstract terms. They delineate the type of change that would indicate problem solving, such as reduced forest death or healthier fish stocks, but go no further than requiring that regimes make a "positive contribution" (Keohane, Haas, and Levy 1993, 7) or have "contributed significantly to solving the problem" (Stokke and Vidas 1996a, 16), or "move the system in the right direction" (Young and Levy 1999, 6). Such abstract yardsticks can make sense in various empirical settings, but they offer little guidance as to where to place the thresholds between various degrees of problem solving; they pay for abstract validity and high generality with low determinacy.

A few analysts have derived statistical measures of the difference a regime makes to the outcome of interest and have thereby achieved high determinacy and generality. The general approach is to compile evidence on a core aspect of problem solving among members and nonmembers of international regimes and then control statistically for other factors. Thomas Bernauer (1995, 372–373) briefly reviews several early applications of this quantitative approach. Mitchell (2002) develops the argument further, linking it directly to the notion of a no-regime counterfactual. In an illustrative study of the effectiveness of the regime based on the

Convention on Long-Range Transboundary Air Pollution, he measures differences in discharges of pollutants among members and nonmembers, and then uses partial regression analysis to control for such nonregime factors as population size and energy intensity, which might influence both membership and the behavior in question. As Mitchell (2002, 63) notes, such a statistically derived coefficient for regime membership expresses the distance between a member state's actual emissions and the emissions likely in a counterfactual situation of nonmembership. The validity of these yardsticks for measuring causality will depend on the quality of the models and of the variable measurements.

A chief merit of statistical measures of the distance between actual outcomes and estimates of no-regime outcomes is that they use a general standard of measurement that supports cross-regime comparison. By measuring annual percentage change rather than absolute change in relevant behavior, Mitchell (2002, 70–71) can meaningfully compare regimes in different issue areas, at least within clusters of regimes where the behavioral adaptation required is roughly similar. Examples could be a pollution cluster, a living resources cluster, or a habitat cluster. Another means of enhancing comparability is to control for the difference between regimes with respect to the difficulty of the problem they seek to deal with, for instance by weighting the annual percentage change in behavior with the corresponding abatement cost (Mitchell 2002, 71).

These various yardsticks focus on the causal dimension of effectiveness. Qualitative versions obtain generality by abstract, highly aggregate assessment with low determinacy, whereas quantitative yardsticks combine generality and determinacy. On the other hand, quantitative yardsticks based on extensive analyses usually derive from more superficial knowledge of each case and are therefore more vulnerable to low validity owing to missing or poorly measured model variables. None of the yardsticks reviewed so far pays much attention to adequacy, or the distance between actual and full problem solving.

Incorporating Adequacy: The Oslo-Potsdam Approach
We may measure the causality and adequacy dimensions of effectiveness separately, but combining them is more elegant. As Underdal (1992, 231) points out, distance from a no-regime state of affairs and distance from a collective optimum both make sense as standards of effectiveness, and they do not necessarily covary (see chapter 1). Following Underdal's (2002b, 53) procedures, the case study contributors to the comparative project reported by Miles and associates (2002) provide separate scores

on those dimensions, seeking generality through such broadly applicable verbal qualifiers as "small," "significant," and "major" improvement on the no-regime counterfactual or regimes falling short of meeting the requirements of an optimal solution "by a large margin" or coming "close to" those requirements (Miles et al. 2002, 483–484). To obtain higher validity, these case study authors have, whenever feasible, consulted experts for review of their scores. Their study was the first to measure effectiveness in a way that systematically considered not only improvement on the no-regime situation but also the adequacy of that improvement.

Helm and Sprinz (2000) further advanced Underdal's (1992) approach by combining the causal and adequacy dimensions of effectiveness into one compact formula. They proposed measuring regime effectiveness as actual improvement on the no-regime situation divided by potential improvement. Actual improvement is the difference between the actual and the counterfactual (no-regime) situation; potential improvement is the difference between the optimal solution and the counterfactual situation. This elegant formula generates effectiveness scores that range from 0 (no improvement) to 1 (optimal improvement). The high level of abstraction that characterizes this yardstick—which Hovi, Sprinz, and Underdal (2003) have called "the Oslo-Potsdam solution" to measuring regime effectiveness—implies a high score on generality.

Assigning values to the parameters of the Oslo-Potsdam formula can be done in various ways. Case study contributors to the project reported by Miles and associates (2002) assessed them qualitatively. The validity of findings based on cross-case comparison depends on whether the contributors apply the research design and key concepts in the same way and on whether the design permits analysis of the most important causal factors in each case. A rather different approach has been delineated by Sprinz and Helm (1999, 362–363), who sought a more objective basis for ascribing values to the parameters. Employing certain concepts in game theory, they recommended measuring the no-regime counterfactual as the noncooperative optimum, specified in the environmental realm by summarizing the policies that a state would take if it were acting solely with a view to its own damage and abatement costs. The collective optimum they operationalized as the sets of policies that the state would adopt when considering damage to other states as well. By not referring to any particular policy instrument or actor, this game theory version retains high generality and can therefore be applied across issue areas and at various levels of aggregation.

Unfortunately, the validity and determinacy of Sprinz and Helm's (1999) game theory version of the Oslo-Potsdam solution are less impressive. The validity of conceiving the no-regime counterfactual as the noncooperative optimum is debatable, since complete disregard for damage to others is scarcely the normal situation in international affairs (Young 2001, 111). A persuasive counterfactual should be compatible with established facts about the actual world (see below and Tetlock and Belkin 1996a, 23–30), and if the noncooperative optimum is an overly pessimistic estimate, the yardstick will exaggerate regime effectiveness. Even more troubling are the conceptual and methodological challenges involved in applying the game theory version of the Oslo-Potsdam approach reliably across cases (see also Sprinz and Helm 1999, 365–367). In most issue areas, damage and abatement cost functions are available only for a subset of relevant states, and then usually only in rough terms. The form of those cost functions depends on environmental and technological thresholds that are subject to considerable disagreement within states and among scientists. Further, the relationship between such cost categories and the readiness of the various states to act, with or without an international regime, involves domestic political processes that reflect differing patterns of influence among societal groups. All of these conditions are likely to change over time. It would be unrealistic to expect analysts to solve such formidable conceptual and methodological challenges to the same extent, and in corresponding ways, for different countries and across issue areas—but that is necessary for valid measurement of effectiveness. In short, then, Sprinz and Helm (1999) pay for high generality and conceptual elegance with questionable validity and low determinacy.

These various challenges to qualitative and game theory–based versions of the Oslo-Potsdam approach are fully recognized by Hovi, Sprinz, and Underdal (2003). They point out that many of these problems are inevitable if one defines effectiveness, as most regime scholars now do, in terms of actual and counterfactual levels of problem solving and some notion of an optimal situation. A manageable way forward, they argue, is to attack those challenges from several angles by seeking to estimate the parameters in several different ways and then exploring whether the results are compatible (Hovi, Sprinz, and Underdal 2003, 89–93). Accordingly, Underdal's (1992, 2002b) case study–based qualitative assessment and Sprinz and Helm's (1999) formalized and quantitative versions stand as limiting cases of the set of procedures that may be devised for using the general Oslo-Potsdam approach to measuring regime effectiveness.

The Oslo-Potsdam approach is clearly the most sophisticated effectiveness yardstick developed to date, which is why I have applied it in this study, with some minor adaptations. By combining the causal and adequacy dimensions of effectiveness in a single formula and offering considerable flexibility with respect to procedures for specifying parameter values, this yardstick allows the balancing of case-specific validity and cross-case generality. As I explain in the section below, in presenting the fuzzy set QCA approach to deriving regime-effectiveness scores, the version of the Oslo-Potsdam yardstick used here achieves higher determinacy than previous versions because it disaggregates the problem addressed by the regime, thereby allowing more concrete specification of categorical thresholds.

To use this yardstick, the analyst must estimate the most plausible counterfactual level of problem solving that would pertain without the regime. In the next section we examine how such analysis can be done persuasively.

Persuasive Counterfactuals

Using counterfactual analysis in causal assessment is controversial. Regime scholars generally recognize that an effectiveness claim—indeed, any causal claim (see King, Keohane, and Verba 1994, 77–79)—harbors a counterfactual statement (see, e.g., Underdal 1992, 231; 2002b; Mitchell 1994, 23; Stokke and Vidas 1996a, 17; Young and Levy 1999, 18–19). In contrast, some scholars outside the regime-effectiveness line of research have questioned the usefulness of counterfactual analysis in substantiating causal accounts. However, as I will show, the practices they criticize are very different from those advocated in this study.

Although granting that the disciplined use of counterfactuals may be helpful, Bennett (2004, 25–26) maintains that they involve "an obvious danger of confirmation bias and spuriousness" and could amount to "an open license to rewrite history." George and Bennett (2005, 168) add that "counterfactual analysis, though frequently employed, has lacked strong criteria and standards for distinguishing good practice from the highly speculative." Similarly, while acknowledging that counterfactuals may support theory building, Weber (1996, 268) doubts they have any role in empirical assessment except in "a very few isolated cases about which we already know an enormous amount and have a high degree of confidence."

Yet the most sweeping of these general warnings about counterfactual analysis exaggerate the point. George and Bennett (2005, 168) correctly point out that specifying a persuasive counterfactual case requires a plausible explanation of the actual, observable case. In presenting this requirement as a limitation of counterfactual analysis, however, they seem to conflate such analysis with "mental experimentation." The latter refers to something that would, were it an actual case, shed light on a specific causal account by complementing other cases in terms of causal conditions and the outcome of interest. They are correct in noting that a comparison between such a counterfactual case and actual ones provides no evidence on the causal account; rather, it is the causal account that has defined the counterfactual. However, such mental experimentation is not what analysts such as Elster (1978), Fearon (1991), and the contributors to Tetlock and Belkin (1996b) have in mind when elaborating standards for sound counterfactual analysis. Their standards concern the construction of a *plausible* counterfactual, one that is transparent and makes maximal use of available information on actual cases.

Three standards for persuasive counterfactuals are *explicitness*, *projectability*, and *compatibility*. Explicitness, argue Tetlock and Belkin (1996a, 19–21), is essential: it involves a counterfactual antecedent as well as a counterfactual consequent. In our case, the counterfactual antecedent describes the characteristics, or scores, on the drivers and impediments of problem solving that would pertain if there were no regime, while the counterfactual consequent is the level of problem solving that those characteristics would most plausibly produce, given what we know about actual cases. Thus, estimating an explicit counterfactual involves specifying and validating an explanatory model of problem solving (Underdal and Young 2004, 365).

Projectability concerns the generalizations the researcher uses when inferring from the counterfactual antecedent to the consequent problem-solving estimate. It requires that such generalizations be able to predict outcomes in cases not yet observed (Tetlock and Belkin 1996a, 30–31; see also King, Keohane, and Verba 1994, 11). For instance, in chapter 4 I argue that regime-based collaboration on fisher-independent scientific surveys was decisive for cognitional problem solving in the early 1990s because in those years, the high availability of cod relative to the quota worked to undermine the quality of catch reports, which had been the major basis for stock assessment. The generalization underpinning this argument is that fishers will be less inclined to report catches fully if such reporting is likely to force them to stop fishing before the season is over. Several implications may be drawn, such as that the quality of catch reports declines with the introduction of quota regulations, which seems confirmed by empirical evidence (Halliday and Pinhorn 1996). Such projectability makes it possible to evaluate the robustness of the causal connections between the counterfactual antecedent and the counterfactual consequent.

And now to the third requirement, compatibility with substantive and theoretical knowledge about actual cases that involve the same actors or that place similar actors in similar situations.[1] An estimate of the problem-solving level that would pertain if the regime had not existed should take account of actual cases that are similar or equal to the counterfactual antecedent. It should also be compatible with available evidence about the case under study. For instance, the argument in chapter 6, that Norwegian coastal vessels would have taken considerably more cod than they did in the early 1980s without the heavy diplomatic pressure exerted by the Soviet Union through the regime, rests on historical facts established in chapter 5: Norway regularly pushed for much higher quotas than scientists advised in the period; this policy enjoyed full support among domestic fisheries organizations and the parliamentary opposition; Norway stubbornly rejected Soviet demands for stricter regime rules; but, when such strengthening finally occurred, various domestic measures were taken to constrain the coastal vessel sector, which had been basically unregulated. Persuasive counterfactuals are compatible with—indeed, they draw on—available evidence about the case in question as well as similar cases.

Jointly, these requirements for explicitness, projectability, and compatibility forge a crucial link between persuasive counterfactual analysis and sound empirical analysis. Constructing a persuasive counterfactual means employing, as far as is possible, the same set of operations necessary in any effort to trace a causal relationship: identifying a possible connection, specifying a broader model on the basis of previous knowledge, and examining the empirical tenability of the various propositions in the model. Good counterfactual estimates of problem solving derive from scrutiny of the case under study as well as "otherwise similar" cases, that is, cases similar to it except that they are not under regime influence.

The contrast sometimes implied between counterfactual analysis and methods for causal substantiation is therefore misleading: process tracing, comparison, statistical inference, and other methods for confronting theories with evidence are techniques for doing counterfactual analysis well. To employ such techniques meaningfully, the analyst needs a good model of the factors that drive or impede the outcome of interest. To this we now turn.

Modeling Actual Problem Solving

Few regime scholars doubt that factors outside international institutions as such, for example power relationships among states or competing material interests, carry weight in explaining outcomes in international affairs. And yet a main rationale for studying international regimes is the expectation that they can explain part of the diversity among states in the goals states pursue and their ability to achieve them. Indeed, regime scholars have paid special attention to this issue of causality—whether a regime makes an actual difference—in part because one competing strand of international relations theory, political realism (Strange 1982; Mearsheimer 1995), typically dismisses such institutions as merely reflecting underlying relationships of power and interests.

A general way to substantiate the causal relevance of institutions is to point to the resilience of international regimes despite considerable change in the circumstances that shaped their creation (Keohane 1984; Young 1992). As an example, we may consider the Bretton Woods institutions, which have remained important factors in interstate coordination of trade and finance even after substantial shifts in the relations of power and interests that triggered their creation and shaped their norms and structures.[2] Such resilience, and the fact that governments continue to invest substantial resources in international regimes, provides significant (if somewhat general) evidence that regimes are not mere epiphenomena in world affairs.

Seeking to understand better the extent to which, and under what conditions, international institutions may improve the ability of states to solve important problems, researchers launched a series of empirical investigations in the 1990s, frequently involving comparative case studies (see Haas, Keohane, and Levy 1993; Stokke and Vidas 1996c; Victor, Raustiala, and Skolnikoff 1998b; Young 1999b; Miles et al. 2002). All of these projects sought in one way or another to "determine the proportion of observed changes in target variables . . . occurring in the aftermath of regime formation that can be attributed persuasively to the operation of the regime" (Young 2001, 100). Another common feature of most of these early regime-effectiveness projects was their "mechanism approach" to causal analysis, which this section examines in greater detail.

Causal Mechanisms

Regime effectiveness scholars have delineated a range of mechanisms to structure their causal analysis,[3] but the many specific versions may be subsumed under three more general mechanisms: cognitional processes of learning, normative processes of obligation, and utilitarian processes of interest calculation.

Among effectiveness scholars, the understanding of a "mechanism" is compatible with that of Bunge (1997, 414): "a mechanism is a process in a concrete system, such that it is capable of bringing about or preventing some change in the system or in some of its subsystems."[4] Case-oriented regime scholars conceive of a mechanism as a real-world process that may under certain conditions connect the regime and outcomes relevant to problem solving (Stokke 2004a). The process inherent in the mechanism is typically simpler, more readily comprehensible, and closer to description than the causal connection it supports. As Bunge (1997, 461) argues, mechanism hypotheses "burrow into the details of the composition or inner workings of the system they refer to," or, in the words of Elster (1983, 24), they "open up the black box and show the nuts and bolts . . . [and] reduce the time lag between the explanans and explanandum."

Some authors have posited that mechanisms are means for microreductive explanation, which would imply that mechanisms operate at a lower level of analysis than the phenomena they explain (Stinchcombe 1991, 367, 371–173; Little 1995, 35–36). To illustrate, Allison (1969) reinforces one of his models of foreign policy behavior by pinpointing mechanisms at the level of bureaucratic organization, including socialization within organizations and competition between them, which jointly support the adage, "where you stand depends on where you sit."[5] However, reserving the mechanism concept for microreductive explanation does not follow from Bunge's (1997) definition, nor does it correspond to usage among regime-effectiveness scholars, who sometimes posit mechanisms at the same level as the *explanandum* (Hovi 2004).[6] Most mechanism explanations combine elements of agency and structure (Bunge 1997, 440–441; George and Bennett 2005, 145), and processes that drive or impede change may occur at either level or both.

In a project on environmental regimes, for instance, Keohane, Haas, and Levy (1993, 19) identify certain "concrete mechanisms around which institutions can alter the behavior of state actors, and in turn improve environmental quality." First, regimes may raise the level of concern in societies and state leaderships about the problem in question, for instance by supporting scientific investigations that promote learning about challenges and solutions. Second, these authors argue, regimes may improve the contractual environment by providing means for entering into and monitoring mutually beneficial agreements; and third, they may enhance state capacity to implement such agreements (Levy, Keohane, and Haas 1993, 398–408). Each of those three mechanisms, while clearly "capable of bringing about or preventing some change," is conceived at a high level of abstraction and covers a range of more concrete variants. For instance, a regime may affect the level of concern not only by raising levels of knowledge but also by providing normative standards; such norms can make it easier for external actors or domestic constituencies to criticize a state's policies. Similarly, an international regime may enhance the contractual environment by providing regularly scheduled meetings or by compiling information on rule compliance. Regimes may build national capacity through, for example, technology transfer, financial support, or programs for administrative training. A general mechanism directs attention to a certain type of process, but the set of cases displaying it may still be heterogeneous.

Other projects have approached causal modeling in a similar but substantively broader way. One group of case study authors agreed to "frame a set of models that appear important on theoretical grounds and then turn to the case studies to assess the relevance and relative importance of the behavioral mechanisms associated with each of the models under real-world conditions" (Young and Levy 1999, 21). Additional to the mechanisms highlighted by Keohane and associates, that project pinpoints such regime-triggered processes as bestowal of authority, redefining of roles, and realignment among domestic groups. Authority bestowal refers to the internalization of norms at the individual or organizational levels. Role definition concerns placing states in new social positions: a prominent example is how changes in the international law of the sea during the 1970s endowed coastal states with sovereign rights to resource management in areas that had previously been high seas. Domestic realignment means that a regime affects internal political processes in a member state by promoting new social alliances or strengthening the ability of certain domestic groups to shape policy at the expense of others.

In a project on Antarctic regimes, this broader set of general mechanisms formed the starting point for defining specific variants tailored to the characteristics of one particular institution. Stokke and Vidas (1996a, 18) instructed case study contributors to bring out the details of how a particular outcome came about, noting that "different mechanisms can be invoked when spelling out this process, accounting for *how* international regimes may affect behaviour." After examining the applicability of Young and Levy's (1999) general mechanisms in a series of case studies involving regimes for the management of Antarctic issues, Stokke and Vidas (1996b) concluded that five more specific versions are especially relevant to understanding change and continuity in governance of this region.[7] Hence, general mechanisms can be specified to obtain sets of cases that are similar enough to allow meaningful comparison in support of causal analysis.

The mechanism approach to regime-effectiveness analysis sensitizes the analyst to a broad range of processes that may connect the operation of the regime with variation in problem solving. Such broadness helps ensure that analyses will cover not only processes that flow from actors' pursuit of self-interest within existing incentive structures (always important in international affairs) but also processes such as cognitional learning and normative obligations. More specific versions of such general mechanisms can be defined to sharpen the analysis and to explore triggering conditions within more homogeneous subsets of institutions.

From Mechanisms to Variables

Research on international regime effectiveness will be more cumulative if the attention to mechanisms is complemented with specific causal models of problem solving. Scholars of regime effectiveness often have a generalizing purpose for structuring analysis around causal mechanisms, since a mechanism evident in one study may sensitize analysts to similar processes in other regimes, or in the same regime at another point in time. Thus, when discussing the possibility that the causal connections found in one case may be capable of "traveling" (Sartori 1991) to another, Young (1999a, 258) points out that although the particular combination of causal factors may be unique, "the causal tendency of each of the individual forces may be similar from case to case."

All the same, the contribution of case-based, mechanism-oriented effectiveness projects to cumulative research has been somewhat constrained since the sets of mechanisms in focus and the delineation of each mechanism differ from one project to another. Such diversity is quite natural and may even be useful in view of the role played by these case-oriented projects in opening up regime effectiveness as a field of research (Stokke 1997). Conceptual diversity nevertheless complicates the assessment of whether the findings of one study support, complement, or contradict those of another. This situation is compounded by a second characteristic of many early projects, the frequently complex relationships between the abstract mechanisms and the observable factors that support empirical assessment. For example, Levy, Keohane, and Haas (1993, 400) see international regime rules primarily as drivers of governmental concern, whereas Young (1999a, 269–271) has viewed them through lenses that reveal legitimization and normative enmeshment through social practice.

Thus we see that using causal mechanisms to derive explicit causal models can further enhance their contribution to cumulative research on regime effectiveness. Such modeling is conducted here in chapters 4 to 6, tailored to the specific aspect of problem solving under study. The cognitional aspect involves whether regime participants reach a shared and empirically valid understanding of how to achieve the social purpose of the regime, here balancing utilization and conservation. The regulatory aspect concerns how well joint regulations correspond with the best available knowledge. And the behavioral part refers to the ability to influence the actions of target groups. In the remainder of this section, I briefly outline five causal variables central to this study and to research on international regime effectiveness in general. Three of the five derive from utilitarian considerations (malignancy, collaboration and transparency), one is cognitional in nature and concerns the state of knowledge about the problem in focus, and one factor involves normative obligation.

Malignancy
Regime scholars frequently start out from the actors and their interests (see Hasenclever, Mayer, and Rittberger 1997, 23–44). For instance, Young (1999a, 272–275) notes that some types of problem are more conducive to the operation of institutions than others. Compliance-type regime activities are more likely to succeed if the number of actors who must cooperate in order to monitor target-group behavior is low (see also Jacobson and Brown Weiss 1998b, 521). This proposition derives from the more general argument that collective action becomes more difficult as the number of participants grows (Olson 1971).

Another aspect of problem type is the arrangement of actor preferences. Studies of regime effectiveness have found, for instance, that the need for monitoring behavioral compliance with regime rules is less decisive in cases that involve one or more Pareto optimal equilibria, thus presenting coordination problems with few incentives to defect from an agreed-upon solution (Levy, Keohane, and Haas 1993, 403; Young 1999a, 275). Underdal (1987, 2002a) uses the term "malignancy" to describe such differences. Some problems addressed by international regimes are rather benign in the sense that individual and collective interests are congruous: the actors have similar preferences as to outcomes, and will all suffer loss or forgo benefits if they fail to coordinate their behavior. Severe malignancy, in contrast, involves incongruity between individual and collective interests due to asymmetry—negatively correlated preferences on outcomes—or to externalities or competition.

Negative externalities are effects on others that an actor fails to take into consideration, as in the "tragedy of the commons" metaphor (see chapter 1), typically generating more of the activity than is socially desirable. Competition denotes effects on others that are calculated inversely, as for relatively assessed goods (Grieco 1988). The concerns of some industrialized states that differentiated commitments on reducing greenhouse gas emissions will severely impair their own competitiveness relative to that of rising developing-state economies have hampered regulatory as well as behavioral progress under the Kyoto Protocol (Stokke, Hovi, and Ulfstein 2005). Summarizing a broad comparative and statistical analysis of international regimes, Underdal (2002c, 460) finds that regimes facing highly malign problems can be effective only if they provide significant selective incentives for cooperative behavior, linkages to more benign problems, or what he terms strong "problem-solving capacity" deriving from decision rules, power distribution between leaders and laggards, and various kinds of leadership (see also Underdal 2002a, 22–36).

This study applies a simple four-value scale to measure the causal variables. I use Underdal's (2002b, 56) criteria to differentiate levels of malignancy. Thus, malignancy is full if it involves severe incongruity through strong elements of asymmetry and competition. It is substantial if the incongruity is large, with no clear significant asymmetry or competition; modest if the problem involves some incongruity, but contingency or synergy predominates; and insignificant if no incongruity exists.

The malignancy variable derives from the rationalist mainstream of regime analysis. It concerns actors' incentives to avoid international obligations or to defect from existing obligations. As chapters 4 to 6 show, this variable is highly relevant to all three aspects of problem solving.

Collaboration

International institutions provide means for overcoming barriers to collective action by identifying focal points for negotiation, by helping to build trust among participants, or by enabling cost-efficient coordination. This is an important thrust in utilitarian as well as cognition-oriented regime analysis (Schelling 1960; Keohane 1984; Levy, Young, and Zürn 1995). Miles and associates (2002, 483) define such collaboration as "jointness of planning and implementation," thus echoing distinctions well known in the study of policy integration (Lindberg 1970). They refer to the means that states use for coordinating their activity— common standards, joint planning, and joint implementation of plans— and these distinctions can be used to scale this variable. On my yardstick, collaboration among two or more parties is insignificant if no explicit coordination occurs, modest if it involves common standards only, substantial if there is joint planning of activities, and full if those plans are also implemented jointly. Underdal (2002a, 36) expects collaboration to intervene in a positive way in the causal relationship between malignancy, various institutional features, and problem solving.

In this study, collaboration is a part of the models that account for variation in cognitional and regulatory success. It indirectly enters the model of behavioral problem solving as well, since steadily more intensive collaboration among the enforcement agencies of participant states is one of the factors underlying variation in behavioral transparency.

State of Knowledge

A third causal factor that looms large in regime-effectiveness analysis, especially in studies of environmental governance, is the credibility and perceived legitimacy of expert input to decision making. Credibility refers to the extent to which decision makers see scientific input as reflecting the best available knowledge of the problem in question (Mitchell, Clark, and Cash 2006, 316). This line of research draws on broader scholarship on the significance of factors such as consensual knowledge (Haas 1990) and the existence of an "epistemic community"—a transnational network of experts well connected to national decision makers and in rough agreement on the severity, causes, and preferred remedies of a problem (Haas 1989; Adler and Haas 1992).

Knowledge building within international institutions may enhance credibility by diffusing research findings (Levy, Keohane, and Haas 1993, 410–412) and leveling the factual ground for the assessment of risks and options (Young 1999a, 262–263). In some cases, such activities may even lead states to redefine their national interests on matters of controversy (Goldstein and Keohane 1993, 24). For example, monitoring and modeling of air pollution flows in the 1990s under the Convention on Long-Range Transboundary Air Pollution revealed that the UK was a much greater importer of toxic pollutants than scientists had thought (Wettestad 2002a). That discovery explains in part the subsequent change in Britain's posture on the desirability of stricter international regulation in the area: its interests had been reassessed on the basis of credible scientific input.

Legitimacy, in the context of regulatory-problem solving, refers to perceptions among the decision makers that the expert input reflects serious consideration of their concerns, values, and data provision (Mitchell, Clark, and Cash 2006, 320). Broad participation in the process of developing input may prove decisive for generating normative commitment to the measures advised by scientists (Stokke and Vidas 1996b, 447).

Several empirical studies of international regimes report evidence in support of these general propositions concerning scientific credibility and legitimacy. "To be effective," conclude Jacobson and Brown Weiss (1998b, 525) from a comparative analysis of implementation in nine polities of five international environmental treaties, "accords need to include provisions for gaining and utilizing scientific and technical advice, and for ensuring that there is a broad consensus among the parties on the scientific and technical issues." Similarly, in summarizing seven in-depth case studies, Adler and Haas (1992, 385) warn that "when an epistemic community loses its consensus, its authority diminishes and decision makers tend to pay less attention to its advice." Substantively compatible but with a broader outcome category, Breitmeier, Young, and Zürn (2006, 220–224) infer from an analysis of numerous international regimes that one factor positively correlated with problem solving is the extent to which a regime promotes understanding of the problem that gave rise to the regime and the consequences of various policy options.

I show in chapter 5 how the state of knowledge can be measured on the four-value scale used in this study, relating it to cognitional problem solving.

Obligation

International norms differ in how compelling they are—in the extent of obligation they exert on states and target groups. Determinacy and formal bindingness are important when grading such normative pull. Determinacy derives from textual precision or agreed-upon procedures for interpreting rules in cases of disagreement (Franck 1990). Jacobson and Brown Weiss (1998b, 523–524) conclude that "the more precise the obligations, the easier it is to assess and promote compliance," but they also emphasize substantive aspects such as the differential treatment of wealthy and developing countries. Young (1999a, 266), too, highlights regulatory precision: while even vague norms may become "more and more influential as . . . the regime itself enmeshes the participants in a web of institutionalized activities from which they cannot easily extricate themselves," such influence derives in part from expectations of there being binding and precise rules in the future (Young 1999a, 267). Similarly, Abbott and Snidal (2000, 421) see a tendency to "legalization" in many international regimes, involving greater rule precision, bindingness, and more frequent delegation of authority to third parties for interpreting and implementing rules. Those three dimensions are also in focus for Breitmeier, Young, and Zürn (2006, 79–95), who report empirical findings on two of them: in their dataset, behavioral impact appears to correlate with rule precision but not with legal status.

The attention among regime-effectiveness scholars to determinate and legally binding rules is in line with the broader literature on international legitimacy. According to Franck (1990, 24), legitimacy in international affairs is "a property of a rule or rule-making institution which itself exerts a pull towards compliance on those addressed normatively because those addressed believe that the rule or institution has come into being and operates in accordance with generally accepted principles of right process." Determinacy builds legitimacy because "right process" requires a clear message about what is expected of those addressed by the rule, whereas vagueness or elasticity facilitates justification of noncompliance (Franck 1990, 53–54). Legal bindingness builds legitimacy by requiring explicit acceptance by states, which is foremost among the procedures available for validating rules (Abbott et al. 2000, 409). A lower but still significant level of acceptance is evident in "soft law"—norms that are deliberately nonbinding legally but still have legal relevance, located "in the twilight between law and politics" (Thürer 2000). Important examples are resolutions by international organizations, international plans of action, or codes of conduct. Similar to unilateral declarations, soft law norms are "politically binding" in the sense that breaking them may cause political criticism and pressure, but not legal action.

My yardstick is based on those two dimensions: obligation is full if norms are highly determinate and legally binding, substantial if norms are legally binding with medium determinacy or politically binding with high determinacy, modest if norms are legally binding with low determinacy, and insignificant if no international norm applies.

This yardstick cannot capture the full range of processes in focus for scholars who argue that international regimes may shape behavior through the force of obligation. For instance, it makes no reference to distributive justice, which many authors see as complementary to legitimacy when assessing the normative pull of an institution or rule (Albin 1995; Franck 1995; Breitmeier, Young, and Zürn 2006, 91). Criteria for distributive justice are notoriously difficult to specify, as well as presumably being less relevant in a bilateral relationship involving advanced industrial nations in the Northern Hemisphere than in many other international regime contexts. Nor does my yardstick explore other procedural characteristics besides acceptance that may help validate an international norm. In environmental governance, validation by involvement of target groups or prestigious scientific expertise are two such characteristics (Bodansky 1999), but both are constants rather than variables in the regime studied here.

Differentiating cases according to the determinacy and bindingness of norms captures two aspects of obligation that are substantively essential and vary over time and among regime members.

Transparency

Many conceptual and empirical studies of regime effectiveness emphasize systems of information that enable states to cross-check the reports provided by target groups or their governments. Such transparency regarding information on rule adherence is in focus for two strands of analysis that otherwise disagree on how to explain regime effectiveness. The "enforcement school" considers transparency primarily as a means of deterrence, allowing states to expose and punish rule violations (Downs, Rocke, and Barsoom 1996, 393), while proponents of the "management school" see behavioral information as clarifying impediments to compliance that allow appropriate rule amendment, learning, or capacity enhancement (Chayes and Chayes 1995; Victor, Raustiala, and Skolnikoff 1998a, 19).

The concept of verification requires both self-reporting and other-reporting; it refers to evaluation of the completeness and accuracy of compliance information (Loreti, Foster, and Obbagy 2001, 3). Such evaluation requires access to alternative sources of information; the *scope* of such verification can be used to scale the transparency variable. My yardstick gives a full transparency score if all or most of the self-reporting by target groups can be verified by their government *as well as* by other regime members. Verifiability by other states is important whenever suspicion exists that a regime member is implementing its commitments too leniently. Transparency is deemed substantial if all or most target-group reports can be verified by their own government only, modest if a significant portion of the reports cannot be verified even by the group's own government, and insignificant if little or no verification occurs.

In an early regime-effectiveness study, Levy, Keohane, and Haas (1993, 399–402) found that publicity about national commitments and the monitoring of compliance exert political pressure on governments and reduce fears among regime participants that others will exploit their cooperation. Mitchell (1998, 119) distinguishes between self-reporting and other-reporting: the latter is especially important when actors have incentives for concealing information, as in malign situations. Jacobson and Brown Weiss (1998b, 525–527) conclude that information measures are more effective when they complement national reports from other sources, and when capacities exist for processing and using the information for review of progress under the regime. Similarly, Breitmeier, Young, and Zürn (2006, 75–78) find that, unlike the case with soft and nonintrusive information requirements, procedures allowing verification correlate positively with rule compliance.

Transparency in behavioral problem solving, as studied in this book, is a matter of whether target-group reports on activities are subject to independent verification. Earlier research indicates that this factor can be important for regime compliance whenever problem malignancy is high.

Summary

I have highlighted these five causal variables because they are applied broadly in regime-effectiveness analysis and because each one is helpful for understanding one or more of the general aspects of problem solving. Thus, in the chapter on cognitional problem solving I combine malignancy and collaboration with two other factors to account for success and failure. The other factors are substantive intricacy, which concerns major shifts in the marine environmental conditions, and the extent to which stock-forecast models incorporate data on such changes. The chapter on regulatory problem solving examines the impacts of malignancy, collaboration, the state of knowledge, and an additional factor, urgency, caused by exogenous "shocks," on the ability of negotiators to agree on rules reflecting the best available knowledge. In the chapter on behavioral problem solving I combine malignancy, obligation, and transparency with one more variable, shaming, to account for ups and downs in rule compliance.

The next section reviews various techniques for evaluating the hypotheses underlying such causal models and thereby obtaining the explanation of problem solving necessary for estimating the most plausible counterfactual level of problem solving.

Confronting Models with Evidence

A persuasive estimate of the level of problem solving that would pertain if there were no regime requires a good explanation of actual problem solving. Methods available for confronting causal models with empirical evidence vary, but one important determinant is the number of observations that go into the analysis. This section reviews the strengths and limitations of some major methods and explains why the present study of the Barents Sea fisheries regime triangulates methods while leaning heavily on the fuzzy set version of QCA.

Process Tracing

One important technique for building a causal account within a singular case is process tracing. This technique involves examining the chain of events that leads to an outcome in light of competing theoretical accounts, and eliminating any accounts that are incompatible with intermediate observations (George and McKeown 1985, 35; George and Bennett 2005, 207). Thus, each link in the causal chain provides an opportunity for projecting observable implications of competing causal accounts— for instance, accounts that do not include an international regime—and seeing how compatible they are with the available evidence (King, Keohane, and Verba 1994, 24; Coppedge 1999, 471–472). Convincing process-tracing evidence of, for example, the theory that regime-generated scientific investigations constrain overfishing could include observations of scientists offering joint advice after the creation of the regime but not before, managers proceeding to adopt compatible regulations, and harvesters complaining that low quotas constrain them but nevertheless reducing their catches, even though the fish stocks in question are demonstrably plentiful. Any break at decisive links in that chain of evidence—such as regulators ignoring advice, or fishers ignoring regulations—would undermine that particular causal account and direct attention to other explanations.

As chapters 4 to 6 show, process tracing is important as a tool in the disaggregate approach to regime effectiveness because it can help clarify the most plausible no-regime scores on drivers of and impediments to problem solving—that is, the counterfactual antecedent—which are important in identifying the upper and lower bounds of plausible counterfactual problem-solving scores (discussed in the next section).

By focusing on a singular chain of events, process tracing is "fundamentally different from methods based on . . . comparison across cases" (George and Bennett 2005, 207). A good explanation can draw on both. Process tracing may provide persuasive evidence that the regime served as a decisive link in a causal chain that produced a high level of problem solving, but that is not quite enough to demonstrate that the no-regime level of problem solving would have been lower. That counterfactual becomes persuasive only after the analyst has evaluated and rejected the possibility that other conditions could do the same job through some other causal chain that does not include the regime. There might be evidence to support such an evaluation within the process traced, but systematic analysis of several cases can make the argument more convincing.

Comparative and Statistical Control on Nonregime Factors

The comparative methods pioneered by John Stuart Mill are important in many effectiveness studies, but they suffer from certain limitations that call for complementary techniques. Were it possible to control the characteristics of all causal factors relevant to problem solving, estimating a persuasive no-regime counterfactual would be straightforward. We could simply remove the international regime while keeping other modeled factors constant, and examine any impacts on the level of problem solving. In his overview of the logical operations that comparative analysts use to identify and reject explanatory candidates, Mill ([1853] 1904) termed such experimental design the "method of difference" and contrasted it to the "method of agreement," which involves searching for a single common condition among cases "agreeing" on the outcome.

Both methods are important for discovering connections between phenomena, but only that of difference is reliable for substantiating causality (Mill [1853] 1904, 256–258). The method of agreement cannot differentiate cause from effect and makes it difficult to rule out a spurious relationship—that is, covariation among causally unrelated variables. Unfortunately, while the method of agreement is unreliable, the experimental design inherent in the method of difference is generally not available to scholars of regime effectiveness because they are dealing with causal factors beyond their control.

When experimental design is infeasible, as is common in the social sciences, Mill ([1853] 1904, 258–259) recommends the "indirect method of difference." This involves sequential application of the method of agreement, first to positive cases, to identify a causal candidate, and then to negative cases, to ascertain that the causal candidate is absent. This method is one of difference because it pinpoints differentiating features among cases that "disagree" with respect to the outcome. The method is indirect because it proceeds not by examining the effects of an actual change in the causal candidate but by selecting cases that agree in every respect except for the outcome and the causal candidate (Ragin 1987, 36–42).[8] To the extent that the cases do agree in all other relevant respects, this indirect method of difference approximates the laboratory situation and provides a "natural experiment" that allows us to observe the effect of the presence or absence of a condition. As Mill ([1853] 1904, 259) noted, however, the number of potentially relevant factors is infinite, so the approximation of a natural experiment to a real one can never be complete.

The method of "structured, focused comparison" aims to maximize the causal leverage of natural experiments by narrowing in on a small number of theoretically interesting variables while remaining sensitive to the specific context of each case (George 1979). This approach is "focused" in that it deals only with cases that are instances of the phenomenon under scrutiny and solely with those aspects of a complex case that are relevant to a sharply defined theoretical question. The procedure is "structured" in standardizing data requirements and "interrogating" each case with the same set of questions (George and McKeown 1985). Organizers of comparative projects on regime effectiveness have found this approach useful; they frequently include "templates" or other means for coordinating data collection, interpretation, and analysis within each case to enhance the cross-case comparability of findings. The present study, which breaks down the general resource management problem into cognitional, regulatory, and behavioral aspects, demonstrates another way to make an intensive study more focused and structured.

Useful as it is to select cases that facilitate comparative control by agreeing in some theoretically important ways and disagreeing in others, applying this logic remains difficult whenever there are many factors other than the regime that may explain the diversity of outcomes and few similar units of analysis. As Mill ([1853] 1904, 249–250) bemoaned, "nature, being constructed on a quite different scheme from that of facilitating our studies, is seldom so friendly as to bestow upon us . . . the precise *sort* of variation which we are in want of for discovering the law of the phenomenon."[9] "Institutional arrangements in international society," concurred Young (1999a, 257), provide analysts with "small numbers of cases, and there are often good reasons to suspect that individual cases differ from one another in significant ways." To counter this problem of limited diversity, which typically renders analysis less conclusive, Miles and associates (2002) split the operation of international regimes into distinct temporal phases and normative components— separate protocols or other documents that specify distinct sets of commitments. Those two moves make it possible to distinguish numbers of observations large enough to allow the use of techniques for analytical reduction that would otherwise be unavailable, including multivariate logical comparison. With the same objective, Mitchell (2002) increased the number of observations that went into his statistical analysis of regime effectiveness by defining and measuring the variables of his model at the level of states, and not at more aggregate levels.

The analyst working with a large data matrix may cross-tabulate an outcome variable with a set of control variables and calculate the partial effects of an operational variable by observing differences in outcome scores between cells that comprise cases agreeing on the control variables (Hellevik 1988).[10] Depending on the mode of selection, the number of observations, and the frequency distribution, the quantitative analyst may derive coefficients that describe correlation among dependent and independent variables and then estimate the probability that such correlation is due to random causes. Although knowing less about each observation than her qualitative colleague, the analyst can allow for measurement error and missing variables by means of confidence intervals and, more generally, the underlying assumption of probabilistic relationships among variables (Goldthorpe 1997, 6–7). The larger the number of observations, the smaller the problem of limited diversity— which is a major rationale for the decomposition of the empirical evidence that marks the disaggregate approach.

Whereas process tracing compiles heterogeneous evidence about one case to evaluate a specific causal proposition, comparative and statistical procedures compile homogeneous evidence about several cases to evaluate a general causal proposition. Scholars of regime effectiveness try to overcome the limited-diversity problem inherent in logical comparison by selecting cases to approximate an experimental situation or by expanding the number of observations. The disaggregate approach advanced in this book does both: splitting the resource management problem into three specific parts helps make each set of observations more homogeneous and thus closer to a natural experiment, while breaking down the empirical data by year, and in part also by the nationality of harvesting operations, raises the number of observations to enhance the comparative or statistical leverage.

QCA and Multiple, Configurative Causation

Another challenge with Mill's methods of comparison, besides limited diversity, is that the logical operations become increasingly complex and unwieldy when the number of variables or cases grows beyond a handful. Mill ([1853] 1904, 255–259) bases those operations on paired comparison and eliminates from the explanation causal candidates that are either absent in some cases where there is agreement on the outcome (by the method of agreement) or present in some cases where there is disagreement on the outcome (indirect method of difference). Neither of those eliminations holds if more than one condition is capable of producing the outcome (multiple causation) or if such capacity depends on the characteristic of another factor (configurative causation) (Ragin 1987; Little 1995). Accordingly, Mill's methods of logical comparison may tend to reject too many causal candidates, especially when causal relationships are complex and the number of observations is intermediate or high. Excessive elimination of causal candidates will yield explanations that are less conditional—bolder, more simplistic—than the empirical evidence warrants.

A set-theoretic technique developed by Charles Ragin (1987, 2000, 2008) formalizes Mill's logical operations and helps reduce their vulnerability to multiple and configurative causation. The original, "crisp set" version has been applied in earlier studies of regime effectiveness (Underdal 2002c; Stokke 2004a, 2007c); it builds on the binary language developed by George Boole in the mid-1800s, which also forms the mathematical basis of computer technology. "Crisp sets" imply that cases are either inside or outside a given category. For instance, if a researcher expects that regime rules on openness in terms of access to information are important for problem solving, the only characteristics available would be "open" or "closed."

Like Mill's methods, the QCA procedure identifies causal conditions that, according to the dataset at hand, may be either necessary or sufficient for producing a given outcome. Boolean algebra does not manipulate numbers, it systematizes logical expressions. The backbone of the QCA technique is a *truth table,* an ordering device that lists all possible combinations of scores on the causal variables under study and imputes the outcome—for instance, high or low problem solving—for each empirically observed occurrence of those combinations. A causal condition, which may involve one or more variables, that *always* occurs in cases with a given outcome merits closer scrutiny as a possible necessary condition for that outcome. More relevant in the study of social systems, which typically display several pathways leading to the same outcome, are causal conditions that occur *only* in cases with a given outcome: such conditions are possible sufficient conditions for that outcome.

The main value added by the QCA procedure to Mill's methods is set-theoretic algebra, which formalizes the analytical reduction of the list of causal conditions that are reliably associated with the outcome of interest. Such reduction aims to formulate the simplest, most general statements of causal sufficiency that the empirical evidence allows. The formalization inherent in set-theoretic reduction helps avoid overelimination of causal conditions under multiple and configurative causality: a condition is eliminated, if logically redundant, only in the specific context defined by the characteristics of the other modeled factors.

Causal configurations empirically shown to reliably deliver either high or low levels of problem solving can be powerful tools for estimating the most plausible no-regime counterfactual level. If, for instance, a regime-driven condition emerges as the sole difference between a causal combination that reliably delivers success and one that reliably delivers failure, that can directly indicate the most plausible no-regime level of problem solving. The same would be true if a reliable success combination did not include regime-driven conditions, or if a reliable failure combination included them.

The QCA technique is relatively novel but has already overcome several initial limitations. Ragin (2000, 2008) extends the applicability of this method to fuzzy sets, by which the analyst can differentiate degrees of membership in a set—thus moving from dichotomous to multichotomous categories. A management regime that allows nongovernmental organizations to participate as observers at regulatory meetings is more open than one that merely issues post facto reports, even if neither of them is closed. This extension to multichotomous categories is important for the applicability of QCA to the present study, which uses four-value scales to measure variation in problem solving and causal factors. If the number of observations permits, the analyst may also impose a frequency threshold on such sufficiency tests by requiring a certain number of cases before judging a configuration sufficient for the outcome. Also possible are probabilistic procedures that allow one or more cases that deviate from the patterns, and then judging a causal configuration "almost always" or "usually" sufficient, depending on the frequency distribution, the number of cases, and the probability criterion (Ragin 2000, 109).

By occupying a middle ground between intensive, case-oriented methods and quantitative procedures, fuzzy set QCA offers a promising tool for examining complex phenomena such as regime effectiveness on the basis of intermediate numbers of observations. Being configurative, it permits a more disciplined reduction of causal statements than does Mill's method of agreement or the indirect method of difference.

Triangulation

The relative strengths of process tracing, logical comparison, and statistical inference for evaluating causal propositions depend crucially on the nature of information that is available, especially the number of observations. As Underdal (2002b, 57–58) comments, "the [regime effectiveness] field at large would be well advised to work with research designs that combine *complementary* approaches."[11] The present study of the Barents Sea fisheries regime does so by triangulating several methods for causal inference. First, multivariate comparison by means of QCA identifies, for each aspect of problem solving, the causal combinations that reliably result in success or in failure. Second, process tracing is important when specifying the most plausible no-regime scores on causal factors. Third, for one of three aspects, behavioral problem solving, statistical procedures are also applicable since this part of the effectiveness analysis distinguishes between Norwegian and Russian behavior and therefore involves more observations. The possibility of examining the same dataset with different methodological tools allows comparison of findings and, when they prove to be compatible (see chapter 6), enhances their reliability.

Among these techniques, QCA is central to this study since it allows configurative analysis even when the number of observations is not very large. The next section explains in greater detail how its fuzzy set version can provide firm evidence on the most plausible no-regime level of problem solving, so that regime effectiveness scores can be assigned.

Fuzzy Set QCA and Regime Effectiveness

The QCA procedure, then, can identify causal combinations that reliably yield either low or high levels of problem solving. As this section shows, such proven paths to failure or success help to assign effectiveness scores whenever the counterfactual path fits a failure path more, or a success path less, than does the actual case. A counterfactual path is the set of scores on the causal factors that would pertain if the regime had not existed. Set theory allows precise measurement of its fit with success and failure paths, and the associated scores help provide upper and lower bounds on plausible estimates of no-regime problem solving.

Reliable Paths to Success and Failure

Fuzzy set QCA identifies reliable paths to a certain outcome, such as success or failure in problem solving, in essentially the same way as the crisp set version does: by examining whether certain combinations of scores on the causal variables consistently yield a high outcome score. However, such examination can quickly become intractable with multichotomous and continuous variables, because the number of logically possible causal combinations rises exponentially with the number of values on each variable. As this subsection shows, the fuzzy set version overcomes that challenge by centering the comparative analysis on the crisp set categories that come closest to describing the observations in the dataset accurately.

Unlike crisp sets, which categorize cases as either inside or outside, fuzzy sets allow cases with partial membership and thus sit better with the four-value categorization of factors and outcomes in this study. Any QCA analysis starts out from the truth table—the multidimensional property space of logically possible combinations of the causal conditions modeled (Ragin 1987). Crisp set cases belong to one of the "corners" of this property space, involving either full score or zero score on each variable, whereas fuzzy sets locate cases by vectors corresponding to their variable scores (Ragin 2000, 183). Each property-space corner is therefore an ideal-type (in the Weberian sense, not the utopian one) combination of characteristics of the modeled factors that fuzzy set cases may fit more or less, depending on their spatial proximity.

Characterizing actual cases according to how well they fit those ideal-type combinations simplifies the QCA analysis tremendously. Rather than comparing for each case the outcome score and the causal-combination scores associated with the 256 (4^4) logically possible vector space locations inherent in four variables with four values each, the number of ideal-type combinations to examine is a mere 16.

Two set-theoretic rules are necessary for determining how well a fuzzy set case fits an ideal-type causal combination—those of intersection and negation. According to the rule of intersection, a case's membership in the intersection of two or more sets is the minimum (not the average) of its memberships in the intersecting sets (Ragin 2000, 172). The underlying logic is obvious with crisp sets: despite its impressive GNP per capita, Switzerland is in no way to be found in the set of wealthy American states. This rule of intersection, whereby a high score on one factor cannot compensate for a low score on another, also applies to fuzzy sets. With fuzzy sets, however, the score expressing the degree of fit with a causal combination—its score on the combination, derived from the minimum of its scores on the variables—can also assume values in between zero and full.

To illustrate the use of this intersection rule to derive how a case scores on a causal combination, let us consider two of the factors that, according to chapter 4, can be expected to influence cognitional problem solving, measured here as the accuracy of scientific forecasts of fish stocks. One such factor is likely to complicate forecast accuracy, namely, substantive intricacy in the form of major shifts in the stock's natural environment, especially food availability. Another factor is expected to promote accuracy: collaboration on scientific surveys, allowing scientists to complement catch reports with fisher-independent data from the entire ecosystem. One ideal-type combination of those causal factors is a full score on intricacy, implying very severe environmental disturbances, and a full score on collaboration, implying joint planning, intercalibration of equipment, and extensive joint surveys (see chapter 4). The score for any given observation on that causal combination is the lowest of its scores on either variable: appendix 5, table A5.1, shows that in the year 1996, for instance, there was both full intricacy (a score of 1) and substantial collaboration (a score of 0.67), yielding substantial fit (a score of 0.67, the lower of the two variable scores) with the combination in question. This case, in other words, is described quite well, but not perfectly, by the causal combination of full intricacy and full collaboration.

The set-theoretic rule of negation is necessary for determining fit scores because half of the logically possible crisp-set combinations to be examined involve factor scores that are zero rather than full. For instance, with regard to the category combining insignificant intricacy with full collaboration, to derive the fit score of a case on that causal combination it is necessary first to determine its score on the insignificant intricacy category, which is the negation of intricacy. A case's membership in the negation of a fuzzy set is obtained by subtracting from full membership (a score of 1) its membership in the original set (Ragin 2000, 173). Thus, the modest intricacy that marks the year 1988 (a score of 0.33) implies substantial membership (a score of $1 - 0.33 = 0.67$) in the set of cases with insignificant intricacy. As collaboration, too, was substantial that year, this case has a substantial fit with the ideal-type combination of insignificant intricacy and full collaboration.

The score that a case achieves on an ideal-type causal combination is one of the two parameters needed for determining whether the case supports a causal-necessity or a causal-sufficiency claim. The second parameter is the outcome score. The crisp set version of QCA narrows in on factors or combinations that are present for all cases with a given outcome because this pattern could suggest—if backed up by a causal theory and corroborated by other evidence—that those conditions are *necessary* for the outcome. The corresponding fuzzy set pattern is that no case achieves an outcome score higher than its score on the causal combination (Ragin 2000, 212–218). An example is a scatterplot that locates each case on or below a rising diagonal, which might indicate that a case cannot obtain a high score on the outcome without an equally high or higher score on the causal condition. This necessity pattern does not emerge for any of the causal combinations examined in this study; one may suspect that substantively interesting necessary conditions for a given outcome are rare in complex societal affairs. Checking for them is nevertheless important because failure to do so might undermine the subsequent analysis of causal sufficiency (Ragin 2000, 105–106, 254).

Highly relevant in regime-effectiveness analysis are possible *sufficient* conditions for an outcome, and the fuzzy set pattern that would support such sufficiency is that each case achieves a score on the outcome that is equally as high as or higher than its score on the causal combination (Ragin 2000, 234–238). On a scatterplot, this pattern would locate all cases on or above a rising diagonal, indicating that a high score on the causal combination reliably delivers an equally high or higher score on the outcome. As we shall see in chapter 4, on one additional condition concerning the use of ecosystem modeling, that causal-sufficiency pattern in fact emerges for the combination of insignificant intricacy and full collaboration.

Reliable paths to *failure* are no less useful for substantiating counterfactual problem-solving scores. Examining whether certain causal conditions consistently yield a low problem-solving score is an integral part of the QCA approach and is logically distinct from the analysis of conditions for a high score: reliable paths to failure are not necessarily mirror images of those that deliver success (Ragin 2006). Identifying possible failure paths proceeds in the same way as identifying success paths except that the outcome score is negated since a case with a modest score (0.33) in the success category has a substantial score (1 − 0.33 = 0.67) in the failure category.

In short, fuzzy set QCA overcomes the challenge of exponentially rising numbers of causal combinations by determining, for each case, the fit with a smaller number of ideal-type categories that allow only full or zero score. The set-theoretic rules of intersection and negation allow us to assign to each case a numerical value that describes its fit with those crisp-set combinations: we call that value its score on the causal path in question. The score is important because the QCA technique identifies sufficient conditions, or reliable paths, by comparing for each case the path score and the outcome score. If all observations in the dataset have scores on success or failure in problem solving that are equal to or greater than their scores on an ideal-type causal combination, the latter will stand out in the dataset as a reliable path to the outcome. While such reliable paths are stated in crisp set terms, they imply a distinct empirical pattern among *all* cases that fit the ideal-type combination to some extent. One part of that pattern is especially useful in effectiveness analysis: all cases that score high (substantial or full) on the ideal-type combination score equally high or higher on problem-solving success or failure.

Evaluating the Evidence: Consistency and Coverage

Causal conditions that always deliver a certain outcome without being trivial are exceptions rather than the rule in societal affairs, which may provide reason for relaxing the reliability criterion somewhat and for allowing some variation among causal paths in their consistency with it. As this subsection shows, reliable causal paths also vary in the coverage, or explanatory power, they provide in accounting for variation in problem solving.

With fuzzy sets, the same unit of observation may be a case of more than one causal combination, fitting some more than others. The 1988 cognitional problem-solving case referenced above was characterized by a substantial score on the combination of insignificant intricacy and full collaboration. Using the set-theoretic rules of intersection and negation, we see that the same case achieves a modest score on the path combining full intricacy and full collaboration. Units of observation achieving a substantial or a full score on a causal combination are strong cases of that combination, whereas those achieving a modest score are weak cases of it. An insignificant (zero) score means that an observation is not at all a case of a causal combination and cannot shed any empirical light on the combination. The fact that each case in the dataset fits several combinations implies that findings derived from fuzzy set QCA typically draw on more cases than do their crisp set counterparts, which build only on cases with a perfect fit. Since each empirical case has the potential of deviating from the sufficiency pattern, fuzzy set analysis usually involves a greater number of reliability tests.

For a dataset to provide firm empirical evidence on a causal combination, however, it must include one or more strong cases of it, since the reliability criterion would be too lenient otherwise: all cases would meet the criterion even if none of them achieved more than a modest score on the outcome. That is why, on the candidate list of reliable paths, the fuzzy set QCA procedure includes only those among the logically possible causal combinations that are represented by strong cases in the dataset. With one exception not relevant here, each case in the dataset is a strong case of only one combination of the causal factors under study,[12] and cases that have their best fit with the same combination of scores on the causal factors belong to the same grouping (Ragin 2000, 186). Hence, all cases with a positive score on a causal path can shed empirical light on the hypothesis that the path reliably delivers an outcome, but strong cases shed more light.

To understand why it can be reasonable to relax the full-consistency requirement for a reliable path, let us consider the nine causal combinations represented by strong cases in the analysis of cognitional problem solving in chapter 4. In addition to intricacy, collaboration, and ecosystem modeling, the causal hypotheses under evaluation also include malignancy, which here concerns fisher incentives to underreport catches. Among the nine, only the category combining insignificant scores on malignancy and intricacy with full scores on collaboration and ecosystem modeling is fully consistent with the reliability criterion. It is not surprising that this combination of causal factors should emerge as a reliable path to forecast accuracy: each property, according to the theory arguments underlying the model, is conducive to problem solving. Zero malignancy implies few incentives to underreport catches, full collaboration ensures that researchers can complement reliable fisher reports with internally comparable survey data, zero intricacy means that ecosystem conditions are not extraordinary, and full ecosystem modeling means that the researchers monitor those conditions and take them into consideration in their stock forecast. The configuration is therefore *theoretically potent* in terms of forecast accuracy, and the empirical analysis corroborates this expectation through a pattern fully consistent with sufficiency.

Another causal path represented in the dataset, equal to the first except that the malignancy score is full, is theoretically somewhat less potent (since fisher reports might be unreliable), yet it comes very close to meeting the full-sufficiency mark: six out of seven cases of this category have outcome scores that are equally as high as or higher than their path score. A simple way to measure how consistent this category is with the sufficiency pattern is to calculate the proportion of cases that meet the criterion, 6/7 = 0.86. This consistency measure requires no more than ordinal-level variable measurement.[13]

However, Ragin (2006) points out two reasons for using a more sophisticated consistency measure that can take account of the important diversity that may exist among cases deviating from the sufficiency pattern: a wide deviation from the pattern is more damaging to a reliability claim than a narrow one, and deviation by a strong case is more damaging than deviation by a weak case. To understand why strong cases should count more than weak ones when evaluating consistency, we need only consider that Robert Mugabe's Zimbabwe would achieve a non-zero score on the democracy measure since some mechanisms exist linking elections and the population of some positions of authority. Few researchers, however, would regard this case as critical for the hypothesis that sharp economic decline is a sufficient condition for high voter turnout in pluralistic democracies. At present, Zimbabwe is a weak case of the pluralistic democracy category and cannot provide firm evidence of it.

A better score of consistency takes account of these important differences by calculating not the proportion of consistent *cases* but the proportion of the total *scores* on the causal combination that is consistent with the sufficiency pattern (Ragin 2006). Unlike the simpler version, this consistency measure requires interval-level measurement of the causal and outcome factors—in other words, it should make sense to judge the qualitative step separating an insignificant score from a modest score on a variable as being equal to the step from modest to substantial or the step from substantial to full score. I consider this judgment a reasonable simplifying assumption allowing the use of QCA measures that are more sensitive than their simpler, case-proportional versions to important diversity within and among groupings in the dataset.

Ragin (2006, 293) warns against accepting a causal category as a "mostly sufficient" condition for an outcome if consistency is less than 0.75. He recommends a cutoff point at 0.85, noting that "17 out of 20 (85%) is substantial enough to indicate, to a social scientist at least, that there may be some sort of integral connection." For the near fully consistent causal category mentioned above (concerning cognitional problem solving), combining full scores on malignancy, collaboration, and ecosystem modeling with insignificant intricacy, this more sophisticated QCA consistency measure raises the score from 0.86 to 0.90, which indicates that this second causal combination, too, is a quite reliable path to forecast accuracy.

Coverage is another important QCA measure. It concerns the explanatory power of the reliable paths, or the proportion of the total problem-solving scores in the dataset that are covered consistently by those causal combinations (Ragin 2006, 301). For each case, a reliable path covers, or accounts for, a problem-solving score only as high as the score of that case on the causal path; that is as far as the evidence goes. Thus, any problem-solving score that a case achieves beyond that score must result from its fit with other causal combinations. We find the coverage of a reliable path by summarizing the consistent path scores of all cases involving significant problem solving and dividing it by the total problem-solving score in the dataset. Among the two reliable paths in the example above, the near fully consistent one involving full malignancy covers nearly twice as much of the total problem-solving score than does the one fully consistent category (see chapter 4). One way to visualize this difference in coverage is that the full-malignancy path is the one most traveled: it has greater empirical weight in this dataset simply because more and stronger cases fit it.

The QCA coverage measure can be further specified to characterize the model as a whole and the relative explanatory contribution of each reliable path (Ragin 2006). Calculating the *joint coverage* score of all reliable paths proceeds in the same way as for individual paths, except that the consistent path score to be summarized is for each case the highest among its scores on the reliable paths; that follows from the set-theoretic rule that a case's membership in a union of two or more sets is the maximum (not the sum) of its memberships in the united sets (Ragin 2000, 174–175). Assuming interval-level measurement, this joint coverage score can be interpreted as the model's explanatory power, the proportion of the total problem solving it accounts for.

Some cases are covered by more than one reliable path, so the joint coverage score is often lower than the sum of the separate scores. Calculating the *unique coverage* scores of each path—the proportion of the problem solving not accounted for by other reliable paths—proceeds in a way that parallels the partitioning of explained variation in multiple regression analysis (Ragin 2006, 304–305) by calculating the drop in the joint coverage that would result if the path in question had not met the reliability criterion. A high score on unique coverage indicates a path accounting for much problem solving that would otherwise be unexplained—one that is vital to the model's joint coverage, or explanatory power.

Accordingly, the QCA consistency and coverage measures can help identify reliable paths to success or failure based on a reliability criterion set by the analyst (conventionally a consistency score of 0.85) and to differentiate among those paths in terms of explanatory power in the dataset. A reliable path with many strong cases has greater coverage than one with fewer and weaker cases, so it will contribute more to the explanation. We may determine the consistency of the empirical data with the pattern indicating a reliable path, and the coverage of any such path, either by comparing each case's scores on the causal combinations and on the outcome and proceeding as explained above, or by running a computer program downloadable at http://www.u.arizona.edu/~cragin.

Widening the Reliable Paths: Logical Minimization and Simplifying Assumptions

The next step in the QCA procedure is to examine whether the empirical pattern allows bolder, more wide-ranging causal statements than those on the initial list of reliable causal paths. Those statements are as complex as the causal model and sometimes involve more conditions than are strictly necessary. Logical minimization and simplifying assumptions are two important means for removing unnecessary conditions on the causal statements, thus widening the reliable causal paths. Such widening corresponds to the analytical reduction that statistical procedures achieve by estimating, for instance, the steepness of the regression line that best fits the distribution of numerous observed cases.

Set-theoretic minimization removes logically redundant factors and combinations from an initial list of reliable causal paths to an outcome. It may proceed in three rounds (Ragin 1987), two of which are applied here. First is a complete round of *paired comparisons*, allowing us to remove redundant factors: if two paths that differ on only one causal condition both reliably deliver the outcome, the distinguishing factor must be irrelevant. In the two reliable paths to cognitional problem solving described above, malignancy is such a singular distinguishing factor, and since the two paths are both reliable, we may merge the two statements into one bolder, more general statement. Thus, whatever the level of malignancy, the combination of insignificant scores on intricacy and full scores on collaboration and ecosystem modeling is a reliable path to cognitional problem solving. A second round of minimization removes any reliable path that is *contained* by another reliable path, that is, that forms a subset of a more general category. Thus, minimization by paired comparison and containment simplifies the causal statements without losing any information.

A third round of simplification supported by the QCA procedure is not applied in this study because it narrows the range of causal path identified in the analysis (Stokke 2007c). If the goal is to achieve the most parsimonious causal statement covering the evidence, causal paths that do not uniquely cover any problem-solving score in the dataset are superfluous and should be removed. In real life, however, explanatory richness is often a merit, since the logically "superfluous" path could very well be of greater practical value—for instance, if the factors involved are easier for social actors to change. In effectiveness analysis, too, we want to identify all reliable paths to either success or failure evident in the dataset, because those paths can help us estimate the counterfactual level of problem solving.

Besides logical minimization, the QCA procedure also supports the reasoned introduction of simplifying assumptions, relevant whenever limited diversity constrains the analysis. Limited diversity shows up as empty cells in the data matrix, here logically possible ideal-type combinations that lack strong cases. Whatever the method of causal inference applied, the typical effect of limited diversity is to render findings less conclusive, for instance by disabling statistical or comparative control on competing variables. In QCA analysis, this problem shows up as great heterogeneity among the causal categories that are consistent with the reliability criterion, inhibiting minimization by paired comparison and containment. Statistical procedures can get around the limited-diversity problem by making certain assumptions about nonexisting observations— usually that variable relationships are additive, homogeneous, and linear. The high level of abstraction that marks such assumptions complicates substantive evaluation of their plausibility. In contrast, the assumptions that allow simpler, more general statements in QCA analysis are concrete and concern the outcome scores that selected counterfactual cases would have.

This more concrete framing of the simplifying assumptions enables a plausibility assessment that draws on existing observations and other substantive or theoretical knowledge (Ragin 1987). Elsewhere I have argued that a simplifying assumption in QCA analysis is reasonable if it does not contradict the available empirical observations and is compatible with the theory argument underpinning the model (Stokke 2004a, 107–108).[14] To illustrate, in the cognitional failure analysis in chapter 4, no strong case exists of the ideal-type category combining full scores on malignancy and intricacy with zero scores on collaboration and ecosystem modeling. However, the singular difference between that category and one represented in the dataset, and meeting the reliability criterion for failure, is a characteristic that should make cognitional failure even more likely: full rather than insignificant intricacy. It is therefore highly reasonable to make the simplifying assumption that a strong case of that category would deliver failure. That will allow a new round of paired comparisons to simplify the causal statement, thereby widening the reliable path to the outcome of interest.

Logical minimization and the introduction of reasonable simplifying assumptions are QCA means for arriving at the most general causal statement permitted by the dataset when it comes to reliable paths to success or failure in problem solving. The next step in the disaggregate approach to regime effectiveness is to use those paths to derive plausible estimates of the level of problem solving that would pertain had the regime not existed.

Counterfactual Path Analysis: Upper and Lower Bounds on Plausible Estimates

Proven paths to success or failure offer the most persuasive basis for estimating what levels of problem solving would be achieved in a hypothetical situation where there was no regime. Estimating such counterfactual problem-solving scores is necessary because effectiveness refers to the *difference* a regime makes in solving a problem—here specified as the ratio of the actual to the potential improvement on a counterfactual situation. Underlying the disaggregate approach to counterfactual analysis is the observation that specifying the counterfactual antecedent—the causal factor scores that would pertain if the regime had not existed—is much closer to actual, traceable processes than is the ultimate counterfactual consequent. To derive the latter, we would need the counterfactual antecedent *as well as* a solid understanding of the relative strength of the modeled causal factors, how they interact, and whether non-regime-driven factors can substitute for regime-driven ones. As Underdal (2004, 39) notes, "to determine in what respects and to what degree the present regime differs from the previous order . . . is the easy part." Chapters 4 to 6 show that the specification for each year of the counterfactual causal path is quite tractable by means of process tracing. This subsection shows that such counterfactual antecedents, when combined with empirical findings about reliable paths to success or failure, can help narrow the plausible range of what is the more difficult counterfactual estimate, the level of problem solving that would pertain had the regime not existed.

A good fit with a success or a failure path can help set upper and lower bounds on the plausible range of counterfactual problem-solving scores. We recall that an ideal-type causal combination qualifies as a success path only if actual cases reliably achieve problem-solving scores equal to or greater than their score on the path itself. The same should hold true for counterfactual cases: any problem-solving estimate below its score on the success path would contradict the empirical pattern among actual cases and thus violate the compatibility standard for sound counterfactual analysis. Thus, how a counterfactual case scores on a success path defines the lower bound of its range of plausible problem-solving scores.

Conversely, how a counterfactual case scores on a reliable failure path helps define the upper bound of its plausible problem-solving scores. By the same logic as above, a counterfactual case should achieve a failure score equal to or greater than its score on the failure path: a lower failure estimate would contradict the pattern among actual cases. That lower bound on the range of plausible failure scores defines an *upper* bound on plausible problem-solving scores because failure is simply the negation of problem solving: full failure is insignificant problem solving, and vice versa. To conclude that a plausible failure score cannot be lower than a value f, therefore, implies that a plausible problem-solving score cannot be *higher* than $(1 - f)$. Thus, the negation of a counterfactual case's score on a failure path is the upper bound of its plausible problem-solving scores. Whenever the upper bound and the lower bound are the same, the counterfactual path analysis yields a point estimate: any other level of counterfactual problem solving would be implausible.

Such upper and lower bounds, based on counterfactual path analysis, prove highly useful when estimating the counterfactual problem-solving scores needed in effectiveness analysis, but there are also other considerations of importance. Of particular interest is the *extent* of the regime's impact on the causal factors. First, whenever the regime has failed to influence any of the factors shown to affect problem solving, we have no basis for arguing that the counterfactual level of problem solving would be lower than the actual score. In such cases the regime is either ineffective or irrelevant; the latter term is appropriate when actual problem solving is full. Second, counterfactual path analysis typically narrows the range of plausible problem-solving scores, but it often leaves more than one option. In such cases I choose among the remaining options based on the number of causal factors that are "weaker" in terms of problem solving—that is, have scores shown in the actual case analysis to be less conducive—in the counterfactual case than in the actual one. For instance, I select the option one step below the actual score if one causal factor is weaker and the option two steps below if two factors are weaker. The rationale for this rule is straightforward: it provides transparency and consistency of treatment across cases, keeps the counterfactual problem-solving estimate within the range substantiated by the comparative analysis, and differentiates among cases according to the extent of difference the regime makes on empirically proven drivers of or impediments to problem solving.

The counterfactual problem-solving estimates derived from the disaggregate approach therefore build on three theoretically and empirically substantiated sets of evidence: a process-tracing-based specification of how the regime affects the modeled factors, reliable paths to failure, and reliable paths to success.

Assessing Effectiveness
Equipped with these empirically based estimates of the counterfactual level of problem solving, we may calculate the effectiveness score by the Oslo-Potsdam formula, which divides actual improvement by optimal improvement. The qualitative specification of the Oslo-Potsdam parameters advanced here differs slightly from Underdal's (2002b) version and achieves higher determinacy than other variants of this general yardstick for measuring regime effectiveness.

Like previous versions of the Oslo-Potsdam yardstick, mine allows effectiveness to vary from 0 to 1. Unlike Sprinz and Helm's (1999) game theory and quantitative version, which uses continuous scales for measuring formula parameters, my scales are designed for categorical assessment, differentiating among four levels of problem solving. As noted in chapter 1, using four values permits somewhat nuanced differentiation without requiring very precise measurement; this makes it appropriate in a relatively new field of research and when drawing on heterogeneous evidence.

With the slight modification that "problem solving" replaces terms such as "performance" and "state of affairs," equation A below states the basic Oslo-Potsdam formula that sees effectiveness as the ratio of actual improvement (difference between actual and counterfactual problem solving) to potential improvement (difference between full and counterfactual problem solving) (see Helm and Sprinz 2000, 637; Hovi, Sprinz, and Underdal 2003, 76).

(A) Effectiveness score = (PS − C′PS)/(1 − C′PS).

Here, PS denotes the actual problem-solving score, C′PS is the counterfactual problem-solving estimate, while 1 is the highest possible score: it requires full problem solving.

Two limitations exist on the applicability of the Oslo-Potsdam formula for measuring regime effectiveness. First, it cannot handle situations when the most plausible counterfactual problem-solving estimate is full problem solving (a score of 1): in such cases, the denominator would be 0 and the formula would be undetermined. This limitation is unproblematic, as it means simply that the formula does not apply if there is no problem left for the regime to solve. Such regime irrelevance is established not by computing the ratio of actual to potential improvement, since that ratio is indeterminate, but by concluding qualitatively that problem solving would most plausibly be full even with no regime.

Another instance in which equation A does not apply directly is when a regime is detrimental to problem solving.[15] In such a case, the equation would yield a negative effectiveness score, but since I prefer a scale varying from 0 to 1, such cases receive instead a 0 value (see also Miles et al. 2002, 483–484). A pragmatic reason for this choice is to avoid using part of a few-values scale to characterize somewhat more accurately the presumably small number of instances in which a regime is counterproductive. Equation A, therefore, applies to all cases in which the most plausible counterfactual level of problem solving is less than full and not higher than the actual level.

To illustrate the use of this yardstick, we may consider a regime that, according to the analyst, has helped raise problem solving from a modest level (a score of 0.33) in the counterfactual no-regime situation to full problem solving (a score of 1). The actual improvement would be (1 − 0.33 = 0.67), which is the same as the potential improvement (also 1 − 0.33 = 0.67), implying that effectiveness is full (0.67/0.67 = 1). Equation A would yield a full score also if the most plausible counterfactual level of problem solving were insignificant (a score of 0) or substantial (a score of 0.67), and that is appropriate: a regime that exhausts the potential for improvement has proved itself fully effective.

At the other end of this effectiveness scale, let us consider a regime that fails to raise problem solving beyond the most plausible no-regime level. Whether that level of problem solving is insignificant, modest, or substantial, equation A would yield an effectiveness score of 0, which is highly appropriate since the regime has not made any significant difference. A regime that fails to improve on the most plausible no-regime level of problem solving is obviously ineffective.

In between the highest and the lowest value, equation A may yield three effectiveness scores.[16] That score is modest (0.33) if the regime raises problem solving from an insignificant to a modest level; it is substantial (0.67) if the regime raises problem solving from an insignificant to a substantial level; and it is medium (0.5) if the increase is from a modest to a substantial level. Thus, with four-value problem-solving scales, the yardstick used here differentiates five levels of effectiveness.

The procedure for measuring effectiveness in this study combines validity and determinacy better than do previous applications of the Oslo-Potsdam approach. Instead of relying on theoretically complex and empirically elusive concepts such as cooperative and noncooperative optima (Sprinz and Helm 1999) or Pareto optimality (Underdal 1992, 2002b), this study links the yardstick's parameters to a concrete formulation of three aspects of the problem addressed by the regime: the cognitional, the regulatory, and the behavioral aspects. Each of those aspects concerns an important set of regime activities—scientific research, negotiation of rules, and efforts to ensure compliance—which facilitates the elaboration of operational thresholds. Moreover, the substantiation of counterfactual problem-solving estimates is far more thorough and transparent than is common in the field. Each estimate builds on a broad range of information sources and triangulation of various techniques for confronting the underlying causal model with empirical evidence. Appendix 1 explains that, while this yardstick applies mathematical subtraction and division, it does not require interval-level measurement of problem solving in order to differentiate validly among cases; it works well also with an ordinal scale.[17] Such validity and determinacy are not obtained by yielding on generality because the three aspects in focus are relevant to most international institutions whatever the issue area (see chapter 1).

Hence, the effectiveness yardstick advanced here retains the high validity and generality of the Oslo-Potsdam approach, which incorporates both the causality and the adequacy dimensions of effectiveness. It achieves higher determinacy than previous versions of this approach by disaggregating the problem addressed by the regime, which in turn permits more concrete specification of categorical thresholds.

Summary and Implications

This chapter has specified a version of the Oslo-Potsdam yardstick for measuring international regime effectiveness and has shown why the counterfactual analysis required by this yardstick should build on empirical findings from actual cases. Two distinctive features of my yardstick are the disaggregation of the problem addressed by a regime into three—the cognitional, regulatory, and behavioral aspects—and the specification of a simple four-value scale for each, requiring no more than ordinal measurement from "insignificant" to "full." An Oslo-Potsdam yardstick incorporates not only the causality dimension of effectiveness—the regime's contribution to problem solving—but also an adequacy dimension that compares actual improvement with potential improvement.

Both actual and potential improvements are measured by reference to the most plausible state of affairs that would pertain if the regime had not existed. The disaggregate approach to international regime effectiveness makes such counterfactual analysis more tractable and transparent by decomposing it into three parts: explaining the actual pattern of problem solving, specifying the most plausible scores on the causal factors involved in that explanation, and using findings about the actual cases to estimate the most plausible counterfactual level of problem solving.

The first part of such evidence-based counterfactual analysis involves explaining the diversity of actual problem solving. That means modeling the drivers of and impediments to success, including those factors under regime influence, and employing methods such as process tracing, logical comparison, and statistical inference to validate those models. The modeling benefits from the sharper analytical focus gained from partitioning of the problem. Separate explanatory models are developed for the cognitional, regulatory, and behavioral aspects in chapters 4 to 6, but we have already examined some variables that were identified in earlier effectiveness research and are relevant here as well. Among these variables are malignancy (incongruity between individual and collective interests among those engaged in the activity that causes the problem), the state of relevant knowledge, and the levels of international collaboration, obligation, and behavioral transparency.

The empirical validation benefits from the larger number of observations achieved through the decomposition of data by year and (for the behavioral aspect) by the major states involved. Particularly well suited for such validation is the fuzzy set QCA technique because it can identify configurative patterns in a dataset even when the number of cases is not very high. Central to this technique is the examination of outcome scores among cases with some degree of fit with ideal-type (in the Weberian sense) causal combinations that allow only full or zero scores on each variable. Such a fit can be specified accurately by applying the set-theoretic rules of intersection and negation. An empirical pattern in which all or nearly all cases in the dataset achieve outcome scores equal to or higher than their scores on a causal combination supports a claim that this combination is sufficient for delivering the outcome—that it is a reliable path to it. Logical minimization and the introduction of reasonable simplifying assumptions are means for stating such findings about sufficient conditions as generally as the empirical data permit. Two outcomes of particular interest are success and failure, because reliable paths to those outcomes help place the counterfactual analysis on an empirical footing.

The second part of such analysis entails specifying the counterfactual antecedents, that is, the combinations of scores on the modeled factors that the cases would have had the regime not existed. This counterfactual question is far more limited and manageable than is the ultimate counterfactual question faced in effectiveness analysis, regarding the consequent level of problem solving. Answering that ultimate question requires not only a persuasive counterfactual antecedent but also good answers as to the relative strength of the causal factors, as well as their substitutability and interaction.

The third and last part of the counterfactual analysis advanced here involves using the empirical findings from the first step to provide those answers, here by examining how well the counterfactual cases fit the proven paths to success or failure. A good fit with either of those reliable paths helps narrow the plausible range of problem-solving estimates because sound counterfactual analysis is compatible with what we know about actual cases. Since the defining property of a success (or a failure) path is that actual cases reliably achieve problem-solving (or failure) scores equal to or greater than their score on the path itself, the same should be true for counterfactual cases. Thus, whenever a counterfactual case has a positive score on a reliable success or failure path, we may derive lower or upper bounds on the plausible range of counterfactual problem-solving estimates. In conjunction with related pieces of information, such as the actual level of problem solving and the extent of regime impact on the causal factors, those upper and lower bounds provide empirically based estimates of the counterfactual problem-solving scores needed for assessing regime effectiveness by the Oslo-Potsdam yardstick.

An important merit of the disaggregate approach to effectiveness is transparency, a property often lacking in the field. Transparency is high here because the analyst is required not only to specify and validate empirically a set of factors influencing actual problem solving but also to substantiate what the most plausible scores on the same factors would have been without any regime. Moreover, all inferences that link this counterfactual antecedent with the counterfactual consequent—the level of problem solving that would pertain if there were no regime—are based on explicit findings about existing cases and, where appropriate, on explicit assumptions about nonexisting cases. Such transparency permits concrete, substantive plausibility and robustness probes; it also allows replication.

The approach to regime effectiveness presented in this chapter breaks up, or decomposes, the counterfactual analysis in order to minimize that part of it that cannot build on actual observation. The next chapter prepares the ground for applying this approach to the specific case of Barents Sea fisheries regime by outlining the major national and international institutions involved in managing shared fish stocks in the Barents region and how these institutions have interacted with other institutions with broader membership.

3

Means for Governance

This chapter describes the components of the Barents Sea fisheries regime, how it is nested in the global regime for fisheries, and its connections to national bodies for fisheries management and to the fishing industries in the region. Each of these aspects of the regime has changed significantly in the period studied, affecting the regime's ability to influence cognitional, regulatory, and behavioral problem solving.

The first section outlines the high and rising economic and political salience of fisheries in the Barents Sea. Next I discuss important continuities, changes, and contrasts regarding the national means for governance of regional fisheries. Both the Norwegian structure and the Russian structure differ markedly from the earlier Soviet-style integration of management, production, and distribution activities within a single entity. The subsequent section shows how the regional regime is situated within the global fisheries regime and linked to broader international institutions for coordinating research and compliance control: the two coastal states predominate, but the Barents Sea fisheries regime itself is multilateral. Thereafter I examine certain sovereignty issues that complicate regional fisheries management and identify the strategies employed by the coastal states, individually or jointly, in dealing with those complications.

Regional Fisheries

The activities dealt with by the Barents Sea fisheries regime span a wide geographic area and are important to the regional economies and to coastal state relations alike.

The Barents Sea covers 1.4 million square kilometers, equivalent to roughly four times the land territory of Norway, and some of its main species migrate south and west into other parts of the Northeast Atlantic. It is a relatively shallow sea, with depths rarely exceeding 300 meters, and is highly productive. Cold water from the central Arctic Ocean meets warmer and saltier masses from the south, generating conditions favorable for plankton and numerous fish species, including capelin, haddock, Greenland halibut, and cod, which occur in the zones of both states. Of the regional fish stocks, Northeast Arctic cod has by far the greatest commercial value.

Whereas other internationally managed cod stocks in the Atlantic, such as those outside Canada or in the North Sea, have collapsed and have yet to recover, annual catches of Northeast Arctic cod have exceeded half a million tons for most of the past two decades (appendix 2). That harvesting level has a landing value of more than U.S. $1.5 billion, before the value further added through the processing and distribution chains.[1] Northeast Arctic haddock also commands high prices but the catches are usually much smaller, around a quarter of the amounts for cod. The third major species, capelin, is a short-lived pelagic species, and the Barents Sea stock fluctuates widely from one year to another. Prior to a collapse around 1985, annual capelin catches were frequently very high (at times beyond two million tons), but since then the maturing component has only occasionally been large enough to justify significant harvesting, and the unit price is a mere fraction of that of cod. From the 2010 season, a fourth stock, Northeast Arctic Greenland halibut, is included among the shared stocks under the Barents Sea fisheries regime. It obtains high prices but has so far been taken only in small quantities.

Harvesting, processing, and trade of Northeast Arctic cod have historically provided the main basis for human settlement in the region, especially in Norway. Even today, this stock looms large economically. The fishery used to concentrate on the large amounts of mature cod—skrei, in Norwegian—that aggregate for spawning around the Lofoten archipelago during late winter and spring. Over time, operations spread to the feeding areas in the Barents Sea, and a summer fishery at the Svalbard banks emerged in the second half of the 1800s (Nakken 1998, 23–24). In Norway's cod fisheries, some five thousand relatively small but often well-equipped and effective coastal vessels predominate, using conventional gear—gill net, long line, hand line, and Danish seine. The ocean-going fleet, including the trawlers, takes far less—around a third of the catch (Norway, Ministry of Fisheries [Norway MF] 2002–2003, 15). Large-scale international trade in dried and salted cod to Europe dates back to medieval times, and various cod products still account for a large part of Norway's seafood exports; only petroleum and metals are bigger export items than seafood (Statistics Norway 2008, table 315). In 1990, no less than two-thirds of the industrial employment in the northernmost county, Finnmark, was in fish processing (Hersoug 1992, 235). Even today, some one-fifth of northern Norway's GDP in primary or secondary industries comes from the fisheries sector (McDonald, Glomsrød, and Mäenpää 2006, 57).

In Northwest Russia, the fisheries were historically of far less economic importance than in Norway. Beginning in the 1920s and continuing throughout the Soviet period, large capital infusions to the Kola Peninsula ensured the development of a high-capacity, vertically integrated fisheries industry capable of exploiting resources in the Barents Sea as well as in distant waters (Borgström 1968). Around 1990, the regional fisheries sector employed as many as 80,000 persons, including those engaged in the construction and maintenance of fishing vessels and equipment and in other services to the industry. In Murmansk oblast, those working onboard fishing vessels accounted for more than 20 percent of industrial employment (Castberg 1992, 19–20).[2] At that time, the fleet consisted of around 450 trawlers, mostly medium-sized (50–70 meters) or larger (Hønneland 2004, 80–81), but in the Soviet era only a fraction of these vessels gave priority to the Barents Sea. The emphasis on proteins and production volume, coupled with subsidized fuels, made distant-water pelagic species more attractive. In the late 1980s, the Northwest Russian fishing fleet took between 50 and 70 percent of its catches *outside* the Barents Sea, mostly in the Northwest and Central Atlantic (Matishov et al. 2004, 25). Whereas total catches and fisheries employment declined sharply in the early 1990s, when higher fuel prices rendered many pelagic fisheries uneconomic (Hønneland 2004, 82), the significance of cod rose as the Murmansk-based industry turned toward resources that were physically closer and also in high demand in the nearby Norwegian processing industry.

The fisheries sector weighs heavily in the bilateral relationship between the two coastal states. Until the end of the Cold War, this sector was the only one for which Norway and the Soviet Union, at that time members of competing military alliances, had developed institutions for handling matters of common interest in the Barents Sea region (Stokke 1990). Bilateral relations were inevitably marked by the strategic sensitivity of the Barents Sea, stemming from the role of nuclear submarines deployed in Arctic waters to maintain military deterrence between the two superpowers: the Soviet and later the Russian Northern Fleet is based in Murmansk oblast. In some ways, this strategic sensitivity may have served to bolster fisheries cooperation, since it implies a shared interest in avoiding political tension in the region (Stokke, Anderson, and Mirovitskaya 1999, 148). In 1987, Mikhail Gorbachev launched an initiative for broader and deeper collaboration with his nation's Arctic neighbors, thereby triggering a wave of collaborative initiatives in the North (Stokke and Tunander 1994; Stokke and Hønneland 2007). By then the Barents Sea fisheries regime had already demonstrated, over more than a decade, how international institutions could help insulate the solving of issue-specific problem of common interest from oscillations in the more general relations between the participating states.

Accordingly, sound management of regional fisheries—especially for Northeast Arctic cod, now the most valuable harvest target for both coastal states—is of great importance not only in terms of production, employment, and trade but politically as well. A central difference between the harvesting sectors of the two states is that Russia's is trawler-based, whereas several thousand relatively small coastal vessels take the lion's share of Norway's catches of cod.

National Means for Fisheries Management

If an international institution is to influence target-group behavior, it must affect the national governance machinery ultimately responsible for the various tasks of fisheries management. The national or subnational agencies in question frequently invite representatives of industry or civil-society organizations to participate during the national and international stages of resource management. The rationale behind involving societal groups in this way is to capitalize on their expertise, impute their views in a manageable way, or build commitment and loyalty to regime outputs, which in turn may improve their implementation (Victor, Raustiala, and Skolnikoff 1998a). This section sketches the domestic means for fisheries management in each state, including the deep involvement of target groups, and the changes such means have undergone. In particular, the transition from the Soviet Union to Russia posed new and severe challenges for the regional fisheries regime.

Norway

The structure of the Norwegian fisheries administration has remained fairly stable throughout the period under study. Overall responsibility for fisheries management rests with the Ministry of Fisheries and Coastal Affairs, with the Directorate of Fisheries as the main implementing agency. At-sea inspection is conducted by the Norwegian Coast Guard, which is part of the Norwegian Navy.

Other institutions also provide important means for conducting research, regulation, and rule enforcement regarding the Barents Sea fisheries. Scientific research—including international cooperation on survey investigations, data analysis, and management advice—is conducted largely by the Institute for Marine Research (IMR), based in Bergen. Since 1988 this institute has been administratively independent of the Fisheries Directorate, but the provision of inputs to the management remains a central task; around half of the IMR's activities are currently financed by the ministry. The Directorate of Fisheries takes note of such inputs and elaborates proposals for regulatory measures; it also implements ministerial decisions by allocating licenses, closing fishing areas, and the like. Part of the directorate's preparatory work concerns involving the major target-group organizations, including the Norwegian Fishermen's Association, which organizes the trawler and the coastal vessel sectors, and the main association of processing industries. Throughout most of the period studied, a key instrument for such involvement was a Regulation Council, replaced in 2006 with a Regulation Meeting open to any interested party. Since the 1990s, environmental organizations have also been represented at these regular meetings.

Monitoring and enforcement are largely the business of the Coast Guard, the Directorate of Fisheries, and various fishermen's sales organization (Norway, Office of the Auditor General [Norway OAG] 2007, 69–113). Each of these sales organizations has a monopoly on the first-hand sales of fish within its region. It is obliged to register landings and sales reports, review their conformity with the vessel's individual quota if appropriate, and report to the Directorate of Fisheries. The directorate aggregates such reports, reviews their conformity with total quotas for each species and any vessel-group quotas, and conducts sample port inspections to verify them. The Coast Guard does the same at sea, based on the logbooks that domestic and foreign vessels are required to keep. A foreign vessel must report its inventory to the Fisheries Directorate upon entering and leaving the Norwegian exclusive economic zone (EEZ), in addition to a weekly catch report; and when leaving it must pass through one of seven Coast Guard checkpoints for inspection (Norway MF 2008–2009, 16).

Thus, the Norwegian system for managing regional fisheries is centralized but with heavy target-group involvement. The overall structure has changed little over the past three decades. As the remainder of this section shows, the Soviet Union/Russia has experienced far greater variability in its domestic structures for regional fisheries management.

The Soviet Union

The first half of the existence of the present Barents Sea fisheries regime overlaps roughly with the final period of the Soviet Union, whose world-wide fisheries activities were orchestrated by the Fisheries Ministry and implemented largely by five regional "main administrations." Of those administrations, Sevryba ("north fish") covered regional and distant-water activities based in Murmansk, Arkhangelsk, and Karelia. An extension of the ministry, Sevryba was a highly complex, vertically integrated institution whose main branches were two large fishing vessel organizations, one organization operating shipyards, freighters, and tankers, and the Murmansk Fisheries Combine, which conducted onshore processing of fish and provided port and construction services (Stokke, Anderson, and Mirovitskaya 1999, 96).

Several other regional bodies under the Fisheries Ministry performed specific management functions and continue to do so in Russia today, although within a different institutional framework and with narrower competences. The main institution responsible for scientific research on the fish stocks of the Barents Sea remains the Knipovich Polar Marine Research Institute of Marine Fisheries and Oceanography (PINRO) in Murmansk, which is connected to the central oceanographic institute, the Russian Federal Research Institute of Fishery and Oceanography (VNIRO), in Moscow. As regards fisheries regulation, the ministry delegated to Sevryba not only industrial decisions, such as when and where to fish for various species or the distribution of raw material among its processing facilities, but also resource management functions, such as fisheries surveys and quota allocation (Nilssen and Hønneland 2001, 317). Another regional ministerial body, Murmanrybvod, was responsible for compliance control activities, including at-sea inspections. However, the main means of monitoring the levels of harvesting throughout the Soviet period was by comparing fisher reports with reports from the receiving port or processing unit where the harvest was landed.

Within a closed production and distribution system, any leeway for falsifying catch reports was limited. The same applied to incentives for overfishing, since remuneration for overfulfillment of production plans was small. In the final few years of the Soviet Union, this system opened up, especially with the growing opportunities to deliver catches abroad (Stokke 1992), but the overall pattern was a high level of integration between resource management activities and a wide range of industrial activities aimed at the domestic market.

The Russian Federation

Following the dissolution of the Soviet Union in December 1991, the Northwest Russian fisheries industry was gradually privatized, and the central roles of the federal fisheries bureaucracy and its regional bodies were soon challenged by other federal and regional actors. Sevryba disintegrated into a number of private joint-stock companies, but part of the structure, including the name, remained as an instrument that enabled the regional industry to uphold de facto control over the quota allocation (Hønneland and Nilssen 2001, 478). Throughout much of the 1990s, Sevryba's director headed the Technical-Scientific Catch Council, a regional corporate body established toward the end of the Soviet era and still in existence today.

Among the implications of privatization was that vessel operators no longer benefited from administrative allocation of fuels, shipyard services, and other necessary inputs but now had to finance them from the sales of fish. During most of the 1980s, the Soviet Union had traded considerable parts of its Northeast Arctic cod quotas to Norway in return for much larger quantities of pelagic species under exclusive Norwegian management. With privatization, cod became a far more lucrative target than distant-water pelagic species as cod fishing required less fuel and could command higher prices from Norwegian processors. Thus, the integration of Northwest Russia's harvesting industry into the Western market economy came to link vessel-operator incomes directly to the catches of Northeast Arctic cod. At the same time, it undermined the traditional system of monitoring harvesting by cross-checking fisher reports with recipient reports, thereby posing new challenges for the fisheries management system.

The bureaucratic entity that used to be the Soviet Fisheries Ministry has experienced several shifts in status and competence scope, on a long-term downward slope. Except for a few years after the major federal administrative reform in 2004, this entity has remained largely intact, however. In some periods it has been a unit under the Ministry of Agriculture, but more often it has been a State Committee on Fisheries, with formal independence from other ministries but no separate seat in the federal government (Hønneland 2005a, 2005b). Undisputedly within the committee's scope of competence was fisheries research, with PINRO remaining the body most heavily involved in international research and advisory collaboration on Barents Sea stocks and VNIRO becoming an increasingly active participant from the turn of the millennium (Aasjord and Hønneland 2008). Regarding competence for regulation and compliance control, however, the federal fisheries bureaucracy has been challenged from several quarters. The State Committee on Fisheries has sought to reverse or contain some of the changes in the regional industry and has defended traditional values from the Soviet era, such as job security and local processing, while critics see it as ridden with inefficiency and corruption (Hønneland 2005a, 186; Jørgensen 2009, 102). A former deputy head of the committee was sentenced in 2007 to six years in prison for extortion (*RIA Novosti*, 15 February 2007). The continuous flow of hard currency generated by the industry is presumably part of the explanation for the external interest in its management, but among the concerns that challengers have championed are environmental sustainability, regional autonomy, and federal revenues.

The first regulatory challenger to the federal fisheries bureaucracy was the State Committee on the Environment, which briefly, at the end of the Soviet era, had been formally (though never in practice) in charge of licensing, as well as some control functions (Nikitina and Pearse 1992, 374). Slightly more successful were attempts in the 1990s by the regional authorities to acquire a bigger say in the allocation of quotas. When Sevryba lost its de facto control over the Technical-Scientific Catch Council in the late 1990s, the regional fisheries departments—especially those of Murmansk and Arkhangelsk oblasti—for some years played central advisory roles to the State Committee on Fisheries in the allocation of quotas within their regions (Hønneland 2005b, 627). Interregional allocation was a federal matter, however: the 2004 Fisheries Act confirmed the consolidation of central power under President Putin by making it clear that fish resources were federal property and that the formal advisory role of federal subjects was limited to coastal fisheries of minor economic significance (Hønneland 2005a, 180). The act also put an end to the quota auctions that for a few years had been organized by the Ministry of Economic Development and Trade (Hønneland 2005a, 181–182), and allowed the State Committee on Fisheries to reclaim a principal role in quota allocation within a broader, interagency commission. Fee-based quota shares were first given on a five-year basis; they now have a ten-year duration (Jørgensen 2009, 98).

Concerning compliance control, however, in 1997 the State Committee on Fisheries lost the competence to conduct at-sea inspections of fishing vessels in the EEZ to the Federal Border Service (Hønneland 2005a, 183), a part of the semimilitary Federal Security Service (FSB) under the president (Russia 2007, 263). While the 2004 reorganization of the federal administrative structure divided the tasks of policymaking, implementation, and monitoring and enforcement among several entities under the Ministry of Agriculture (Russia 2007, 255–268), the federal fisheries bureaucracy reemerged as a consolidated entity in 2007 independent of any ministry, first as a state committee and then as the Federal Fisheries Agency under the prime minister (Jørgensen 2009). The priority now accorded to interagency coordination is evident in the establishment in 2008 of the Governmental Fisheries Commission, headed by the deputy prime minister, which is intended to ensure efficient cooperation between the various federal organs on fisheries-related issues and to consider legislative proposals in this sector (Russia 2008).

In short, the disintegration of Sevryba and the privatization and global market orientation of the fishing industry are the most striking contrasts between the Soviet and the Russian fisheries sectors. The federal fisheries bureaucracy has engaged in a series of bitter institutional turf struggles, losing its ministerial status and the right to conduct at-sea inspections, but it remains a central player in most aspects of Russian fisheries management.

Brief Comparison

While Norway's system for governing regional fisheries activities has remained quite stable since the formation of the Barents Sea fisheries regime, considerable variability has marked that of the Soviet Union/Russia. A persistent feature of both systems has been high target-group involvement in the management process, with industry associations playing important roles in the preparations for Joint Commission meetings, in delegations, and in the domestic processes of implementing agreed-upon regulations. In the Soviet era, the predominance of the Fisheries Ministry not only in management but also in production and distribution chains contrasted with the Norwegian structure, but developments since the early 1990s have narrowed that difference. Today, both the Norwegian and the Russian governance systems involve clear institutional boundaries between industrial activities and fisheries management, with at-sea inspections conducted by agencies that are also charged with national defense responsibilities.

International Means for Fisheries Management

The Barents Sea fisheries regime is a nested one. That means that important parameters are set forth within a broader institution (Aggarwal

1983, 620)—here the body of international customary and treaty law concerning fisheries, primarily the 1982 Law of the Sea Convention. This global regime provides default rules concerning the regulation of fisheries activities and its enforcement, rules that apply whether or not more specific institutions exist for managing regional stocks. The coastal state right to claim sovereign rights over fish resources within 200 nautical miles from a state's baseline is one such global rule that shapes the relevant membership of many regional fisheries institutions.[3] Previously, management of stocks like the Northeast Arctic cod required participation and agreement among numerous states engaged in the fishery; now it is often enough that two or three states agree. A regional regime can help strengthen global rules when its members agree among themselves on innovative rules or procedures (usually to accommodate distinctive regional challenges) that become models for those negotiating or operating other institutions (Stokke 2000; Oberthür and Stokke 2011). Thus, regime nesting denotes a normative hierarchy, but change may originate also in the subordinate, narrower institution.

This section begins by outlining important changes in the global fisheries regime that affect regional management. We then turn to the international structures for research, regulation, and compliance control concerning fisheries in the Barents Sea.

Rising Coastal State Dominance and Its Limits

With the evolution of the law of the sea in its modern meaning, from the sixteenth century, flag-state jurisdiction eventually gained a prominent position concerning fisheries regulation and enforcement. After World War II, however, this prominence has been circumscribed by a mix of unilateral actions and international diplomacy at regional as well as global levels (Stokke 2001c).

The 1958 Convention on the High Seas listed fishing as one of the freedoms of marine areas beyond coastal state jurisdiction, but added that states are to exercise that freedom with "reasonable regard to the interests of other States" (Article 2). This vague qualification was specified somewhat by another of the 1958 Geneva Conventions, that on High Seas Living Resources, which provides for compulsory and binding dispute settlement whenever user states fail to reach agreement on conservation measures (Articles 4–12); however, this convention obtained few ratifications and has remained largely a dead letter (Churchill and Lowe 1999, 287). Some of its less ambitious provisions are echoed in the 1982 Law of the Sea Convention, including that states "have the duty to take, or to co-operate with other States in taking, such measures . . . as may be necessary for the conservation of the living resources of the high seas" (Article 117). Codifying a practice that had already become widespread, the Convention adds that states "shall, as appropriate, co-operate to establish subregional or regional fisheries organizations to this end" (Article 118). Until the extension of coastal state jurisdiction, major fishing grounds in the Barents Sea were in high seas areas, and the international body for managing the fishery was the North-East Atlantic Fisheries Commission (NEAFC), created in 1959 (Underdal 1980; Sen 1997). Accordingly, circumscription of the high seas freedom of fishing began well before the emergence of EEZs.

Acceptance of extended coastal state jurisdiction has typically been the outcome of heated, sometimes violent regional conflicts over stocks that "straddle" existing national zones and the high seas, as occurred in the UK-Iceland "cod wars" over Iceland's unilateral proclamations of 12-mile and 50-mile fishing limits in the late 1950s and early 1970s, respectively (Thór 1995). Since 1977, however, it has not been controversial under international law for a coastal state to set up a 200-mile EEZ. By then, the states negotiating the Law of the Sea Convention had reached consensus on the EEZ concept, and the major states had either established such zones or were preparing to do so (Burke 1994). The EEZ concept places the coastal state in the driver's seat for most activities undertaken within such a zone, including resource utilization, environmental protection, and scientific research—but not navigation, which remains a high seas freedom within the EEZ (Articles 58 and 87). Indeed, these zones are not national spaces since the coastal states do not have full sovereignty, only specified sovereign rights and aspects of jurisdiction. This concept reflects the balance that had to be struck between the coastal states that argued that multilateral resource management had failed to conserve living resources and those major states, including the United States and the Soviet Union, that were set on retaining the freedom of navigation for commercial and naval vessels (Stokke 2007b). With respect to fisheries, however, a coastal state under the Law of the Sea Convention enjoys "sovereign rights for the purpose of exploring and exploiting, conserving and managing" the fish stocks, and regulations set forth in accordance with the Convention can be acted on by the full range of enforcement activities, including "boarding, inspection, arrest and judicial proceedings" (Articles 56 and 73).

Also in the remaining high seas areas, some encroachment has occurred on the traditional jurisdictional monopoly of the flag state. Canada,

spurred by the collapse of the northern cod stock and substantial unregulated harvesting in high seas parts of the Grand Banks, mustered support
from a group of Latin American countries and managed to place high
seas fisheries on the agenda of the 1992 UN Conference on Environment
and Development (Stokke 2001c). Negotiations over the jurisdictional
balance between flag states and coastal states were conducted in several
international fora, the most prominent of which adopted the UN Fish
Stocks Agreement in 1995 (Balton 1996). This agreement strengthens the
duty to cooperate with other states on high seas fisheries by providing
that only states that are members of a regional fisheries regime, or that
agree to apply the conservation and management measures taken under
such a regime, shall have access to the fishery (Article 8). With respect
to enforcement, it confirms heavier flag-state responsibilities and emu-
lates procedures developed within the Northwest Atlantic Fisheries Organization (Warbrick, McGoldrick, and Anderson 1996; Joyner 2001) that
permit nonflag states, under certain conditions, to inspect and detain
fishing vessels on the high seas (Article 21).

Thus we see that long-term trends in international ocean law have
involved spatial contraction of the high seas and more specific constraints on the freedom to fish on the high seas. Most fishing for Northeast Arctic cod takes place within areas under the jurisdiction of Norway
or Russia. That explains their dominant position in the Barents Sea fisheries regime, whose structures for research, regulation, and compliance
control are in focus in the remainder of this section.

Regional Regime Structures
Several treaties involving Norway and Russia can provide useful starting
points for describing the Barents Sea fisheries regime, but other important sources add a multilateral dimension.[4] The bilateral Framework
Agreement of 1975 defined regime objectives—conservation, rational
resource use, and good-neighborly relations (Preamble)—and created the
Joint Commission on Fisheries as the institutional hub (Article III).[5] A
1976 Mutual Access Agreement obliges Norway and Russia to permit
fishing vessels flagged by the other party to operate within their EEZs
in accordance with coastal state regulations (Articles 1–4). Jointly or
independently, these two coastal states have drawn up treaties granting
fishing rights for Northeast Arctic cod to European Community members,
the Faeroe Islands, Greenland, and Iceland, whereas Poland and Canada
may harvest some other species. These noncoastal states operate within
the framework for regulation and enforcement that Norway and Russia
define in the Joint Commission.

Upon forming the Barents Sea fisheries regime, Norway and the Soviet Union pledged to "ensure the conservation, rational use and reproduction of the living resources . . . [p]aying special attention to the importance of scientific research" (Framework Agreement, Preamble). It did not provide for any separate scientific body, however—mainly because there already existed a multilateral organization, the International Council for the Exploration of the Sea (ICES), that would continue to provide research coordination and scientific advice. This organization has developed a reputation for impartial input of high quality (Gullestad 1998), but that quality depends on the data and analysis provided by its member states. At its first meeting, the Joint Commission on Fisheries established a working group for coordinating survey activities (JCF 1976a, item 7). This bilateral research collaboration soon deepened and now consists of a rolling bilateral research program on living marine resources, including joint surveys, as well as several ad hoc scientific working groups on matters of particular interest to the commission. PINRO and IMR scientists predominate in the ICES working group responsible for Northeast Arctic cod; at a recent meeting, twenty-three of the twenty-eight participants were from Norway or Russia (ICES 2010, 529–531).

The ICES procedure for developing advice involves independent peer review to ensure impartiality. First, the relevant working group compiles available data and conducts the necessary analyses. Then a review group or a review process involving experts from states without any stake in the fishery examines the analysis in light of the best-available-science objective and develops a draft advice statement. Finally, the ICES Advisory Committee reviews that draft, modifies it as appropriate, and adopts the final advice.[6] Thus, the generation and provision of scientific advice under the Barents Sea fisheries regime are placed in a multilateral setting with third-party peer review, but the substantive basis is provided by researchers from the two coastal states.

As regards regulation, the Joint Commission on Fisheries meets annually and adopts the total allowable catch for each shared stock and technical regulations such as mesh-size rules. Recommendations are binding on the two states unless they opt out within two months (JCF 1983, annex 2); such opting out has occurred only twice. The important question of how to allocate fishing rights for Northeast Arctic cod was settled in a simple way: although Norway had argued that zonal attachment and historical catches indicated a 70/30 division in its favor (Hønneland 2006, 23), the solution was an equal split, with two qualifications (JCF 1976b, item 4).[7] First, coastal vessels may continue harvesting even after the quota is taken—a provision clearly beneficial to Norway, since the Northwest Russian fleet consists mostly of trawlers, not coastal vessels. Second, and clearly favoring the Soviet Union, the parties agreed to consider one segment of the Northeast Arctic cod as an exclusively Soviet stock, "Murman cod." The quota set for this "political stock"—ICES has never recognized the existence of a "Murman cod" stock—always corresponds to that of Norwegian coastal cod, which is distinct from Northeast Arctic cod and occurs solely in waters under Norway's jurisdiction. Yet another regime feature has proved very significant for its effectiveness (see chapters 5 and 6), especially during the 1980s: the practice under the Joint Commission of negotiating transfers of part of the Soviet and Russian cod quotas to Norway in return for larger quotas of pelagic fish (Stokke and Hoel 1991). Accordingly, the commission has simplified the allocation of cod by adopting de facto a fixed key, while retaining the flexibility to adjust this division by means of reciprocal quota transfers.

Regarding technical regulations, the Mutual Access Agreement stipulates that the parties "shall co-operate . . . with a view to ensuring the harmonization of any new measures . . . in so far as practically feasible" (Article 4). The Soviet and later the Russian authorities have seen this formulation as implying that all management measures pertaining to the shared stocks shall be equal throughout their migratory range; by contrast, Norway has held that the commission sets *minimum* standards, and that states may opt to set stricter rules in waters under their own jurisdiction (see, e.g., JCF 1982, item 4.3). Throughout the 1980s these different interpretations acquired political significance because Norway advocated stricter technical regulations rather than quotas whenever the stock was in decline (see chapter 5). The Soviets held the opposite view and often complained over Norway's implementation of more stringent rules, especially concerning mesh size, in waters under Norwegian jurisdiction. The longstanding disagreement over the minimum mesh size was put aside for many years, in part because of the development of a technical solution—sorting grids—acceptable to both states (Stokke, Anderson, and Mirovitskaya 1999, 131), but it was back on the agenda in 2008 and was finally resolved the year after (JCF 2009, annex 7).

The agreements under the Joint Commission on mutual access to each other's zones and gradually more stringent technical regulations contribute to a more rational harvesting pattern by reducing the pressure on young fish. As a result of the migratory pattern, the cod is generally older and bigger in Norway's zone, so a westward shift of the fishery means that the total allowable catch removes fewer individual fish.

Regulatory activities under the Joint Commission are becoming increasingly transparent, in line with general developments in international fisheries management (e.g., the Food and Agriculture Organization's Code of Conduct, Article 6.13). From the outset, a protocol from each meeting, with information about the agenda, the participants, the research activities, and the agreed-upon measures for conservation and allocation, was available on request from the Norwegian Ministry of Fisheries; now the ministry posts it on its official website. Meetings of the Joint Commission are closed to the public, however, and information about national positions on substantive issues is available only at the discretion of regime participants. There is a tradition whereby delegation members maintain contact with interested media during the annual negotiations. As a result, the coastal state fishery press frequently provides general insights into the state of play on contested matters, including who favors what solution and the distance between the positions of the two states. Especially in Norway, firm demands for greater openness were voiced early in the 2000s, when the commission had set the quotas drastically higher than the scientific recommendations. As a result, some of the organizations and agencies that had put forward such criticism were invited into Norway's delegation on a permanent basis (Hønneland 2006, 117–119).

The compliance system of the Barents Sea fisheries regime is far more decentralized than are the arrangements for providing scientific advice and regulations, but it also exhibits dynamism. A decentralized compliance system makes little use of joint, collaborative structures and leaves verification, review, and response largely to each state, acting on its own (Hovi, Stokke and Ulfstein 2005). Initially, the regional regime failed to add much to the default structure offered by international customary law—coastal state enforcement—which is already strong, since most regional harvesting occurs in waters under coastal state jurisdiction. The main contribution was a 1978 Grey Zone Agreement, with a system of parallel jurisdiction in an area that includes waters claimed by both Norway and Russia (see below). Each state surveys fishing operations by means of vessel reports, landings data, port and at-sea inspections, and, since 2000, satellite-based tracking of own vessels. The main limitation of a decentralized compliance system is lack of insight into how strictly *other* parties implement commitments within their jurisdiction. The creation in 1993 of a Permanent Committee for Management and Enforcement under the Joint Commission, involving the leading fisheries enforcement agencies of the two states, reflected the ambition for deeper collaboration that had been prompted by the disclosure of very severe overfishing in the preceding years (see chapter 6).

Since its creation, the Permanent Committee has been important as a point of contact between commission meetings and as an arena for elaborating joint measures to improve the implementation of regime rules. Notable initiatives subsequently adopted by the Joint Commission have included regular exchanges of information about national fisheries legislation, annual joint seminars involving enforcement personnel (JCF 1993), the dispatch of Russian observers to participate in inspections of Russian vessels landing fish in Norwegian ports (JCF 1994), annual exchanges of observers on each other's control vessels (JCF 1995), common conversion factors between whole fish and the processed products that enforcement personnel find on board during inspections (JCF 1994, 1996), and the coordination of satellite tracking systems (JCF 2000). An important addition is the exchange of vessel-level data on quotas and catches so far, allowing inspectors to expose cumulative overfishing not necessarily apparent from a snapshot comparison of logbooks and inventory.[8] Since 2006, Norway and Russia have shared tracking data on a continuous basis concerning the entire Barents and Norwegian Seas area (JCF 2008).

These various arrangements, which are also formalized at the agency level in regularly updated memoranda of collaborative control, can greatly improve the flow of information among the bodies responsible for fisheries control in the two states and help remove practical impediments to rule enforcement, making the overall compliance system somewhat less decentralized. Another indication of dynamism in bilateral compliance cooperation is the recent joint audit of the Barents Sea fisheries management system conducted by Norway's and Russia's respective offices of general audit (Norway OAG 2007; Russia 2007).

Since 2007, the compliance structure of the Barents Sea fisheries regime has been reinforced by a multilateral component in the form of port-state measures under a more stringent Scheme of Control and Enforcement under the NEAFC, which retains regulatory competence over high seas stocks in the region (Stokke 2009). Port-state measures involving noncoastal states became more important for effective fisheries enforcement in the Barents Sea when, around 2000, Russian vessels increasingly began to transship their catches for final delivery in EU member states (see chapter 6). Under the new scheme, members are not to allow a NEAFC vessel to land or transship frozen fish in its port unless the flag state of the vessel that caught the fish confirms that the vessel has sufficient quota, has reported the catch, and is authorized to fish in the area, and that satellite tracking information data correspond with vessel reports (NEAFC 2006). Unlike earlier NEAFC schemes, the new system applies not only to regulated resources on the high seas but to all "frozen catch of fisheries resources caught in the Convention Area"; the latter includes the regional EEZs as well. This broadening of scope makes the NEAFC Scheme of Control and Enforcement directly applicable to stocks managed under the Barents Sea fisheries regime.

In short, the bilateral Joint Commission holds center stage in the international management of fisheries in the Barents Sea but delegates the scientific advisory task to a multilateral organization. As regards compliance control, for many years this international regime left most of those tasks up to the individual initiatives of the coastal states, but the trend is now toward greater collaboration, bilaterally and multilaterally.

Nested Bilateralism
The distinction between bilateralism and multilateralism is helpful when summarizing the international means for governance of fisheries in the Barents Sea. A bilateralist regime is dyadic in its mode of coordination; of note, it differentiates participants on a case-by-case basis, depending on their strategic position with respect to the dominant actors (Ruggie 1992, 568).

The Barents Sea fisheries regime is bilateralist, based on treaties that the coastal states have drawn up among themselves or have entered into with *selected* noncoastal states in return for fishing rights in their waters. The European Community, the Faeroe Islands, Greenland, and Iceland currently have fishing rights for cod, haddock, saithe, and several other species in the Barents Sea (Norway MF 2007–2008, 66–69), but their vessels must operate according to the rules defined by the two coastal states. In contrast, the key characteristics of a multilateralist regime are inclusiveness and nondiscrimination (Ruggie 1992, 571). In international fisheries, multilateralist regimes typically manage stocks that occur in waters where coastal state jurisdiction is either absent (as on the high seas), disputed (as in Antarctic waters), or otherwise difficult to enforce (Stokke 2000).

The main explanation for the bilateralist form of the Barents Sea fisheries regime is its nestedness in a global institution that grants to coastal states wide competences in the management of fisheries within their 200-mile EEZs, which is where most of the Northeast Arctic cod occurs. The jurisdictional basis for conducting fisheries management nevertheless varies in this region, as we will see in the next section.

Sovereignty Issues as Management Constraints

Pending boundary delimitation or other unsettled jurisdictional issues are not uncommon in international fisheries management, sometimes pitting sovereignty concerns against those for sound fisheries management (Churchill 1993). Thus, when preparing for joint management of their shared stocks in the mid-1970s, Norway and the Soviet Union took pains to avoid any negative impacts on the status of their non-compatible territorial claims in the Barents Sea. In general, jurisdictional competition among members of an international regime may complicate cooperative management because of the "principle of effectiveness" in international law, which implies a linkage between actual, accepted exercise of authority and the strength of a territorial claim (Jennings 1963, 22–23). Enforcement measures are particularly sensitive in this respect since they ultimately rest on the ability to take coercive measures and are therefore closer to the core of sovereignty than are regulatory measures.

These considerations are relevant in the Barents Sea case, in part because of a delimitation of the continental shelf and the EEZs that was achieved only in 2010. Parts of the shelf area contain large amounts of proven oil and gas reserves, and the disputed area is promising in terms of undiscovered resources (Gautier et al. 2009). Other difficult jurisdictional issues concern the differing views on the legal status of a fisheries zone around Svalbard and the appropriateness of noncoastal state harvesting of cod in the Loophole, a pocket of high seas between the Norwegian and Russian EEZs. Figure 3.1 shows these contested areas, whose special management challenges are the subject of this section.

The Disputed Area and the Grey Zone

A major effect of the longstanding boundary dispute in the Barents Sea on regional fisheries management has been to shrink the area where a coastal state can exercise compliance control over vessels flagged by the other state. When formal negotiations on the maritime delimitation began in 1974, both Norway and the Soviet Union cited the 1958 Convention on the Continental Shelf, but with differing emphases on its two key concepts, the "median line" and "special circumstances" (Article 6;

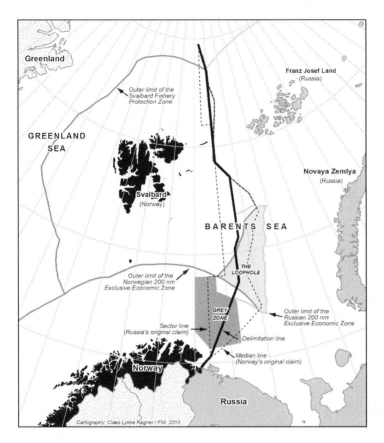

Figure 3.1
Jurisdictional zones in the Barents Sea. Map drawn by Claes Lykke Ragner, the Fridtjof Nansen Institute.

Oude Elferink 1994, 228). According to the Soviet position, several special circumstances, including national legislation from the 1920s, would indicate that the boundary should follow the sector line, and not the median line, as argued by Norway (see figure 3.1). The 2010 Norway-Russia Maritime Delimitation Agreement divides the disputed area between those lines more or less equally. The general concern that collaborative management may influence the status of sovereignty claims is evident in the Framework Agreement's assurance that "Nothing in this agreement shall affect the rights, existing or future claims or legal positions of the Contracting Parties regarding the nature and scope of fisheries jurisdiction" (Article V).

The Grey Zone Agreement was the main regime instrument for balancing sovereignty concerns with those for fisheries regulation and control in the disputed area. This agreement acknowledged, as a provisional arrangement until a delimitation line was agreed upon, parallel regulatory and enforcement jurisdiction in an "adjacent area," usually referred to as the "Grey Zone," which includes most of the disputed part of the EEZs but also undisputed parts. By stipulating that in this area, neither of the parties is competent to inspect or arrest vessels flagged or licensed by the other party (Articles 3 and 4), the two states hoped to safeguard their competing sovereignty claims while acquiring an undisputed basis for rule enforcement concerning own vessels and those of third parties.

The inclusion of large segments of nondisputed EEZ areas originates in a Soviet request, on the argument that it would reduce the "impression of conflict" (Fisheries Minister Ishkov, cited in Tamnes 1997, 297; my translation). One effect of such inclusion was to loosen the link between the acceptance of enforcement activities by the other party in the disputed area and the weakening of one's own jurisdictional claim, since such activities occur also in areas where national jurisdiction is not an issue (Stokke, Anderson, and Mirovitskaya 1999, 139). The price of any such gain, however, has been to shrink the area where one regime participant is entitled to monitor and enforce rule compliance on vessels flagged by the other party. For Norway, an additional cost was that the Grey Zone includes far greater areas to the west than to the east of the disputed area—which, critics argued, could be interpreted as an acknowledgment that the basis for Norway's claim is less weighty (Stortinget 1977–1978, 3). Mostly for this reason, the agreement only narrowly passed the Storting, following an unusually acrid debate (Stortinget, 9 March 1978, 2170–2220).

Since its adoption, the Grey Zone Agreement has been renewed annually by both states without any domestic controversy, despite its geographic asymmetry and the effect it has in confining the spatial area where each coastal state may enforce fisheries regulations on vessels of the other state. Such smooth renewal indicates that no other solution for balancing the sovereignty and fisheries-management concerns in the region appeared politically feasible prior to the 2010 adoption of the maritime delimitation agreement.

The Svalbard Fisheries Protection Zone
Partially disputed jurisdiction also characterizes a second distinctive segment of the Barents Sea. Here as well the effect is to constrain the

enforcement of fisheries rules, although less so over time. Norway established a Fisheries Protection Zone around Svalbard in 1977.[9] The disputed status of this zone is rooted in different interpretations of the 1920 Svalbard Treaty, which grants to Norway sovereignty over this archipelago, with some specified limitations. Norway must give equal access to, and equal treatment of, nationals of any signatory state to specified economic activities, it must refrain from collecting more tax than is needed for administering the archipelago, and it must keep the area demilitarized (Articles 1, 3, 8, and 9). According to Norway, those limitations apply only to the onshore areas and the territorial sea, not to the continental shelf or to waters beyond the territorial sea. That is why the zone is legally based on Norway's EEZ legislation, whereas fisheries regulations in Svalbard's internal waters and its territorial sea are based on Norway's Svalbard Act.[10] The Soviet Union (and later Russia) openly rejected Norway's right to establish unilaterally any zone beyond Svalbard's territorial waters, and several other states have reserved their opinion on whether such a zone falls within the ambit of the Svalbard Treaty (Ulfstein 1995, 422). From the perspective of fisheries management, the challenge is again to find procedures for exercising enforcement authority that touch as lightly as possible on a contested jurisdictional issue.

The modus vivendi that Norway has achieved with other states with fishing rights in the Fisheries Protection Zone involves a combination of coastal state restraint in the exercise of management authority and practical acceptance of such authority by all user states, with some differences in their degree of acceptance. Norwegian restraint is evident in the decision to abstain "for the time being" from implementing the general ban on nonlicensed foreign fishing in the EEZ in this particular zone; hence the term "fisheries protection zone," which denotes nondiscrimination.[11] Moreover, Norway has tended to choose rather mild responses when exposing rule violations by foreign vessels (Pedersen 2008a, 917), usually no more than written warnings (see, e.g., Norwegian Coast Guard 2004). This cautious approach has always been openly acknowledged by the representatives of Norwegian policymaking and enforcement agencies.[12] In return, most other regime participants have instructed their fishers to adhere to Norwegian information as well as conservation measures in the zone, and to accept inspections. Although Russian captains are instructed not to sign inspection papers—which Moscow considers would be too much of an acceptance of Norwegian jurisdiction—they usually do not impede at-sea inspectors. In 2002, the Norwegian Coast Guard conducted more than 350 inspections of Russian vessels, accounting for some two-thirds of the total number of inspections in the Fisheries Protection Zone (Norwegian Coast Guard 2002, 6). Content analysis of all reports from inspections in this zone from 1986 to 1992 indicated that overall compliance with conservation measures had been high, only slightly lower than in Norway's EEZ, where the responses to rule violations are far more severe (Hønneland 2000, 86).

These practices of mutual accommodation add up to a case of "bifocalism," an institutional solution that conveniently allows diverging interpretations by regime participants whose disagreement over an underlying issue might otherwise disrupt cooperation (Stokke and Vidas 1996b, 443). Whereas Norway focuses on the facts that the Fisheries Protection Zone is based on its EEZ legislation, that it actually conducts enforcement activities, and that the level of compliance is usually acceptable, Russia and other user states have focused on the nondiscriminatory nature of the zone. The latter implies that Norway in practice goes no further in its exercise of sovereignty than it could if the Svalbard Treaty were to apply to the waters outside the territorial sea. According to Article 2 of the Treaty,

Norway shall be free to maintain, take or decree suitable measures to ensure the preservation and, if necessary, the re-constitution of the fauna and flora of the said regions, and their territorial waters; it being clearly understood that these measures shall always be applicable equally to the nationals of all the High Contracting Parties without any exemption, privilege or favor whatsoever, direct or indirect to the advantage of any one of them.

The limits of what such bifocalism can achieve are evident in the cases of international dispute that have nevertheless occurred, largely serving to raise the level of ambition in Norway's regulation and rule enforcement. Mostly in response to challenges by other states, and beginning with the 1986 decision to cap the amounts of cod that noncoastal states may take in the zone (Churchill and Ulfstein 1992, 116), Norway has gradually become less cautious in its exercise of regulatory and enforcement authority in the zone and has achieved a practical level of acceptance through the use of quotas and coercion.

Allocating EEZ quotas to challengers is a widespread strategy among coastal states seeking to manage high seas fisheries (Stokke 2000) and has worked well also in the Fisheries Protection Zone. In the late 1980s, practical acceptance from Poland and the German Democratic Republic was obtained by playing the quota card (Churchill and Ulfstein 1992, 111); and Greenland's acquisition of fishing rights for cod in Norway's EEZ in 1991 occurred as a consequence of its engagement in unregulated fishing in the Loophole and the Fisheries Protection Zone.[13] When other vessel operators from other states tried to follow this example, however, Norway shifted tactics and used its Coast Guard instead—as it had earlier threatened to do in 1986 during a confrontation with Spain over the noncoastal state quota (Pedersen 2008b, 248).

The first subject of Norway's tougher line in the Fisheries Protection Zone was a Faeroese vessel flying a Caribbean flag of convenience. A warning shot was fired, and the vessel was chased from the zone (*Nordlys*, 29 July 1993, 2). The year after, two Icelandic vessels had their trawl bags cut, and a third was fired at, arrested, and brought to a Norwegian port for legal prosecution (Pedersen 2008b, 249). The latter incident induced Norway to specify in its domestic regulation which states, on the basis of historical catches, are entitled to take the noncoastal state quota. In 1998, the policy of using coercion if necessary was extended to Russia: the Norwegian Coast Guard initiated an arrest of one out of some thirty Russian fishing vessels working in an area that had been closed for juvenile-density reasons, after the vessels ignored a Coast Guard request to leave (*Aftenposten*, 14 July 1998, 4). The vessel was released following the departure of all the Russian vessels from the area in question, so the arrest in 2001 of the trawler *Chernigov* was the first involving a Russian vessel in the Fisheries Protection Zone to result in legal prosecution (Pedersen 2008b, 249). While that arrest triggered a Russian protest and strong language in the Russian media by the chairman of the State Committee on Fisheries (Hønneland 2003), Russia's de facto acceptance of Norway's gradually more ambitious regulation and enforcement activities in the zone reflects an underlying reality for any state with significant cod quotas in the Barents Sea: uncontrolled fishing in a large area where Northeast Arctic cod is highly available is simply not in its interest.

Thus, we see that disagreements over the legal status of the zone around Svalbard have rendered fisheries enforcement more lenient but have not prevented regular inspection also of noncoastal state vessels. Mostly in response to cases involving explicit challenges to its management authority, Norway has gradually become more ambitious concerning regulation and enforcement in the Fisheries Protection Zone, especially from the early 1990s on.

The Loophole
While Northeast Arctic cod occurs mostly in waters under coastal state jurisdiction, in some periods with high temperatures in the Barents Sea

it can also be found in the high seas Loophole, and that has given rise to some management challenges (Churchill 1999; Stokke 2001d). The fishing is usually better closer to the coast, so this high seas area is of interest mostly to vessels without access to the regional EEZs—which in practice today means those flying flags of convenience. However, during the first half of the 1990s, the most recent period of high cod availability in the Loophole, it was Iceland that predominated. At the time, Iceland had no agreed-upon access to cod in the Barents Sea and therefore lacked weighty incentives for complying with Norwegian and Russian requests to abstain from fishing there. Noncoastal state cod harvests in the Loophole peaked at some 50,000 tons in 1994, or 7 percent of the total (Stokke 2001d).

Despite pressure from industry organizations calling for "emergency measures," Norway and Russia refrained from handling the Icelandic challenge in a way that might have stretched international law, for instance by using such coercive measures as noncourtesy boarding or the detention of foreign vessels. According to a prominent international lawyer, any such unilateral action on the high seas could be legitimate only if bona fide attempts to reach agreement with the user states had failed and if the stock were unequivocally in jeopardy due to the activity in question (Burke 1989, 285). In the case at hand, those conditions were not present. Even at the peak, the unregulated catches of Northeast Arctic cod amounted to no more than a third of the *increase* in the total quota from the preceding year, and thus posed more of a nuisance than a sustainability threat. Moreover, Iceland clearly indicated its willingness to negotiate with the two states.

The difficulty of justifying coastal state unilateralism under international fisheries law induced Norway to introduce trade-related measures instead—notably, the blacklisting of vessels with a history of Loophole fishing from access to EEZ quotas and port calls, and collaborative port-state denial of landings of Loophole catches. Such blacklisting would stick with the vessel even after a change of ownership, thus reducing its value on the second-hand market. One instance of port denial induced Iceland to file a complaint to the body overseeing compliance with the European Economic Area Agreement, but no action was taken (Stokke 2001d). While such trade-related measures are generally promising for combating unregulated harvesting on the high seas (Stokke 2009), they are less potent when the harvesting vessels deliver their catch at home, as the Icelanders did with Northeast Arctic cod. In the end, the quota card proved decisive for achieving external acceptance of coastal state rules on the high seas (Stokke 2001d). The 1999 Loophole Agreement gives Iceland a small share of Northeast Arctic cod quota in return for a pledge to take it in the EEZs, to allow coastal state rule enforcement (Articles 2–4).

As in many other regional attempts to manage high seas fisheries, therefore, allocation of EEZ quotas and to a lesser extent trade-related compliance measures have played important roles in dealing with the Loophole problem, which never became severe enough to justify unilateral coercive measures.

Coping with Jurisdictional Constraints

In summary, then, we see that bifocalism, reward, and coercion are the main measures used by the coastal states and other regime participants to tackle the threats to sound fisheries management posed by unsettled jurisdictional issues and the near monopoly of flag states on the high seas. The Grey Zone Agreement and the practice of mutual accommodation concerning fisheries around Svalbard both display bifocal solutions, with productive unclarity allowing states to delink in part certain undesired consequences of regulation and enforcement activities. In the Svalbard case, additional measures have been taken, notably the allocation of quotas to some challengers of Norway's management authority and the use of force against others. The grudging acceptance of such coercive measures derives from the interest that any state with a piece of the Northeast Arctic cod quota has in avoiding a management vacuum. Coastal state efforts to manage cod fisheries in the high seas Loophole primarily involve rewarding those who adhere to regime regulations with EEZ quotas. The legal basis for non-flag-state regulation and enforcement is weaker in the Loophole than in the other two zones, but large-scale harvesting in that area is only occasional and therefore less of an actual risk to sustainable fisheries management.

Summary and Implications

This account of the Barents Sea fisheries regime and how it relates to broader institutions, the regional fisheries industries, and the national structures for fisheries management feeds directly into the effectiveness analyses in the chapters that follow. While centered on the Joint Commission, this regime is nested within the broader institution of global fisheries law, notably the right that coastal states have to establish and implement 200-mile EEZs. Such zones enable the strategic use of the quota card and thus form the basis for coastal state dominance in the management of Northeast Arctic cod, even in waters where their jurisdiction over vessels flagged by foreign states is weak or contested, as in the high seas Loophole, in the Svalbard Fisheries Protection Zone, and in the Grey Zone prior to the coastal state delimitation agreement of 2010.

The longstanding importance of the cod fisheries for regional settlement, production, and trade implies favorable conditions for cognitional problem solving by justifying sizable investment in scientific research on how to balance use and conservation. As elaborated in chapter 4, when the Murmansk-based research institute PINRO experienced various financial uncertainties in the transitional period following the dissolution of the Soviet Union, one consequence was significantly deeper collaboration with its Norwegian counterpart.

Similarly, the cross-state difference in industry structure, with trawlers predominating in the Russian industry and relatively small coastal vessels taking the majority of Norway's cod catches, affects both the nature of the regulatory problem and the means available for dealing with it. Chapter 5 shows that the lesser ability of small coastal vessels to pursue alternative fishing opportunities in distant waters was among the factors behind Norway's reluctance to accept scientifically advised quota cuts during the 1980a. This structural difference also underlies the regime-based quota exchange, a flexibility mechanism that has helped reduce the overall costs of regulatory quota cuts. As brought out in chapter 6, such quota exchange also shaped behavioral problem solving by directing parts of the Soviet harvesting pressure toward other species than the troubled cod stock. The economic value of the fishery and the structure of the industries have influenced the material interests of regime participants and thereby the basis for regime-based problem solving.

Similar comments apply regarding the national and international structures for Barents Sea fisheries management. At the national level, the most dramatic case in point is the reshuffling of the Northwest Russian fisheries sector during the 1990s. The privatization process not only influenced research funding, and thereby the basis for cognitional problem solving, it also prompted a shift in the Russian vessel-deployment pattern from distant pelagic stocks to Northeast Arctic cod. As chapters 5 and 6 show, these developments had profound effects on regulatory and behavioral problem solving, removing the basis for large-scale quota exchange and boosting the incentives for Russian quota overfishing at a time when the national fisheries bureaucracy was expending much of its energies on defensive turf struggles with competitors at the regional and federal levels.

Thus, the challenges of joint management associated with Russia's transition to a market economy have triggered a stepwise strengthening of the Barents Sea fisheries regime especially with respect to compliance control, but also as regards scientific research and advice and regulatory decision making. As we will see in the next four chapters, such strengthening of the international regime has enhanced its ability to influence the ultimate problem addressed by it, the balancing of utilization and conservation.

4

Cognitional Effectiveness

The cognitional problem in focus for international regimes is to build a shared, well-founded understanding of how best to achieve the social purpose of the regime. In fisheries management, that means generating research-based advice that differentiates accurately among alternative management programs in terms of the impacts on the state of targeted and related stocks. Some of the factors that have improved cognitional problem solving in the Barents Sea case are regime-driven and include deepening collaboration among Norwegian and Russian research institutions and the stepwise incorporation of ecosystem modeling in the basis for scientific advice. By treating the quality of scientific advice as something that an international regime may explain, at least in part, this chapter differs from most other contributions on the interface of science and politics in resource management. The focus has usually been on the converse causal connection: how aspects of research activities and scientific advice influence decision making.

This chapter applies the disaggregate approach to international regime effectiveness developed in chapter 2. Central here is the Oslo-Potsdam formula for measuring effectiveness as the ratio of actual improvement to potential improvement. Thus, we begin by specifying a scale for measuring actual cognitional problem solving based on two dimensions of scientific advice: its salience, or practical usefulness to managers, and its accuracy in forecasting the impacts of various levels of harvesting pressure. Every year, the scientific advisory body provides a menu of harvesting options, each including a forecast on the future level of the spawning stock that will emerge as a result. The accuracy of those forecasts can be measured because the advisory body also publishes retrospective spawning stock assessments; the most recent assessment is the most reliable, because time-series data are available for more years. This procedure helps specify concretely and validly what would qualify as *full* problem solving, as well as reasonable thresholds for the three lower scores for describing the outcome of interest: substantial, modest, or insignificant levels of cognitional problem solving.

Besides a conception of full problem solving that allows comparison with actual achievements, the effectiveness yardstick used here needs an estimate of the most plausible counterfactual level of problem solving. As explained in chapter 2, determining whether an outcome would be markedly inferior if there were no regime requires a good account of actual problem solving. That is why the subsequent section develops a specific model of cognitional problem solving based on earlier findings in the study of regime effectiveness. This model is then tested with relevant empirical evidence from twenty-five years of scientific advice on the stock in question. Use of the qualitative comparative analysis (QCA) technique helps pinpoint certain ideal-type combinations of causal properties that reliably deliver either cognitional success or cognitional failure.

Those findings about causal combinations reliably delivering either success or failure among actual cases prove very useful in substantiating the most plausible level of problem solving that would pertain if the regime did not exist. The disaggregate approach tackles that large counterfactual question by first answering one that is much smaller and more tractable, namely, what scores the case would achieve on the modeled factors if there were no regime. In the section assessing effectiveness, I examine how well those counterfactual cases fit the success and failure paths. Such a fit is measurable by the set-theoretic rules of intersection and negation and helps to estimate the most plausible outcome, since counterfactual cases should behave in the same way as actual cases do. Actual cases reliably achieve problem-solving scores equal to or higher than their scores on a success path; they likewise achieve failure scores equal to or higher than their scores on a failure path. Accordingly, a good fit with a reliable success or failure path helps to derive lower or upper bounds on the plausible range of counterfactual problem-solving estimates, the last parameter needed for assessing regime effectiveness by the Oslo-Potsdam yardstick.

The Problem: Generating Salient and Accurate Advice

Building a shared and empirically valid understanding among the participants of a regime on how its social purpose can best be achieved is particularly important in sectors involving resource and environmental management, and states typically create or use separate scientific bodies to provide relevant input. Such input varies in salience (Parson 2003; Clark, Mitchell, and Cash 2006, 15), that is, whether it differentiates among the policy options under consideration as to forecasted impacts on the policy objectives. This dimension of cognitional problem solving has a long pedigree. A nearly forty-year-old *FAO Manual of Fisheries Science*, for instance, notes that "the practical fisheries biologist collects data to answer two main questions: 'how much fish is there in the area that it is intended to fish?' and 'what is the maximum amount which can be caught annually without affecting the ability of the stock to produce that yield?'" (Holden and Raitt 1974, item 9.1). A crucial second dimension, accuracy, concerns the difference between such forecasts and actual developments in the resource stock.

This section specifies those dimensions, merges them into a single scale of cognitional problem solving, and assigns problem-solving scores under the Barents Sea fisheries regime for each year under study.

A Scale of Cognitional Problem Solving

A good scale for measuring cognitional problem solving should incorporate both the salience and the accuracy dimensions, without necessarily according them equal weight. With respect to salience, an ongoing dialog among scientists, managers, and conservation groups has generated several stock-specific biological reference points in order to differentiate among policy options. For many years, maximum sustainable yield was the main standard underlying the recommendations provided by ICES and other advisory bodies in fisheries management. It denotes the highest long-term average annual catch that can be taken from a stock under the given pattern of exploitation (ICES 1990a, 56).[1] Behind that concept is the frequent empirical observation of a bell curve relationship between the pressure on a stock and the catch per unit effort, indicating that intensive exploitation may jeopardize future use. The concept of "optimum yield" as defined in U.S. fisheries legislation also starts out from the long-term yield but takes account of nonbiological concerns as well, including broader economic and social goals.

On the basis of such biological reference points, scientific bodies provide advice involving different levels of salience. Advice involving *several policy options* gives managers a basis for setting priorities between current and future use and therefore implies high salience. Thus, for stocks that are not depleted or suffering from recruitment failure but are fished "largely in excess of the levels indicated by biological reference points," ICES decided in 1982 to provide a range of "options inside safe biological limits, and . . . recommend one of those options, according to the general principles of aiming at more stable levels" (ICES 1982, 3). Perhaps more common in international fisheries management is what we may term medium-level salience, whereby the scientific body offers *a single recommendation* without specifying whether other levels of harvesting pressure might also be sustainable and how those other levels would compare with the recommendation in terms of the policy objective. Whenever scientists are *unable to identify* any recommended level of harvesting deserve, a low salience score is appropriate—as is often the case in the early periods of a fishery when there is little information available to support assessment work. As shown by the boom-and-bust experience with several Antarctic fisheries for demersal species in the mid-1970s (Stokke 1996), low salience can prove disastrous when it comes to fisheries management.

My yardstick for measuring cognitional success and failure combines salience and accuracy on a four-value scale. Cognitional problem solving is deemed full if both salience and accuracy are high, substantial if one of them is high and the other is medium, modest if salience is medium and accuracy is low, and insignificant if no advice is offered (low salience) or accuracy is very low. This yardstick gives priority to accuracy at the lower end because even the most differentiated and well-substantiated assessment will be of scant use if the underlying forecasts of how the harvesting pressure will affect the state of stocks prove to be widely off the mark. Forecasts that seriously underestimate the detrimental stock impacts of a certain level of harvesting may encourage unsustainable quotas.

Salience
Scientific advice on Northeast Arctic cod is highly salient, in great part because of the long history of fisheries research in the region. As an economically crucial stock in a technologically advanced part of the world, Northeast Arctic cod has been subject to systematic collection of relevant data ever since fisheries research emerged as a distinct area of activity in the second half of the nineteenth century. The range of activities that fall under the rubric of fisheries research has expanded over time. At first the term denoted primarily biology and oceanography, but as early as the 1950s economics and other social sciences had been incorporated (Walford 1958).

Norway launched the world's first government-sponsored research and monitoring program for saltwater fisheries in 1860, with Northeast

Arctic cod among the species of interest from the start. The geographic distribution of the stock throughout the year is now well known, as are its migratory and spawning patterns. We have long time-series data on abundance in the form of catch and effort data, from the Lofoten fishery even back to the 1860s (Godø 2003, 123). Scientists determined long ago such key biological parameters as fecundity, age of spawning, and the mean relationships among length, age, weight, and growth; these parameters are regularly monitored and updated. Taken together, such data permit age-structured stock assessment. In 1965, researchers conducted the first virtual population analysis (Aglen, Drevetnyak, and Sokolov 2004)—more than a decade before the formation of the Barents Sea fisheries regime.

When ICES adopted the options form of advice in 1982, that approach had already been tried out for two years with Northeast Arctic cod (ICES 1979, 151–152). Among the factors that determine whether a stock is within safe biological levels are fishing mortality, its distribution over the age groups, and the size of the spawning stock, which for Northeast Arctic cod comprises fish aged six years or older. Reflecting greater concern with how to deal with uncertainty in the advisory process, during the 1980s ICES explored other biological reference points to identify levels of fishing that would make it either "probable" or "doubtful" that long-term recruitment would be "sufficient to sustain a stable stock" (ICES 1988, 5). The backdrop for this development was the great fluctuations in important fish stocks, such as the Northeast Arctic cod, and the stock collapses that had affected major harvesting activities in earlier decades, including those for the Antarctic blue whale and the Atlanto-Scandian herring.

In its advice for 1998, ICES introduced a precautionary approach to fisheries advice, following extensive work on how best to implement the relevant provisions of the UN Fish Stocks Agreement (Stokke and Coffey 2004). That approach defines stock-specific "limit reference points," associated with "unknown population dynamics or stock collapse," and derives "precautionary reference points" for fishing mortality and the spawning stock so as to minimize the risk of the stock falling below the limit reference point (ICES 1998, 6). The advisory body continued its practice of calculating and providing forecasts for several higher levels of harvesting as well. Those higher levels are, however, now "considered inconsistent with the precautionary approach" (ICES 1998, 24).

The precautionary reference point for the spawning stock of Northeast Arctic cod, initially placed at 500,000 tons (ICES 1998, 24), reflects considerable continuity.[2] Citing earlier work, the ICES Advisory Committee thirty years ago had already considered a spawning stock range between 500,000 and one million tons as optimal; the lower threshold was "a minimum requirement to reduce the probability of recruitment failure" (1982, 241). Soviet scientists too referred to 500,000 tons as a scientifically agreed-upon lowest "norm" for the spawning stock when they argued that lower quotas were preferable to stricter mesh-size rules to promote stock recovery (PINRO 1982).

In short, demands from governments and regional fisheries management bodies for policy-relevant input led ICES to introduce the option form of advice, which implies high salience. Since 1980 the Advisory Committee has recommended one among several options for Northeast Arctic cod, based on biological reference points that were further developed with the introduction in 1998 of a precautionary approach to fisheries advice.

Accuracy

While it is certainly of interest that a scientific body considers the evidence solid enough to offer differentiated advice, cognitional problem solving also requires that the underlying assessment be accurate. Here ICES performance has varied considerably over time. Given the centrality of scientific expert advice as a standard for evaluating the performance of international environmental regimes (see, e.g., Jacobson and Kay 1983a; Andresen and Wettestad 1995, 2004; Stokke, Anderson, and Mirovitskaya 1999; Miles et al. 2002), it seems odd that so few studies have tried to evaluate the empirical validity of such advice.

One indicator of accuracy is how well the annual assessments of the spawning stock have stood up against the quality control ICES performs annually by providing updated and revised versions of earlier stock assessments in light of new information. Odd Nakken (1998, 33) has found that, with only one exception in the period from 1984 to 1994, the initial assessment of the spawning stock biomass for Northeast Arctic cod proved to be overly optimistic. Thus, the retrospective, more reliable assessments have tended to be considerably lower than the first; and this pattern is more pronounced for cod than for species of lesser economic significance, such as haddock and saithe.[3]

This study uses an even more direct indicator of accuracy, based on the spawning stock forecasts underlying the catch levels included in the ICES options range. After all, managers act not on the assessment itself but on the forecasted impacts of alternative levels of harvesting. Such

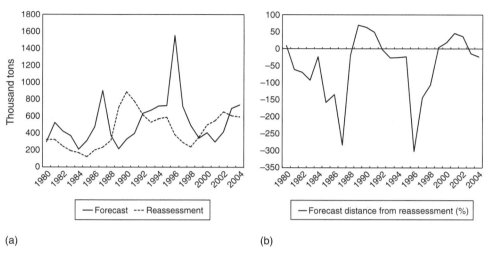

(a)   (b)

Figure 4.1
Distance between initial forecasts and retrospective assessments, Northeast Arctic cod. Figure 4.1a shows spawning stock forecasts and retrospective assessments in absolute numbers. Figure 4.1b gives forecasts as a percentage of the retrospective assessments. Data from the annual ICES Report of the Advisory Committee on Fisheries Management; calculations of distances in appendix 3.

forecast accuracy is what figure 4.1 shows for Northeast Arctic cod. Figure 4.1a compares the spawning stock forecast underlying each year's advice with the most recent assessment of how the spawning stock developed. The forecasts are interpolated or extrapolated linearly from the two options in the ICES advice that are the closest to the best estimate of the actual catch.[4] For example, in 1984 the Advisory Committee forecasted that 1985 catches at 300,000 tons would bring the spawning stock to 216,000 tons by the end of the year. According to the latest assessment, however, that level of harvesting reduced the spawning stock to 170,000 tons, indicating that the forecast underestimated the impact of such harvesting pressure by 46,000 tons. That difference between forecast and assessment constitutes around 25 percent of the spawning stock as retrospectively assessed. To allow comparison over time, figure 4.1b plots the corresponding distances for each year from 1980, the time that ICES provided the options necessary for calculating such accuracy, to the 2004 forecast.[5]

Figures 4.1a and b bring out the variation over time in the accuracy of Advisory Committee forecasts concerning Northeast Arctic cod. Whenever the line in figure 4.1b is below the horizontal axis, scientists have been too optimistic, underestimating the impact of harvesting on the spawning stock. The figure reveals two periods of extremely low accuracy, in the mid-1980s and the mid-1990s, ICES forecasts concerning spawning stock size were up to three times greater than the figures identified in the retrospective assessment. Moreover, for nearly three-fourths of the observations, the assessed spawning stock proved to be less than the forecast, which reinforces and extends earlier finding that stock assessments tend to be overly optimistic.

Thus, we find radical variation in the accuracy of annual ICES forecasts of how various levels of harvesting will affect the size of the spawning stock biomass of Northeast Arctic cod. Depending on the robustness of the stock, forecasts as widely off the mark as in the mid-1980s and mid-1990s could encourage unsustainable quotas, setting in motion a chain of events leading to a recruitment failure, especially if the error is largely on the optimistic side, as it has been with Northeast Arctic cod.

Assigning Cognitional Problem-Solving Scores
Since salience is high throughout the period under study, variation in cognitional problem-solving scores follows the ups and down of forecast accuracy. Thus, I derive the most reasonable thresholds between levels of problem solving from the forecast–assessment distances, measured in percentage of the spawning stock (see figure 4.1b). The procedure for placing those thresholds is outlined in chapter 1. While paying attention to potential "qualitative anchors" (Ragin 2000, 317) that help to determine whether a certain threshold is reasonable, I examine whether the observations cluster around a small number of values that could provide a basis for categorization. On a line plotting the forecast–assessment distances from the lowest to the highest absolute value, such a cluster would show up as a rather flat segment for cases with similar levels of accuracy.[6] Since cases with similar accuracy should not be assigned different problem-solving scores, such flat parts of the line are to be avoided when placing the category thresholds. In contrast, particularly steep parts of that line would indicate big leaps in accuracy and might justify a category threshold. A secondary distributional criterion, used only if the qualitative or the steepness criteria do not allocate cases determinately, is that the four categories should capture roughly the same number of observations.

Applying this procedure to the forecast versus assessment distances listed in appendix 3 yields a cutoff point for full cognitional problem solving at a 10 percent distance. Only three cases achieve this score, but the only alternative candidate, the next steep part of the line, would yield a full-score category considerably bigger than the others and, even worse, would include a forecast that misses the mark by more than one-third, which seems unreasonable. The same line of reasoning places the cutoff point for substantial problem solving at a 30 percent distance from the most recent spawning stock assessment and that for a modest score at 70 percent; an even greater distance constitutes insignificant problem solving. These thresholds allocate a clear majority of cases to the lower end of the cognitional problem-solving scale, which would appear reasonable from figure 4.1. Exact problem-solving scores are given in appendix 5. Later in this chapter I examine whether the findings concerning the causal combinations that drive this variation in problem solving are robust to various alternative placement of thresholds.

To summarize, for most of the years studied, the effects of harvesting proved more depressive on the spawning stock than expected by the scientists, with forecast accuracy dropping to low or very low levels in the mid-1980s and the mid-1990s. Such accuracy can be measured, thanks to the ICES practice of conducting and publishing each year a revised version of earlier assessments of the state of stocks. Advice on the harvesting levels of Northeast Arctic cod is highly salient, the second dimension of cognitional problem solving, because it includes separate stock forecasts for a range of harvesting options within safe biological limits, but the accuracy of forecasts has varied significantly. The next section builds an explanatory model that can account for this variation.

Modeling Cognitional Problem Solving

When specifying a model to explain variation in cognitional problem solving, we may usefully combine theoretical knowledge about the general phenomenon under study and substantive knowledge about the specific cases at hand (Ragin 1994, 60).

The role of scientists and experts is frequently prominent in the study of international environmental regimes, but the emphasis has mostly been on the influence that scientific input may have on political decisions (Underdal 1989; Haas 1989; Adler and Haas 1992; Litfin 1994; Andresen et al. 2000; Clark, van Eijndhoven, and Jäger 2001; Parson 2003; Mitchell, Clark, and Cash 2006), which is among the themes of chapter 5. The relatively few studies that do examine institutional impacts on the provision of scientific knowledge in international resource management have not systematically evaluated the *quality* of scientific advice. Walsh (2004, 38–40), for instance, draws attention to three mechanisms for fixing accepted beliefs within fisheries institutions: those mechanisms concern the individuals who occupy leading positions, the formal rules on knowledge generation, and the practices for arriving at group beliefs within a scientific advisory committee. While her analysis reveals processes that serve to insulate science institutions from pressures by governments or interest groups, Walsh does not seek to derive from those processes any general model to identify factors likely to promote such insulation under given sets of conditions. Surprisingly little has been written about the factors that may explain variation in the quality of scientific advice.

My development of a cognitional problem-solving model starts from the observation that no scientific advice can be better than its underlying data. Accurate forecasting requires reliable information on numerous factors, including the stock's geographic distribution, abundance, growth rate, and migratory and spawning habits, and on aspects of the marine environment that influence those factors. In fisheries research, the two main sources of relevant data are catch reports and fisher-independent surveys, and two explanatory candidates presented in chapter 2 and specified below concern the reliability and validity of such data: *malignancy,* in the form of strong incentives to underreport catches, and the depth of survey *collaboration* among the coastal states. Two other factors derive more from scrutiny of the pattern of forecast accuracy evident in this particular study than from general theory, but both make intuitive sense as well: substantive *intricacy,* here referring ecosystem complexity and rapid shifts in the environmental conditions of the cod stock, and the extent of *ecosystem modeling* under the regime. Figure 4.2 places those four factors in a causal model and illustrates the hypotheses that malignancy and intricacy affect cognitional problem solving negatively, whereas survey collaboration and ecosystem modeling do so positively.

In line with the disaggregate approach to international regime effectiveness, the remainder of this section specifies the causal variables in the model and substantiates the actual and the most plausible counterfactual scores for them in the case of Barents Sea fisheries.

Malignancy
Catch reports by fishers provide an important basis for scientific stock assessment but they are not always reliable, since fishers may benefit from underreporting their catches. That observation forms the starting

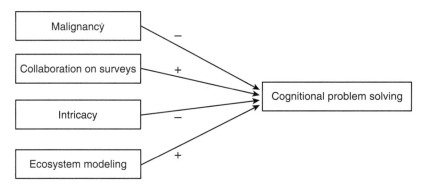

Figure 4.2
Causal model of cognitional problem solving.

point for defining cognitional malignancy, which is expected to complicate problem solving.

In the Barents Sea, vessels are required to keep logbooks of catches
and effort, reporting them to the flag state as well as the coastal state—in
the Norwegian case, on a weekly basis.[7] These reports on catch and effort
feature prominently in stock assessment by providing information on
total removal, changes in stock size, and, if complemented by a sampling
system, the length distribution of the commercial stock, which for Northeast Arctic cod comprises fish aged three years or more. When such data
are combined with biological information, including data obtained from
study of age-variant bony structures, they permit assessment of the
stock's age composition, which is among the requirements of virtual
population analysis (Kock 1992, 129). That method relies on estimates
of the total number of fish in the population and their distribution over
age classes, or cohorts, which in turn allows separate attention to the
spawning and commercial parts of the stock, highly useful in preparing
management advice. The centrality of catch reports for accurate advice
is reflected in the frequent complaints about reliability. In one of many
similar statements, ICES (2003, 4) expressed grave concern "over the
quality of the catch and effort data from most of the important fisheries
in the ICES area. . . . Trends in stock size and the overall status of the
stock can sometimes be evaluated from research vessel surveys, but such
information alone cannot be used to give the short-term TAC advice
usually required." Since catch reports form a critical basis for the elaboration of scientific advice, it is important to understand the conditions
that affect their reliability.

Explaining variation in the reliability of catch reports may usefully start out from the concept of malignancy presented in chapter 2, concerning the relationship between individual and collective interests. Scientific research on Northeast Arctic cod has clear elements of contingency or synergy and thus poses a relatively "benign" problem (Underdal 1987): Russian and Norwegian researchers save costs and put scarce resources to better use by collaborating on survey activities, pooling data, and conducting stock assessment jointly. Yet their dependence on reliable catch reports makes them vulnerable to incongruity between the fishers' collective interest in sound science and their individual interest in taking as much fish as possible. Compliance with reporting requirements in the Northeast Atlantic declined sharply in the late 1970s, when quota limitations replaced technical regulations as the main tool of international management (ICES 1983, 4; Halliday and Pinhorn 1996). That occurred because, with quota regulation, a linkage was created between catch reports and the closure of a fishery once the quota had been taken, thereby introducing externalities and competition to a relationship otherwise marked by contingency and synergy.

Since the malignancy of catch reporting derives from the constraints that quotas place on harvesting activities, one way to grade this factor is to calculate the ratio of the commercial stock size to the total allowable catch (TAC). This ratio, which I call "relative availability," is a good measure of malignancy because with high relative availability, keeping within quotas requires forgoing considerable harvesting opportunities. That situation generates weighty incentives to underreport catches, thus implying a more malign cognitional problem.

The relative availability of Northeast Arctic cod varies substantially over time, as appendix 3 shows. We may use that variation to generate appropriate malignancy scores for the years under study. I proceed in the same way as with the cognitional outcome scores, sorting the annual relative availability ratios from the lowest to the highest value and applying the steepness and category size criteria while considering whether the results are reasonable in qualitative terms.

This procedure yields a threshold separating full from substantial malignancy at a stock to quota ratio of 3.8, which makes seven years fully malign. A qualitative anchor for this threshold is the observation that the two periods when relative availability was higher, 1990–1993 and 2002–2003, include the years for which ICES (2008a, 51), retrospectively and based on a wide range of evidence, provided estimates of very high unreported catches (Stokke 2009, 342; see also chapter 6).

The next steep part of a rising relative availability line occurs around a ratio of 2.8, which also matches the category size criterion by capturing eight substantially malign cases. A threshold between modest and insignificant malignancy at the next steep part, at a ratio of 2.1, is qualitatively anchored in the fact that the four years with lower relative availability, 1987–1988 and 1997–1998, are the only years in the study when actual catches were considerably lower than the agreed-upon quotas (ICES 2006a). In those years, apparently, nature constrained fishers more than regulators did and removed any incentive to underreport catches: an insignificant malignancy score seems appropriate. As with the outcome thresholds, I examine below the robustness of the empirical findings concerning malignancy and other causal factors in the model to alternative reasonable placements of scale thresholds.

As noted above, the disaggregate approach to regime effectiveness tackles the big and complex counterfactual question of what the problem-solving outcome would be if the regime did not exist by answering first the simpler question of what the no-regime scores on the *causal* factors would be (see also chapter 2). For malignancy, the most reasonable counterfactual score for each year is the same as the actual one. True, chapters 5 and 6 show that the Barents Sea fisheries regime does affect quotas and fisher behavior in parts of the period studied, thereby impinging on the two components of relative availability. However, also numerous nonanthropogenic factors have intervened in these relationships, so we have an inadequate basis for making any specific assertions about altered scores.

Therefore, the counterfactual malignancy scores most compatible with existing theoretical and empirical knowledge map onto the actual scores derived from the relative availability ratio and plotted in figure 4.3.

This figure shows malignancy as either full or substantial in the mid-1980s, when forecast accuracy was particularly low, which corresponds with our expectations. On the other hand, malignancy was modest or insignificant in 1996–1997, the other period of extreme inaccuracy. Moreover, the full or substantial malignancy that marks the early 1990s and the early 2000s did not seem to constrain cognitional problem solving, which in both periods was considerably higher than in preceding years. Reasonable as it may seem that strong incentives to underreport catches due to high relative availability will complicate cognitional problem solving, therefore, any such effect of malignancy is only partly evident in forecast accuracy.

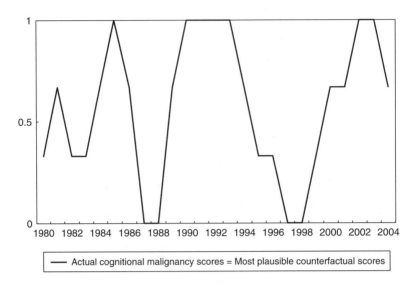

Figure 4.3
Cognitional malignancy scores. 1 = full = severe incongruity, owing to very high relative availability; 0.67 = substantial = large incongruity, owing to high relative availability; 0.33 = modest = some incongruity, owing to medium relative availability, but mostly synergy; 0 = insignificant = no significant incongruity, owing to low relative availability. Thresholds between severe, large, some, and no incongruity are relative availability ratios of 3.8, 2.8, and 2.1.

One possible explanation is that researchers have found ways to reduce their dependence on reliable fisher reports, as the next subsection argues.

Collaboration
Since the late 1980s, survey results have formed the main input for stock assessment of Northeast Arctic cod (Aglen, Drevetnyak, and Sokolov 2004, 34). The growing emphasis on fisher-independent survey investigations using standardized equipment is due in part to less reliable catch reports, but even more to rapid technological advances that have undermined the validity of catch-per-unit-effort indicators in the assessment work. The best approach combines survey- and report-based data and then uses survey results to fine-tune the virtual population analysis (Kock 1992, 129) or vice versa (Pennington and Strømme 1998, 105).

The rising importance of fisher-independent investigations directs attention to a second factor, besides malignancy, that may influence cognitional problem solving—collaboration on fisheries surveys. We recall from chapter 2 that collaboration among two or more parties is modest if it involves nothing more than common standards, substantial if the parties enter into joint planning of activities, and full if those plans are also implemented jointly. Applying these criteria to the Norwegian-Russian scientific collaboration on Northeast Arctic cod reveals four stages in the period under study.

The two states began systematic investigation of ocean resources in the Barents Sea in the late 1800s (Schwach 2000), and such pioneers as Norway's Johan Hjort and Russia's Nikolai Knipovich were in regular correspondence (Serebryakov and Solemdal 1993). Collaborative ties between the two leading institutes, PINRO in Murmansk and the Institute for Marine Research (IMR) in Bergen, preceded the Barents Sea fisheries regime. Already in the mid-1960s, Soviet and Norwegian vessels were conducting annual joint 0-group surveys during the autumn, mapping the survivors (0-agers) from each year's spawning, by combining acoustic equipment and standardized trawl hauls (ICES 1965). Around 1980, the two institutes expanded their national survey activities, aiming to cover in addition juvenile and mature cod during the spring, fall, and winter. On the scale above, therefore, modest collaboration occurred under the regime from the outset, primarily through the use of joint ICES standards as specified in an annual Joint Research Program approved by the Joint Commission, and supported by an annual research vessel call in either Bergen or Murmansk that allowed direct contact between scientists from the visiting and the host institutions (JCF 1981, annex 4).

A qualitative shift in this scientific survey collaboration occurred in 1984, when the IMR and PINRO invited each other's researchers to participate in their respective surveys in order to improve the compatibility of data, especially through intercalibration of gear and acoustic equipment (JCF 1984, annex 5). Such researcher exchange for intercalibration purposes has continued up to the present; each exchange may last for several weeks prior to the actual surveys (JCF 2001, annex 5). This combination of partial joint planning of survey investigation and intercalibration of equipment justifies a rise in the survey-collaboration score from modest to substantial in 1984.

A new shift that occurred in 1991 substantiates a full score on collaboration, as the number of jointly implemented surveys rose and also became more central to the spatial scope of survey investigations. The economic reforms that followed Gorbachev's ascent to power brought severe financial constraints to all institutions relying on Soviet state funding, and several marine biological laboratories were forced to close

(Stokke, Anderson, and Mirovitskaya 1999, 118). By the end of the Soviet period, staff numbers at PINRO had dropped markedly, and worries grew among Norwegian researchers that the financial situation would jeopardize PINRO's contribution to the collaborative research program.[8] Interruptions in the time-series data collected by scientists reduce the value of the data for stock assessment, so in this period of financial strain, the Norwegian authorities granted additional funds for maintaining and strengthening IMR ties with the Russian counterpart. A primary motivation was to ensure continuity in terms of personnel, equipment, and quality of activities particularly important to the stable monitoring of the Barents Sea ecosystem.[9] PINRO used this support to upgrade its computer systems, to format data to improve compatibility with Norwegian data and facilitate computer-based processing, and to enable broader interaction among researchers from the two institutes.[10]

In addition to financial transfers, collaboration during the first half of the 1990s expanded into new areas, including a long-term project on the significance of ocean currents for regional bioproduction and a series of joint experiments with new sorting-grid technology.[11] Norwegian and Russian scientists jointly planned a range of survey investigations relevant to stock assessment, collaborated closely on the purchase and application of computer equipment to enhance the use of survey and other data, and expanded their coordination of activities into such salient areas as ecosystem modeling and fishing-gear technology. Through 1995, therefore, cognitional collaboration remained at the highest level.

In 1996, however, the Russian authorities rather unexpectedly introduced impediments to the joint implementation of research surveys. Since then, Norwegian research vessels have experienced either full rejection or severe restriction of their access to the Russian Exclusive Economic Zone (EEZ). The 1996 JCF protocol notes that the joint research program has been implemented "with certain exceptions," adding that the "Parties agree that research cruises are necessary for the management and research cooperation. . . . [T]he ability to conduct such cruises in the zones of the other is necessary . . . [and parties] agree to prepare the ground for smooth processing of research cruise applications" (JCF 1996, item 13; my translation). Those asked to provide scientific advice have mentioned, with increasing concern, these constraints on the implementation of the joint survey program: "Such reduced survey coverage seriously jeopardizes the scientific basis for providing advice on this stock" (ICES 1998, 24).

There is little to indicate that Russian fishery managers and researchers were responsible for these impediments to the joint survey program from 1996. On the contrary, Russian regime participants had worked hard to obtain permits for the Norwegian vessels,[12] and protocols from the Joint Fishery Commission meetings since 1998 show that they have accepted rather harsh criticism of those impediments.[13] No, the decline in survey collaboration appears to stem from interagency differences inside Russia, with naval and intelligence organizations being more critical of cooperative ties with Western partners than were fisheries institutions (Stokke 2000).[14] Such restrictions on foreign research vessel operations have not been confined to the fisheries sector: the Russian authorities first introduced them within the Russo-Norwegian environmental cooperation in connection with measurements of radioactivity in waters close to locations where Soviet reactors had been dumped in violation of international rules (Stokke 1998). Nor has the restrictive policy been limited to the Barents Sea: U.S. marine researchers have reportedly experienced similar problems in the Bering Sea.[15] Whatever the origins of this policy, these impediments to the implementation of the joint research program from 1996 meant that survey collaboration dropped from a full score to a substantial level—and, although constraints have varied somewhat from one year to another, this situation continued throughout the period under study (ICES 2008a, 45).

For specifying the most plausible *counterfactual* levels of cognitional collaboration in a hypothetical situation with no Barents Sea fisheries regime, process-tracing evidence suggests that these levels would be lower than the actual ones but never insignificant, since ICES exists independently of the regional regime and provides a multilateral means for coordination. The two states were members of ICES for several decades before creating the bilateral fisheries regime, and they subscribe to this organization's various standards and methods for conducting scientific surveys. On the other hand, we have no basis for assuming that the gradually deeper collaboration that evolved from the 1980s and accelerated in the early 1990s would have occurred had it not been emplaced within the joint management regime. The only preregime collaboration activity above a modest level, annual joint 0-group surveys, emerged within another regional management framework, the North-East Atlantic Fisheries Commission, which would not have existed in a no-regime situation.

Since survey investigations generate information relevant to fish finding, the collaborative problem has clear elements of malignancy, and incentives to collaborate would be far weaker if the coastal states were not to negotiate joint regulations. Moreover, the IMR and PINRO initiated

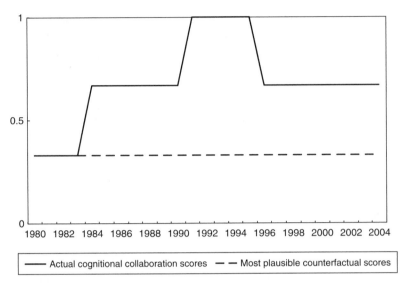

Figure 4.4
Cognitional-collaboration scores. 1 = full = joint planning and joint implementation of many surveys; 0.67 = substantial = joint planning, joint implementation of some surveys; 0.33 = modest = coordination by joint standards in ICES and regime; 0 = insignificant = no explicit coordination.

their regular exchange of personnel for purposes of intercalibration at a time when the general political climate was otherwise rather hostile to collaboration, owing to the two states' membership in competing geopolitical blocs during the "second Cold War" that followed the Soviet invasion of Afghanistan. Thus, the most plausible counterfactual collaboration scores remain modest throughout the period 1980–2004.

Figure 4.4 plots actual collaboration scores on the solid line and counterfactual scores on the dashed line.

We see that the regime raised the level of collaboration on fisher-independent survey investigations from a modest to a substantial level in 1984 and to the highest level in 1991. Later, Russian constraints on implementation of the joint survey program from 1996 brought collaboration back down to the substantial level.

Examining figures 4.2 through 4.4 together, however, indicates that malignancy and collaboration alone cannot account for the variation over time in cognitional problem solving with respect to Northeast Arctic cod. While the dramatic drop in forecast accuracy in the period 1996–1998 coincided with the introduction of survey impediments, accuracy improved quickly thereafter and remained high despite continual access limitations for Norwegian survey vessels and sharply rising malignancy.

One thing the 1996–1998 interlude has in common with the earlier period of very low accuracy, in the mid-1980s, is a major disturbance of the Barents Sea ecosystem involving the collapse of the regional stock of capelin, which usually figures prominently in the cod's diet. The suspicion of a connection between those two phenomena—ecosystem disturbance and low forecast accuracy—draws attention to a third general factor that may influence cognitional problem solving: the substantive intricacy of the problem at hand.

Substantive Intricacy

Some problems are substantively more complicated than others, in the sense that adequate description and diagnosis require greater intellectual capital and energy (Underdal 2002a, 15). Such intricacy may vary across issue areas or over time. For instance, assessing the economic costs of mitigating environmentally harmful emissions is far more difficult for greenhouse gases than for ozone-depleting substances since the latter originate from a narrower set of activities. Similarly, a simple ecosystem with few species at each trophic level is easier to model and analyze than is a highly complex web of interactions.

This concept of intricacy is distinct from Underdal's (2002a, 16) notion of intellectual complexity, which highlights "the amount of descriptive and theoretical uncertainty pertaining to the knowledge base" (see also Miles et al. 2002, 483; Underdal 1989, 259–265), and from Breitmeier, Young, and Zürn's (2006, 203–206) notion of "problem understanding." Those concepts refer to rough consensus on what the most important factors and mechanisms are and how well these relationships are understood, which is an aspect of cognitional problem solving, not a factor that drives it. They do not constitute, as substantive intricacy does, characteristics of the basic subject matter: the ecosystem, the set of socioeconomic processes that generate greenhouse gases and ozone-depleting substances, or any other relevant object of analysis. After all, predators are going to eat prey in more or less complex patterns and will be more or less sensitive to changes in temperature or salinity regardless of whether researchers monitor such relationships or succeed in building solid descriptive and analytical models of the system components involved in all these interactions.

Since this study examines cognitional problem solving within a single ecosystem, variation in substantive intricacy derives not from levels of ecosystem complexity but from the stability of the ecosystem components that affect the size of the spawning stock of cod. Rapid shifts that are particularly interesting concern the abundance of prey and of predators. For Northeast Arctic cod, smaller fishes such as capelin and herring feature heavily in the diet, along with crustaceans such as shrimp and krill, and the main predators on cod are minke whale, harp seal, and, in years of food scarcity, larger cod (Aglen, Drevetnyak, and Sokolov 2004, 29).

Ideally, a measure of substantive intricacy should build on information concerning all those components and their temporal and spatial overlaps, but for reasons of data availability, figure 4.5 narrows in on two types of evidence on rapid shifts in food availability: the relative abundance of capelin and cod cannibalism. The columns portray fluctuations in the availability of the cod's major food item, capelin, and specifically the ratio of the nonharvested capelin biomass to the commercial stock of Northeast Arctic cod.[16] The two lines plot natural mortality due to can-

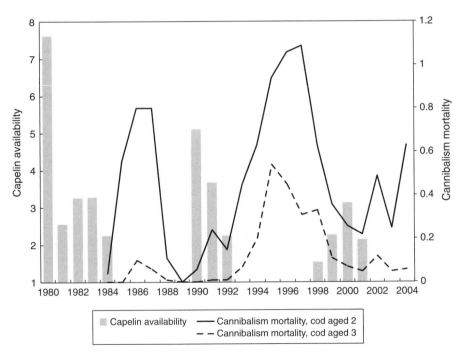

Figure 4.5
Capelin availability and cannibalism mortality for cod. Underlying data are given in appendix 3. Capelin availability is the biomass ratio of nonharvested capelin and the commercial stock of cod (aged 3 years or more); cannibalism mortality is natural mortality due to cod cannibalism.

nibalism for cod two and three years of age, which the ICES Arctic Fisheries Working Group has estimated back to 1984 (ICES 2006b, 161). Cannibalism mortality provides a more direct indication of food scarcity since cod cannibalism appears to rise rapidly in emergency situations.

We can clearly see two rapid shifts in the environmental conditions of cod in the period studied here. One such change originated in the summer of 1983, when the first rich cohort of Norwegian spring-spawning herring in two decades spread into the Barents Sea to feed on capelin larvae and juveniles. The rising regional abundance of herring has been seen as the main cause of the recruitment failure of the capelin stock that occurred from 1984 (ICES 1998, 45), which coincided with the migration of young herring out of the region to mix with the adult part of the stock. With the capelin stock in collapse and the young herring gone, the cod were unable to find ready substitutes. As a result, annual growth dropped drastically, while natural mortality rose from starvation and cannibalism. Accordingly, a rapid shift in ecosystem conditions in the mid-1980s severely complicated the task of accurate stock assessment and forecasting the impacts of harvesting. The second crash in the capelin stock occurred in the early 1990s. Although several rich herring cohorts compensated somewhat from the cod's perspective (ICES 2003, 66), the rapid rise in cod cannibalism from 1993 onwards, even among three-year-olds, indicates considerable ecosystem disturbance.

I differentiate levels of substantive intricacy by combining these three indicators of cod-relevant ecosystem disturbance, as figure 4.5 details. Cutoff points between high and low levels of relative capelin availability and cod cannibalism emerge from the same general procedure as was undertaken for forecast accuracy and malignancy, through a combination of distributional and qualitative considerations that yield threshold ratios of 1.7 (capelin availability), 0.3 (cannibalism on two-year-old cod) and 0.15 (cannibalism on three-year-old cod).[17] The Arctic Fisheries Working Group reports estimates of cod cannibalism only from 1984 (ICES 2006b, 161), but since capelin was amply available in the years prior to this and the 1984 cannibalism estimates are close to zero, a low-cannibalism assumption seems reasonable. These various decisions imply intricacy scores ranging from insignificant in the early 1980s to full in the mid-1990s.

The most plausible *counterfactual* scores on intricacy equal the actual ones, as figure 4.6 shows, for the same reasons as for malignancy: the causal chains that may connect the regime and changes in category scores are too long and too fragile to be pursued empirically.

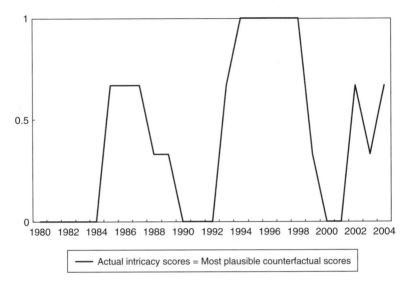

Figure 4.6
Intricacy scores. 1 = full = capelin availability low, high cannibalism on 2- and 3-year-olds; 0.67 = substantial = capelin availability low, high cannibalism on 2-year-olds; 0.33 = modest = capelin availability low, cannibalism low, or capelin availability high, cannibalism on 2-year-olds high; 0 = insignificant = capelin availability high, cannibalism low. The threshold between high and low capelin availability is a ratio at 1.7; cannibalism on 2-year-olds is high if above 0.3; cannibalism on 3-year-olds is high if above 0.15.

Unlike malignancy and collaboration, intricacy is substantial or full during both of the dives in accuracy in the mid-1980s and mid-1990s, which supports our suspicion that intricacy is partly responsible for these poor outcomes. However, the rising intricacy toward the end of the period under study does not appear to hold back cognitional problem solving. This observation links up to a fourth explanatory candidate, explored in the next subsection: if substantive intricacy due to ecosystem disturbance undermines the basis for forecast accuracy, how do advances in regional ecosystem modeling affect cognitional problem solving?

Ecosystem Modeling
The existence of functional relationships between the abundance of capelin, herring, and marine mammals in the Barents Sea ecosystem and important cod population parameters—notably recruitment, growth, and natural mortality—has long been recognized, but only in the past few decades have these relationships been described in some detail. Two devel-

opments in particular triggered greater effort directed toward multispecies modeling in the region (Tjelmeland and Bogstad 1998, 128). One was the capelin collapse in the mid-1980s, which created a sense of urgency among managers and scientists to obtain a better understanding of interspecies connections, especially among capelin, herring, and cod. A second factor was the publicity and international criticism of Norwegian whaling, which encouraged the inclusion of mammals in the models in order to examine their predatory impact on commercially exploited fish stocks.

Since the late 1980s, the IMR and PINRO have coordinated their ecosystem modeling efforts within the framework of the Barents Sea fisheries regime. The cornerstone of those efforts is a database containing information from two decades of cod stomach sampling; each year, researchers analyze an average of eight thousand individual stomachs (Bogstad and Gjøsæter 2001, 199). This long time series provides unique insight into the consumption habits of cod under widely changing levels of prey availability. The expansion of research collaboration in the early 1990s led to systematic data collection of a broader set of environmental parameters, including the level of pollution to understand its influence on primary production, reproduction, and the state of commercial stocks (JCF 1990, 14). In 1991, the regular Norwegian-Russian research symposium addressed interrelations between fish populations in the Barents Sea.[18] Research conducted by the Joint Working Group on Seals similarly turned increasingly toward multispecies connections by focusing on feeding and trophic relationships, especially those involving harp seals and commercially important fish stocks (see JCF 1994, annex 4). Thus, systematic empirical work to support the development of ecosystem modeling in the Barents Sea began in the late 1980s and accelerated in the first half of the 1990s.

The traditional approach to dealing with highly uncertain and environmentally sensitive model parameters is to examine the robustness of the yield estimates to variations in parameter values (Walford 1958, 46). Advances in computer technology have greatly facilitated such simulation, permitting multiple model runs for assigning probabilities to the various outcomes. While this may be adequate in times of normal ecosystem variance, simulation remains vulnerable to rapid changes in the environmental conditions that shape cod recruitment, growth, and natural mortality.

Figure 4.7 applies three thresholds for grading ecosystem modeling based on the amount of ecosystem information scientists use to predict those model parameters and whether such incorporation is qualitative or based on explicit, quantitative models.

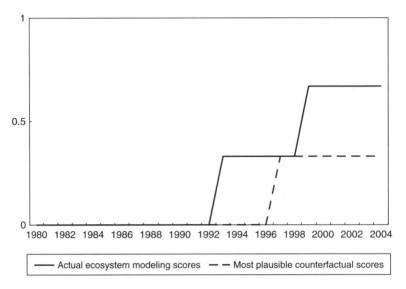

Figure 4.7
Ecosystem modeling scores. 1 = full = quantitative modeling using data on ocean climate, predator abundance, and prey abundance to predict population parameters; 0.67 = substantial = quantitative modeling using data on prey abundance to predict parameters; 0.33 = modest = qualitative estimation of ecosystem impact on parameters; 0 = insignificant = ecosystem information not used in forecast. The cod population parameters in question are recruitment, growth, and natural mortality.

Regular attention to interspecies connections has been evident in ICES advice since the late 1980s, but such connections were not incorporated into the quota advice until 1993. The scientists had concluded in 1989 that high cod cannibalism due to food shortage had led them to severely overestimate the 1983–1986 cohorts and to provide excessively high quota advice in subsequent years (ICES 1990b, 10; see also figure 4.1). Recalling that bad experience, ICES (1993, 9) warned four few years later that an ongoing decline in capelin might slow down cod growth but decided against lowering the single-model-based cod forecast out of uncertainty as to the extent of compensation that would derive from an expected increase of herring. That ICES advice, offered in the autumn of 1993, implied a rise in ecosystem modeling from an insignificant to a modest level: it was the first to build explicitly on qualitative multispecies considerations, with separate cod forecasts corresponding to low- and medium-growth parameters (ICES 1994, 9; see also Tjelmeland and Bogstad 1998, 132). This advice shows that knowledge of functional ecosystem relationships may support the estimation of population parameters even when the data are not yet in a form that permits direct incorporation into stock forecast models.

As Filin and associates (2008, 135) note, however, one limitation of such qualitative incorporation of ecosystem information is high subjectivism, and ecosystem modeling is more valuable when it reaches the point at which interspecies and other ecosystem relationships can be quantified. Managers want to know how much they should hold back catches as a consequence of adverse ecosystem circumstances; or conversely, how much more their fishers may be allowed to take in years when ecosystem conditions are favorable.

For Northeast Arctic cod, there was gradual progress toward quantification of ecosystem relationships during the second half of the 1990s, along with accumulation of data on cod cannibalism (ICES 1996, 21). The advice offered in 1999 used for the first time models relating capelin and cod cannibalism to predict the two parameters marked by the greatest uncertainty, growth and natural mortality (ICES 2000, 16). In figure 4.7, the threshold for substantial ecosystem modeling is placed at that point, requiring the use of data on prey abundance to predict crucial population parameters.

Work is under way to also include in the assessment models data on the strength of *predator* stocks of harp seal and minke whale (Aglen, Drevetnyak, and Sokolov 2004). These various interspecies relationships are also shaped by oceanographic conditions, so incorporating such information into the stock forecasts will be important for reducing uncertainty (Filin et al. 2008, 133). Studies confirm hypotheses from the early 1900s on a close relationship between climatic conditions (notably water temperature) and the productivity of Northeast Arctic cod (Godø 2003). Shorter-term phenomena such as inflows of warmer, plankton-rich water from the south can influence temporal or geographic overlaps between cod and its various prey and predators (Tjelmeland and Bogstad 1998, 129). A full score on ecosystem modeling, therefore, would require advice on the Northeast Arctic cod that quantifies and incorporates data not only on prey and predator abundance but also on relevant ocean climate information—but that is not yet the case.

Although ICES would exist as a means for coordination of ecosystem modeling even without the regime, the most plausible *counterfactual* scores on ecosystem modeling are lower than actual levels. The main reason is the deepening of collaboration involved in the compilation and the analysis of multispecies and other ecosystem data from the mid-1980s. The coordination of such core activities as sampling cod stomachs, generating a joint database, and developing models that relate the state of prey stocks to cod forecast parameters would be far more difficult without the cohesive force of a joint management responsibility.

Caution is nevertheless required when estimating the difference that such lower coordination would make on the level of ecosystem modeling: both the IMR and PINRO had initiated multispecies investigations before joining forces, and both were aware of the proposition that capelin availability affects cod growth. On the other hand, even with the benefit of collaborative ecosystem data collection and analysis, as recently as 1992 the scientists were too uncertain about that effect to employ it in their forecast (ICES 1993, 9), and the wide inaccuracy of forecasts in the mid-1980s had become evident only around 1990. All things considered, a delay in the application of multispecies knowledge in cod forecasts by more than four years seems unlikely and implies that counterfactual ecosystem modeling would have been modest from 1997 on.

The step from modest to substantial ecosystem modeling is no smaller, since quantifying multispecies relationships is far more data-intensive than are the qualitative considerations that may substantiate a choice among low, medium, or high growth estimates for any given year. This observation indicates that the most plausible time lag from actual graduation to substantial ecosystem modeling to counterfactual graduation is longer than for achieving modest ecosystem modeling. Pointing in the same direction is that while mammal experts nearly two decades ago, endorsed by the Joint Commission, focused increasingly on clarifying the dietary composition and feeding patterns of two key predators of cod, harp seals and minke whales (JCF 1993, annex 4), ICES has remained unable to incorporate such data into its assessment models of Northeast Arctic cod (Aglen, Drevetnyak, and Sokolov 2004, 35). Even with the deep collaboration that marks studies of cod–prey relationships, the researchers crossed the "substantial" ecosystem modeling line only in 1999. Thus, it seems that, without that regime-based collaboration, counterfactual ecosystem modeling would most likely have remained modest throughout the remainder of the period under study.

Figure 4.7 gives the general criteria for various levels of ecosystem modeling, substantiates the allocation of actual cases, and compares them with the most plausible counterfactual ecosystem modeling scores.

The regime has affected the extent of ecosystem modeling by facilitating collaboration among the leading regional fisheries research institutions on joint sampling and analysis of cod stomachs and, from 1993, direct application of ecosystem data in cod forecasts. Toward the end of that decade, scientists succeeded in quantifying these relationships and incorporating prey abundance and related estimates of cod cannibalism in forecast models of Northeast Arctic cod—which shows a substantial level of ecosystem modeling. A full score on this factor would incorporate also predator abundance and oceanographic conditions that affect inter-species relationships.

Summary
The quality of scientific advice as something to be *explained* (in part) by institutions has not received much attention in international regime analysis. Therefore, to construct an explanation of the diversity in forecast accuracy depicted in figure 4.1, this section started out from the assumption that good forecasts require good data and identified explanatory candidates by deductive as well as inductive reasoning. Collective action theory drew attention to variation in malignancy, here fishers' incentives to underreport catches, which in turn will depend on the availability of cod relative to the quota. The other major source of data is survey investigation, increasingly important because it allows researchers to standardize sampling methods and obtain data independently of the fishers, but the quality of survey data depends on a second modeled factor that has varied over time, the level of coastal state collaboration.

Cross examining these variations in malignancy and collaboration and the outcome diversity indicated that a broader model was required. The experience of severe falls in accuracy in periods of ecosystem disturbance pinpointed two additional and closely connected explanatory candidates: substantive intricacy, which here concerns major shifts in the cod's environmental conditions, and the extent to which stock forecast models incorporate data on relevant environmental conditions.

Process-tracing evidence suggests that the Barents Sea fisheries regime has affected the levels of collaboration and ecosystem modeling, but the regime has no influence on the level of substantive intricacy. As regards malignancy, the regime is among the factors influencing the relative availability of the catch, but those causal connections are too complex and variable to justify counterfactual scores different from the actual ones.

This initial model of factors to account for variation in cognitional problem solving derives from theories and evidence about the process of developing stock forecasts, but also from side glances at the specific pattern of accuracy characteristic of Northeast Arctic cod forecasts in the period under study. The next section confronts the model more systematically with the empirical evidence on variation in cognitional problem solving under the Barents Sea fisheries regime.

Paths to Cognitional Success and Failure

The empirical analysis reported in this section reveals that, in this dataset, certain combinations of properties on the modeled causal factors reliably deliver either high or low forecast accuracy. Those paths to cognitional success or failure are identified by the fuzzy set QCA technique explained in chapter 2. Central to this technique is examination of outcome scores among cases fitting to some extent certain ideal-type causal combinations. A pattern in which all or nearly all cases achieve outcome scores that are equally as high as or higher than their scores on the causal combination would support a claim that the causal combination is sufficient for that outcome to occur, that it is a reliable path to it. The section focuses first on conditions for successful cognitional problem solving, involving high forecast accuracy, and then turns to paths to forecast failure. Finally, I examine the robustness of findings to minor adjustments of the category thresholds or to removal of one or a few strong cases of the causal combinations in question.

Success Paths
The conditions surrounding spawning-stock forecasts on Northeast Arctic cod from 1980 to 2004 indicate that whatever the level of malignancy, a combination of low intricacy, deep survey collaboration, and intensive ecosystem modeling reliably delivers high accuracy, as measured by the percentage distance to the most recent and reliable assessment.

This reliable path to cognitional success emerges from the fuzzy set QCA analysis that chapter 2 referred to when illustrating the main concepts, procedures, and measures used in this technique, and I will keep repetition to the minimum required for a complete argument. The twenty-five cases of cognitional problem solving described in the preceding sections are strong cases in nine out of sixteen corners in the property space defined by the four modeled factors (the scores are given in appendix 5). Of those nine, only the category combining insignificant malignancy and intricacy with full collaboration and ecosystem modeling is fully consistent with the sufficiency pattern. The dataset contains five cases of this category, all of them occurring toward the end of the timeline. As chapter 2 notes, it is not surprising that this combination is a reliable path since each factor property, according to the theory argument behind the model, is conducive to accurate forecasting. That theoretical potency is now validated empirically.

Almost fully consistent with the sufficiency pattern is the theoretically less potent category that combines insignificant intricacy with a full score on the other factors, including malignancy. Its QCA consistency score is 0.90. On the simplifying but non-necessary assumption made throughout this study that the outcome and the causal factors are measurable at the interval level (see chapter 2 and appendix 1), this score means that 90 percent of the total case scores for this combination are consistent with the sufficiency pattern that outcome scores equal or exceed the causal path score. No other causal combinations meet the conventional 0.85 consistency criterion for a reliable path to cognitional problem solving (see Ragin 2006; see also chapter 2).

The two reliable paths differ in their coverage or explanatory power, meaning that they account for unequal proportions of the total cognitional problem solving in the dataset. The full malignancy path is the one most traveled by, with a QCA coverage score of 0.28, nearly twice as high as that of the zero malignancy path (0.16). This coverage score implies that 28 percent of the total problem-solving score in the period is covered consistently by the full malignancy path. The difference between the two reliable paths in empirical weight is even greater when we turn to their unique coverage scores, 0.16 versus 0.03. Those scores refer to the amounts of problem solving that the other reliable path does not cover. In other words, both paths contribute to the model's explanatory power, but the high malignancy path in particular does so. Their joint coverage score is 0.31, meaning that the model's reliable paths to forecast accuracy account for less than a third of the cognitional problem solving occurring in the period 1980–2004. With more than two-thirds of the cognitional problem solving in this period *not* covered by any reliable path, the model's explanatory power concerning forecast accuracy remains unimpressive.

One comment is in order regarding the empirical pattern that might indicate that a causal combination is a necessary condition for an outcome. Each of the consistent paths identified here involves full scores on the two regime-driven factors in the model, collaboration and ecosystem modeling, and a zero score on intricacy. Those properties are not thereby necessary conditions for cognitional accuracy since the two paths cover only a relatively small portion of the total problem-solving scores in the period under study. In fact, as noted in chapter 2, none of the causal combinations examined for any aspect of problem solving in this study stands out as a necessary condition.

To summarize the analysis so far: two out of nine causal paths represented by strong cases in the dataset meet the reliability criterion that all, or nearly all, cases should achieve cognitional problem-solving scores equal to or exceeding their scores on the path. Both paths involve insignificant intricacy and full scores on collaboration and ecosystem management, but they differ in terms of malignancy. The model's coverage, or explanatory power, is less than one-third, which means that numerous cases of forecast success involve causal combinations that are unreliable.

Statement A below lists the two reliable causal paths to cognitional problem solving, stated in ideal-type terms but derived from observation of all cases fitting them to some extent. These ideal-type terms distinguish only between absence of a property (a score of 0), represented by the symbol "~" in the statement, and the presence of a property (a score of 1). An asterisk means "combined with," whereas an arrow means "delivers reliably," that is, the causal combination meets the reliability criterion in use, here a QCA consistency score of 0.85.

(A) ~malignancy * ~intricacy * collaboration * ecosystem modeling → cognitional success

malignancy * ~intricacy * collaboration * ecosystem modeling → cognitional success

As explained in chapter 2, various means for set-theoretic minimization help widen the reliable paths by removing logically redundant characteristics or combinations to derive less restricted statements about the conditions for success. Among those means, only paired comparison is applicable here: with or without malignancy, the combination of insignificant intricacy and full collaboration and ecosystem modeling delivers cognitional problem solving reliably. By logical implication, those two sufficiency claims may be merged into one more general statement with no restriction on malignancy: statement A logically implies the more general causal statement B:

(B) ~intricacy * collaboration * ecosystem modeling → cognitional success

Thus, the set-theoretic comparative analysis indicates that high forecast accuracy cannot be reliably obtained without high scores on collaboration and ecosystem modeling, and even then only if the environmental conditions (here, for the cod) render substantive intricacy low. The significance of ecosystem modeling for accurate forecasts even in years with scarce environmental disturbance indicates that the ecosystem modeling category also captures other aspects of maturation regarding assessment work. In the concluding chapter 8, I examine how the empirical findings in this study relate to previous research on cognitional problem solving. Since the regime contributes significantly to the level of collaboration and ecosystem modeling, statement B is highly relevant to the question of what the level of cognitional problem solving would be if the regime did not exist.

Failure Paths

Turning to reliable paths to cognitional failure, the QCA analysis indicates that both malignancy and intricacy can be lethal to forecast accuracy unless counteracted by regime-driven ecosystem modeling or survey collaboration, or both.

As explained in chapter 2, the failure path analysis uses negated problem-solving scores, since failure is the negation of success: substantial problem solving (a score of 0.67) implies modest failure (a score of $0.33 = 1 - 0.67$). Using the same notation as above, statement C lists the two causal paths that meet the reliability criterion for cognitional failure.

(C) malignancy * ~intricacy * ~collaboration * ~ecosystem modeling
   → cognitional failure

   ~malignancy * intricacy * collaboration * ~ecosystem modeling →
   cognitional failure

The first of those reliable failure paths combines full malignancy with zero scores on the remaining factors, while the second combines zero scores on malignancy and ecosystem modeling with full scores on intricacy and collaboration. None of them is as theoretically potent as the most reliable success path: one and two, respectively, of their four factor properties are expected to promote forecast accuracy and thus make failure less likely. Yet both paths achieve a consistency score of 0.87, and their joint coverage score is 0.58, which indicates that my four-factor model does a better job of explaining failure than success: nearly 60 percent of the total forecast failure in the dataset is covered consistently by reliable failure pathways. Unlike the success paths, the two paths to failure are equally vital to the explanation—each covers one-third of the forecast failure in the dataset consistently, and one-quarter of it uniquely.

Statement C cannot be minimized directly by paired comparison since the categories differ on more than one causal property, but inserting reasonable simplifying assumptions helps reduce it. As explained in chapter 2, a simplifying assumption in QCA analysis responds to limited diversity in the dataset: it is a statement that a certain causal combination not represented by strong cases in the dataset would have met the reliability criterion if it had been represented. That assumption is reasonable only if two conditions are met: the causal combination inserted into the list of reliable paths should be compatible with existing observations, and it should be theoretically more potent than an existing combination that meets the reliability criterion.

Two out of three simplifying assumptions, or paths, inserted into rows 3 to 5 of statement D, below the two empirically proven paths, are fully reasonable. The simplifying path in row 3 equals the first proven path except that full intricacy should make failure even more reliable; and similar comments are in order for the simplifying path in row 4, which equals the second proven path except that collaboration is insignificant. The simplifying path in row 5 is more dubious since that combination is in fact represented by strong cases in the dataset and fails the reliability criterion, if rather narrowly. Its consistency score is 0.80 alone, rising to 0.83 when merged with the second proven path to failure to form a superset combining full scores on intricacy and collaboration with insignificant ecosystem modeling. Such examination of superset consistency, which proceeds by calculating the scores of all cases in the union of the two sets, is helpful because it increases the number of cases fitting a category, thereby reducing the sensitivity to outliers. Since this superset is so close to meeting the reliability criterion, I accept the third simplifying path as rather reasonable. I also make a mental note that the second proven path to failure is less reliable than the first, since merging it with a theoretically more potent set yields lower consistency. Statement D shows the simplifying paths in italics to distinguish them from the proven paths listed first.

(D) malignancy * ~intricacy * ~collaboration * ~ecosystem modeling → cognitional failure

~malignancy * intricacy * collaboration * ~ecosystem modeling → cognitional failure

*malignancy * intricacy * ~collaboration * ~ecosystem modeling → cognitional failure*

*~malignancy * intricacy * ~collaboration * ~ecosystem modeling → cognitional failure*

*malignancy * intricacy * collaboration * ~ecosystem modeling →*
cognitional failure

By minimizing statement D through paired comparison, we achieve the most general causal statement on cognitional failure that the theoretical model and the empirical evidence permit:

(E) malignancy * ~collaboration * ~ecosystem modeling → cognitional failure

intricacy * ~ecosystem modeling → cognitional failure

The two paths to failure differ somewhat in generality and reliability. The first term states that, without survey collaboration or ecosystem modeling, cases involving great incentives to misreport catches reliably fail to generate accurate cod forecasts, whatever the state of the ecosystem. The second term is more general and states, somewhat less reliably, that unless researchers engage in ecosystem modeling, a rapid environmental shift affecting capelin availability and cod cannibalism will generate a widely inaccurate cod forecast, whatever the levels of malignancy or collaboration. Accordingly, both malignancy and intricacy appear to be lethal to cognitional problem solving unless counteracted by factors under regime influence: malignancy seems amendable by either collaboration or ecosystem modeling, whereas only ecosystem modeling can stop intricacy from generating reliable failure.

Since the regime influences the levels of both counterforces, this failure analysis provides additional support to the general claim that cognitional problem solving would be lower without the regime. Before specifying that general claim and assigning effectiveness scores, I examine the robustness of these various findings about reliable paths to forecast success and failure.

Robustness

The results from this comparative analysis are robust in the sense that findings do not change much as a result of small adjustments of the thresholds separating scores on the outcome or causal factors, or of the removal of one or two observations. Among the strengths of QCA is that examining such robustness is relatively simple and can be done without losing contact with the underlying cases (Stokke 2007c).

Certain more lenient placements of the thresholds on the problem-solving scale could be justified on quantitative grounds; the results would be a somewhat wider path to success but the same paths to failure. Placing the cutoff point for substantial problem solving at 40 percent distance from the best assessment rather than at 30 percent, for instance, would remove the low-intricacy restraint in statement B above: high scores on both collaboration and ecosystem modeling would be a reliable path to success, regardless of the cod's environmental conditions. This widening of the path would occur because one more case, the year 2002 with a forecast–assessment distance at 35 percent, would pass the threshold for substantial problem solving and thereby raise the consistency of certain paths with the sufficiency pattern. Such widening would also improve the coverage of the reliable success paths, from 31 percent to 43 percent of the total problem solving.

An even more lenient conception of forecast accuracy could in addition raise the cutoff point for modest problem solving from 70 percent distance to the next major leap, at 110 percent. Such placement would yield an additional reliable success path combining full collaboration with insignificant scores on malignancy and intricacy. The price to pay for this new reliable path, which is not particularly interesting in terms of theory since both impediments to problem solving are absent, would be the uphill battle of convincing a skeptical audience that forecasts more than twice as high as the retrospective assessment still constitute significant, if modest, cognitional problem solving.

Accordingly, these more lenient thresholds on the outcome scale would confirm the reliable paths to success already reported, as well as adding one or two new ones by stretching the concept of accuracy, without affecting the set of reliable failure paths.

Reasonable adjustment of thresholds for the two causal factors that are scaled in part by the two quantitative criteria would not affect the results significantly. Steepness inspection of the line plotting the relative availability ratios from the lowest to the highest value reveals that a somewhat more inclusive category of full malignancy, including all cases involving a ratio above 3.5, could be justified on the quantitative criteria used, but such a change would affect neither the success paths nor the failure paths. For intricacy, likewise, moving the cutoff point for high capelin availability from a ratio of 1.5 to one of 1 is justifiable on grounds of steepness and category size, but would still yield the same paths to success and failure as those listed in statements B and E.

Random removal of one or a few cases from the database is unlikely to affect any of the findings, but strategic removal of years that constitute strong cases of either the success or the failure paths could have an effect, since strong cases are scarce for some categories. For instance, the years

2000 and 2001 are two out of three strong cases of one of the reliable paths to success, but removal of either or both of them would affect neither the success nor the failure paths. The year 1999 is the only strong case of the other reliable success path, but overlapping coverage of the two success paths ensures that not even removal of that case would alter the success findings. The effect on failure paths would be more extensive: removal of 1999 would affect none of the initial failure paths in statement C, but that year blocks three other paths from meeting the reliability criterion. Thus, removing it from the dataset would widen the failure paths in statement E as well as adding a third path that combined full malignancy with full intricacy. That would disperse any remaining illusions about the likelihood of accurate forecasts under such difficult conditions, whatever the levels of collaboration and ecosystem modeling.

Also one of the failure paths has mainly weak cases. However, removing of the sole strong case, 1981, would only add the same unsurprising success path as would an overly lenient concept of accuracy, while otherwise upholding all the findings on reliable paths to success and failure in this section.

Accordingly, neither reasonable alternative placement of outcome or causal factor thresholds nor strategic removal of scarce strong cases of the paths in question would invalidate any of the findings reported in this section. The only effect would be additional and theoretically compatible paths to cognitional success or failure, in a few cases.

Summary
The comparative analysis reveals reliable paths to forecast success as well as to failure. As long as substantive intricacy is low, combining high scores on collaboration and ecosystem modeling reliably delivers accurate forecasts. With severe malignancy, in contrast, the combination of shallow collaboration and scarce ecosystem modeling seems lethal to forecast accuracy, as does scarce ecosystem modeling whenever substantive intricacy is high.

My model explains cognitional failure better than it explains success: the reliable success paths cover only some 30 percent of problem-solving scores in the period under study, whereas nearly 60 percent of the forecasts that are widely off the mark involve reliable failure paths. All of these findings are robust to various other reasonable ways of coding the outcome and the causal factors, and to removal of one or a few cases from the data matrix, although some such adjustments would yield additional paths to failure.

In some but not all years under study, the levels of survey collaboration or ecosystem modeling, or both, would be lower without the regime. In many cases, such lower counterfactual causal factor scores would imply a better fit with the reliable failure paths or a lesser fit with the reliable success path. The next section uses these findings to estimate the most plausible levels of counterfactual problem solving and to derive cognitional effectiveness scores.

Assessing Cognitional Effectiveness

The effectiveness of the Barents Sea fisheries regime in raising the accuracy of the forecasts underlying scientific advice was insignificant throughout most of the 1980s. Thereafter the cognitional effectiveness improved, however, to reach especially high levels in periods when severe malignancy or intricacy would otherwise have kept accuracy low, as in the early and late 1990s and toward the end of the timeline. An indication of such improvement over time is that the total effectiveness score achieved during the last half of the timeline is more than twice the score achieved during the first half.

These findings derive from a combination of counterfactual path analysis and the Oslo-Potsdam effectiveness yardstick. Counterfactual path analysis involves examining how well the counterfactual antecedents—the combinations of the causal factor scores that would pertain if the regime had not existed—fit the reliable paths to success or failure. Chapter 2 explains and justifies this procedure, so here I only recapitulate the decision rules. Whenever actual problem solving is insignificant or the regime fails to influence any of the causal factors, the most plausible counterfactual estimate is the same as the actual score. Whenever the counterfactual path fits a reliable success or failure path, the fit score places a lower or an upper bound on the plausible counterfactual estimates. Finally, whenever the counterfactual path analysis leaves more than one plausible option, I choose among them based on the number of causal factors that are weaker in the counterfactual case than in the actual case—that is, that have scores empirically shown to be less conducive.

To demonstrate how these considerations allow determinate estimates of the counterfactual problem-solving scores, we may consider the year 1984. Its counterfactual collaboration score is lower than in the actual case because the regime allowed joint planning of surveys and intercalibration of equipment (see figure 4.4). The combination of substantial malignancy, insignificant intricacy, modest collaboration, and insignificant ecosystem modeling implies substantial fit (a score of 0.67) with the first reliable failure path in statement E above, which combines full malignancy with insignificant collaboration and ecosystem modeling. Thus, any failure estimate below 0.67 would contradict the pattern among actual cases; and since problem solving is the negation of failure, this finding places an *upper* bound on plausible problem-solving estimates at a modest level (1 − 0.67 = 0.33). That leaves two plausible options: modest or insignificant problem solving. Since the regime has altered only one causal factor (collaboration), and the actual problem-solving score that year is substantial, I select the higher of those options (0.33) as the most plausible counterfactual estimate.

In other cases, the counterfactual path analysis yields determinate estimates because the lower bound on the range of plausible counterfactual problem-solving scores equals the actual score—indicating that the same score would be achieved without the regime—or equals a lower bound. The year 2000 illustrates the latter situation. Figures 4.4 and 4.7 show that the regime had raised both collaboration and ecosystem modeling from modest to substantial levels that year. Since malignancy was substantial and intricacy was insignificant, its score on the first failure path in statement E is substantial, again placing an upper bound of the plausible estimates at a modest level. However, this case also has modest fit with the reliable success path in statement B, which combines insignificant malignancy with full collaboration and ecosystem modeling. Since among actual cases, such fit reliably implies problem solving at a modest level or higher, this finding places a *lower* bound on the counterfactual estimate at a modest level. Here the upper and the lower bounds are the same, so the counterfactual path analysis yields a point estimate: any level of problem solving other than modest would be implausible. This estimate builds on three theoretically and empirically substantiated sets of evidence: process-tracing based estimates of how the regime affects the modeled factors, a reliable path to cognitional failure, and a reliable path to cognitional success.

Table 4.1 reports such counterfactual path analysis for each year under study and lists the counterfactual problem-solving estimates that result from it; the counterfactual paths and their scores on the success and failure paths are given in appendix 5, table A5.1. The table then gives the cognitional Oslo-Potsdam effectiveness scores that derive from each year's combination of actual scores and counterfactual estimates.

Although table 4.1 shows the Barents Sea fisheries regime to be ineffective in cognitional terms in as many as eleven of the twenty-five years

Table 4.1
Cognitional Effectiveness Analysis

Actual Problem Solving		Counterfactual Problem Solving		Effectiveness Score
Year	Score	Substantiation	Estimate	Score
1980	1	No regime influence on drivers of problem solving	1	IR
1981–82	0.33	No regime influence on drivers of problem solving	0.33	0
1983	0	No regime influence on drivers of problem solving; and insignificant even in actual case	0	0
1984	0.67	Counterfactual path analysis narrows range to 0.33–0; highest option chosen since only collaboration is weaker than in actual case	0.33	0.5
1985–87	0	Insignificant even in actual case	0	0
1988	0.67	Counterfactual path analysis narrows range to 0.67–0; mid-option chosen since collaboration only is weaker than in actual case	0.33	0.5
1989–91	0.33	Counterfactual path analysis narrows range to 0.33–0; option below actual score chosen since collaboration is weaker	0	0.33
1992	1	Counterfactual path analysis narrows range to 0.33–0; higher option chosen since only collaboration is weaker than in actual case	0.33	1
1993	0.67	Counterfactual path analysis narrows range to 0.33–0; lowest option chosen since both collaboration and ecosystem modeling are weaker than in actual case	0	0.67
1994–95	0.67	Counterfactual path analysis yields point estimate	0	0.67

Table 4.1
(continued)

Actual Problem Solving		Counterfactual Problem Solving		Effectiveness Score
Year	Score	Substantiation	Estimate	
1996–98	0	Insignificant even in actual case	0	0
1999	1	Counterfactual path analysis narrows range to 0.67–0.33; lowest option chosen since both collaboration and ecosystem modeling are weaker than in actual case	0.33	1
2000	0.67	Counterfactual path analysis narrows range to 0.67–0.33; lowest option chosen since both collaboration and ecosystem modeling are weaker than in actual case	0.33	0.5
2001–02	0.33	Counterfactual path analysis yields point estimate	0.33	0
2003–04	0.67	Counterfactual path analysis yields point estimate.	0.33	0.5

Note: Scores: 1 = full; 0.67 = substantial; 0.5 = medium; 0.33 = modest; 0 = insignificant; IR = irrelevant. Counterfactual paths and their fit with success and failure paths are listed in appendix 5, table A5.1. Effectiveness scores are calculated by the Oslo-Potsdam formula.

under study, it also shows that the performance improves over the period. Thus, the summarized effectiveness score achieved during the first twelve years is 2, whereas the corresponding score for the last twelve years is 4.5. Significant variation in this positive trend line is evident in figure 4.8, which plots the regime's cognitional effectiveness scores from 1980 to 2004.

We can now offer a concise, substantive summary of these findings on the cognitional effectiveness of the Barents Sea fisheries regime regarding Northeast Arctic cod. Until the deeper survey collaboration inherent in the intercalibration of equipment and methodology from 1984, the regime failed to influence any of the drivers of problem solving. The leading research institutes in the two states maintained the modest level of survey collaboration that had existed prior to the present regime, with

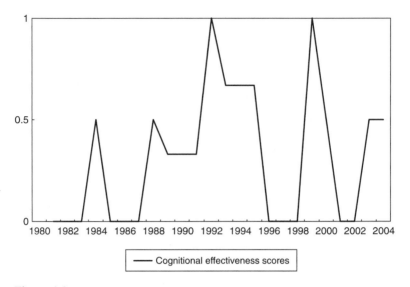

Figure 4.8
Cognitional-effectiveness scores. Line discontinuity in 1980 indicates that the regime was irrelevant in that year.

the multilateral ICES as the key institution. The 1984 advance in collaboration helped raise forecast accuracy to a substantial level that year—an impressive achievement, since malignancy in the form of incentives to misreport catches was more severe than before—but unfortunately, this effect on problem solving proved short-lived. Collaborative surveys were inadequate to tackle the drastic rise in substantive intricacy that hit the ecosystem with the capelin collapse and the ensuing rise in cod cannibalism from 1985, and the effectiveness level dropped to insignificant.

Only when this ecosystem disturbance declined in the late 1980s was the regime able to raise forecast accuracy, which it did for a long good period until 1995, often with substantial and even full forecast accuracy despite severe malignancy and sometimes severe intricacy as well. These regime contributions were due largely to the collaborative surveys, which by the late 1980s had produced fisher-independent data over a sufficiently long period to make assessments less vulnerable to unreliable catch reports. Such regime-induced broadening of data sources proved crucial in the early 1990s, when quota overfishing and thus underreporting of catches was particularly severe. The high accuracy that marked stock forecasts in 1993–1995 is similarly impressive, since intricacy rose to the highest level in this period—and the best explanation for the high accuracy is the breakthrough in ecosystem modeling inherent in qualitative estimation of model parameters based on capelin availability.

In the second half of the 1990s, however, two developments conspired to complicate assessments, pushing both accuracy and effectiveness down to insignificant levels. Several years of growing intricacy combined with a decline in survey collaboration resulting from Russian constraints on the area coverage of Norwegian, later also domestic, research vessels in Russia's EEZ. The result of those constraints was interruption of some of the time series of survey data that supported the assessment work.

The rise in accuracy and effectiveness to substantial or full levels in 1999–2000 is best explained by a drop in intricacy. Very high intricacy had constrained the effect of a new leap in ecosystem modeling that involved the use of models that quantified the relationships between key population parameters for cod, the abundance of capelin, and the extent of cod cannibalism. Finally, in the 2000s, the evidence is somewhat mixed but nevertheless permits optimism regarding the efficacy of ecosystem modeling and collaboration for jointly overcoming the main impediments to cognitional problem solving. The forecasts in 2003 and 2004 were highly accurate despite severe malignancy, combined in the last year of the study with severe intricacy as well.

The counterfactual path analysis underlying these findings uses process-tracing evidence to specify the most plausible scores on the causal factors that would pertain if the regime did not exist and the empirically proven paths to cognitional success or failure to estimate the most plausible counterfactual level of problem solving.

Summary and Implications

In keeping with the disaggregate approach to international regime effectiveness, this chapter has focused on one aspect of resource management, cognitional problem solving, measured on a scale that combines the notions of advice salience and accuracy. Salience is about the usefulness of scientific advice to political decision making, a concept firmly established in the field of regime effectiveness, although attention to the accuracy of such advice has been scant so far. This chapter has used retrospective ICES stock assessments to evaluate the accuracy of the spawning stock forecasts underlying quota advice. On the whole, initial assessments have tended to underestimate the impact that harvesting levels have on the future state of the stock, with forecasting failure reaching dramatic levels in the mid-1980s and from 1996 to 1998. Accuracy improves toward the end of the period studied.

The disaggregate way of assessing what proportion of such improvement can be ascribed to the regime involves decomposing even the difficult counterfactual analysis that is necessary for such assessment. A first step is to explain the pattern of problem solving among actual cases, which requires causal modeling and empirical confrontation. For the cognitional aspect of resource management, earlier studies provide little guidance beyond certain general mechanisms that highlight incentives, obligation, and learning. Thus, one contribution here is a more specific explanatory model of forecast accuracy that includes factors outside as well as within regime influence. A fully external factor is substantive intricacy in terms of ecosystem complexity or shifts. A second factor may be influenced by the regime but in complex and untraceable ways: malignancy, here the incentives that fishers have for misreporting catches, great whenever cod is highly available relative to quotas. In contrast, the last two factors in the model are clearly regime-driven and involve efforts to counteract the complications arising from malignancy and intricacy through coastal state collaboration on surveys and through incorporating relevant environmental data into forecast models.

This model is better at explaining cognitional failure than at explaining success: the causal combinations shown by the fuzzy set QCA analysis to reliably deliver failure cover a greater proportion of the forecasting failure in the dataset than the success path does for accurate forecasts. The failure paths indicate that severe malignancy is lethal to forecast accuracy unless counteracted by collaboration or ecosystem modeling, and that the same is true for severe intricacy not counteracted by ecosystem modeling. As to the success path, an accurate forecast is a reliable outcome only when substantive intricacy is low and deep collaboration is combined with intensive ecosystem modeling.

These explanations of variation in actual problem solving are important for the subsequent step in the effectiveness approach advanced here: specifying the counterfactual antecedents, or the combinations of scores on the modeled factors that the cases would have if the regime had not existed. That counterfactual question is easy compared to the counterfactual question of what the problem-solving scores would be if there had been no regime. Whenever the counterfactual paths fit to some extent the proven paths to success or failure, however, they provide crucial means for narrowing the plausible scope of counterfactual problem-solving estimates.

The Oslo-Potsdam effectiveness yardstick combines such estimates with levels of actual problem solving and their distances, if any, from the highest score. Considerable variation from one year to another remains, owing in particular to the effects of malignancy and intricacy, but the regime contributed much more to the levels of cognitional problem solving during the last half of the period under study than it did during the first. Those contributions derived primarily from the regime's effects on the planning and implementation of scientific surveys and on a range of activities aimed at modeling functional relationships between the cod, its main prey and predators, and the ocean climate.

The salience and accuracy of advice are of considerable inherent interest, but even full cognitional effectiveness would not constitute regime effectiveness. Instead, cognitional effectiveness draws its significance from the other two aspects of resource management studied here: the regulatory problem of overcoming barriers to agreement on adequate regulations, and the behavioral problem of shaping target-group behavior in ways that affect the pressure on the resource. As we have seen in this chapter, international regimes can help improve the salience and accuracy of scientific advice. They can also help diffuse research findings, level the factual ground for debate over conservation measures, and render such measures more appropriate in the eyes of target groups. The next two chapters elaborate on those functions and examine their relationship to certain other causal factors that may influence the regulatory and behavioral effectiveness of the Barents Sea fisheries regime.

5

Regulatory Effectiveness

The regulatory problem in focus for international regimes is to establish a set of behavioral rules that jointly reflect the best available knowledge on how to achieve the social purpose of the regime. In fisheries management, that purpose is to maximize the long-term yield from the resource, which includes safeguarding its ability to replenish—in other words, it is a question of balancing utilization and conservation. Chapter 4 showed that the Barents Sea fisheries regime has helped improve the accuracy of scientific forecasts of how levels of harvesting will affect replenishment and sustainability. In this chapter we will see how the state of such scientific knowledge is one of the factors that can explain variation in regulatory problem solving.

This chapter is the second to apply the disaggregate approach to international regime effectiveness developed in chapter 2, centered on counterfactual path analysis and the Oslo-Potsdam yardstick. This yardstick compares actual problem-solving scores with those that would most plausibly be achieved if the regime had not existed, so the first section examines various bases for measuring the regulatory problem. The scale used here is based on the scientific advice that ICES provides concerning various options for total harvesting levels and allows us to specify in concrete terms what would constitute full problem solving. Considerable variation emerges when we apply this scale to twenty-five actual decisions on cod quotas under the regime.

Substantiating the most plausible level of problem solving that would pertain if there were no regime requires a good account of the drivers of and impediments to problem solving. That is why I will specify a model for explaining the observed variation in regulatory problem solving. Among the factors included here, two emerge from utilitarian considerations: malignancy is about short-term incentives to exceed the quota advice, whereas collaboration concerns ways to reduce the costs of heeding the advice. The knowledge factor derives from theories of persuasion and learning, while a fourth causal factor, urgency, refers to a bargaining dynamics that includes utilitarian considerations as well as learning.

Validating this model empirically is the business of the subsequent section, which identifies, by means of fuzzy set qualitative comparative analysis (QCA), certain ideal-type combinations of causal properties that reliably deliver either high or low regulatory problem solving. Those success and failure paths allow us to rephrase the ultimate counterfactual question in regime-effectiveness analysis, concerning what the outcome would have been if the regime had not existed, into a much simpler one—what the scores on the causal factors would be. Whenever such counterfactual paths fit one or more reliable failure or success paths, we can place upper or lower bounds, or both, on the plausible range of counterfactual outcome estimates. That is because counterfactual cases should be expected to behave similarly to what equivalent actual cases do—and actual cases reliably achieve problem-solving scores equal to or greater than their score on the ideal-type causal combination. Equipped with actual problem-solving scores and empirically based estimates of counterfactual scores, both defined by their distance to a full problem-solving score, we can proceed to calculate regulatory effectiveness scores for each year under study.

The Problem: Keeping Quotas within Scientific Advice

Since the mid-1970s, the setting of annual total allowable catches (TACs) for individual stocks has served as the foremost regulatory instrument in international fisheries management and thus is a natural point of departure for examining regulatory problem solving. The main purpose of such quantitative caps is to retain enough of the spawning stock to ensure replenishment and, where ecosystem concerns are prominent, to accommodate the needs of other predators besides man. The Norwegian-Russian Joint Commission on Fisheries meets annually to adopt and allocate total quotas and other regulations for each of the shared stocks, including Northeast Arctic cod. These quotas and regulations are binding on both parties unless they opt out within two months.

This section first considers how to specify the best available knowledge on balancing utilization and conservation. It then develops a yardstick for measuring degrees of regulatory problem solving, and finally it assigns actual problem-solving scores to each of the years under study.

Specifying Regulatory Problem Solving

Scientific advice is not a self-evident reference for evaluating the quota decisions of the Joint Commission, but it is the best one. At least two complementary or alternative yardsticks deserve attention: stakeholder satisfaction and subsequent stock developments.

One objection to using scientific advice as a referent is that ICES harvesting-impact assessments have frequently proved to be widely off the mark (see chapter 4). Given such revealed uncertainty, it is not surprising that fishers and other stakeholders sometimes find it difficult to accept advice that may run counter to fishing-ground experiences as well as economic incentives. If cod is highly available and fishers take their quotas with comparative ease, resource users tend to question any scientific advice warning that the stock is in jeopardy.

While such stakeholder perceptions of the state of a stock may be valid, high availability is hardly a reliable indicator in itself. For example, the existence of a few impressive year classes among older and larger fish can easily mask a situation involving poor recruitment to the commercial part of the stock, which for cod comprises fish aged three years or more. Further complicating the use of stakeholder satisfaction as a yardstick of regulatory problem solving is the fact that scientific advice regularly comes under fire on opposite grounds as well, often from environmental groups that reject stock estimates as being overly optimistic (Aasjord 2001). As we saw in figure 4.1, ICES advice on Northeast Arctic cod has mostly been overly optimistic in the period studied when judged against the latest and most reliable assessments. Such diversity of stakeholder perceptions links up to a practical impediment to incorporating them in a standard for evaluating regulatory measures: collecting reliable and representative information would be very difficult and costly. Because of these various threats to validity and determinacy, we can rule out using stakeholder satisfaction in measuring regulatory problem solving.

Another possible reference for evaluating quota decisions is the ensuing stock development. For instance, we might judge regulatory problem solving at a particular point in time as being high if the state of the stock improves subsequent to a quota regulation or remains stable at a high level, and low if the stock declines or fails to recover from a low level. Such a reference would be in line with the underlying idea that effectiveness is anchored in the problem domain rather than in outputs or behavior alone, as noted in chapter 1.

One challenge to this stock-development approach is that fishers frequently overfish quotas, making it difficult to test the substantive merits of the regulatory decision. A more fundamental methodological objection is that such a yardstick would require highly demanding causal analysis, since numerous factors beyond the reach of regimes and human behavior may also affect stock developments, including water temperatures, species interactions, and other environmental circumstances. A stock-development indicator of regulatory success would have to incorporate the behavioral and the cognitional aspects of problem solving, thereby undermining the benefits derived from disaggregating the problem. It would also require causal control for all non-quota-related factors that influence stock developments. Like stakeholder perception, therefore, subsequent stock developments could in principle provide a yardstick of regulatory problem solving, but this tool would suffer from either low conceptual validity or low determinacy due to causal complexity. In chapter 7 I return to the relationship between regulatory problem solving and subsequent stock development.

In contrast, using scientific advice as the basis for measuring regulatory problem solving can make good sense in a wide range of issue areas. It is both valid and determinate, provided certain conditions are met. One such condition is the existence of a scientific body that provides advice on regulatory decisions. Since procedures for adopting scientific advice in international regimes typically give a single dissenting state the power to veto a specific recommendation (Stokke 2000), a second condition is scientific integrity relative to various stakeholders such as managers and the industry (Underdal 1989). As early experience with the Scientific Committee in the regime for managing Antarctic marine living resources showed, building such integrity can be a difficult and time-consuming process (Orrego Vicuña 1989; Stokke 1996).

In the Northeast Atlantic, however, various ICES bodies have been providing quota advice to European fisheries management bodies for more than forty years; and they have developed procedures that insulate the advice from political pressure, including a peer review process that involves scientists from states not engaged in the fishery (see chapter 4). Another indication of scientific integrity is the fact that the Joint Commission has in practice frequently chosen *not* to heed advice offered by ICES: had integrity been low, we would have expected scientists to give only such advice as managers were prepared to accept.

Scientific advice, then, stands out as the best among three imperfect options for evaluating the adequacy of regulatory measures under international regimes. While such alternatives as stakeholder perceptions and subsequent development in the state of the resource would also make sense in many management contexts, their validity and determinacy are much lower. The frequency of cognitional failure constrains somewhat the validity of an advice-based yardstick as well, but the possibility of such failure is among the predicaments of resource management and only serves to underline that the regulatory aspect of resource management is one of several ingredients in regime effectiveness, which also include the cognitional and behavioral aspects.

Scaling and Case Assignment
The set of quota options that ICES provides annually for Northeast Arctic cod offers a compelling qualitative anchor for scaling a yardstick of regulatory problem solving and for assigning cases to categories. Among those options, the *recommendation* aims to balance high long-term yield against the risk of overexploitation and recruitment failure; my scale considers quotas at or below this recommendation as meeting the requirements for full regulatory problem solving. In contrast, a quota above the *highest ICES option* clearly qualifies for the insignificance score. The intermediate threshold, separating modest from substantial problem solving, is set according to the quantitative criteria set out in chapter 1.

Identifying the highest ICES option—the cutoff point between modest and insignificant regulatory problem solving—is straightforward until 1998, when the precautionary approach was introduced. Up till then, ICES vocabulary required that all harvesting options given be "inside safe biological limits" (ICES 1982, 3; see also chapter 4). When the spawning stock was relatively low, the highest option typically involved forecasts of a stable or slightly increasing spawning stock. With the introduction of the precautionary vocabulary, however, ICES began to shade the forecasts corresponding to a TAC in excess of its recommendation (e.g., ICES 1998, 24), and the fishing mortality rate implied by the highest ICES option was frequently much higher than in earlier years.

Should, then, the shaded forecasts in the ICES advice after 1997 be considered options of the same type as the previous ones? The answer is a qualified yes. To disregard all the shaded forecasts when identifying the highest ICES option would be too radical, for three reasons. First, ICES does not state explicitly that those options should not be considered in the management of the stock, as it did in the past (e.g., ICES 1981, 220); it merely notes that they are inconsistent with the precautionary approach. Second, even after 1997 the pattern remains the same: at relatively low levels of the spawning stock, the highest-option forecasts would keep the spawning stock on a stable level. Third, while ICES considered the setting of *limit* reference points (those of danger; see chapter 4) to be entirely within its purview, it has recognized that the setting of *precautionary* reference points concerns the amount of risk acceptable to the fishery managers (Hilborn et al. 2001, 101), so it only "proposes" them (ICES 1999, 17). To balance the need for continuity in how the "highest ICES option" is measured with recognition of the significant change inherent in the precautionary approach, I also count as ICES options those shaded advice options that do not exceed the limit reference point for fishing mortality.

To help derive the intermediate threshold between substantial and modest problem solving on a quantitative basis, and to assign cases to the scale, figure 5.1a portrays for each year the ICES recommendation and highest option, as well as the TAC set by the Joint Commission, for the period 1980–2004. Figure 5.1b shows the distance between the recommendation and the TAC, measured in percentage of the recommendation. This helps in placing the threshold that separates modest from substantial regulatory problem solving.

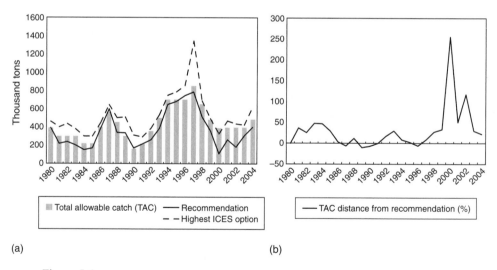

(a)   (b)

Figure 5.1
Scientific advice and agreed quotas, Northeast Arctic cod. Figure 5.1a shows the scientific advice and the agreed-upon quotas in absolute numbers. Figure 5.1b gives the agreed-upon quotas in percentage of the advice. Data from annual reports of the ICES Advisory Committee on Fishery Management, 1978–2004.

We see that Northeast Arctic cod quotas exceed the ICES recommendation in most years, but also that the Joint Commission has only once, in 2000, set the quota beyond the highest ICES option: only for that year is regulatory problem solving insignificant. At the other end of the scale, six of the quota columns remain at or below the recommendation line, which implies full problem solving.

A simple way to allocate the remaining observations is to examine the distance of each quota from the recommendation. Consider, for instance, the 1986 and 1995 quotas. They diverged only slightly from the recommendations in percentage terms but nevertheless involved distances of 13,000 and 18,000 tons, respectively, indicating that we should not consider including them in the category of full problem solving. To put those distances in perspective, Norway as well as Russia challenged as irresponsible Iceland's unregulated cod catches in the high seas Loophole, which in 1996 were only somewhat higher, at 23,000 tons (Stokke 2001d). As seen in figure 5.1b, a few other years show extremely high distances: for instance, the 2002 quota was twice the ICES recommendation. Between those low and very high distances (all listed in appendix 4), sixteen cases exceed the recommendation by 8 to 50 percent, with no clear clustering of values.

On the basis of the steepness and category-size criteria, a reasonable threshold between modest and substantial problem solving is a distance of 20 percent from the ICES recommendation. When that threshold is used, twelve cases are allocated to categories with a high score (substantial or full problem solving) and thirteen cases to categories with a low or zero score, and the last case involving substantial problem solving exhibits a markedly smaller percentage distance from the recommendation than does the first case receiving a modest score. Appendix 5, table A5.2 gives the precise regulatory problem-solving scores derived from these thresholds.

In summary, regulatory problem solving is measured on the basis of ICES options that are believed by scientists to be within safe biological limits and varies considerably over the period under study. Only once has the Joint Commission exceeded the highest ICES option, which is the threshold for insignificant problem solving, and regulatory problem solving remained generally high from 1986 through 1997. On the other hand, no more than modest scores were achieved in the first half of the 1980s and after the introduction of the precautionary approach in the late 1990s.

As the next section shows, those two periods of low problem solving were also years of considerable coastal state controversy over quotas, with one party rejecting scientific advice and the other party supporting the advice wholly or in part. This observation forms our starting point for building the explanation of regulatory problem solving that is necessary in order to substantiate counterfactual problem solving and assess regime effectiveness.

Modeling Regulatory Problem Solving

In seeking to explain the diversity of regulatory problem solving concerning catch levels of Northeast Arctic cod, I first examine differences of opinion between the two states concerning the desirability of heeding scientific advice, and then relate the areas of controversy to earlier studies of regulatory problem solving. In focus are impediments to collective action and various institutional responses to them.

Disagreement over quota levels of Northeast Arctic cod has been particularly high in two periods, early and late in the period studied. The reasons offered by regime participants and observers can help identify impediments to and drivers of regulatory problem solving. From the late 1970s, ICES recommended sharp cuts in harvesting levels, but the biggest cod harvester, Norway, was reluctant to heed this advice fully. Many North Norwegian communities relied heavily on the harvesting, processing, and marketing of cod (Sagdahl 1992); moreover, the general opinion was that the stock decline was mostly a result of the marked increase in activities of foreign trawlers *(Nordlys,* 6 November 1979, 4). By contrast, Norway's own cod fisheries mostly involve relatively small coastal vessels with limited range and few alternative uses (JCF 1981, item 4).

In part because Soviet trawlers in the region were better equipped to exploit other species or seek out distant fishing grounds, the Soviet authorities clearly preferred quota cuts to certain other ICES-recommended measures for achieving stock recovery, especially larger mesh size (Stokke, Anderson, and Mirovitskaya 1999). In some years the Soviets even pressed for quotas below the scientific advice. On Norwegian insistence (Sagdahl 1992, 31), the 1979 quota was set 100,000 tons higher than the recommendation, adding one-sixth of the recommended level; in the following year as well, Norway pressed for and achieved a higher quota than that preferred by the Soviet Union *(Nordlys,* 11 November 1979, 6). Similarly, the 1982 quota of 300,000 tons was much closer to the initial position of Norway than to the lower Soviet proposal *(Aften-posten,* 17 November 1981, 8). This pattern, with Norway favoring quotas well above the scientific advice and the Soviets favoring quotas well below, or even a moratorium, continued in subsequent years *(Nordlys,* 16 November 1982, 10; *Nordlys,* 16 November 1983). The Norwegian Commissioner described the negotiation of the 1984 quota as "the toughest I have experienced" *(Nordlys,* 19 November 1983; my translation). Gradually higher ICES quota recommendations from the mid-1980s explain why the quota level thereafter became less contentious in the Joint Commission's deliberations.

When the cod stock declined again toward the end of the 1980s, it became clear that Norway would no longer play the role of a "quota laggard" in the Barents Sea fisheries regime. The two states were now in full agreement on the need for drastic quota cuts. In preceding years, Norway had adopted domestic rules that enabled far better control over coastal vessel harvesting than before (see chapter 6). In contrast to past policy, its fisheries minister characterized a large quota reduction mid-season in 1988, following revised ICES advice, as being "very good for Norway" *(Aftenposten,* 29 June 1988; my translation). In fact, from the late 1980s to the late 1990s there is no longer much evidence of any significant disagreement among the two coastal states over the quotas.

Toward the end of the 1990s, however, open controversy over quotas reappeared in the Joint Commission's sessions, but now with Norway as the party more inclined to heed the scientific advice. Differences of view peaked with the 2000 quota, when the recommendation plummeted from the preceding year's 360,000 tons to a mere 110,000. Russian industry representatives were cited as claiming that the negotiators had paid too much attention to a scientific recommendation that, in their view, was not backed up by solid evidence; indeed, it was seen as part of a Norwegian plot to strangle Russian competitors *(Nordlys,* 18 November 1999, 6). While Norway, too, found the ICES recovery plan excessively ambitious (Fisheries Minister Peter Angelsen, cited in *NTBTekst,* 8 November 1999), it was sufficiently uncomfortable with the agreed-upon quota of just under 400,000 tons to insist on a highly unusual protocol statement. In Norway's view, notes the protocol, "the quota level for cod . . . is disturbingly high relative to the existing stock assessment and ICES advice" and was acceptable only "in consideration of the significance of fisheries for the troubled population in Northwest Russia" (JCF 1999, item 5.1; my translation). Fisheries Minister Angelsen explained that Norway had had to accept the Russian high-quota request since negotiations would have broken down otherwise *(Aftenposten,* 20 November 1999, 25). While Norway's initial proposals remained lower than Russia's in the following years as well, the differences narrowed as the recommendation rose. During the 2000s, negotiations gradually reverted to the amiable atmosphere that has generally characterized the Joint Norwegian-Russian Fisheries Commission (Hønneland 2006).

This brief sketch of quota controversies under the regime, and the circumstances surrounding the negotiations, brings out several themes identified by earlier research on regulatory problem solving (see chapter 2): the *state of knowledge,* as apparent in the accuracy of recent forecasts; regulatory costs, including the possibility that measures may affect regime participants asymmetrically, here termed *malignancy,* and the *urgency* of the stock situation. A fourth factor also mentioned in the previous chapter and discussed below influences regulatory problem solving under this regime as well as others: regulatory *collaboration* aiming to facilitate decision making and reduce the costs of heeding scientific advice by a "flexibility mechanism," quota transfers. Figure 5.2 places these four factors in a causal model, hypothesizing that severe malignancy is an impediment to regulatory problem solving, whereas high scores on knowledge, collaboration, and urgency are drivers of regulatory success.

The remainder of this section specifies these causal variables and substantiates their actual scores, as well as the most plausible counterfactual scores for each year under study.

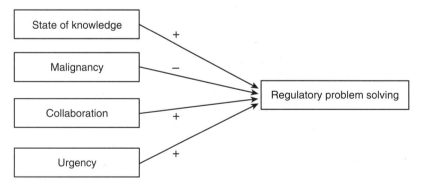

Figure 5.2
Causal model of regulatory problem solving.

State of Knowledge

An important strand in the study of how scientific advice affects international regulatory decisions highlights the credibility and legitimacy of the scientific input concerning environmental risks and options. The case of the Barents Sea can shed light on several of the propositions that have emerged. Earlier findings, reported in chapter 2, indicate that scientific inclusiveness and consensus are among the drivers of regulatory success, but, as this chapter makes clear, they are hardly sufficient conditions. The provision of scientific advice on Northeast Arctic cod has for several decades involved expertise from numerous user as well as non-user states in the form of consensual and authoritative ICES advice, yet considerable outcome diversity exists, which must be due to other factors.

More specific findings can be obtained concerning a second driver of credibility besides consensus: the conclusiveness of the state of knowledge as perceived by the users (Underdal 2000a, 15). One way to investigate the causal potency of this knowledge factor is to narrow in on the ICES forecasts examined in chapter 4, concerning how various levels of harvesting will affect the state of the spawning stock. The underlying argument is that if new data seem to confirm an earlier forecast, this would send a clear message to managers and fishers that the state of knowledge is sound, which in turn should enhance the persuasiveness of scientific advice. Conversely, when the latest scientific input contradicts earlier assessments, managers could be forgiven for considering scientific advice as less certain and thus less compelling, especially if the recommendations happen to involve unpopular restraints on harvesting. Forecasting accuracy, in short, is a sensitive barometer of the state of knowledge as perceived by the users.

A tempting procedure for measuring the perceived state of knowledge is simply to use the cognitional problem-solving score that chapter 4 substantiates, but a small modification is necessary. For cognitional success, the referent is the most recent retrospective assessment (here, from 2008; see chapter 4), which may differ considerably from the rolling ICES reassessment that is available to stakeholders at any given time. A much better referent is the spawning stock forecast for the quota year, which is reported to the users prior to the annual negotiations. By spanning two successive scientific reports rather than three, this comparative exercise should also reflect better what the users of scientific advice might actually do.[1] For example, during the 1997 Joint Commission meeting, ICES (1998, 24) forecasted, in view of that year's catches, an initial 1998 spawning stock of just over 800,000 tons. That report must have been a nasty shock, since the preceding ICES report (1997, 16) had forecasted that such a level of catches would deliver more than 1,500,000 tons of spawners—a 91 percent distance. When negotiating the 1998 quota, therefore, the coastal state representatives had reason for seriously questioning the state of knowledge of harvesting–stock relationships. In fact, the managers had had cause for surprise at the previous Joint Commission meeting as well, but on that occasion the new reported forecast had been 43 percent *higher* than the foregoing. The most recent retrospective assessment for these years confirms forecasting accuracy as very low, mainly owing to severe ecosystem disturbance (see chapter 4), but the distinction between cognitional problem solving and the state of knowledge as perceived by managers at the time remains important. Among the implications are slightly different cutoff points for the categories: for the state of knowledge, the steepness and category-size criteria imply thresholds at 15, 35, and 50 percent distance (see appendix 4)—more generous than for cognitional problem solving at the high and intermediate part of the scale, and somewhat stricter at the low end. The two sets of scores, measuring cognitional problem solving and the state of knowledge as perceived by users on the basis of reported accuracy, differ the most in the years when the latest retrospective stock assessment had considerably revised the first report.

This approach to measuring the state of knowledge generates scores for all years in the timeline except the two earliest ones, which cannot build on multiple-option forecasts since only single options were provided until 1980. An ad hoc procedure for those two years compares the spawning stock assessment that managers received before entering the quota talks with the preceding year's forecast. When the 1980 quota was under negotiation, the most recent assessment was a spawning stock estimate for 1979 at just over 300,000 tons (ICES 1980, 25), whereas the preceding year's forecast had been 241,000 tons—a distance of some 20 percent from the assessment, implying a substantial score on the state of knowledge. The following year's performance was even stronger: the assessment of 222,000 tons (ICES 1981, 219) indicated that the preceding year's forecast of 200,000 tons (ICES 1980, 26) had apparently missed the target by only 10 percent, thus qualifying for a full score on the state of knowledge.

The purpose of identifying possible drivers of and impediments to regulatory problem solving is to clarify whether problem solving would be lower without the regime; hence, the most plausible *counterfactual* scores of the causal factors are crucial in the analysis of regime effectiveness, and require specification (see chapter 2). On the basis of comparative and process-tracing evidence indicating an upper bound of the plausible counterfactual scores lower than the actual scores, chapter 4 substantiated the proposition that, in certain years, the accuracy of the cod forecast would have been significantly lower without the Barents Sea regime. Because of the conceptual difference between cognitional problem solving and perceived knowledge, it would be inappropriate to use those scores directly in estimating the counterfactual knowledge scores. Since they both concern forecasting accuracy, however, it does seem likely that the *difference* that the regime makes for the most plausible counterfactual accuracy is the same for each year, although the scores may differ.

The approach underlying the counterfactual knowledge scores plotted in figure 5.3, therefore, is to implement the same distance between the actual and the counterfactual scores as that between actual and counterfactual cognitional problem solving (see appendix 5). Those counterfactual time series must be time-lagged by two years, since the forecast

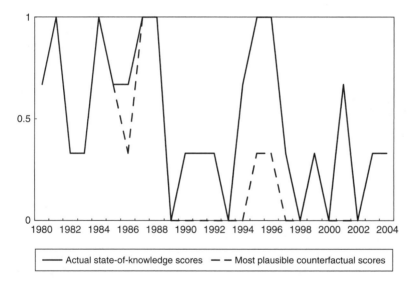

Figure 5.3
State-of-knowledge scores. 1 = full = high reported accuracy; 0.67 = substantial = medium reported accuracy; 0.33 = modest = low reported accuracy; 0 = insignificant = very low reported accuracy. Thresholds separating high, medium, low, and very low reported accuracy are at 15, 30, and 50 percent. The timeline refers to the quota year.

whose accuracy benefits from the regime is the forecast provided one year prior to negotiations on the subsequent year's quota. For example, it was only when negotiating the 1986 quota that managers could evaluate the 1984 forecast on the basis of a new forecast. This procedure implies lower counterfactual knowledge scores in the quota years corresponding to forecasts that, according to chapter 4, would have been significantly less accurate without the regime. The main merits of this procedure are parsimony, determinacy, and rough validity—but we should recall that cognitional problem solving is not quite the same as the state of knowledge.

The solid line in figure 5.3 shows variation over time in the state of knowledge, as reported to the users, on how various catch levels are expected to affect the spawning stock of Northeast Arctic cod. The dashed line gives the most plausible counterfactual scores.

Unlike such other potentially relevant aspects of scientific advice as consensus and legitimacy, which are stable as regards Northeast Arctic cod, the state of knowledge in terms of reported accuracy varies considerably: it was strong in the mid-1980 and the mid-1990s but mostly weak otherwise. Differences between the actual and the most plausible counterfactual knowledge scores reflect how the regime has contributed to accuracy in forecasting, as explained in chapter 4. Other things being equal, high knowledge scores should make managers more inclined to heed scientific advice.

Malignancy

Even scholars who stress the state of knowledge and processes of learning when explaining scientific influence on political decisions are usually quick to point out an additional important factor, the substantive content of the advice, and notably the costs of heeding it. Adler and Haas (1992, 383), for instance, report from their comparative analysis of epistemic community influence that "it was much easier for politicians to accept a community's policy approach after military or economic conditions changed sufficiently to minimize the costs of compliance with the approach." Sebenius (1992, 361) states the point firmly: "the path of influence of an epistemic community can be traced to its effects on perceptions of a zone of possible agreement." More indirectly, Goldstein and Keohane (1993, 26) note that lack of clarity about regulatory costs can induce states to heed authoritative knowledge claims: when "power relations are fluid and interests and strategies are unclear or lack consensus . . . articulations of principled and causal beliefs that were ignored earlier may exert an impact on policy." Examining scientific persuasiveness requires attention to the perceived costs of advised policy options.

No other analyst of the science–politics relationship in international environmental governance has more vigorously and persistently emphasized this utilitarian factor of how a policy distributes costs among actors than Arild Underdal (1989, 2000a, 2000b, 2002b, 2002c). As explained in chapter 2, his concept of malignancy refers to incongruity between an actor's share of the overall benefits from a given policy and the actor's share of the overall costs, for instance as a result of externalities or asymmetric affectedness. In an early work on the science–politics relationship, Underdal (1989, 262) noted that "political conflict tends to exploit and even reinforce uncertainty by infusing political energy into diverging interpretations of available evidence." Drawing on scientific advice and regulatory decision making in five environmental regimes, Underdal (2000b, 190) later concluded that malignancy can affect regulatory problem solving to such an extent that "even sophisticated models and fairly accurate and reliable knowledge are likely to be neglected." While in another comparative study the outcome category is broader, Underdal (2002c, 460) finds that the combination of scientific uncertainty and severe malignancy can be lethal to problem solving under international regimes.

The case of the Barents Sea fisheries sheds further light on these propositions. The malignancy of heeding the scientific recommendations varies with the amount of constraint that the quotas imply for fishers, which in turn will depend on the ratio of the commercial stock to the quota. The preceding chapter related cognitional malignancy to the incentives fishers have to misreport catches, and a similar approach is appropriate as regards regulatory malignancy. The underlying mechanism is the same: fears that others will appropriate the gains from one's own restraint may complicate international negotiations and impede the adoption of ambitious conservation measures. Such fears become especially keen in years when managers have reason to believe that their own fishers may be taking considerably more than the scientists recommend. The small differences from the cognitional malignancy measure are that, for regulatory malignancy, the relevant comparison is between the *preceding* year's commercial stock (and not that of the quota year, since such information is not yet available) and the *recommended* quota. When negotiating a new quota, the managers receive the most recent catch and effort data, including whether fishers are likely to keep within the current quota. If availability is relatively high, this is likely to trigger complaints that the scientists are out of touch with fishing-ground realities (see, e.g., *Fiskaren,* 8 June 2005, 4; see also chapter 4). The ratio of the preceding year's commercial stock to the recommendation is thus a valid measure of regulatory malignancy and gives determinate scores for all the years under study.[2]

As the malignancy columns in appendix 4 show, the criteria of steepness and category size yield reasonable thresholds at stock–advice ratios of 2.8, 3.5, and 4.8. For the same reasons as with cognitional malignancy (the harvesting pressure is only one of many factors influencing the state of the stock), the most plausible *counterfactual* scores map onto the actual ones, as shown in figure 5.4, since we lack sufficient basis for substantiating specific no-regime estimates of the commercial stock.

We see that regulatory malignancy is high during the first halves of the 1980s, the 1990s, and the 2000s. This result relates to the nature and severity of the collective action problem addressed by a regime, here

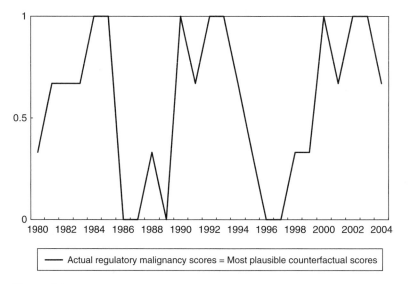

— Actual regulatory malignancy scores = Most plausible counterfactual scores

Figure 5.4
Regulatory malignancy scores. 1 = full = severe incongruity, owing to very high relative availability; 0.67 = substantial = large incongruity, owing to high relative availability; 0.33 = modest = some incongruity, owing to medium relative availability, but mostly synergy; 0 = insignificant = no significant incongruity, owing to low relative availability. Thresholds between severe, large, some, and no incongruity are relative availability ratios of 4.8, 3.5, and 2.8.

measured by the ratio of two conditions that shape the costs an actor may suffer if others exploit that actor's regulatory restraint—the size of the commercial stock and the size of the quota. In years of severe malignancy, we may expect managers to experience especially heavy pressure to set quotas above the scientific recommendation.

Collaboration

Collaboration matters for the regulatory aspect of problem solving no less than for the cognitional aspect. As laid out in chapter 2, I follow Miles and associates (2002, 483) in grading collaboration by the extent to which states coordinate their activities on the relevant aspect of management: modest collaboration relies solely on common standards, substantial collaboration involves joint planning, and full collaboration means joint implementation of resource management. In focus here are two such collaborative means: the Barents Sea fisheries regime has contributed certain common standards for addressing the regulatory problem, as well as a "flexibility mechanism" associated with quota exchange that has helped reduce the costs of heeding scientific advice.

Throughout the period under study, both Norway and the Soviet Union/Russia made extensive use of *joint standards* to achieve science-based agreement on annual quotas. In the Preamble to the Framework Agreement underlying the Barents Sea fisheries regime, they emphasized "in particular the significance of scientific investigations for the maintenance of a sustainable yield from the ocean's resources" and the role of such research in identifying "measures for conservation and rational utilization of the marine living resources." Both states have ratified the Law of the Sea Convention, which commits them to take "into account the best scientific advice available . . . [and] ensure through proper conservation and management measures that the maintenance of the living resources in the exclusive economic zone is not endangered by over-exploitation" (Article 61); similar provisions concern high seas areas (Article 119). The practice of requesting annual quota advice from ICES frames regulatory problem solving within the Joint Commission and facilitates agreement.

Similar comments apply regarding the fixed keys that determine the initial allocation of shared-stock quotas. If the quota distribution were also up for grabs during annual negotiations, that might tempt the two states to dampen disagreement on allocations by increasing the quota (Stokke, Anderson, and Mirovitskaya 1999; see also chapter 3). Together with the shared commitments to scientific advice, these practice-based standards for allocation imply that the level of regulatory collaboration has always been at least modest under the Barents Sea fisheries regime.

Elements of *joint planning* are also evident in the setting of Northeast Arctic cod quotas since representatives of both states meet annually to scrutinize scientific and other inputs with a view to adopting joint regulations. Meetings of the Joint Commission and its various working groups enable recurrent exchanges of information and views on any impediments to heeding scientific advice, as well as on measures that might improve the level of regulatory problem solving. In the early 1980s, for instance, when Norway found the ICES recommendation on quotas excessively ambitious, Joint Commission meetings provided a venue for discussing possible responses to the stock decline and for explaining particular difficulties that stemmed from the structure of Norway's fisheries (see JCF 1981, item 4.1, and especially JCF 1983, item 4), notably the predominance of relatively small vessels highly dependent on cod fishing. In itself, however, this venue function involves no commitment on how to tackle the regulatory problem, which means that any joint planning is still too meager to raise the collaboration score beyond the modest level.

In contrast, the major collective *response* to the quota controversy arising from Norway's reluctance in the early 1980s to constrain the coastal vessel sector involved a measure of joint implementation of the regulatory task. In 1982, the Soviet Union began to transfer considerable amounts of fishing rights for cod in return for access to various other species found in waters under Norwegian jurisdiction, especially blue whiting and redfish. In international environmental governance, the most salient flexibility mechanisms are certain instruments under the 1997 Kyoto Protocol to the UN Framework Convention on Climate Change, such as tradable assigned amount units of emission and credit for certified emissions reductions in other countries, aimed at reducing the costs of mitigating global warming (Stokke, Hovi, and Ulfstein 2005). The quota exchange under the Barents Sea fisheries regime provides a corresponding flexibility mechanism, a means for implementing regulations more cost-efficiently, thus facilitating the adoption of ambitious conservation measures.

An important condition for the relevance of quota transfer as a flexibility mechanism in the management of Northeast Arctic cod has been the difference between the structures of the Norwegian and the Soviet fleets (see chapter 3). Soviet oceangoing trawlers were better placed than Norwegian coastal vessels to exploit fishing opportunities elsewhere when faced with shrinking Barents Sea cod quotas. They also valued pelagic species relatively higher, largely because these trawlers were operating in an economic context unlike that of Norway. Whereas the large amounts of blue whiting that the Soviets purchased in return for cod were destined for human consumption, Norway has typically used this relatively abundant source of protein largely as animal and aquaculture fodder.

When such quota transfer, or joint implementation of the regulatory aspect of management, makes up a substantial part of the coastal-state quotas, a higher collaboration score is warranted. In the 1980s, when Norway was a regulatory laggard during the quota negotiations, the Joint Commission decided to transfer from approximately 70,000 tons (1983, 1987) to around 20,000 tons (1990) of fishing rights for Northeast Arctic cod from the Soviet Union to Norway (appendix 4).[3] Those transfers constituted from 15 to 48 percent of Norway's quota and must have considerably alleviated its difficulties in accepting the low quotas that the scientists advised during the period. While joint implementation of such magnitude hardly constitutes full regulatory collaboration, since most of the initial quota did not change hands, a substantial score seems reasonable here.

After 1990, however, transfers have been insignificant, around 10,000 tons or less, typically representing a few percent of Norway's quota. The main explanation for this change is the gradual removal of two vital conditions for quota transfer to be mutually beneficial: the practical separation of the markets served by Soviet and by Norwegian vessels and their different valuation of pelagic species relative to cod. Perestroika, the societal reshuffling propelled by Gorbachev in the late 1980s, gradually undermined both conditions: in the fisheries sector, the new order implied a decentralization of economic decisions and greater leeway for transactions with foreign entities. Direct deliveries of cod by Soviet vessels in Western ports became legal when Sovrybflot, the foreign trade organization under the Ministry of Fisheries, lost its monopoly on international transactions (Stokke 1992; see chapter 3). Such direct deliveries generated hard currency and were more attractive to vessel operators than were landings in Northwest Russia. These tendencies were accelerated by the subsequent dissolution of the Soviet Union and the large-scale privatization that ensued (Hønneland 2004). The turn to Western markets in the Northwest Russian fishing industry after 1990 made the flexibility mechanism inherent in quota trade less relevant, and the regulatory collaboration score returned to a modest level.

A decade later, however, joint planning expanded markedly in connection with the implementation of the precautionary approach to fisheries, which involves predefined biological reference points and the political commitment to take forceful action whenever the spawning stock falls below certain levels. Those changes triggered multiyear management planning with respect to Northeast Arctic cod ambitious enough to qualify as substantial regulatory collaboration.

Thus, responding to the recurrent quota controversies in the late 1990s, the two states sought to develop a more long-term approach to quota setting, one that could balance the precautionary approach with industry's need for stability. When agreeing on the 2001 quota, Norway and Russia committed themselves to retain the agreed-upon harvesting level for a three-year period except in the event of unexpected stock developments (JCF 2000, item 5.1). In subsequent years, that simple decision rule was refined and formally adopted by the Joint Commission. The two states pledged to set the total allowable catch as a rolling average of the TAC levels for the coming three years, corresponding to the precautionary reference point for fishing mortality, while making sure that any distance from the preceding year's quota remained within 10 percent, unless such stability would depress the spawning stock below the precautionary reference point (JCF 2002, item 5.1). Should that occur, a special procedure for reducing the TAC would apply (JCF 2004, item 5.1; see also Bogstad et al. 2005; ICES 2005, 39). This harvest control rule involves a high degree of joint planning, linking the quota negotiations directly to the ICES advice, and clearly qualifies for a substantial regulatory collaboration score from 2001.

Figure 5.5 contrasts these trends in regulatory collaboration with respect to quotas for Northeast Arctic cod (solid line) with the most plausible *counterfactual* level in a hypothetical situation in which there was no Barents Sea fisheries regime (dashed line). We see that counterfactual collaboration is modest throughout the period studied. If there were no regime, the two coastal states would have received ICES recommendations regarding the TAC, but they would have set their quotas unilaterally, without the means for coordinating decisions that the Joint Commission provided or the fixed keys for initial division of the shared stocks that have emerged from practice. General commitments under customary and conventional international law to heed the best available scientific advice would have provided an important joint standard, so regulatory collaboration would have been at least modest. In contrast, as the difference between the solid and the dashed lines in figure 5.5

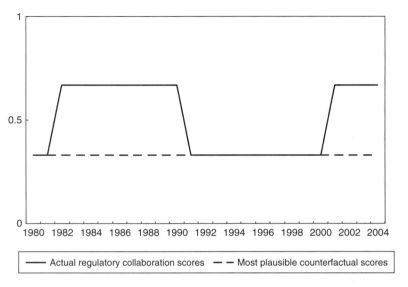

Figure 5.5
Regulatory collaboration scores. 1 = full = joint planning and implementation;
0.67 = substantial = substantial joint implementation by quota transfer or substantial planning by harvest control rule; 0.33 = modest = coordination by joint
standards only; 0 = insignificant = no explicit coordination.

reflects, neither the exchange of quotas that raised the collaboration
score in the 1980s nor the harvest control rule for multiyear planning of
quota regulations in the 2000s would have been plausible without the
venue for negotiating joint conservation measures provided by the Joint
Commission.

In short, collaboration on cod regulation under the Barents Sea fisheries regime has never been insignificant; indeed, it was substantial through
most of the 1980s and the 2000s. Even without the regime, collaboration
would probably have been modest, since both states were committed to
international norms on science-based management. The regime has added
to these joint standards by providing a venue for joint planning, especially relevant with the 2001 introduction of a multiyear harvest control
rule, and the joint implementation inherent in the transfer of fishing
rights from the Soviet Union to Norway during most of the 1980s.

Urgency
Another strand of rationalist regime analysis focuses on contextual
factors that affect the process of international bargaining (Stokke 1997).

Charging that mainstream utilitarian approaches, with their emphasis on interest configurations, fail to capture some important drivers of international accord, Young (1989) has drawn attention to exogenous "shocks" that may motivate states to cut through a distributive deadlock, providing a more forceful political response. One commonly cited illustration of this factor in international environmental governance is the discovery of an ozone hole over Antarctica, which played a role in the negotiation of the Montreal Protocol aimed at combating emissions of ozone-depleting substances (Young 1989, 372; Haas 1992, 202; but see Parson 2003, 250). More specifically concerning the influence of experts on policy, Underdal (1989, 260) likewise considers that rapid, dramatic developments in a specific problem addressed by states are likely to make a significant difference. Similarly, Adler and Haas (1992, 380) summarize research showing that "crises and dramatic events have the effects of alerting decision makers to the limitations of their understanding . . . increasing their reliance on a community with an established foothold." In times of crisis, according to this line of argument, negotiators work under the pressure of strong societal expectations and are more likely to heed scientific input.

The explanatory weight of this variable, which I term "urgency," can be explored in the context of Northeast Arctic cod management by narrowing in on variations in ICES evaluations of the state of the stock. Here we may consider the high regulatory problem solving that the two states achieved in the years 1989 to 1992, despite severe malignancy, which should have complicated adherence to scientific advice. Urgency provides a plausible explanation: midway in the 1988 season, ICES revised the recommendation for the ongoing season downward by more than a third, arguing that with "reduced stock biomass . . . [and] the declining trend in recruitment, the need for a reduction in fishing mortality has become more urgent" (ICES 1989, 8). To this the managers responded forcefully, agreeing to cut the quota mid-season by nearly as much as the scientists advised (Christensen and Hallenstvedt 2005, 268). However, subsequent scientific inputs proved no more reassuring: "the recent level may have been the lowest in the stock history" (ICES 1990b, 9).

An operational measure of urgency may use the biological reference points that scientists have elaborated for the stock in question. Long time series of catch and effort data for Northeast Arctic cod enabled ICES to develop early a biological reference point indicating whether the stock was within "safe biological limits." This concept provides an appropriate qualitative anchor for separating cases that are mostly within the urgency category from those that are mostly outside it—that is, for the threshold between substantial and modest urgency. A spawning stock level of 500,000 tons has been used, under different labels, as a reference for this stock, including when ICES implemented the precautionary approach in 1998.[4] Of the twenty-five spawning stock assessments that the Joint Commission received from ICES between 1980 and 2004, fourteen were below that threshold. No similarly clear qualitative bases exist for the two other cutoff points, those separating substantial from full urgency and modest from insignificant levels. Under such circumstances, it is appropriate to use the quantitative steepness and category-size criteria. From the urgency columns in appendix 4 we see that the most reasonable thresholds are spawning stock levels of 310,000, 500,000 and 750,000 tons.

As with malignancy, we lack sufficient basis for substantiating *counterfactual* urgency scores distinct from the actual ones. ICES preceded the current fisheries regime and would most likely have offered evaluations of urgency also if Norway and Russia had managed Northeast Arctic cod autonomously: the political force of scientific worry would pertain as well in the counterfactual situation. Chapters 4 to 6 substantiate that, in some periods, the Barents Sea fisheries regime has affected research, regulatory practice, or fisher behavior, thereby indirectly influencing the level of the spawning stock. However, translating this aggregate assessment into specific counterfactual spawning stock estimates for each year would clearly stretch the evidence. It is more appropriate to consider, as figure 5.6 does, that ICES urgency reports would have been same without the Barents Sea fisheries regime.

In short, urgency means that the state of the stock under regulation is reported to be so low as to jeopardize replenishment, and that in turn should encourage managers to take the scientific advice more seriously than otherwise. For Northeast Arctic cod, such urgency was high throughout most of the 1980s and in the early 2000s.

Summary
Unlike cognitional problem solving, the regulatory side of resource management has received considerable attention in the study of international regimes. This section has drawn on such earlier research in building a causal model to account for the outcome diversity indicated in figure 5.1. Propositions as to the role of inclusiveness and consensus in the generation of advice cannot account for that diversity (since those factors

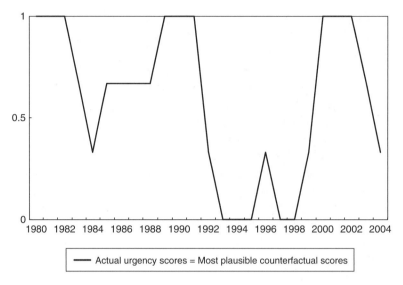

Figure 5.6
Urgency scores. 1 = full = severe urgency; 0.67 = substantial = high urgency; 0.33
= modest = some urgency; 0 = insignificant = no urgency. Thresholds between
severe, high, some, and no urgency are spawning stock assessments at 310,000,
500,000, and 750,000 tons.

remain stable at a high level in Barents Sea fisheries management), but
there is another component of the state of knowledge that varies considerably in the dataset and provides one explanatory candidate: the conclusiveness of the evidence, here measured as the reported accuracy of
the annual ICES spawning stock forecasts. Various strands of collective
action theory identify three additional factors: malignancy, measured as
the ratio of the commercial stock to the recommended quota; collaboration, highlighting the use of joint standards, joint planning, or joint
implementation to facilitate regulatory adherence with scientific advice;
and urgency, operationalized by the biological reference points used by
ICES to indicate whether the stock is within or outside safe biological
limits. The Barents Sea fisheries regime affects the state of knowledge
and the level of collaboration, but not malignancy and urgency.

This initial model of explanatory factors is derived in part from previous research on regulatory problem solving, so its empirical application
may illuminate earlier findings. It also takes cues from various observations of industry complaints, researcher warnings, and regulatory distances from scientific advice specific to the international management of

Northeast Arctic cod in the period under study. The next section confronts the model more systematically with the empirical evidence on variation in causal properties and regulatory problem solving under the Barents Sea fisheries regime.

Paths to Regulatory Success and Failure

In the management of Northeast Arctic cod, certain combinations of modeled factor properties reliably yield either high or low adherence to the scientific advice. These paths to regulatory success or failure derive from the fuzzy set QCA analysis, whose main concepts, procedures, and measures were explained in chapter 2. This set-theoretic technique examines outcomes scores among cases that to some extent fit certain ideal-type combinations of scores on the causal variables. High consistency with a pattern whereby all cases achieve outcome scores that are equally as high as or higher than their score on the causal combination may, if supported by other theoretical and substantive knowledge, indicate that the causal combination is a sufficient condition—a reliable path to the outcome. This section identifies two paths to success and two paths to failure, then examines how robust those findings are to adjustments of category thresholds and to the removal of one or a few strong cases of the ideal-type causal combinations.

Success Paths

Agreed-upon quota decisions on Northeast Arctic cod over two and a half decades indicate that, as long as malignancy remains low, a strong state of knowledge or the combination of high urgency and deep collaboration is sufficient for achieving high adherence to scientific advice. In contrast, no grouping of cases involving severe malignancy consistently achieves a high problem-solving score.

The reliable paths to regulatory success become evident from examining the twenty-five combinations of causal property scores and regulatory problem-solving scores described in the previous sections, which populate thirteen of the sixteen corners of the four-factor property space (scores are given in appendix 5). While no necessary condition for regulatory success is indicated by the QCA analysis, four causal combinations consistent with the sufficiency pattern can be reduced to two more general, reliable paths to regulatory problem solving.

At the outset, as many as eleven paths satisfied the conventional criterion for reliability (a consistency score of 0.85; see chapter 2) but this apparent richness of reliable paths is an artifact resulting from a nearly empty category of cases with insignificant problem solving. With only four outcome categories, this distribution makes every weak case of any causal combination consistent with the sufficiency criterion: weak cases have a modest score (0.33) on the category and cannot be inconsistent when problem solving is either modest or higher. As regards regulatory problem solving, therefore, only strong cases of an ideal-type combination are capable of failing the test, and that necessarily inflates the QCA consistency scores. An example is the high consistency score (0.91) achieved by a highly unlikely success path candidate: the combination of full malignancy and zero scores on urgency, knowledge, and collaboration. One of two strong cases of this combination (1993) fails the test, which is closer to what we would expect on grounds of theory. The special circumstance that only one case receives an insignificant problem-solving score clearly invalidates the standard consistency criterion, so some modification is needed.

One way to avoid inflated consistency scores is to redefine the category of insignificant problem solving in order to capture more of the twenty-five quota decisions (for instance, those that depart the most from the ICES recommendation), but such a redefinition would reduce construct validity. Managers who set quotas within the range of options provided by the scientists do, in fact, significantly reflect the best available knowledge, even if they depart widely from the recommended option. A better approach, therefore, is to evaluate a sufficiency claim solely on the merit of cases that are capable of failing—the strong cases. Given the moderate number of observations, this criterion in practice accepts no failure among strong cases, and the four causal combinations that meet it, listed in statement A, are fully consistent with a causal-sufficiency claim. As in the previous chapter, the reliable paths are stated in ideal-type terms that distinguish only between absence of a property (a score of 0), represented by the symbol "~" in the statement, and presence (a score of 1), but they derive from observation of all cases fitting them to some extent. In the statement, an asterisk means "combined with," whereas an arrow means "delivers reliably":

(A) ~malignancy * urgency * knowledge * collaboration → regulatory
    success

    ~malignancy * urgency * knowledge * ~collaboration →
    regulatory success

~malignancy * urgency * ~knowledge * collaboration →
regulatory success

~malignancy * ~urgency * knowledge * ~collaboration →
regulatory success

The reliable path listed first in this statement is hardly surprising, given its zero score on the model's impediment to problem solving (malignancy) and the full scores on all three drivers: a failure by this combination would have cast severe doubt on the explanatory model. Appendix 5 indicates the limits to what those drivers can achieve: the path combining full scores on the drivers with *full* malignancy fails the sufficiency test and is therefore not included in the list.

The second reliable path to success indicates that, as long as malignancy is low, high scores on urgency and knowledge yield regulatory success, even when collaboration is shallow. As the analytical reduction below confirms, this path indicates that the collaboration part of the first combination is not decisive in achieving regulatory success. The third reliable path highlights the combination of urgency and collaboration, which seems potent even when the forecasting accuracy is reported to be low—but again, only at low levels of malignancy: the corresponding full-malignancy path fails the sufficiency test. The fourth and final category in statement A speaks for the significance of forecasting accuracy. As long as low malignancy constrains any fear of forgoing large catches, a strong forecast record seems to persuade managers to heed scientific advice even under conditions of low urgency and without cost-saving collaboration.

A fifth path also seemed to qualify as reliable but failed, following consideration of a theoretically more potent superset. At first glance, the regulatory success of the one strong case of the category combining full scores on malignancy and knowledge with scores of zero on urgency and collaboration (see appendix 5) would seem to indicate that recent forecast success is highly potent and may also suffice for reliable problem solving when malignancy is high. That interpretation crumbles, however, when we consider the failure among all other strong cases of the superset of *all* categories combining full scores on malignancy and knowledge, which incorporates as well those with full scores on one or both of the other problem-solving drivers besides knowledge.[5] If a strong state of knowledge alone were sufficient for regulatory success, that property, reinforced by high urgency or deep collaboration, should do the same.

Theoretically more potent supersets usually involve more observations and are thus less sensitive to outliers, and examining them can prevent inflated lists of sufficient causal conditions. The four reliable paths to regulatory success in statement A all involve low malignancy, and none of them has theoretically stronger supersets that fail the sufficiency test.

As to the explanatory power of the model, the joint coverage scores for those four paths are 0.54, implying that they cover consistently 54 percent of the regulatory problem solving achieved in the period under study. This joint coverage is considerably higher than the corresponding value for the reliable paths to cognitional success, yet nearly half of the regulatory problem solving occurs under conditions that are unreliable in yielding regulatory success. The first path in the statement, with high scores on all the drivers of regulatory problem solving, covers a somewhat greater proportion of the success in the period than do the others (0.35), which indicates greater empirical relevance in the dataset. In contrast, the second and the fourth paths, highlighting the knowledge factor with and without urgency, have the highest unique coverage (0.12), and that indicates a contribution to problem solving that no other reliable path covers.

As explained in chapter 2, logical minimization and the introduction of reasonable simplifying assumptions can help formulate statement A more generally. Paired comparison of the first and second terms in the statement shows that, with or without collaboration, the combination of full malignancy and full scores on knowledge and collaboration is reliable for achieving regulatory problem solving. We may therefore, as the first term in statement B does, merge those two arguments into a more general statement without restrictions on the state of knowledge. Similarly, paired comparison of the first and third terms in statement A indicates that their restriction regarding the state of knowledge is redundant, as is the restriction on urgency in the second and fourth term:

(B) ~malignancy * urgency * knowledge → regulatory success

~malignancy * urgency * collaboration → regulatory success

~malignancy * knowledge * ~collaboration → regulatory success

An even less restricted statement is warranted on the reasonable simplifying assumption that, if it had been represented the dataset, the category combining scores of zero on malignancy and urgency with full scores on knowledge and collaboration would have met the reliability criterion. This assumption is reasonable because the only difference to the fourth reliable category in statement A is a property that should further strengthen regulatory problem solving—deep collaboration. Inserting this simplifying assumption allows another round of paired comparison, yielding statement C:

(C) ~malignancy * knowledge → regulatory success

~malignancy * urgency * collaboration → regulatory success

~malignancy * knowledge * ~collaboration → regulatory success

Here, the third term is contained by the first: it forms a subset of the first, more general term. Accordingly, shallow collaboration is not only an implausible restriction on the regulatory potency of robust forecasts (as long as malignancy is low) but one that is logically redundant as well:

(D) ~malignancy * knowledge → regulatory success

~malignancy * urgency * collaboration → regulatory success

Analysis of the twenty-five cases of regulatory problem solving reveals two fairly general paths to success. Whenever malignancy is low, a strong forecasting record or the combination of high urgency and deep collaboration reliably delivers quotas that heed scientific advice, fully or substantially. In the concluding chapter 8, I examine how the findings in this study relate to earlier research on the science–politics interface. Since the regime contributes significantly to both the level of knowledge and the level of collaboration, these findings substantiate in a general way that regulatory problem solving would have been lower without the regime. In specifying that substantiation, I draw not only on the success paths but also on the reliable paths to regulatory failure.

Failure Paths

Low scores on all three drivers of regulatory problem solving reliably yield regulatory failure in this dataset, even under benign conditions, as does the combination of severe malignancy and low urgency. From the perspective of regime effectiveness, reliable paths to regulatory failure are no less interesting than the paths to success, as both can help substantiate the most plausible level of problem solving that would pertain without the regime.

Unlike the analysis of regulatory success, the failure analysis can proceed without having to disregard weak cases, since they too may be inconsistent with the sufficiency criterion for failure: weak cases of regulatory success are strong cases of failure (on the negation of sets, see chapter 2). Using the same notation as above, statement E lists the five causal combinations that meet the conventional consistency criterion for a reliable failure path.[6]

(E) malignancy * ~urgency * knowledge * collaboration → regulatory failure

malignancy * ~urgency * knowledge * ~collaboration → regulatory failure

malignancy * ~urgency * ~knowledge * collaboration → regulatory failure

malignancy * ~urgency * ~knowledge * ~collaboration → regulatory failure

~malignancy * ~urgency * ~knowledge * ~collaboration → regulatory failure

Those five reliable paths achieve a joint coverage score of 0.59, roughly the same as for the cognitional problem-solving model. Two rounds of logical minimization by paired comparison permit the following statement:

(F) malignancy * ~urgency → regulatory failure

~urgency * ~knowledge * ~collaboration → regulatory failure

No assumption that would further simplify this statement is reasonable: all nonrepresented combinations have low malignancy and are therefore, as both theory and actual cases suggest, less prone to failure than the combinations listed in statement E. Statement F, therefore, is the most general finding about reliable paths to regulatory failure permitted by the evidence reported here. The first term implies that severe malignancy reliably yields failure unless the state of the stock is severe enough to add urgency to the scientific recommendation. The second term adds that whenever the reported state of the spawning stock is relatively strong, regulatory failure is inevitable (even with low malignancy) unless either the state of knowledge or the level of collaboration is high.

Given the regime's influence on two of the counterforces to failure, this analysis provides additional support to the general claim that regulatory problem solving would be lower without the regime. Before specifying that claim over time, as the next section does, we should examine the robustness of these findings concerning reliable paths to regulatory success and failure.

Robustness
Most of the findings from the comparative analysis of regulatory problem solving are robust to various reasonable ways of coding the outcome and the causal factors, as well as to strategic removal of one or a few observations.

If we coded very high distances between the quota and the recommendation as insignificant problem solving even when the quota keeps within the highest option, with a reasonable cutoff point at 40 percent, considering curve steepness and category size (see appendix 4), that would remove the third, collaboration-driven path among the four in statement A. And that removal would deprive statement D of the second term, implying that high urgency and collaboration would not suffice for reliable success, even in benign circumstances; only strong knowledge would do. The knowledge factor, therefore, is somewhat more robust than are the other model drivers to an alternative but arguably less valid approach to measuring regulatory problem solving. In contrast, the set of reliable paths to failure would be exactly the same.

Similar comments apply with respect to alternative reasonable codings of the causal factors. The regulatory malignancy columns in appendix 4 show that a cutoff point between modest and substantial malignancy at a stock–advice ratio of 3.7 (rather than 3.5) could also be justified on distributional grounds. This change would reduce the malignancy score of two cases from substantial to modest levels, which again would remove the third, collaboration-driven success path in statement A. Such removal would result whether we applied the more valid robustness test (involving only strong cases) or the alternative approach that involves all cases and considers a 40 percent distance or more as insignificant problem solving. Again, the analysis of paths to failure would yield the same result: the third term in the failure statement E would have no strong cases but would enter the minimization as a reasonable simplifying assumption.

The findings are also robust to modifications of urgency and collaboration codings. Reducing the spawning stock threshold between modest and substantial urgency levels from 500,000 to 460,000 tons—the latter is the more recent ICES (2003, 12) precautionary target—would not alter any coding and therefore would not change any of the analysis above. No other adjustment of urgency thresholds would be reasonable (see appendix 4). A more fine-grained differentiation among the cases involving high quota transfers relative to the quota would most reasonably place the threshold to substantial collaboration at 30 percent. That would depress the collaboration scores from substantial to modest levels for two years in the late 1980s but would not affect the findings on reliable paths to regulatory success or failure.

The findings above are also robust to strategic removal of those years that constitute individual strong cases of either a success path or a failure path, as 1989 was for success and 1984, 1993, 1994, and 2004 were for failure. Of these, only removal of 1984 would affect the findings, and then only slightly so: the rather depressing first reliable path to failure in statement E, which indicates the impotency of the two regime-driven factors in the face of severe malignancy and low urgency, would no longer have any strong case in the dataset, and no theoretically stronger actual case would justify its inclusion as a simplifying assumption. The effect would be to narrow the first reliable path to failure in statement F, which would require, in addition to full malignancy and insignificant urgency, scores of zero on either collaboration or knowledge.

In short, the findings in this section on reliable paths to regulatory success or failure would not change much even if we were to opt for other reasonable ways of coding the outcome and the causal factors or undertook strategic removal of scarce strong cases of the paths in question. The collaboration-driven path to success is sensitive to the coding of problem solving and malignancy; an alternative but less valid approach to the coding of knowledge would similarly narrow one success path and remove one path to failure.

Summary
The comparative analysis identifies two factors not readily under regime influence as crucial for explaining variation in regulatory problem solving under the Barents Sea fisheries regime, but regime-driven factors also matter. Thus, all reliable paths to regulatory success include low regulatory malignancy, and the combination of severe malignancy and low urgency proves lethal to regulatory problem solving even when counteracted by regime-induced strong knowledge and deep collaboration.

As long as malignancy is low, however, the characteristics of the two regime-driven factors are highly significant for regulatory problem solving. Low scores on both knowledge and collaboration are certain to yield failure unless urgency is high.[7] In contrast, a strong recent record of forecasting accuracy induces managers to keep quotas reasonably close to scientific advice, regardless of the level of urgency and collaboration. Even without such accuracy, the combination of high urgency and deep collaboration, through quota transfers or the harvest control rule, reliably yields regulatory success, provided malignancy is low.[8]

The four-factor model does a better job of accounting for regulatory success than does the model in chapter 4 for forecasting accuracy, covering consistently more than half of the regulatory problem solving in the dataset and around 60 percent of the failure. The paths to regulatory success and failure prove very useful for estimating the most plausible levels of problem solving that would pertain if the regime had not existed, which is necessary for assessing regulatory effectiveness.

Assessing Regulatory Effectiveness

The effectiveness of the Barents Sea fisheries regime in bringing coastal state quota regulations more in line with the best available scientific advice has been significant in most years since 1984 and generally high in the period from 1989 through 1997, but thereafter low or insignificant. Unlike cognitional effectiveness, which improved markedly over the timeline, regulatory effectiveness was significantly lower during the second half of the period under study than during the first half.

These findings emerge from the combination developed in this book of counterfactual path analysis and the Oslo-Potsdam effectiveness yardstick. Counterfactual path analysis proceeds by examining the fit between the counterfactual antecedents—the combinations of causal properties that would pertain if the regime had not existed—and the reliable paths to success or failure. Chapter 2 explained and justified the following simple decision rules. First, in years when actual problem solving is insignificant or the regime fails to influence any of the causal factors, the most plausible counterfactual estimate is the same as the actual score. Second, whenever the counterfactual path fits a reliable success or failure path, the fit score places a lower or upper bound on the plausible counterfactual estimates. And third, whenever the counterfactual path analysis leaves more than one plausible option, my choice is based on the number of causal factors that are weaker in the counterfactual case than in the actual case—that is, factors with scores empirically shown to be less conducive.

To illustrate how this procedure yields determinate and empirically based estimates of counterfactual problem-solving scores, we may consider the year 1984. The counterfactual collaboration score is lower than in the actual case because the regime allowed substantial transfers of cod quotas to the regulatory laggard, Norway. The combination of modest scores on collaboration and urgency with full scores on malignancy and knowledge implies substantial fit (a score of 0.67) with one of the reliable failure paths—the one that combines full malignancy with insignificant urgency. Thus, any failure estimate below 0.67 would contradict the pattern among actual cases; and since problem solving is the negation of failure, this finding places an upper bound on plausible problem-solving estimates at a modest level (1 − 0.67 = 0.33). That leaves two plausible options: modest or insignificant problem solving. Since the regime has altered only one causal factor (collaboration), and the actual problem-solving score that year is modest, the lower option is the most plausible counterfactual problem-solving estimate. The counterfactual paths and their scores on the success and failure paths for all years in the timeline are given in appendix 5.

This 1984 estimate based on counterfactual path analysis and the extent of causal path influence is firmly supported by process-tracing evidence from the negotiation of the 1984 quota, as reported above. First, as in preceding years, Norway entered the talks with a quota preference considerably higher than that of the Soviet side. Second, Norway accepted the agreed-upon quotas only after receiving a quota transfer of 40,000 tons each year. Third, until then Norway had insisted on a right under the regime to allow coastal vessels with passive gear (nets, longlines, handlines, etc.) to continue harvesting after the quota had been taken—this despite considerable Soviet pressure, clear ICES advice, and evidence that these fisheries had in some years pushed catches well beyond the highest ICES option (see chapter 6 for details). Norway's high initial quota positions, its requests for large quota transfers, and its general unwillingness to constrain its coastal vessels all indicate that a Norwegian unilateral quota would have been considerably higher than the levels agreed to under the regime. Fourth, partly because historical fishing practice is an important criterion for allocation in many international fisheries regimes (Stokke 2000), the Soviet Union had raised its cod catches to Norway's level in the years prior to the formation of the present regime in the 1970s (ICES 2001, 9), which indicates that, if there had been no regime, it would most probably have matched Norway's unilateral quotas. A final consideration is that additional quotas for each state of no more than 40,000 tons would reduce the level of problem solving from modest to insignificant. Thus, the finding from the counterfactual path analysis is highly compatible with process-tracing evidence based on the positions taken by the two states during the quota talks.

Table 5.1 reports such counterfactual path analysis for each year under study as well as the resulting counterfactual problem-solving estimates. Thereafter the table gives the regulatory effectiveness scores that derive from imputing the actual problem-solving scores and the corresponding counterfactual estimates into the Oslo-Potsdam formula, calculating for each year the ratio of actual improvement to potential improvement.

The table shows the Barents Sea fisheries regime to be ineffective in regulatory terms in ten out of the twenty-five years under study. Moreover, performance declines over time: the summarized effectiveness score achieved during the first twelve years is 4.16, whereas the corresponding score for the last twelve years is 3.16, around 25 percent lower. Figure 5.7 provides more details on the variation in the regime's regulatory effectiveness from 1980 to 2004.

A concise, substantive summary of these findings on the regulatory effectiveness of the Barents Sea fisheries regime regarding Northeast Arctic cod would highlight the following. Through 1983, the regime failed to influence the drivers of problem solving, or the effect was insufficient to raise problem solving above the most plausible counterfactual level. Thereafter, however, and for most years up to 1997, the regime accounted for a significant part of the regulatory success, first because of quota transfers to the regulatory laggard, Norway, and then because of a conducive effect on the reported accuracy of stock forecasts, which made scientific advice more credible and persuasive.

During the mid-1980s the levels of problem solving would most likely have been rather high even without the regime, owing to a combination of low malignancy (fish availability was low compared to the quotas) and high urgency (the stock was reported to be below biological thresholds). Toward the end of that decade, and especially in the early 1990s, the regime became more important for regulatory success, as rising malignancy would otherwise have constrained the level of problem solving. Regulatory effectiveness was particularly high in the mid-1990s, when several years of reassuring spawning stock reports had removed urgency as a problem-solving driver and, combined with low malignancy, created very difficult conditions for those seeking to keep quotas within scientific recommendations. The high level of regulatory success achieved in this period is impressive: it can best be explained by the regime's ability to raise the reported accuracy of stock forecasts and thereby the persuasiveness of scientific advice.

Toward the end of the 1990s, unfortunately, the regime's contribution to the state of knowledge was shattered by a major ecosystem shift, yielding low scores on regulatory problem solving despite low malignancy. From the turn of that decade, the combination of rising malignancy and rising urgency rendered the counterfactual path less determinate. Regime effectiveness remained insignificant or low in this period, and was modest in 2002 and 2003 as a result of regulatory collaboration in the form of a long-term harvest control rule.

Table 5.1
Regulatory Effectiveness Analysis

| Actual Problem Solving | | Counterfactual Problem Solving | | Effectiveness Score |
Year	Score	Substantiation	Estimate	
1980	1	No regime influence on drivers of problem solving	1	IR
1981	0.33	No regime influence on drivers of problem solving	0.33	0
1982–83	0.33	Counterfactual path analysis identifies 0.33 as lowest plausible estimate	0.33	0
1984–85	0.33	Counterfactual path analysis narrows range to 0.33–0; option below actual score chosen since collaboration is weaker	0	0.33
1986	0.67	Counterfactual path analysis narrows range to 1–0.33; option below actual score chosen since both collaboration and knowledge are weaker	0.33	0.5
1987	1	Counterfactual path analysis identifies 1 as lowest plausible estimate	1	IR
1988	0.67	Counterfactual path analysis identifies 0.67 as lowest plausible estimate	0.67	0
1989	1	Counterfactual path analysis narrows range to 1–0.33; mid-option chosen since only collaboration is weaker than in actual case	0.67	1
1990	1	Counterfactual path analysis is indeterminate; 0.33 chosen since both collaboration and knowledge are weaker than in actual case	0.33	1
1991	1	Counterfactual path analysis narrows range to 1–0.33; mid-option chosen since knowledge only is weaker than in actual case	0.67	1

Table 5.1
(continued)

Actual Problem Solving		Counterfactual Problem Solving		Effectiveness Score
Year	Score	Substantiation	Estimate	
1992	0.67	Counterfactual path analysis narrows range to 0.33–0; higher option chosen since only knowledge is weaker than in actual case	0.33	0.5
1993	0.33	No regime influence on drivers of problem solving	0.33	0
1994	0.67	Counterfactual path analysis narrows range to 0.33–0; highest option chosen since only knowledge is weaker than in actual case	0.33	0.5
1995	0.67	Counterfactual path analysis narrows range to 0.67–0.33; option below actual score chosen since knowledge is weaker	0.33	0.5
1996	1	Counterfactual path analysis narrows range to 1–0.33; mid-option chosen since only knowledge is weaker than in actual case	0.67	1
1997	0.67	Counterfactual path analysis is indeterminate; 0.33 chosen since knowledge (and no other factor) is weaker than in actual case	0.33	0.5
1998–99	0.33	No regime influence on drivers of problem solving	0.33	0
2000	0	No regime influence on drivers of problem solving; and insignificant score even in actual case	0	0
2001	0.33	Counterfactual path analysis identifies 0.33 as lowest plausible estimate	0.33	0
2002	0.33	Counterfactual path analysis is indeterminate; option below actual score chosen since collaboration is weaker	0	0.33

Table 5.1
(continued)

Actual Problem Solving		Counterfactual Problem Solving		Effectiveness Score
Year	Score	Substantiation	Estimate	
2003	0.33	Counterfactual path analysis narrows range to 0.67–0; option below actual score chosen since collaboration is weaker	0	0.33
2004	0.33	Counterfactual path analysis yields point estimate	0.33	0

Note: Scores: 1 = full; 0.67 = substantial; 0.5 = medium; 0.33 = modest; 0 = insignificant; IR = irrelevant. Counterfactual paths and their fit with success and failure paths are listed in appendix 5, table A5.2. Effectiveness scores are calculated by the Oslo-Potsdam formula.

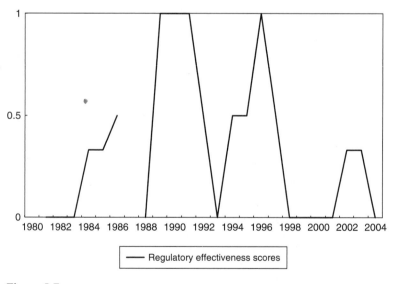

Figure 5.7
Regulatory effectiveness scores. Line discontinuities in 1980 and 1987 indicate that the regime was irrelevant in those years.

The counterfactual path analysis underlying these findings is empirically based insofar as it uses process-tracing evidence when specifying the most plausible causal properties that would pertain had the regime not existed and uses proven paths to regulatory success or failure when estimating the most plausible counterfactual level of problem solving.

Summary and Implications

The aspect of resource management dealt with in this chapter is the regulatory aspect—reaching agreement on conservation measures that reflect the best available knowledge on how current resource use will affect future availability. In the Northeast Atlantic, this standard gives a central place to ICES, which provides authoritative advice to numerous international fisheries management bodies, including the Joint Commission. On the scale developed here, full regulatory problem solving means that the fisheries managers heed the ICES recommendations, whereas a quota in excess of the highest advised ICES option returns an insignificant score. In between those scores, problem solving is modest or substantial, depending on the distance from the recommendation. Whereas the Joint Commission has only once exceeded the highest ICES option, regulatory problem solving was low in the first half of the 1980s and in most of the years after 1997.

The disaggregate approach to regime effectiveness proceeds by building a causal model capable of accounting well for such variation in regulatory problem solving. The model developed here combines a factor relating to cognitional processes, the state of knowledge about the stock in question, and three factors deriving from the rationalist mainstream of regime analysis. Those three are malignancy (here, the availability of cod relative to the recommendation), regulatory collaboration in the form of a mutually beneficial quota exchange or joint planning, and urgency arising from a dangerously low spawning stock. Of the causal factors, only the state of knowledge and collaboration are readily and traceably under regime influence.

Based on this causal model, QCA analysis of the empirical data helped identify configurations of causal properties that reliably deliver either high or low levels of problem solving under the Barents Sea fisheries regime. Regulatory success is reliable only when malignancy is low, and even then only if the state of knowledge is strong or if deep regulatory collaboration is reinforced by high urgency. With severe malignancy, only high urgency can prevent reliable failure. These reliable paths are robust and consistently cover around 55 percent of the regulatory success in the period under study and some 60 percent of the regulatory failure. They support the effectiveness analysis by helping to narrow the range of plausible counterfactual problem-solving estimates whenever the counterfactual antecedents—the causal factor properties that would pertain if the regime had not existed—fit to some extent either a failure path or a success path. The Oslo-Potsdam effectiveness yardstick combines such estimates with the levels of actual problem solving and their distances, if any, from the highest score.

We have seen that regime-driven factors, at first regulatory collaboration but later also the state of knowledge, have triggered significant regulatory effectiveness in most of the years from 1984 to 1997. The regime has also improved the conditions for problem solving in the last period studied, but only on a few occasions enough to counteract sharply rising malignancy. As regards collaboration, the basis for large-scale quota exchange disappeared when the Northwest Russian fishing industry began to exploit Western markets in the years immediately before the dissolution of the Soviet Union. Through most of the 1990s, therefore, the Barents Sea fisheries regime affected quota levels primarily by improving the state of knowledge, and thus the credibility of scientific advice. More recently, joint planning by means of a long-term harvest control rule has fostered the return of regulatory collaboration.

Important as legally binding, agreed-upon quotas are for effective international resource management, regulatory effectiveness does not amount to *regime* effectiveness. Chapter 2 argued that such regime outputs indicate regime dynamism and are usually a necessary condition for effectiveness. Unless conservation measures also affect behavior among the ultimate target groups, however, regime dynamism will be to little avail. In the next chapter, we turn to the relationship between regulatory problem solving and fisher behavior.

6
Behavioral Effectiveness

The behavioral problem in focus for international regimes is to ensure that international rules really influence the actions of the target groups—those that engage in the activities regulated by the regime. Examining target-group impact, as this chapter does, is fundamental to the analysis of regime effectiveness since neither cognitional nor regulatory effectiveness will matter to resource management if there is no effect on the activities that exert pressure on the resource in question.

The disaggregate approach to international regime effectiveness developed in chapter 2 revolves around counterfactual path analysis and the Oslo-Potsdam yardstick, which measures effectiveness as the ratio of the actual improvement on a hypothetical no-regime situation to the potential improvement—or the distance from full problem solving. That is why the first section specifies the behavioral problem and identifies an appropriate standard for measuring degrees of problem solving and for defining what would constitute a full score: no practical deviation from the agreed-upon rules for behavior.

Both parameters of my effectiveness yardstick refer to the most plausible level of problem solving that would pertain in the hypothetical no-regime situation. Substantiating that counterfactual estimate requires a good account of the variation in problem solving among actual cases. Drawing on earlier work as well as on the general mechanisms identified by regime-effectiveness scholars, I develop a causal model that reflects utilitarian and normative considerations on the part of target groups and member states. As in previous chapters, malignancy is among the explanatory factors; others are legal obligation, behavioral transparency, and shaming. The model structures the fuzzy set qualitative comparative analysis (QCA), which reveals causal combinations that reliably deliver behavioral success (high quota adherence), as well as combinations that reliably produce failure. Conceptualizing cases at the state level rather than at the regime level generates more observations than in chapters 4 and 5, which in turn permits various statistical procedures to complement the comparative analysis and support the findings.

The reliable paths to behavioral success or failure help simplify the counterfactual analysis and place it on a firm empirical footing. Rather than immediately tackling the difficult question of what levels of problem solving would be plausible had the regime not existed, the disaggregate approach begins with the easier question of what the properties of the causal factors would be—the counterfactual antecedent. Analysis of those hypothetical paths, notably whether they fit any of the reliable paths to success or failure, helps narrow down the range of plausible counterfactual problem-solving estimates, thereby supporting the assessment of behavioral effectiveness.

The Problem: Keeping Catches within Quotas

Ever since national quotas were introduced as a major instrument in international fisheries management, quota overfishing has been quite common in the Barents Sea and elsewhere. Data are available for a slightly longer period than in the preceding chapters, so this section traces regime impacts on problem solving up to 2006.[1] I first explain why distance from national quotas can provide a good yardstick for measuring behavioral problem solving, then use variation in quota adherence to scale the yardstick, and finally show how Norway and the Soviet Union/Russia have performed on the scale.

Both the quotas and the scientific advice are relevant for evaluating the harvesting pressure exerted by fishers, but in this chapter the latter plays only a modest role, for two reasons. First, scientific advice is essential in the yardstick for *regulatory* problem solving, so using it here would blur the distinction between two aspects of resource management. Second, unlike its cognitional and regulatory counterparts, the yardstick for behavioral problem solving should be applicable at the state rather than at the regime level since the two states have differed considerably over time in their quota adherence and in their scores on several of the explanatory factors. Thus, any effect of *one* state's quota overfishing on the overall compatibility with the ICES option range will depend on catches by the other state(s). In the early 1980s, for instance, the Soviet Union frequently took less than its post-transfer quotas, which served to soften the sustainability impact of severe Norwegian overfishing;

but such softening cannot validly affect the other party's problem-solving score.

Instead, I opt for a solution that mirrors the procedure for grading cognitional problem solving: it differentiates among cases according to the percentage distance of national catches from quotas and uses the highest ICES option as a qualitative anchor for evaluating the threshold placement.

The data underlying figures 6.1a and 6.1b below, which I use to scale the yardstick, are the best available and are used by ICES in its stock assessment work, but parts of the data have been contested by Russia. Whereas the pattern of over- and underfishing of quotas in the 1980s derives from undisputed official landings, the data underlying the dotted line from 1990 include a somewhat rough ascription of Russia's share of the total unreported catches estimated by ICES (2007, 23) in the period to two-thirds. That share corresponds to the information given by the Norwegian fisheries minister when revealing the findings from the NorwegianCoast Guard study of unreported catches that underlies the ICES estimates.[2] The Coast Guard had expanded its scope of control when inspecting Russian vessels by scrutinizing and registering logbook information not only for zones where Norway claims jurisdiction but also for the Russian Exclusive Economic Zone (EEZ) and the Grey Zone (Hønneland 2006, 51). Russia accepted the thrust of this information and soon indicated its readiness to work together with Norway in tackling this overfishing scandal, which triggered the creation of the Permanent Committee for Management and Enforcement.[3]

In contrast, Russia has partly contested the information underlying figures 6.1a and 6.1b concerning the level of Russian overfishing in the 2000s. That information is based on annual studies by the Norwegian Fisheries Directorate, which combined data on landings and satellite tracking evidence of the movements of fishing and transport vessels from the fishing grounds to the main ports with estimates of vessel storage capacity derived from inspections and vessel registers (Norway, Office of the Auditor General 2007, 32–51; Norway, Directorate of Fisheries 2008). Because of uncertainties as to loading extent, species composition, and the mix of filleted and head-and-gutted products, these estimates of unreported catches should be treated with some caution. Russia (Russia 2007, 207–210) considers them to be too high, but has acknowledged that its vessels did undertake substantial unreported fishing in the period. In sum, these data remain the best available information on the amounts

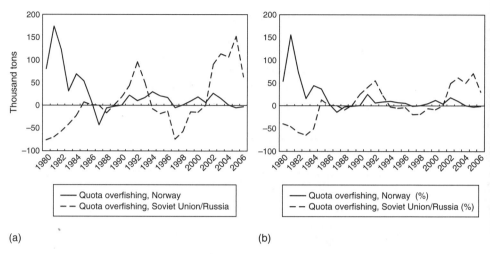

(a)   (b)

Figure 6.1

Overfishing of national quotas, Northeast Arctic cod.

6.1a: Overfishing (in thousands of tons) occurred at different times for Norway and the Soviet Union/Russia and had different drivers. 6.1.b: Overfishing as percentage of quota. Catch data from ICES (2008a); data on quotas, including transfers, from annual JCF protocols.

of quota overfishing, as is evident in their use by the ICES in assessment work and statistical publications (Stokke 2009).

In figure 6.1a this information is used to plot the overfishing of post-transfer quotas by Norway and the Soviet Union/Russia, in thousands of tons. A line that dips below the horizontal axis indicates that catches have been lower than the quota. To help scale my behavioral problem-solving yardstick, figure 6.1b plots this overfishing as a percentage of states' respective quotas. Of the fifty-four observations, twenty-eight exceed the national quota by more than 1 percent. The latter figure reasonably qualifies as full behavioral problem solving.

The placement of thresholds for allocating the twenty-eight cases involving overfishing by more than 1 percent proceeds by a mixture of quantitative and qualitative considerations. Thresholds implying an insignificant score if overfishing exceeds 30 percent, a modest score from that level to 15 percent, and a substantial score from that level to 1 percent (the full-score threshold) are reasonable from the quantitative curve-steepness and category-size criteria, and remain reasonable after the highest ICES option is used as a qualitative anchor. Actual total catches of Northeast Arctic cod exceeded the highest option in around one-fifth of the years in this study. If one party overfished the quota by 14 percent—the worst performance still receiving a substantial problem-solving score—that would push the total catches beyond the highest ICES option far less frequently, in around one-sixth of the years. Conversely, overfishing at 29 percent—the best performance qualifying for a modest score—would do so considerably more frequently than in the actual case, in around one-fourth of the years. Thus, problem-solving thresholds at 30 percent, 15 percent, and 1 percent of quota overfishing are in line with the quantitative criteria and allow high scores to be reserved for cases that jeopardize stock replenishment considerably less frequently than Norwegian and Russian fishers have done under the Barents Sea fisheries regime. The exact behavioral problem-solving scores are given in appendix 5, tables A5.3 and A5.4.

To summarize, only in the late 1980s and the late 1990s did both states achieve high scores on behavioral problem solving. Norway performed poorly during the early 1980s, as did Russia a decade later and toward the end of the period under study. As the next section shows, Norway's period of severe overfishing involved its coastal vessel sector, whereas Russia's overfishing occurred because the regime's compliance system had not yet adapted to the radical changes that had occurred in the organization and management of the Northwest Russian fisheries industry.

Modeling Behavioral Problem Solving

This section specifies a causal model to account for the variation in behavioral problem solving concerning catch levels of Northeast Arctic cod. I build the model by first examining more closely the cases that involve severe quota overfishing and then relating salient features of those cases to earlier studies of how international institutions, through their influence on state action, can affect target-group behavior. Among the distinctive features cognitional of this model is the combination of factors derived from cognitional, utilitarian, and normative regime effectiveness mechanisms: malignancy, obligation, shaming, and transparency.

The first of three waves of severe behavioral failure under the Barents Sea fisheries regime involved very substantial quota overfishing by Norwegian coastal vessels during the early 1980s—which, unusually, did not clearly constitute a violation of regime norms. As part of the compromise on how Norway and the Soviet Union were to divide their shared cod quota under the new Law of the Sea, an important regime provision allowed fishers using passive gear (such as gill nets, longlines, and handlines) to continue harvesting even after the quota had been taken (JCF 1979, item. 6). Although in principle neutral, since the exemption applied to both sides, this provision clearly benefited Norway, as only Norway has a substantial passive gear sector in the region. The exemption implied an acknowledgment that regulatory precision is difficult to achieve with respect to a large and diverse coastal fleet with great annual variation in the number of participants in the fishery and in the availability of cod near the coastline.

Since the passive gear sector predominates in Norway's cod fisheries, this exemption greatly reduced the determinacy of the annual quota agreement. The provision became highly problematic with the sharp quota cuts that began in 1980 and coincided with an unusually high availability of cod near the coast (Christensen and Hallenstvedt 2005, 255). As figure 6.1b shows, Norway's catches were more than twice its quota in 1981; overfishing was very high in other years as well, despite large quota transfers. From the Soviet perspective, such excessive catches threatened the recovery of a regionally important stock but also provided a weighty argument for changing the user rights inherent in the regime's passive gear exemption. After several years of Soviet diplomatic pressure, Norway finally agreed to a more stringent regime provision on passive gear. Another factor that helped reduce and then eliminate Norway's quota overfishing in this period was the significant rise in total quota levels from 1986.

A second wave of quota overfishing, this time largely by Russian vessels, began around 1990 and resulted from the major reshuffling of the Northwest Russian fishing industry as part of the larger perestroika process. Incorporation of the Murmansk-based fishing industry into the global market economy took off in this period, with rapidly increasing landings in Western ports. Several factors drove this development, which lessened the ability of the Russian authorities to monitor harvesting activities and determine compliance with national regulations.

For one thing, the dismantlement of the huge Soviet-era fisheries complex Sevryba loosened the ties between the harvesting fleet and the Murmansk-based processing industry. A second factor was the growing inability of Russian processors to pay for fish. Sevryba had organized most of the regional fisheries industry, including fishing fleets, transportation vessels, tankers, and various onshore functions such as shipyards, port facilities, processing plants, and construction works (Stokke, Anderson, and Mirovitskaya 1999, 95–97). In 1992, after several reorganizations, this huge association was privatized and converted to a joint-stock company. Its component parts soon became independent entities, and new private companies emerged alongside them (Hønneland 2004). Especially in the transitional years, there were no well-functioning markets in place to fill the gap created by the breakdown of vertical organization: perestroika had removed an old engine without installing a new one (Kotov 1994). High inflation had deprived many Northwest Russians of their savings, slashing real incomes and thus considerably weakening the domestic pull of demand in production and distribution. The Murmansk-based processing industry found itself totally unable to compete with its Norwegian counterparts for Russian cod, and was reportedly operating at half capacity or less through 1993 (*Fishing News International*, February 1994, 5; see also Hønneland and Nilssen 2001, 477). A third factor emerged in the second half of the 1990s, as jurisdictional turf struggles and legal complexity in Russia's fisheries enforcement apparatus made domestic landings highly time-consuming and costly endeavors that vessels sought to avoid (Hønneland 2004, 138).

For a growing number of reasons, therefore, Russian vessel operators chose to land more and more of their catch abroad, at first mostly in Norway. That meant that many Russian vessels were no longer subject to the traditional means of monitoring fishing activities, by comparison of fisher reports and recipient reports from domestic processing units. Suspicions arose in Norwegian fisheries quarters concerning the validity of Russian reports of actual landings and triggered the more extensive Coast Guard control of Russian logbook information that exposed the quota overfishing that had taken place in the early 1990s.

Yet another wave of behavioral failure occurred in the 2000s, again closely related to Russian direct landings of Northeast Arctic cod in foreign ports. Whereas deeper collaboration between the fisheries enforcement agencies in Norway and Russia had improved information flows about landings in Norway, the more recent foreign landings had been taking place in third-country ports, in Germany, Spain, the UK, and other EU states. They increasingly involved at-sea transshipment from Russian trawlers to transport vessels, further compounding the problem of monitoring actual catches (Stokke 2009). A joint report by the Norwegian and Russian enforcement agencies concluded that nearly half of the transshipments observed by the Norwegian Coast Guard in 2001 concerned fish that had not been reported to the Russian authorities and that therefore had not been included in the quota count (Ulvatn et al. 2006, 170).

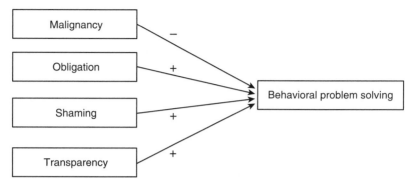

Figure 6.2
Causal model of behavioral problem solving.

This closer look at the ups and downs of quota overfishing directs attention to several factors that loom large in the regime-effectiveness literature (see chapter 2): the availability of the resource relative to the quota, which indicates a *malignancy* problem; the nature of regime *obligations*; the role of the regime as a venue for criticism and *shaming* of member states; and the role of the regime in shaping the *transparency* of harvesting operations to those who monitor compliance with agreed regulations. In figure 6.2 I use those factors to model behavioral problem solving, stating the hypotheses that severe malignancy will impede behavioral success, whereas high scores on obligation, shaming, and transparency are drivers of success.

The remainder of this section builds on earlier contributions on regime effectiveness to specify these causal variables, substantiating for each case the actual score as well as the most plausible counterfactual score.

Malignancy
Individual incentives to violate agreed-upon standards are no less relevant to behavioral problem solving than they proved to be for the cognitional and regulatory aspects of problem solving. Malignancy denotes incongruity between an actor's share of the overall benefits from an activity and the actor's share of the overall costs (Underdal 1987; see chapter 2). In periods of very low quotas for Northeast Arctic cod, incongruity by competition was evident in claims made by the Northwest Russian fisheries industry that quotas had been set artificially low— allegedly because scheming, wealthy Norwegians were seeking to strangle the Russian industry and subsequently appropriate a greater part of

the resources (see Hønneland 2003). More recently, Russian as well as Norwegian industry representatives have similarly warned that harvesting restraint on the part of vessel owners who play by the rules only enhances the profitability of illegal harvesting in the region (Stokke 2009, 342).

This chapter examines the role of malignancy in the same way as in the study of cognitional effectiveness, by relating the size of the commercial stock to the size of the quota. A large commercial stock usually implies great availability, so a high stock to quota ratio means that fishers are asked to take considerably less cod than they would if not constrained by national quotas. That situation provides strong incentive for fishers to violate domestic regulations and take more than they report to their national authorities. Thus, the cognitional malignancy scores plotted in figure 4.3 are also valid for behavioral malignancy.

As in chapters 4 and 5, the most plausible *counterfactual* malignancy estimates, which help substantiate the level of problem solving that would pertain without the regime, are the same as the actual scores. True, with respect to the quota part of the ratio, chapter 5 showed that the most plausible counterfactual quotas would often be higher than those agreed upon within the Joint Commission on Fisheries, but that is not sufficient basis for specifying for each year exactly how much. As before, moreover, any attempt to specify a different no-regime level of the commercial stock, which depends on numerous factors fully or largely beyond human control, would stretch the evidence. Accordingly, figure 6.3 gives the criteria for differentiating malignancy, reproduces the actual and counterfactual malignancy scores from chapter 4, and adds the scores derived from the stock–quota ratios in 2005–2006.

Thus, behavioral malignancy is especially great in the early and mid-1980s, in the first half of the 1990s, and in the final part of the period studied. The face validity of this explanatory factor is substantial since those periods correspond to the years when quota overfishing was severe, but the fact that the coastal states reacted so differently to the shared circumstances suggests that other factors should also be considered.

Obligation
In international law and in political science, the legal bindingness of a norm and its determinacy (how clearly it communicates what the subject is expected to do) are considered important for the ability of the norm to influence behavioral problem solving. The yardstick of obligation developed in chapter 2 was built on those dimensions: obligation is deemed

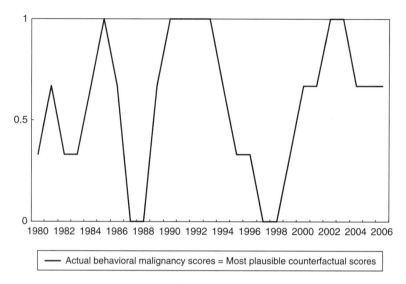

Figure 6.3
Behavioral malignancy scores. 1 = full = severe incongruity, owing to very high relative availability; 0.67 = substantial = large incongruity, owing to high relative availability; 0.33 = modest = some incongruity, owing to medium relative availability, but mostly synergy; 0 = insignificant = no significant incongruity, owing to low relative availability. Thresholds between severe, large, some, and no incongruity are relative availability ratios at 3.8, 2.8, and 2.1.

full if norms are highly determinate and legally binding, substantial if norms are legally binding with medium determinacy or politically binding with high determinacy, modest if norms are legally binding with low determinacy, and insignificant if no international norm applies.

The regulations adopted annually by the Joint Commission are legally binding unless a state opts out within two months. Accordingly, for the Soviet Union and later Russia, the highly precise annual quota agreement has implied full obligation throughout the period under study. For Norway, in contrast, the passive gear exemption for many years kept the level of obligation modest: the agreed-upon regulation was highly imprecise as to what levels of passive gear overfishing were acceptable. The obligation was never insignificant, however, since neither party saw the provision as offering carte blanche to overfish the national quota. Of note in this regard is the response by Norway's fisheries minister to a query in the Storting in 1981 concerning stricter domestic measures on passive gear:

During the negotiations on a quota for Northeast Arctic cod, great emphasis has been placed on retaining the opportunity to continue the fisheries with passive gear after the total quota has been taken. Such a provision requires, however, that the excess catches are kept within reasonable limits.[4]

Similarly, the Joint Commission's protocol records that the Soviet side expressed "serious concern over the significant Norwegian overfishing of its 1981 quota due to the fisheries with net, line, and hand gear and raised the issue of a need for regulation of the fisheries with these gear types within the national quotas" (JCF 1981, item 4.2). The Norwegian obligation score in the early years of the regime, therefore, remained modest up to the agreement, applicable from 1984, that passive gear fishing "should be limited by both parties, taking into consideration the agreed-upon quotas and the state of the stock" (JCF 1983, item 5.2; my translation). Norwegian media emphasized the hortatory language ("should"), which leaves some legal room for continued harvesting (*Nordlys*, 19 November 1983, 1; *Nordlys*, 6 November 1984, 1, 7), but the clause that had explicitly permitted continued fishing was no longer a part of the agreement. Thus, from 1984 a substantial score on obligation is reasonable, which means relatively determinate and legally binding quotas.

Since the 1998 season, the two states have settled on a formulation that leaves no doubt about the substantive contents and thus raises obligation to full score also for Norway: "Fishing with net, line and hand gear shall be conducted within the quotas set by the parties" (JCF 1997, item 5.1; my translation).

When specifying the regime's effect on the level of obligation, the most plausible *counterfactual* situation is not a legal vacuum but two states managing the shared stock without the means for precise commitment that the annual protocols provide. The most plausible counterfactual scores, as the dashed line in figure 6.4 shows, are modest for both states throughout the period. Even without the regime, Norway and Russia would have been committed under the Law of the Sea Convention to "ensure through proper conservation and management measures that the maintenance of the living resources in the exclusive economic zone is not endangered by over-exploitation" (Article 61), with similar provisions concerning high seas areas (Article 119). The linkage from that general commitment to any specific quota level is too vague to qualify as substantial, however.

Obligation, then, reflects substantive determinacy and formal bindingness and is full for Russia throughout the period under study. For Norway, the passive gear exemption rendered obligation modest through 1983, then substantial through 1997, and full thereafter. Global norms

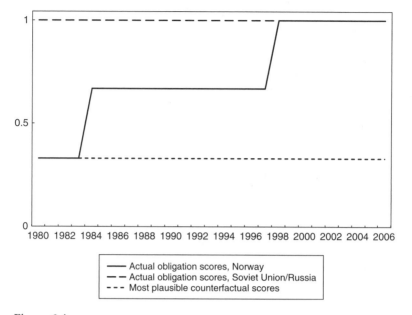

Figure 6.4
Obligation scores. 1 = full = international norm is determinate and legally binding; 0.67 = substantial = international norm is determinate and politically binding; 0.33 = modest = international norm is indeterminate and legally binding; 0 = insignificant = no applicable international norm. Determinacy refers to textual precision or procedures for rule interpretation; politically binding norms include international soft law and unilateral declarations.

imply that the most plausible counterfactual obligation score is modest for both states throughout the period.

Shaming
During each of the three periods of substantial quota overfishing of Northeast Arctic cod, the other party engaged in shaming, or explicit criticism aimed at improving performance. Shaming is a relatively mild form of pressure, as it involves no material reward, punishment, or coercion. Social exposure is at the core of shaming and reflects the conceptual proximity to embarrassment: while embarrassment refers to deviation from one's self-conception, shame concerns deviation from a more widely shared norm (Keltner and Buswell 1997). As noted by Hveem (1970, 58), such criticism can be expected to influence another state's policy more if the sender is generally more powerful than the target yet politically close, and if the "blame behavior," as he terms it, is intensive, sincere, and related to an issue that is salient to the target. Elsewhere (Stokke

2004a, 2007c) I have pointed out that an international regime facilitates shaming when it provides the venue, the standards, or the behavioral transparency that a shamer needs for articulating and justifying criticism; little influence is to be expected if, among other things, malignancy is high or the level of obligation is low.

A simple way to grade shaming is to start from the two basic elements, the criticism and the target. Full shaming combines harsh criticism and explicit naming of the target, whereas substantial shaming is either softer in its criticism or implicitly locates the target within a broader category of actors. Modest shaming means soft criticism of an implicit target, as in the JCF (1993, item 11.1) statement that "Parties agree on the need to strengthen the level of control over Barents Sea fisheries" (my translation) in conjunction with a series of measures aimed at improving transparency concerning the Russian harvesting. An insignificant score is appropriate whenever no state articulates criticism of another's behavior under the regime.

These criteria imply that Soviet shaming of Norway's passive gear excesses in the early 1980s began modestly but soon sharpened. By not referring explicitly to Norway's quota overfishing but calling publicly for more stringent regulation of the Lofoten fishery for the large, spawning cod and for removal of the passive gear exemption, the Soviet commissioner engaged in what would be called modest shaming prior to the 1980 season (*Nordlys*, 2 November 1979, 1). As is evident in the quotation above from the fisheries minister's statement to the Norwegian Storting, passive gear harvesting in excess of the quota was again an issue in the subsequent year, but the Soviet commissioner refrained from including the criticism in the protocol from that meeting.

From the talks prior to the1982 season, in contrast, the commissioner engaged in full shaming by expressing in the protocol "serious concern over the significant Norwegian overfishing" (JCF 1981, item 4.2; 1982, item 4.2; 1983, item 4; my translation). The fisheries media covering the negotiations for 1983 described the Soviet criticism as "very harsh" (*Nordlys*, 16 November 1982, 1, 10; my translation). After the passive gear provision was strengthened, that criticism softened somewhat, with the commissioner merely expressing "concern" over the "significant Norwegian quota overfishing" (JCF 1984, item 3; 1985, item 3). Although such overfishing also occurred the next year, any Soviet criticism went unrecorded in the protocol.

The issue reappeared on the Joint Commission's agenda only in the final few years of the period under study, following changes in Norway's domestic regulations that resulted in substantial quota overfishing (JCF

2004, item 4; 2005, item 4). From a soft start, therefore, the external shaming of Norway's performance activities warrants high scores from 1982 to 1986 and toward the end of the timeline, as plotted by the solid line in figure 6.5 below.

Norway's shaming of Russia's quota overfishing during the 1990s and 2000s was never as harsh as the earlier Soviet criticism had been, even though in these periods Russian harvesting clearly violated legally binding rules and not merely, as in the earlier Norwegian case, stretched a regime loophole beyond reason. Prior to the 1993 season, Norway published evidence that substantiated very high Russian overfishing, but the commission protocol framed the issue as a joint challenge that called for deeper collaboration on monitoring (JCF 1992, item 11). The target was explicit, therefore, but the criticism soft—presumably because of Russia's readiness to cooperate on the matter, as well as an improvement in overall political relations between the two states. In a speech in Murmansk in 1987, the Soviet leader Mikhail Gorbachev had invited other states in the Arctic region to work together more closely with the Soviet Union in several issue areas, triggering numerous cooperative processes at bilateral and regional levels (Stokke 1990). Just when Russia's quota overfishing peaked in 1992, the two states cosponsored a major Norwegian foreign policy initiative resulting in the establishment of the Barents Euro-Arctic Region (Stokke and Tunander 1994). Also, within the Joint Commission the atmosphere was favorable: ICES-recommended quotas were again on the rise, and bilateral research collaboration was expanding into new areas, involving a broader set of institutions. The protocol for 1994 did not explicitly mention Russia's overfishing, merely implying it in emphasizing the significance of the new compliance collaboration (JFC 1993, item 11.2).

Thereafter, and through the remainder of the 1990s, no evidence exists to substantiate Russian quota overfishing, so we cannot interpret protocol records of further advances in collaborative monitoring as implicit shaming of this party's performance. In fact, for a few years the Joint Commission even held that these advances made the Barents Sea fisheries regime an example for emulation by others (JCF 1995, item 11.2; 1996, item 11.2).

Norway's shaming reemerged at a high level in the 2000s. Soft and implicit criticism of the lack of control inherent in the redirection of Russian landings from Norwegian to various EU ports is evident when the parties elaborated measures for 2001 and requested the relevant authorities "to establish as far as possible an overview of landings, also in third countries" (JCF 2000, item 4; my translation). Explicitness about the target of criticism, and thus the level of shaming, rose prior to the 2002 season, with the Permanent Committee for Management and Enforcement (PCME) reporting that the parties had agreed to collaborate more closely with fisheries enforcement agencies in Scotland, Denmark, and the Netherlands to obtain "information on Russian landings in these countries" (PCME 2001, item 7; my translation). Every year thereafter, Norway published a Fisheries Directorate assessment of very high Russian overfishing, implying substantial shaming. From 2004 Norway even submitted this evidence to the ICES Arctic Fisheries Working Group (JCF 2004, item 4), which used it in the analysis underlying the subsequent ICES estimates (e.g., ICES 2004) of aggregate unreported catches of Northeast Arctic cod. Thus, Russia was subjected to modest or substantial shaming prior to the 1993–1994 period and from 2001, as depicted by the dotted line in figure 6.5.

As to specifying the most plausible *counterfactual* level of shaming, such activity would be difficult to conduct without the regime, which provides both the venue (commission meetings) and the substantive

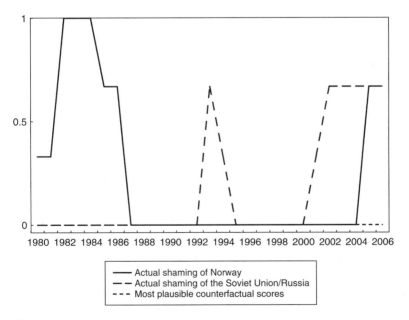

Figure 6.5
Shaming scores. 1 = full = hard criticism of an explicit target; 0.67 = substantial = soft criticism of an explicit target or hard criticism of an implicit target; 0.33 = modest = soft criticism of an implicit target; 0 = insignificant = no criticism.

arguments (quota commitments) that a shamer needs. Even modest shaming requires a behavioral standard that is specific to each state, so the external ICES advice on total catches would not suffice. The most plausible counterfactual level of shaming for both states, as shown by the dashed line that follows the horizontal axis in figure 6.5, therefore remains insignificant throughout the period under study here.

In short, Norway's passive gear overfishing was subjected to substantial or full shaming during the mid-1980s, with criticism that was heavy and explicitly targeted. When Russian quota violations reached alarming levels in the 1990s and 2000s, shaming was generally softer, but it was substantial in the last part of the timeline. No shaming would have been plausible without the regime.

Transparency

Behavioral transparency figures prominently in the debate between the "enforcement school" and the "management school" of international compliance; it concerns whether target-group reports on activities can be verified independently. Verification requires access to alternative sources of information besides target-group reports to cross-check the information. With fisheries management, such alternative sources may be landing reports by port authorities or processors, or they may derive from vessel inspections at sea or in port.

In chapter 2 I scaled this variable by considering the *scope* of such verification. Applied to our cases, full transparency would require that fishers can expect their reports to be cross-checked not only by their own authorities but also by other states throughout their operational range. Such a level of transparency is otherwise unusual in international resource management, but cases include foreign fishing vessels operating in well-surveilled EEZs. For instance, EU vessels operating on a Norwegian license must report catches to Norway as well as to their flag state and the EU; they are also required to keep an updated logbook of catches, carry a satellite tracking device, call at certain checkpoints after entering and before leaving the zone, and accept at-sea inspection at any time.

At the opposite end of the scale, insignificant transparency means that little or no fisher-independent information suitable for cross-checking is available to the flag state or any other state. I define the intermediate categories as follows: transparency is modest if a significant part of the harvesting occurs by fishers whose reports are not verifiable by any state, and substantial if all or most fishers can expect cross-checking throughout the operational range, but only by their own authorities.

For Barents Sea fisheries, each state cross-checks fisher reports by means of recipient reports from processors or sales organizations and through inspections at sea or in port. As long as fishers landed their catches mostly in domestic ports, through the 1980s, that implied substantial transparency for both coastal states. Russian as well as Norwegian vessels frequently operate in the zone of the other state and may encounter inspections there, but such cross-checking has been too limited to qualify as full transparency, as portrayed by the solid and the dotted lines in figure 6.6.

As more and more Russian vessels began landing their catches in Norway during the early 1990s, transparency declined to a modest level for a few years, until deeper collaboration with Norwegian enforcement agencies restored Russia's ability to cross-check fisher reports. In the period of modest transparency, at-sea inspections could not compensate for the loss of port inspection–based transparency because, until recently, the enforcement agencies lacked access to vessel-level information about

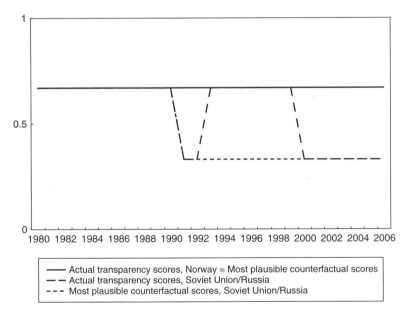

Figure 6.6
Transparency scores. 1 = full = all or most fisher reports verifiable by flag state and other states; 0.67 = substantial = all or most fisher reports verifiable by flag state; 0.33 = modest = significant part of fisher reports not verifiable by flag state or other state; 0 = insignificant = little or no verification of fisher reports.

quotas and aggregate catches. All they could expose were direct discrepancies between logbook data and the amounts of fish found on board.

The transparency of Russian fishing activities returned to a substantial level in 1993, when Norway began to furnish Russia with reports on Russian landings in Norwegian ports and harvesting operations in areas patrolled by the Norwegian Coast Guard. The same year, both parties agreed to monitor more closely third-state harvesting and Russo-Norwegian joint ventures in the cod sector (JCF 1992, item 11.1). These measures were implemented swiftly, giving Russian fishers reason to assume, from 1993, that their own authorities were again in a position to verify their fishing reports.

Since around 2000, the shift by many Russian vessel operators to the EU market (often by means of at-sea transshipment, which complicates the tracing of fish from harvesting to marketing) has again reduced the level of transparency to a modest level for Russian vessels. Other evidence too indicates such lower transparency. In 2002 the Norwegian authorities summed up Russian landings in Norway and concluded that considerable quota overfishing had occurred even among those who did not target the EU market. Many of these landings had not been reported at home, and the absence of attempts to hide the quota overfishing convinced Norwegian officials that the vessel operators did not expect their own authorities to use Norway's port-delivery information for cross-checking purposes (Ulvatn et al. 2006, 170). Such expectations indicate that cross-checking of fisher reports at the level of individual vessels had not occurred for quite some time: and that in turn suggests that the higher level of transparency that followed the exposure of overfishing in the early 1990s was only temporary. Transparency had most likely returned to a modest level already by the turn of the decade and remained so throughout the remainder of the period under study.

A 2007 strengthening of the Scheme of Control and Enforcement under another regional institution, the North-East Atlantic Fisheries Commission (NEAFC), improved the level of transparency regarding Russian harvesting activities (Stokke 2009). Norway, Russia, and the European Community are NEAFC members; none of them may now allow a NEAFC vessel to land or transship frozen fish in its ports unless the flag state of the vessel that caught the fish confirms that the vessel has sufficient quota, has reported the catch, and is authorized to fish in the area, and that satellite tracking information data correspond with vessel reports (NEAFC 2006, Articles 20–23). This system applies not only to regulated resources in the NEAFC Regulatory Area, the high seas, but to all "frozen catch of fisheries resources caught in the Convention Area," which includes also the regional EEZs. Thanks to these developments, the level of transparency concerning Russian harvesting for Northeast Arctic cod is again substantial, but this change came after the period studied here.

Concerning the most plausible *counterfactual* scores on transparency, the regime has significantly influenced this level only in parts of the period under study and only with respect to Russian vessels. Most of the coastal state verification activities preceded the regime and would have occurred without it. For many years, monitoring and enforcement were more or less left to each state within its EEZ—which it would hold independently of the regional institution. The sole regime attribute relevant to transparency in the early years was the Grey Zone Agreement, enabling parallel enforcement jurisdiction in an area that includes a part of the Barents Sea that was disputed until a delimitation agreement was reached in 2010 (see chapter 3). Inadequate evidence exists to substantiate that the two states would have refrained from inspecting their own vessels in this area without the regime, so up to 1993, the most plausible counterfactual score on transparency equals the actual score. Thereafter, as portrayed by the dotted line in figure 6.6, the Russian compliance system would have delivered only modest transparency without the regime-based supply of data on landings in Norway and other collaborative compliance measures. Accordingly, counterfactual transparency scores derive from the difference that the regime has made on flows of information, largely through measures developed under the PCME.

The levels of transparency that fishers experience, therefore, vary between the two states, and for Russian fishers even over time, because burgeoning landings abroad have periodically prevented cross-checking of catch reports. Collaborative compliance control took off in 1993 and restored transparency regarding Russian vessels to a substantial level, but it appears that the risk perceived by fishers that their reports would be cross-checked has been low in the 2000s, implying no more than a modest score. The regime has made little difference to Norwegian transparency, whereas Russian counterfactual transparency would have been lower than the actual level from 1993 to the end of that decade.

Summary
As with regulatory problem solving, the behavioral side of resource management has received considerable attention in the study of international regimes, which this section has benefited from when building a

causal model to account for the variation in behavioral problem solving. Malignancy derives from rationalist regime analysis with its emphasis on interest configurations; obligation concerns normative compellingness and highlights determinacy and bindingness; shaming is about social exposure and therefore invokes the utilitarian, the normative, as well as the cognitional mechanisms; and much the same is true for transparency. As this section has argued, all of these factors except malignancy are directly influenced by the regime.

As with its cognitional and regulatory counterparts, the model also takes some cues from scrutiny of the Barents Sea experience—here, a review of the periods when overfishing of Northeast Arctic cod was especially high. In the next section, we implement more systematically this confrontation of theoretical arguments and empirical evidence on behavioral problem solving.

Paths to Behavioral Success and Failure

In the management of Northeast Arctic cod, certain combinations of the causal factors shown in figure 6.2 consistently yield either high or low levels of quota adherence. Identifying such reliable paths to behavioral success or failure is one way to explain the phenomenon. It also sheds light on earlier findings regarding the drivers of and impediments to regime compliance. This section applies the fuzzy set QCA technique described in chapter 2: high consistency with a pattern that no case has a lower score on the outcome than in a causal combination may, if supported by other theoretical and substantive knowledge, indicate that the causal combination is a sufficient condition—a reliable path to the outcome.

One success path and one failure path emerge from this analysis, and I evaluate the robustness of these findings in two ways. First, and parallel to the procedure in chapters 4 and 5, I examine whether the results change significantly if category thresholds are adjusted somewhat or if a few strong cases are removed. Second, I use the larger number of observations that result from measuring behavioral problem solving at state levels rather than at regime levels and analyze the dataset by two statistical techniques, rank-order correlation and multiple linear regression.

Success Paths
Provided malignancy is modest or insignificant, the combination of strong obligation and high transparency reliably yields behavioral success.

High problem solving can also be achieved under severe malignancy, but no combination of the three regime-driven factors is strong enough to generate reliable success.

These findings derive from scrutiny of the fifty-four cases of Norwegian and Russian problem-solving attempts since 1980, described in the preceding sections, which populate nine of the sixteen corners of the four-factor property space (the scores are given in appendix 5). Only one of those ideal-type combinations achieves a consistency score above the reliable-path threshold of 0.85, and that is the path combining zero scores on malignancy and shaming with full scores on obligation and transparency.

This single reliable path to success can be simplified if we introduce a reasonable simplifying assumption, namely, that the causal combination that equals the reliable path in all respects except that shaming is full would, if it had been represented by strong cases in the dataset, have met the reliability criterion. This assumption is reasonable because the simplifying path differs from one represented in the dataset and meeting the criterion only in a way that should strengthen behavioral problem solving (see chapter 2). Paired comparison of the proven reliable path with the simplifying path indicates that shaming is redundant to behavioral success whenever malignancy is low and obligation and transparency are high, so statement A below summarizes the comparative analysis. As in previous chapters, the reliable paths are stated in ideal-type terms that distinguish only between absence of a property (a score of 0), represented by the symbol "~," and presence (a score of 1), but they derive from observation of all cases that fit them to some extent. An asterisk means "combined with," whereas an arrow means "delivers reliably":

(A) ~malignancy * obligation * transparency → behavioral success

As long as malignancy is low, therefore, the combination of strong obligation and high transparency suffices for achieving high adherence with international quota regulations. A coverage score of 0.49 indicates that this path covers consistently around half of the behavioral success achieved by Norway and Russia in the period under study; the remaining quota adherence is achieved under conditions that do not deliver success reliably. The concluding chapter 8 examines how the findings in this study relate to previous research on regime compliance.

Of the four causal factors, shaming emerges from the QCA analysis as irrelevant to the sole path that achieves behavioral success reliably. As the process-tracing argument above shows, however, shaming has played an indirect role by helping remove the passive gear exemption and thereby raising Norway's obligation. Both of the factors that drive behavioral problem solving reliably whenever malignancy is low are partially influenced by the regime, so statement A provides some general support that the Barents Sea fisheries regime is effective. The same is true for the reliable path that emerges from the analysis of behavioral failure, to which we now turn.

Failure Paths

In the management of Northeast Arctic cod, the combination of severe malignancy, low obligation, and modest or no shaming reliably yields large or very large overfishing of the set quotas.

Failure scores negate success scores; and in this dataset, only one causal category delivers behavioral failure reliably. The path in question combines full scores on malignancy and transparency with zero scores on obligation and shaming. Another path, combining zero scores on malignancy and obligation with full scores on transparency and shaming, initially meets the reliability threshold but fails after we examine a theoretically stronger superset, which captures more cases and thus is less sensitive to outliers (see chapter 4). The superset in question includes all cases that to some extent fit the ideal type that combines zero scores on malignancy and obligation with a full score on transparency. This superset is theoretically more potent in producing failure than the rejected path since it also includes cases with no shaming whatsoever: if weak obligation reliably generates failure among benign cases despite high transparency and shaming, the same conditions *without* shaming should also generate failure. Yet the superset achieves a consistency score of only 0.75, which indicates that the higher score achieved by its less potent subset is merely an artifact resulting from the small number of cases fitting that category. Thus, statement B lists only one reliable path to behavioral failure:

(B) malignancy * ~obligation * transparency * ~shaming →
    behavioral failure

This statement indicates that managers facing severe malignancy are liable to fail unless either obligation or shaming is strong, as transparency alone cannot prevent such failure. To achieve a more concise statement, statement C has accepted the one reasonable simplifying assumption this dataset permits, namely, that the nonrepresented category in all respects equal to the reliable path except for insignificant transparency would have met the reliability criterion. That simplifying path is reasonable because it differs from an empirically proven failure path only in a way that makes behavioral problem solving even more difficult: it involves no possibility of cross-checking fisher reports. Paired comparison with the proven failure path yields the most concise statement of paths to failure that is compatible with the evidence:

(C) malignancy * ~obligation * ~shaming → behavioral failure

According to this analysis, therefore, meeting severe malignancy without strong obligation and shaming is to invite substantial quota overfishing. A coverage score as low as 0.20 indicates that the model accounts far better for behavioral success than for failure: no less than 80 percent of the quota overfishing practiced by Norway and Russia from 1980 to 2006 occurred under conditions that are unreliable for generating failure.

Nevertheless, statement C supports the general proposition that the regime does matter, since two of the factors included in the failure path are clearly and traceably under regime influence. As the next section shows, this path also helps substantiate more specific effectiveness claims, since low scores on shaming and obligation are exactly what would characterize a situation with no Barents Sea fisheries regime.

Robustness

These findings on reliable paths to high or low problem-solving scores are robust to various other reasonable ways of coding the outcome category and the causal factors, and to the removal of one or a few cases.

My yardstick for behavioral problem solving implies that exceeding the quota by less than 1 percent, as five cases do, is de minimis and qualifies as full problem solving. A less generous outcome coding would hold that a distance of, say, 0.7 percent—which was the Soviet official overfishing figure in 1989—in fact implies quota overfishing of one thousand tons of valuable whitefish, and cannot merit the highest score. Recoding the dataset accordingly would generate exactly the same path to success as in statement A, with the same consistency and coverage scores, and the same path to failure as in statement C.[5]

Still on the outcome coding, I noted above that estimates of actual Russian catches in the 2000s are uncertain and contested. Although neither ICES nor the Norwegian authorities had offered any specific overfishing estimate prior to the 2002 estimate (ICES 2007, 23), several considerations indicate that the rise in unreported catches had taken place over several years. First, the Norwegian and Russian authorities had already agreed in 2000 that the increase in Russian transshipment for landings in the EU implied a greater risk of quota overfishing (PCME 2000, item 5). Second, with the commercial cod stock on the rise, the deep quota slash in 2000 raised malignancy from a modest level in 1999 to a full score in 2002. Finally, Russia's official 2000–2001 landings were considerably below 200,000 tons, which is some 40 percent below a reasonable estimate of this fleet's harvesting capacity, considering the size of the commercial stock (Ulvatn et al. 2006, 173). Both before and after, the figures for total official and externally ascribed catches are around capacity. A rough, plausible trajectory would hold that unreported landings emerged gradually as quotas shrank around the turn of the decade, increasing from zero in 1999 to 20,000 tons in 2000 and to 40,000 tons in 2001, before reaching the ICES estimate of 90,000 tons in 2002. That trajectory would reduce the problem-solving scores to substantial in 2000 and modest in 2001, but the findings in statements A and C are fully robust to such changes.

As to the causal factors, we could justify somewhat different codings of the malignancy and the transparency factors. In chapter 4 I noted that the malignancy threshold for full problem solving could reasonably be placed at a slightly lower stock–quota ratio than in figure 6.3, at 3.5. Again, however, such a change would alter neither the success path nor the failure path.

Regarding transparency, we have seen evidence indicating that the Russian authorities have failed to utilize fully the harvesting and landings data they now receive from Norway in their domestic compliance control. If that is so, Russian vessel operators presumably realized such absence of actual cross-checking sooner than the Norwegian authorities did, which would imply that the Russian transparency scores for 1993–1999 in figure 6.6 are too high. A robustness test reveals that modest transparency scores in this period would generate the same paths to success and failure as in statements A and C except that an additional path, combining insignificant malignancy and shaming with full obligation, would also deliver success reliably. This path would imply that obligation is an even more powerful driver than is evident in statement A, and that it is capable of generating high problem solving even without transparency and shaming, as long as malignancy is low. Such a result requires, however, that Russian vessel operators were confident during the second half of the 1990s that their government would not use, for control purposes, information actually in their possession.

The large number of strong cases of the success path in statement A renders this finding robust as well to the removal of one or a few cases from the dataset. For instance, removing either Norway's or Russia's performance in 1987–1988, both strong instances of the success path, would not affect statement A. Such robustness does not mark the failure path in statement C, since Norway in 1981 is the sole strong case in the dataset. Removing that case from the dataset would leave only weak cases of the failure path in statement C, and consistency with the sufficiency criterion would be slightly below the reliability criterion.

Accordingly, the reliable path to success, which combines insignificant malignancy with full scores on obligation and transparency, is robust to a number of reasonable changes in the coding of the outcome and modeled factors. It would even withstand the removal of several strong cases of the causal path. The path to failure is robust to the same changes in outcome and factor coding, but removing the one strong case from the dataset would imply that no causal combination reliably generates failure. Another type of robustness test involves analyzing the same dataset with different techniques, to which we now turn.

Rank-Order Correlations

Whereas the QCA technique examines the combined effect of several causal factors and uses logical minimization and reasonable simplifying assumptions to evaluate less complex causal claims, statistical techniques typically proceed differently: they examine the *separate* effect of each causal factor and then use various procedures to evaluate the more complex causal claims that involve combined effects, or interaction.

Table 6.1 reports Spearman correlations between each causal factor and behavioral problem solving; this statistical measure requires no more than ordinal-scale measurement of categorical data and permits statistical significance tests. As the first row shows, each causal factor correlates sufficiently strongly with the outcome, passing a significance test at the 0.05 level.[6] We must of course exercise caution when interpreting such simple coefficients, since bivariate correlation may disappear when other factors are controlled for. Nevertheless, the directions of three coefficients correspond with theoretical expectations and with the QCA findings: malignancy correlates negatively with problem solving, whereas obligation and transparency correlate positively. Somewhat surprisingly, shaming shows a clear negative correlation with the outcome, which contradicts theoretical expectations and sits poorly with the QCA results. We recall, however, that the QCA analysis rejected a no-shaming path

Table 6.1
Spearman's Rank-Order Coefficients of Correlation between Causal Factors and Behavioral Problem Solving

		MAL	OBL	TRA	SHA	N
All Cases		−0.50**	0.28**	0.41**	−0.53**	54
High malignancy	All	−0.41**	0.12	0.44**	−0.41**	34
	High transparency	−0.47**	0.41**		−0.27	25
	Low transparency	−0.48			−0.46	9
Low malignancy	All	−0.52**	0.71**		−0.76**	20
	High transparency	−0.52**	0.71**		−0.76**	20
	Low transparency					0

Note: MAL = malignancy; OBL = obligation; TRA = transparency; SHA = shaming; *N* = number of observations. *Statistical significance at *P* < 0.1; **statistical significance at *P* < 0.05. An empty cell means that limited diversity prevents calculation of a coefficient. Underlying data are given in appendix 5.

to reliable success only after superset evaluation. Shaming therefore merits closer attention when we move from bivariate to multivariate analysis, as in the subsequent table rows.

The dataset allows control for two of the causal factors, malignancy and transparency; the small numbers of cases involving weak obligation or harsh shaming prevent further decomposition. My four-value scale implies variation in malignancy within the high and low categories, and correspondingly for transparency. The malignancy column shows the correlation between malignancy and problem solving as roughly the same in all subsets. That pattern could indicate that malignancy is a powerful driver of quota overfishing throughout its range and whatever the level of transparency. However, the small number of cases involving low transparency makes the latter claim uncertain, since the corresponding coefficient (0.48) is statistically nonsignificant. While some caution is necessary, since obligation could interfere with these relationships in ways we cannot control for in this dataset, these findings correspond well to the central place of malignancy in the QCA solutions as an ingredient of both the success and the failure paths.

Obligation, transparency, and shaming are also addressed in table 6.1. The obligation column shows a weak (0.12) and nonsignificant correlation in the subset of malign cases and a strong (0.71) and statistically significant correlation among benign cases. Since neither theoretical reasoning nor empirical correlation suggests that one of those factors drives the other, this pattern indicates an interaction effect: obligation seems to drive problem solving only at low levels of malignancy. Such a finding fits neatly with the QCA conclusion that causal paths that reliably deliver success involve no more than modest malignancy and no less than substantive obligation. The QCA success path is more restricted, however, indicating that such reliability requires also high transparency; the very high (0.71) and statistically significant coefficient for the subset involving benign cases with high transparency points in the same direction, but the low transparency category is too small to permit conclusions. The shaming column, finally, makes it clear that controlling for malignancy and transparency does not alter the negative correlation between shaming and problem solving, and also indicates that the negative correlation is stronger among benign cases.

In summary, rank-order correlation analysis shows strong and statistically significant bivariate association between each causal factor and behavioral problem solving. The directions of those bivariate correlations are as expected for three factors, whereas shaming emerges as negatively correlated with problem solving. The dataset also permits some multi-variate analysis, indicating that malignancy correlates strongly with problem solving throughout its range and that the effect of obligation depends on a low score on malignancy. Except for the clear negative association between shaming and quota adherence, these findings are highly compatible with the QCA analysis, but the limited diversity in obligation and shaming prevents statistical control for these potentially intervening factors.

Multiple Linear Regression
Regression analysis requires interval-level measurement of the outcome and causal factors, which usually calls for continuous variables, but researchers sometimes use regression also when analyzing categorical data. Underdal (2002c), for instance, examines the effects of several multichotomous variables on two dimensions of regime effectiveness by multiple regression.

Table 6.2 reports the results of a stepwise entry of the four modeled factors into a linear regression analysis. Unfortunately, auto-correlation disables the statistical significance tests. Generally, the output from a regression fits effectiveness analysis well, since the coefficients have clear interpretations relating each causal factor to an outcome score—here, the average change in problem solving associated with a unit change in the causal factor. A good regression model that includes factors under regime influence therefore provides a means for estimating the difference between the actual and the most plausible counterfactual problem-solving scores (Mitchell 2002), just as the QCA paths to success and failure do.

Thus, row 1 in the table predicts from regression of a simple trivariate model that insignificant scores on both causal factors will deliver problem solving at 0.39 (slightly above a modest score). If obligation does not change, a unit increase in malignancy (from insignificant to full score) generates a drop in problem solving by 0.54 (slightly less than two quali-tative steps), which is close to the *improvement* in problem solving that a unit increase in obligation yields with malignancy held constant (0.64). The adjusted coefficient of determination (R^{2Adj}) indicates the proportion of variance in behavioral problem solving that each model accounts for. The trivariate regression explains a rather low share of the variance, only a third. Adding transparency in row 2 improves the proportion to 54 percent, while the full four-factor model in row 3 accounts for 61 percent of the variance. We recall that the QCA coverage of the success path was 49 percent while that of the failure path was a mere 20 percent.

Table 6.2
Regression Coefficients of Additive Causal Factors on Behavioral Problem Solving ($N = 54$)

Row	Causal Model	a	b_M	b_O	b_T	b_S	R^2_{Adj}
1	BPS $= a + b_M$MAL $+ b_O$OBL $+ e$	0.39	-0.54	0.64			0.33
2	BPS $= a + b_M$MAL $+ b_O$OBL $+ b_T$TRA $+ e$	0.92	-0.43	0.96	1.61		0.54
3	BPS $= a + b_M$MAL $+ b_O$OBL $+ b_T$TRA $+ b_S$SHA $+ e$	0.43	-0.39	0.72	1.24	-0.38	0.61

Note: Additivity means absence of causal interaction: a change in the value of one causal factor does not alter the effect of another causal factor on the outcome. a = intercept, the average outcome value when all causal factors are zero; b = unstandardized coefficient (slope), the average change in problem solving associated with a unit change in the causal factor, subscripts refer to causal factors; e = residual, an error term reflecting that relationships between social science variables are always inexact; R^2Adj = adjusted coefficient of determination (explained variance); N = number of observations; BPS = behavioral problem solving; MAL = malignancy; OBL = obligation; TRA = transparency; SHA = shaming. Statistical significance tests are disabled by positive auto-correlation.

The dataset falls prey to a common threat to valid significance testing in regression analysis of time-series data—auto-correlation—but interpretation of the coefficients remains meaningful. The term refers to correlation among the residuals and implies dependent observations, which violates the assumptions of the significance test: time-series observations are often connected by similar scores on nonmodeled factors. The Durbin-Watson statistics test for the table models indicates positive auto-correlation, which disables the standard regression procedures for evaluating statistical significance. Auto-correlation does not bias the coefficients, however (Lewis-Beck 1980, 28), nor does the dataset display multicollinearity or other properties that might introduce such bias.[7] Visual inspection of the standardized residuals of the four-factor model against predictive scores on problem solving suggests a reasonably good model fit, since the residuals do not show a curvilinear pattern or increasing variance and are distributed evenly around zero with very few outliers.[8] The pattern does indicate a tendency to overestimate problem solving when predicted scores are low, but the generally falling slope of the pattern simply reflects the use of four-value categorical data; forecasts close to the highest value leave little or no scope for overestimation. Accordingly, although we cannot know whether correlations are strong enough to be statistically significant, there is no evidence to indicate that the coefficients are biased—meaning that substantive interpretations are tenable.

The magnitude and direction of the regression coefficients are compatible with the findings from the QCA and rank-order analyses. Although the modeled factors are on the same scale, we cannot read relative factor strength directly from the table since factor variance differs. Not reported in the table are the standardized coefficients, where absolute values in the full model are around 0.35 for all factors, indicating similar strength. Table row comparison reveals that, for each factor, the sign of the coefficients remains the same as the model expands. Accordingly, control for all other causal factors (unavailable in the rank-order analysis) upholds the somewhat puzzling result that shaming correlates negatively with problem solving.

The review of shaming under this regime renders quite implausible the substantive interpretation that shaming is something counterproductive, triggering perverse target responses. In all periods involving shaming, the target has in fact acknowledged that a problem exists and has taken steps to rectify the situation. A simpler and more reasonable interpretation, therefore, is that strong shaming occurs only when quota overfishing is recurrent and high—and under such conditions, soft diplomatic instruments rarely have any immediate effect. Moreover, we noted on process-tracing grounds that an important effect of shaming on problem solving has been *indirect*, by pressuring Norway to assume a firmer obligation to the quota in 1984, which in turn helped reduce the quota overfishing. Such indirect causal effects will show up in the QCA or regression analysis only with an appropriate time lag. A three-year time lag, for instance, reduces the shaming coefficient in the full model to $b_S = -0.02$.[9]

Thus, just as with the rank-order analysis, regressions support the findings from the QCA analysis concerning the directions of impact of malignancy, obligation, and transparency. The effect of shaming is different, but it practically disappears if the series is time-lagged, which seems reasonable from the process analysis.

Table 6.2 also hints at interaction effects between some of the modeled factors. Suspicion of such interaction arises from the considerable changes in the malignancy and obligation coefficients when controlling for transparency, as in row 2. Such changes may indicate differential effects over the range of transparency scores, especially if cases with low scores on malignancy and obligation have transparency scores that are higher than average. That pattern is evident in the data, since cases with low obligation—Norway in the early 1980s—have consistently high transparency scores, whereas cases with low transparency—Russia in the early 1990s and in the 2000s—involve severe malignancy. Such interaction effects are reasonable in terms of theory and map onto the findings from the QCA and rank-order analyses. High transparency implies greater probability that the authorities will expose overfishing, which should counteract in part the greater incentives to exceed the quota inherent in high relative availability. Similarly, strong obligation without means for cross-checking fisher reports may easily become a dead letter, hence a lower obligation effect.

It would be useful to clarify whether inclusion of such interaction effects would improve the explained variance of the model, or shed light on the proportions of the effects from malignancy and obligation that are independent of transparency. Unfortunately, including either of the two relevant interaction variables introduces high multicollinearity and thus biased coefficients. While evident in the QCA and the rank-order analysis, these possible interaction effects are difficult to pursue empirically with linear regression analysis.

In short, positive auto-correlation prevents valid significance tests, and thereby precludes confidence that the coefficients do not reflect random causes. However, the partial regression coefficients in table 6.2 are presumably unbiased—and they are fully compatible with the findings from the QCA and rank-order analyses regarding three out of four causal factors, while a difference with respect to the fourth, shaming, disappears with a reasonable time lag.

Summary

The QCA analysis reveals two robust paths relevant to behavioral effectiveness. First, as long as malignancy is no more than modest, combining strong obligation with high transparency delivers success reliably. Behavioral success solving can be achieved also under severe malignancy, but not reliably. Second, combining severe malignancy with low obligation and shaming reliably delivers failure. While the success path covers around half of the behavioral success in the dataset, the failure path covers no more than a fifth of the failure but still supports the effectiveness analysis by highlighting factors under regime influence.

Both the success and the failure paths are robust to the coding of the outcome and the causal factors, but, of the cases supporting the failure path, only one is strong. The substantive findings from the rank-order and regression analyses concern primarily the direction of each factor's impacts on problem solving and certain causal interactions. All the statistical inferences regarding malignancy, obligation, and transparency are directly compatible with the QCA findings, while the shaming results differ unless a reasonable time lag is introduced. Process-tracing evidence supports the QCA finding that also this factor may make a positive difference to behavioral problem solving. This overall compatibility of results derived from different analytical techniques indicates that the findings reported in this section are robust.

Assessing Behavioral Effectiveness

The effectiveness of the Barents Sea fisheries regime in raising target-group adherence to agreed-upon regulations has been significant for both Norway and the USSR/Russia through most of the period under study, but the extent differs considerably. In the case of Norway, the regime was ineffective in behavioral terms in the first half of the 1980s, whereas for Russia the regime mattered little for quota adherence in the first half of the 1990s and in the final years studied. Taken together, regime contributions to behavioral problem solving were slightly higher during the last half of the period studied than during the first.

These findings derive from using a combination of counterfactual path analysis and the Oslo-Potsdam effectiveness yardstick. Counterfactual path analysis involves examining how well the counterfactual antecedents—the causal factor scores that would pertain if there were no regime—fit the reliable failure or success paths. Such fit can narrow the range of plausible counterfactual problem-solving estimates. In chapter 2, I explained and justified three simple decision rules that guide such estimation. In years when actual problem solving is insignificant or the regime has not influenced any causal factor, the most plausible counterfactual estimate equals the actual score. Whenever the counterfactual path fits a reliable success or failure path, the fit score places a lower or an upper bound on the plausible counterfactual estimates. Finally, whenever the counterfactual path analysis leaves more than one plausible option, I choose among them based on the number of causal factors that are weaker in the counterfactual case than in the actual case—that is, that have scores empirically shown to be less conducive. Appendix 5 gives the counterfactual paths and their scores on the success and failure paths for all years in the period under study. Because the regime's impact on actual harvesting behavior differs between the two member states, it is logical to examine them separately.

Regime Impacts on Norwegian Harvesting

In the early 1980s, Norwegian quota overfishing was severe enough to make effectiveness insignificant, but thereafter the picture becomes less gloomy, mostly because the regime strengthened an important driver of problem solving, obligation. Regime effectiveness was particularly high in the late 1980s and in the final part of the timeline, when severe malignancy would otherwise have constrained quota adherence. Table 6.3 reports the counterfactual path analysis for each year under study, as well as the resulting counterfactual problem-solving estimates and the corresponding effectiveness scores.

From the table we see that the Barents Sea fisheries regime was ineffective in shaping Norwegian quota adherence in six of the twenty-seven years studied and was fully effective in nine. The trend is markedly positive: the sum of the effectiveness scores for the last half of the timeline is 8.83, about 65 percent higher than the corresponding figure for the first half.

The long and nearly unbroken series of medium to high effectiveness scores achieved from 1986 has been driven largely by regime impacts on Norway's obligation to the quotas, which increased from modest to

Table 6.3
Behavioral Effectiveness Analysis: Norway

Actual Problem Solving		Counterfactual Problem Solving		Effectiveness Score
Year	Score	Substantiation	Estimate	Score
1980–82	0	Insignificant even in actual case	0	0
1983	0.33	Counterfactual path analysis identifies 0.33 as lowest plausible estimate	0.33	0
1984–85	0	Insignificant even in actual case	0	0
1986	0.67	Counterfactual path analysis yields point estimate	0.33	0.5
1987–88	1	Counterfactual path analysis narrows range to 1–0.33; mid-option chosen since obligation only is weaker than in actual case	0.67	1
1989	1	Counterfactual path analysis yields point estimate	0.33	1
1990	1	Counterfactual path analysis narrows range to 0.33–0; highest option chosen since only obligation is weaker than in actual case	0.33	1
1991	0.33	Counterfactual path analysis narrows range to 0.33–0; option below actual score chosen since obligation is weaker	0	0.33
1992–93	0.67	Counterfactual path analysis narrows range to 0.33–0; higher option chosen since only knowledge is weaker than in actual case	0.33	0.5
1994	0.67	Counterfactual path analysis yields point estimate	0.33	0.5
1995–96	0.67	Counterfactual path analysis narrows range to 0.67–0.33; option below actual score chosen since obligation is weaker	0.33	0.5

Table 6.3
(continued)

Actual Problem Solving		Counterfactual Problem Solving		Effectiveness Score
Year	Score	Substantiation	Estimate	
1997–98	1	Counterfactual path analysis narrows range to 1–0.33; mid-option chosen since obligation only is weaker than in actual case	0.67	1
1999	0.67	Counterfactual path analysis narrows range to 0.67–0.33; option below actual score chosen since obligation is weaker	0.33	0.5
2000–1	0.67	Counterfactual path analysis yields point estimate.	0.33	0.5
2002	0.33	Counterfactual path analysis narrows range to 0.33–0; option below actual score chosen since obligation is weaker	0	0.33
2003	0.67	Counterfactual path analysis narrows range to 0.33–0; higher option chosen since only obligation is weaker than in actual case.	0.33	0.5
2004–6	1	Counterfactual path analysis yields point estimate	0.33	1

Note: Scores: 1 = full; 0.67 = substantial; 0.5 = medium; 0.33 = modest; 0 = insignificant. Counterfactual paths and their fit with success and failure paths are listed in appendix 5, table A5.3. Effectiveness scores are calculated by the Oslo-Potsdam formula.

substantial levels in 1984 after years of Soviet pressure. The lower counterfactual obligation score is the main reason why the counterfactual problem-solving estimates are lower than the actual scores: obligation is full in the reliable success path and insignificant in the reliable failure path. It is therefore of interest to see whether other evidence available for process-tracing analysis is compatible with this key result from the counterfactual path analysis. Would Norwegian fishers have exerted considerably higher pressure on the resource if Norway had *not* been obliged by the regional regime?

The process-tracing evidence clearly supports the findings from the counterfactual path analysis: Soviet obligation-based shaming triggered a process of strengthening Norwegian domestic regulation of the passive gear sector, which predominates in Norway's cod fisheries. Time closures far more extensive than before were introduced in 1981, and from 1983 group and (occasionally) vessel quotas were introduced for the coastal fleet, along with restrictions on the number of nets (Sagdahl 1992, 83).[10] Group quotas made it more difficult for fishers to compensate for time closures by taking more in the open periods, as they had done in previous years. This gradual tightening in regulation culminated in 1989 with a mid-season closure of the passive gear cod fisheries, followed by new and far stricter access rules (Norway, Ministry of Fisheries 2002–03, 24).

There were nonregime drivers of such stricter regulation as well—notably, Norway's trawler sector was concerned about the lack of real constraints on a competing sector (Christensen and Hallenstvedt 2005, 257). However, three empirical observations indicate that the regulations would have been adopted later and less forcefully if there had been no regime. First, as noted in chapter 5, throughout most of the 1980s Norway proposed considerably higher quotas than the scientists had advised—and apparently few domestic critics stood up against this policy. On the contrary, coastal fishers protested angrily that the measures were too strict, not too weak (Christensen and Hallenstvedt 2005, 257). In the Storting, the opposition sided firmly with the coastal fishers and lamented "the unreasonableness of regulating passive-gear fishing . . . [considering] that the decline of the Northeast Arctic cod stock is not due to passive gear fishing" but to the multinational trawler fleet instead.[11] Only toward the end of the 1980s did Norwegian environmental organizations begin to mobilize on Barents Sea fisheries management.[12] Second, Norway stubbornly defended the passive gear exemption in the Joint Commission despite the enormous quota overfishing that ensued as a result. Permitting continuation of passive gear catches relieved both the political authorities and the Norwegian Fishermen's Association of the political burden that new constraints on the coastal vessels would have entailed (Sagdahl 1992, 30–39). Finally, the intensive Soviet shaming activity over several years indicates that the Soviet Union was clearly not of the opinion that the Norwegian authorities would take on the passive gear sector if left to their own devices. In sum, we can say that external inducement, centered on the regime obligations, most plausibly drove the regulatory strengthening that occurred during the 1980s and reduced Norwegian quota overfishing.

Behavioral problem solving remained high also in the 1990s. However, with some exceptions, the role of the regime was modest to medium, typically raising problem solving one step by the force of obligation, reinforced by a high level of transparency that was not based on the regime, since Norwegian catches are largely landed at home.

To summarize, the Barents Sea fisheries regime mattered little for Norway's quota adherence during the early years, mainly because the passive gear exemption kept the level of obligation low. The removal of this exemption, following intensive regime-based shaming, had only limited effect at first because malignancy was severe—the commercial cod stock was large relative to the quota, providing weighty incentives to overfish the quotas. After 1985, however, the high obligation enabled by the regime, partly through shaming, contributed significantly to generally high quota adherence on the part of Norway. The effectiveness scores are especially high in periods with severe malignancy—in the late 1980s, in 1997–1998, and in the last few years of the timeline. The high levels of problem solving achieved during other years of the 1990s and early 2000s were less regime-driven, either because malignancy was low or, when malignancy was severe, because another important driver of quota adherence, transparency, does not rely on the regime in the case of Norway. However, transparency is a key factor in accounting for regime impact on Russian harvesting, to which we now turn.

Regime Impacts on Soviet and Russian Harvesting

The Barents Sea fisheries regime has been more effective in shaping the quota adherence of the USSR/Russia than in shaping that of Norway, except during the periods of low transparency in the early 1990s and the 2000s. Among the regime-based drivers, obligation is the most important, backed up by a domestic transparency system that became partly regime-based in the second half of the 1990s. Shaming of quota overfishing during the 2000s proved important by triggering more advanced port-state control measures under a broader regime, the NEAFC, but those measures were introduced after the period studied here. Table 6.4

Table 6.4
Behavioral Effectiveness Analysis: The Soviet Union/Russia

Actual Problem Solving		Counterfactual Problem Solving		Effectiveness Score
Year	Score	Substantiation	Estimate	
1980	1	Counterfactual path analysis narrows range to 0.67–0.33; higher option chosen since only obligation is weaker than in actual case	0.67	1
1981	1	Counterfactual path analysis yields point estimate	0.33	1
1982–83	1	Counterfactual path analysis narrows range to 0.67–0.33; higher option chosen since only obligation is weaker than in actual case	0.67	1
1984	1	Counterfactual path analysis yields point estimate	0.33	1
1985	0.67	Counterfactual path analysis narrows range to 0.33–0; higher option chosen since only obligation is weaker than in actual case.	0.33	0.5
1986	1	Counterfactual path analysis yields point estimate	0.33	1
1987–88	1	Counterfactual path analysis narrows range to 1–0.33; mid option chosen since only obligation is weaker than in actual case	0.67	1
1989	1	Counterfactual path analysis yields point estimate	0.33	1
1990	0.33	Counterfactual path analysis narrows range to 0.33–0; option below actual score chosen since obligation is weaker	0	0.33
1991–92	0	Insignificant even in actual case	0	0
1993	0.33	Counterfactual path analysis narrows range to 0.33–0; option below actual score chosen since obligation is weaker	0	0,33

Table 6.4
(continued)

Actual Problem Solving		Counterfactual Problem Solving		Effectiveness Score
Year	Score	Substantiation	Estimate	
1994	1	Counterfactual path analysis yields point estimate	0.33	1
1995–96	1	Counterfactual path analysis narrows range to 0.67–0.33; lower option chosen since both obligation and transparency are weaker than in actual case	0.33	1
1997–98	1	Counterfactual path analysis narrows range to 1–0.33; lowest option chosen since both obligation and transparency are weaker than in actual case	0.33	1
1999	1	Counterfactual path analysis narrows range to 0.67–0.33; lower option chosen since both obligation and transparency are weaker than in actual case	0.33	1
2000–1	1	Counterfactual path analysis yields point estimate	0.33	1
2002–6	0	Insignificant even in actual case	0	0

Note: Scores: 1 = full; 0.67 = substantial; 0.5 = medium; 0.33 = modest; 0 = insignificant. Counterfactual paths and their fit with success and failure paths are listed in appendix 5, table A5.4. Effectiveness scores are calculated by the Oslo-Potsdam formula.

draws together the counterfactual path analysis for each year studied and gives the consequent counterfactual problem-solving estimates as well as the effectiveness scores.

We see that, in terms of raising Soviet and Russian quota adherence, the regime has been ineffective in seven of the twenty-seven years under study but fully effective in seventeen. The summed behavioral effectiveness score is around 25 percent higher than for Norway, but the Soviet/Russian trend line, unlike Norway's, points downward: the sum of effectiveness scores for the last half of the timeline is 8, nearly 20 percent lower than the corresponding figure for the first half.

As to whether the results of the counterfactual path analysis are compatible with the process-tracing evidence, one specific period warrants special comment. The full effectiveness scores in 1980–1984 may seem surprising at first glance, because the Soviet Union considerably underfished its quotas in those years (see figure 6.1). Such underfishing could indicate that other factors, such as cod availability, constrained the Soviet fleet more than regime obligations did. However, what this quota underfishing reflects is not primarily low cod availability in domestic waters but the preference within the Soviet production-plan system for edible species then available in greater quantities than cod, such as blue whiting and redfish. That preference underlies the large cod quota transfers to Norway in the 1980s in return for access to those pelagic species in Norway's zones (see chapter 5). It is evident also from the fact that Soviet vessels refrained from taking all the cod they were entitled to in Norway's EEZ (see, e.g., *Aftenposten*, 13 November 1981), where cod was highly available in the early 1980s.

Had the regime not been in place, the Soviets would have had clear incentives to take as much cod as possible within their own zone, also because catches relatively close to the Norwegian level would have placed them in a better bargaining position should these states try to form a regional regime later on. From economic as well as stock-replenishment perspectives, heavy fishery in the Soviet zone, where the cod is typically younger and smaller, would have been less rational than the actual pattern of harvesting in this period (Stokke, Anderson, and Mirovitskaya 1999, 127). Accordingly, by allowing a mutually beneficial quota transfer and assuring the Soviets that low cod catches would not reduce their future share of this valuable stock, the regime helped to divert Soviet harvesting pressure toward species less troubled than Northeast Arctic cod. Figure 6.7 plots the Soviet and Russian behavioral effectiveness scores for the period studied, together with those for Norway.

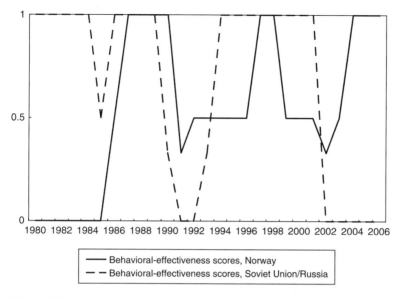

Figure 6.7
Behavioral effectiveness scores.

Thus, we may conclude that the Barents Sea fisheries regime has significantly shaped the Soviet and the Russian harvesting of Northeast Arctic cod, except in the early 1990s and the final part of the years under study. This high behavioral effectiveness results mostly from the obligations the regime emplaces regarding harvesting pressures and from the higher transparency deriving in some years from closer cooperation on rule enforcement. That regime obligation proved insufficient when transparency dropped in the early 1990s and 2000s, however, as Russian vessels increasing delivered their catch in foreign ports, first in Norway and then in EU states, in periods when rising relative availability made the behavioral problem more malign. After the period under study here, an amendment of the NEAFC Scheme of Control and Enforcement again raised transparency to a substantial level. Only during relatively short periods has behavioral effectiveness been high for both main members of the Barents Sea fisheries regime.

As in previous chapters, the effectiveness assessment in this section has centered on estimates of what the scores would most plausibly be in the hypothetical situation in which the regime was lacking. Those estimates derive from the comparative and statistical analyses concerning drivers of and impediments to quota adherence, as well as process-tracing evidence of what the scores on the causal factors would be in a no-regime situation, and the estimates are fully compatible with what is otherwise known about the cases under study.

Summary and Implications

This chapter has focused on the behavioral aspect of resource management: here, in shaping the actual harvesting pressure exerted by the fishers. The simple yardstick used is adherence to national quotas. Periods of very high quota overfishing in the first half of each of the three decades under study formed one starting point for developing an explanatory model. This modeling has also drawn on earlier regime-effectiveness research; it forms an important part of the disaggregate approach to international regime effectiveness by helping to substantiate the most plausible estimates of what problem solving would have been in a hypothetical situation with no regime.

The model employed to account for variation in actual behavioral problem solving includes malignancy, obligation, transparency, and shaming. Malignancy concerns the relative availability of cod, which gives rise to both opportunities and gains from disregarding quota limitations. Obligation denotes normative determinacy and bindingness. Transparency is about governments' ability to cross-check fisher reports against other sources; and shaming refers to criticism by states. The regime is found to have a strong impact on the level of obligation and, in parts of the period studied, also on the levels of transparency and shaming.

Decomposition of the dataset by examining regime impacts on Norwegian and Russian performance separately makes the number of observations large enough to support not only QCA analysis but also two statistical techniques. High overall compatibility of the findings indicates robustness. The success path covers around half of the behavioral success in the dataset, markedly more than the corresponding failure coverage: behavioral success is reliable only when malignancy is low—and even then, only if reinforced by high levels of obligation and transparency. In contrast, severe malignancy reliably yields failure unless counteracted by high obligation or shaming. Such an effect of shaming is not evident in the statistical analyses—unless time-lagged, shaming correlates with *low* behavioral problem solving—which might simply reflect the fact that shaming is used only when overfishing occurs. Shaming has been relatively rare in this regime; the process-tracing evidence suggests that its main contribution to behavioral problem solving has been indirect, by helping to remove the passive gear exemption that kept Norway's quota obligation low in the early years.

In the disaggregate approach to international regime effectiveness, an important role of such explanation of actual success and failure is to support the estimation of counterfactual problem-solving scores and thereby allow assessment of regime effectiveness by use of the Oslo-Potsdam yardstick. The Barents Sea fisheries regime has, in parts of the period studied, contributed to significantly lower quota overfishing of the region's most important stock, Northeast Arctic cod, but the explanatory weight of each regime-driven factor—shaming, obligation, and transparency—differs between Norway and Russia.

During the early years, when Norwegian passive gear catches posed the greatest threat to stock replenishment, the regime helped counter the problem in two ways. In the short term, the clear allocation of user rights assured the Soviet Union that leaving much of the shrinking cod stock to Norway, whose coastal vessels had fewer alternative uses when the cod quotas dropped around 1980, would not jeopardize its own share in the stock, while at the same time providing access to much greater quantities of pelagic fish in Norway's EEZ. In the longer term, the regime-based shaming of passive gear overfishing, and the rising quota obligation it triggered, yielded earlier and more forceful domestic regulation of the coastal vessel sector than would have occurred otherwise. Thereafter, high obligation has been the main value added by the regime to Norway's behavioral performance, with dips in problem solving largely reflecting high relative availability of cod and therefore strong incentives to cheat on the quota.

High relative cod availability also marks the periods of greatest Russian quota overfishing, in the early 1990s and 2000s. Shaming has played a role in combating Russian quota excesses, but the legally binding and precise obligation to the quotas set by the Joint Commission in conjunction with a partly regime-based transparency system has been weightier.

Whereas target-group behavior is close to the core of the regime-effectiveness concept, the ultimate purpose of resource management regimes is to safeguard the long-term ability of the resource base to support a valuable fishery—in other words, to balance utilization and conservation. The next chapter sets about aggregating the evidence on regime impacts on cognitional, regulatory, and behavioral problem solving. It does so by relating those partial effectiveness scores to developments in catches and the state of the stock, as measured by certain biological reference points that have become central to precautionary fisheries management under the Barents Sea fisheries regime.

7

Aggregate Effectiveness

The basic problem or social purpose of an international regime is what motivated states to create it, whether it is avoidance of nuclear conflict, the furtherance of free trade, or the sustainable management of natural resources. Whatever the issue area, the causal chains that might connect the regime and the achievement of that purpose, to whatever degree, are usually long and complex, and therefore difficult to substantiate. The disaggregate approach makes such substantiation more tractable by considering three parts separately before joining them. The partial problems are to build shared and well-based knowledge among regime members on what measures will best achieve the purpose, to create a set of behavioral rules that jointly reflect the knowledge, and finally to ensure that the rules shape the actions of those who can influence the outcome in question.

The preceding chapters have examined each of these cognitional, regulatory, and behavioral aspects of the larger problem, which for resource management regimes is to balance utilization and conservation. As this aggregating chapter shows, the Barents Sea fisheries regime has significantly improved that balance and thereby contributed to the present status of Northeast Arctic cod as the world's biggest cod stock. Near disasters and failures have also occurred in the period under study, however, often because the successes on one aspect of problem solving were undercut or canceled out by poor performance on another.

While this chapter brings together the three aspects of problem solving, the approach to assessing regime effectiveness remains disaggregate. Rather than tackling head-on the difficult and highly complex question of how the balance between utilization and conservation would have been in a counterfactual no-regime situation, I first describe and explain the track record of success and failure for actual cases. Thus, the next section specifies what the balancing of utilization and conservation means in resource management and shows that we can measure the outcome validly for any given year by combining trends in annual catches and the subsequent strength of the spawning stock. On that basis, I derive the aggregate problem-solving scores for the period under study.

In the three preceding chapters, I have specified causal models, including factors that are wholly or partly outside ready regime influence, to account for the variation in problem solving. Here I ask instead how well combinations of cognitional, regulatory, and behavioral problem solving can account for the variation we see in the ability to balance present and future use of the resource. On the behavioral aspect, the levels of problem solving can be measured in two ways: whether both regime members adhere to their quotas or only one of them does. Evaluating those models is again done by the fuzzy set qualitative comparative analysis (QCA) technique, which helps identify any combination of causal properties reliably associated with a certain outcome in a dataset. The hallmark of sound counterfactual analysis is that facts and inferences are compatible with those that apply to otherwise similar actual cases, so those reliable success and failure paths can shed light on what the problem solving would have been if the regime had not existed. I showed in chapter 2 that specifying the counterfactual antecedent—the scores on the modeled factors—is much easier than estimating the consequent outcome. Here we enjoy the additional benefit that the preceding chapters have already substantiated the scores, as well as the most plausible counterfactual estimates, for the three modeled drivers: cognitional, regulatory, and behavioral success.

Before we evaluate that causal model and consider the results according to the Oslo-Potsdam effectiveness yardstick, we must define the aggregate problem more clearly.

The Problem: Balancing Utilization and Conservation

Chapters 4 to 6 of this book have offered in-depth but only partial accounts of how the Barents Sea fisheries regime has helped balance present use and future use. Figure 7.1 combines two trends that help aggregate those accounts. The columns show the development in catches of the main stock managed under this regime, including the best estimates of illegal, unregulated, and unreported catches. The solid line plots the weight of the spawning part of the stock—cod aged around six years or more. Stock replenishment depends on the spawning stock, and the management of living resources revolves around how much of the repro-

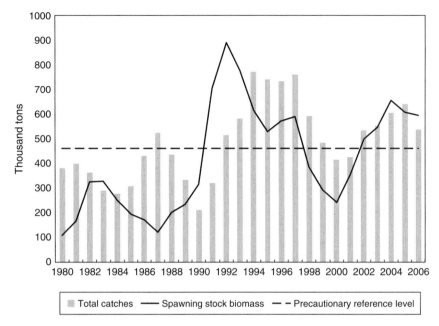

Figure 7.1
Annual catches and spawning stock levels, Northeast Arctic cod. Data on catches and spawning stock levels are from ICES (2008a, 53); data on the commercial stock are from ICES (2008b). Up to 2004, the precautionary reference level was slightly higher, 500,000 tons (ICES 2003, 12).

ducing part of a stock should be conserved to ensure future use. That is why the size of the spawning stock is central to the biological reference points that underlie scientific quota advice. The dashed line in the figure gives the level that scientists consider the lower bound of an optimal range for Northeast Arctic cod, now known as a precautionary reference point.

We see that catches as well as spawning stock levels for cod fluctuate widely in the period. Total catches below 400,000 tons, characteristic of the early 1980s, are only half of what they had been in the preceding decade. Only for a short period during the mid-1990s were catches close to the level of the 1970s, and that level proved unsustainable since the spawning stock dropped steeply. In most years under study, the spawning stock was below the reference level, at times dramatically lower.

The size of the spawning stock is crucial to the future availability of the resource and is seen by managers, scientists, and fishers alike as one of two main items to watch when gauging success in management. The second main item is actual catches, which generates employment and income, as well as valuable food. Since those two parameters compete in the short term, it is natural to include both in a yardstick for measuring aggregate problem solving.

One possible way to combine the two is to consider the *levels* of catches and the spawning stock, but that approach has some problems if we want to assign success scores on a year-by-year basis. A reasonable qualitative anchor for evaluating the level of the spawning stock would be the precautionary reference level, whereas for catches, the average for the period studied would be a reasonable threshold between "high" and "low." The problem with using those levels to grade aggregate management performance is that they are quite dependent on the previous performance. Managers must play with the cards they have, and the cards received, for instance, in 1980—with a spawning stock of little more than a fifth of the reference level—were very different from those received, say, in 1992. It would seem practically impossible, judging by figure 7.1, for managers to have delivered a spawning stock above the reference level in the first of those years and practically impossible to have avoided it in the last. Since this study examines causal and outcome variables on an annual basis, we would like the yardstick to be more sensitive to management accomplishments in a given year.

The yardstick most sensitive to the decisions and actions in a given year would gauge success in the balancing of conservation and utilization based on *changes* in the two parameters of interest, but this approach has its own validity problems. The simplest change-based yardstick would assign, for any given year, a full aggregate problem-solving score if the aggregate results of what scientists, managers, and fishers do are catches higher than in the year before, with enough fertile fish left to deliver a higher spawning stock in the next year. Conversely, aggregate problem solving would be insignificant if both catches and spawning stock are found to be on downward slopes, whereas cases involving catches and a spawning stock that change in opposite directions would achieve one of the intermediate scores.

Such a change-oriented yardstick would make the full range of scores realistically achievable each year and would be far more sensitive to the decisions and harvesting behavior of the year in question than the level-oriented yardstick. The problem is that such a yardstick would have no linkage to the best available knowledge about the optimal range of the spawning stock. It would give priority to the crude qualitative anchors of "higher" and "lower" over the more sophisticated anchors derived from many years of studying the dynamic relationship between the stock's age composition and its replenishment. In an extreme scenario, the yardstick would assign an unbroken series of full scores to combinations of very low catches and dangerously low levels of the spawning stock, as long as their slopes were slightly positive, and zero scores to very high but slowly declining values on both. Clearly, a purely change-based yardstick would be unreliable in use.

My yardstick combines elements of the level- and the change-oriented alternatives by means of an index that weighs the parameters differently. The spawning stock parameter can contribute a maximum proportion of 0.67 of the total aggregate score, based on its level and change, whereas the catch parameter can contribute only a score of 0.33, based on the change. The greater weight thereby placed on the spawning stock reflects the rising prominence of precautionary considerations in international resource management in general, clearly evident in the Barents Sea regime as well. The backdrop for this trend is that as many as a quarter of the world's recorded fish stocks are either overfished or have collapsed (Food and Agriculture Organization 2009, 30). Figure 7.1 shows that for most of the years under study, according to the best available knowledge, the spawning stock of interest here has remained below the range that scientists consider optimal for maximizing long-term yield. Emphasizing the spawning stock in the yardstick is therefore well aligned with the priority expressed by the regime members, based on negative experiences with the opposite priority.

I base the catch component of the index on the change in catches rather than on their level primarily because that makes the yardstick more sensitive to annual decisions and accomplishments—which is important, since the causal drivers are specified annually. Besides, the last year's harvest is more readily available for use as a standard by fishers and managers than is the more abstract notion of a twenty-five-year average. The rising quotas and catches in the mid-1980s, for instance, brought relief and optimism and took much of the controversy out of the quota negotiations (see chapter 5), although a slightly longer backtracking would have shown that catches were far smaller than only a decade earlier.

To summarize, my simple yardstick for measuring aggregate problem solving in any given year considers the short-term changes in the two parameters of greatest interest to all players, catches and the spawning stock, as well as the *level* of the spawning stock. Aggregate problem solving is full if the spawning stock is within its optimality range and rising, and catches are up as well; it is insignificant if none of these three conditions applies. Substantial and modest scores may come from any combination of the three, each capable of contributing a third of the full score.

Applying this yardstick to the developments shown in figure 7.1 yields aggregate problem-solving scores (given in appendix 5, table A5.5) that are mostly modest or insignificant up to 1987, when the spawning stock finally took a turn for the better, joined in 1991 by rising catches as well as moving into the optimality range. Aggregate success in balancing utilization and conservation continued through 1996, primarily because of rising catches: the spawning stock declined but nevertheless remained within the optimality range. Then a difficult period ensued, with modest or insignificant scores resulting from declining catches and a spawning stock that soon crossed the precautionary reference on a downward slope. In contrast, the 2000s have been quite good, as is evident in rising catches and a steadily larger spawning stock. That trend has continued after the period under study.

In the next section, we examine whether this variation in the ability of regime members to balance their concerns with utilization and conservation is explained well by combinations of success and failure on the three aspects of problem solving.

Explaining Aggregate Problem Solving

Insofar as all of the partial problem-solving scores have been measured by yardsticks that relate directly or indirectly to levels of catches and the spawning stock, it is not entirely surprising that certain combinations of cognitional, regulatory, and behavioral scores do in fact reliably yield either high or low aggregate success scores. Strong associations cannot be taken for granted, however, since measurement of each of the aspects of problem solving reflects thresholds placed and justified, without consideration of how they might affect the parameters in my aggregate yardstick. Moreover, the analytical connections between these variables are not so rigid that the aggregate outcome can be safely predicted from the partial success scores.

The thresholds separating lower from higher degrees of success on the various aspects of problem solving have been established through different combinations of qualitative and quantitative considerations. In the cognitional case, the cutoff point for a high score, involving either full or substantial problem solving, was a forecasting accuracy of 30 percent.

Similarly, a high regulatory problem-solving score could be achieved as long as quotas did not depart from the recommendation by 20 percent or more; and behavioral problem solving would qualify as high as long as overfishing did not exceed 15 percent. I have argued in each case that these thresholds are reasonable, based on the aspect of problem solving that they help measure, but it is by no means clear that combining them will yield an aggregate result that corresponds to the outcome score deriving from my aggregate yardstick for measuring management success.

Another reason for caution regarding how well success on the aspects of problem solving can be expected to predict aggregate success is that these variables are not necessarily linked sequentially or rigidly. The analytical links are not necessarily sequential, in part because each causal factor may affect total catches and the spawning stock by influencing only one of the main regime members; I return to this point concerning leaders and laggards below. The analytical links are not rigid because in between cognitional success—accurate forecasts of how any given level of harvesting will affect the spawning stock—and regulatory problem solving we have the scientific advice, with its range of options and pre-ferred recommendation. That advice reflects attention to the levels of catches as well as levels of the spawning stock, but the balance between those criteria cannot be expected to be the same as in my aggregate yardstick. Nor is the balance likely to remain the same over the long period of advice provision studied here. Another flexible analytical link is that between behavioral success and aggregate problem solving. Since the catch parameter of my aggregate yardstick also includes overfishing, a lower behavioral score may raise the aggregate success score if the underlying level of overfishing does not yield a smaller spawning stock in the subsequent year. The analytical connections between the variables modeled here are not so tight as to rule out a low score on aggregate problem solving despite high scores on all drivers. Conversely, success on one aspect of problem solving can affect aggregate problem solving also without high scores on the others.

To summarize, a strong empirical association between partial success and aggregate problem solving is expected but does not necessary follow from the way the variables have been conceptualized or measured. If one or more drivers were found to influence aggregate success independently of the others, that would still make good sense. Confronting the hypoth-eses inherent in the model shown in figure 7.2 with empirical evidence can shed light on the connections between each aspect of problem solving and aggregate success in balancing utilization and conservation, including

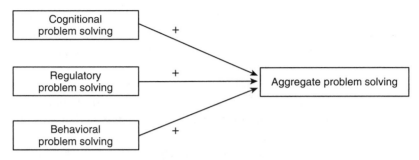

Figure 7.2
Causal model of aggregate problem solving.

whether some aspects are more central than others. Such findings will prove important for the ensuing assessment of how the regime has influenced aggregate problem solving.

First, however, we must ensure that the findings in chapter 6 about levels of behavioral problem solving are comparable to those concerning cognitional and regulatory problem solving.

Behavioral Leaders and Laggards

Thus far, the three drivers of aggregate problem solving modeled here have been specified at different analytical levels. A simple set-theoretic transformation allows us to use the findings from chapter 6 in the aggregate analysis.

Unlike the other drivers of aggregate problem solving, behavioral success is conceptualized and measured at the level of the state, which means that variation in it cannot be used directly in this analysis. Doing so would create a level-of-analysis problem: each of the behavioral success scores substantiated in chapter 6 concerns the harvesting pressure exerted by only one leading regime member, whereas the outcome variable in this chapter reflects the pressure of both members. One possible way to deal with this complication is to consider their joint quota adherence. In some years, both parties have exceeded their quotas; in others, underfishing by one has partly compensated for overfishing by the other. Since we want to use this causal analysis to assess aggregate *effectiveness*, however, such an approach would require an entirely new analysis, corresponding to that in chapter 6 but treating the coastal states jointly. It would require substantiation of new thresholds appropriate for differentiating among levels of joint quota adherence, as well as a new estimation of counterfactual problem-solving scores over the period studied. Even if we were prepared to undertake such a task, the causal analysis would be cruder than that in chapter 6, since the observations would be fewer and we would not benefit from the differences between the coastal states that allowed us to analyze the significance of transparency, obligation, and shaming for behavioral problem solving.

A much better way to place the three aspects of problem solving on the same analytical level is to derive two slightly more abstract behavioral variables and then analyze their possible interaction with cognitional and regulatory success separately. The new variables describe the *scope* of behavioral success: whether both main regime members adhere to their quotas, or only one does so. The leader-only version is the less demanding. In the early 1980s, for instance, the regime under study obtains a high leader-only score since the Soviet Union took significantly less cod than it would have had the regime not existed. Norway's resounding behavioral failure in the same period ensures a low score on the all-member version, which requires adherence by leader and laggard alike.

The two new variables are substantively relevant and conceptualized at the level of the regime, and moreover, it is a simple matter to measure them on the basis of earlier findings. The all-member version is the intersection of the sets of Norwegian behavioral success and that of the Soviet Union/Russia; the more lenient leader-only version is the union of the two. Therefore, as chapter 2 explains, the score on the all-member variable for each year is simply the minimum of the behavioral success scores achieved by the two coastal states, whereas the leader-only score is the maximum of the state-level scores. The same logic and procedure allow practically effortless transformation of the counterfactual estimates substantiated in chapter 6 to the regime-level estimates needed in the aggregate analysis.

The causal models examined in the remainder of this section, therefore, allow us to examine how variation in success on each aspect of problem solving affects the aggregate success score, with the behavioral driver specified in two ways, corresponding to different scopes of rule adherence.

Paths to Aggregate Success and Failure
Success in balancing utilization and conservation can be reliably predicted only when all three aspects of problem solving succeed, including quota adherence by all states. Aggregate failure seems guaranteed if regulatory failure combines with a cognitional failure that underestimates

the effects of harvesting on the spawning stock. Both outcomes may occur under other causal conditions as well, but not reliably.

The reliable paths to aggregate success or failure derive from a fuzzy set QCA analysis of the combinations of cognitional, regulatory, and behavioral problem-solving scores achieved under the Barents Sea fisheries regime from 1980 through 2004, and the levels of aggregate success over the period.[1] This set-theoretic technique, explained in chapter 2, proceeds by examining outcomes among cases with causal scores that fit certain ideal-type combinations to some extent: a pattern whereby all such cases achieve outcome scores that are equally as high as or higher than their score on the causal combination may, if other theoretical and substantive knowledge points in the same direction, indicate that the causal combination is a sufficient condition for the outcome. Chapters 4 to 6 explained the application of this technique in detail, so here I will be rather brief. I first show why the paths qualify as reliable—which they do only when behavioral success is coded strictly, requiring quota adherence by leader as well as laggard. Then I examine how robust the findings are if we code the outcome variable differently and remove one or several strong cases of the ideal-type causal combinations.

The reliable path to aggregate *success* is revealed by considering the eight cases in the dataset that fit the causal category combining full scores on all three aspects of problem solving; their consistency with the sufficiency pattern is 0.83. While this figure is slightly below the criterion of 0.85 used when we examined partial success, it is close enough to be accepted here as evidence of reliability, for two reasons. First, no other causal combination comes anywhere near it in consistency. Second, Ragin's (2006, 294) lower limit for a sound consistency criterion is much lower, 0.75, and I have accepted a consistency score slightly below the 0.85 limit when examining cognitional problem solving also. Since only one causal combination meets the criterion in use, and no simplifying assumption would be reasonable because the single consistent path is also the most potent in theory (see chapter 2), no reduction by logical minimization is possible. Statement A therefore is the most general formulation compatible with the evidence of what is required to obtain reliably a good balance between utilization and conservation. As in previous chapters, an asterisk means "combined with," an arrow means "delivers reliably," and the suffix "(all)" denotes that the behavioral success required is that involving all regime members. Around one-quarter of the total aggregate success in the dataset is covered by this combination:

(A) cognitional success * regulatory success * behavioral success (all)
   → aggregate success

The reliable path to aggregate *failure* becomes evident when we examine cases that fit one out of two causal categories, but only if we are prepared to remove one case from the dataset. Among the sixteen cases with some degree of fit with the ideal-type category combining full cognitional failure with full regulatory failure, consistency with the causal-sufficiency pattern is slightly below 0.80. Closer inspection reveals, however, that consistency with the expected pattern is perfect from 1980 up to 2001, when a modest departure from the pattern occurs that rises to substantial deviation in the subsequent two years. If we remove, for instance, the 2003 case from the dataset, the combination of cognitional and regulatory failure would meet the reliability criterion with flying colors, a consistency of 0.86.

Such removal of one observation from a dataset should never be undertaken lightly, but it seems appropriate here, for three reasons. First, the full consistency with the sufficiency pattern in every consecutive observation from 1980 to 2001 indicates that a connection exists. Second, what sets the subsequent period apart from nearly every other year under study is that the scientists *overestimated* the effect that the actual levels of harvesting would have on the spawning stock (see figure 4.1). Whereas cognitional and regulatory failure have usually reinforced each other, by encouraging harvesting levels that jeopardize the spawning stock in these particular years, one type of failure has reduced the effect of the other. Third, the findings from the aggregate success analysis are fully robust to this removal. I accept the evidence as supporting statement B, therefore, but add that this failure path is reliable only in periods when the scientific forecasts underestimate the effects of harvesting, as they have usually done. With the removal of one observation, this failure path covers consistently around half of the aggregate failure in the dataset:

(B) cognitional failure * regulatory failure → aggregate failure

These findings concerning reliable paths to success or failure are robust to an adjustment in the index of aggregate problem solving and to the removal of a few strong cases of the causal paths. I argued above that, for several reasons, the catch component of the index should be based on the change in, rather than the level of, harvesting. If one is not convinced by that argument and chooses the other basis instead, statements A and B would remain exactly the same. Nor are the results sensitive to strategic removal of one or a few strong cases of the causal combinations that meet the consistency criterion. Removing 1989, for instance, a strong case of the success path, would only raise the consistency of this path while retaining the failure path, and removing it jointly with 2003 would yield exactly the same success and failure paths.

In sum, this analysis indicates that reliable aggregate success requires high scores on the cognitional, regulatory, and behavioral aspects of problem solving. Combining regulatory failure with cognitional failure is usually a reliable path to aggregate failure, and it is always so if the cognitional failure involves underestimation of effect that harvesting will have on the spawning stock. These results are robust; in chapter 8, I examine their relationship to earlier findings on regime effectiveness.

Since the regime contributes significantly to all three partial success scores, the findings provide a somewhat general substantiation of regime influence on aggregate problem solving. To make that substantiation more specific, let us now turn to the most plausible counterfactual estimates of partial success, as derived in the preceding chapters, and see how well they fit the two empirically proven paths to success or failure in balancing utilization and conservation.

Assessing Aggregate Effectiveness

The effectiveness of the Barents Sea fisheries regime in improving the balance between utilization and conservation has been significant in most years from 1984 and high through most of the 1990s. The regime has contributed somewhat less to the relatively high scores achieved during the 2000s, but on the whole, the aggregate effectiveness of the Barents Sea fisheries regime emerges as being far higher in the second half of the period studied than in the first half.

These findings derive, as in previous chapters, from the approach advanced in this book, combining counterfactual path analysis and the Oslo-Potsdam effectiveness yardstick. Counterfactual path analysis involves examining the fit between the counterfactual antecedents—the combinations of causal properties that would pertain if the regime had not existed—and the reliable paths to success or failure. In chapter 2, I explained and justified three simple decision rules. Whenever actual problem solving is insignificant, or the regime has failed to influence any of the causal factors, the most plausible counterfactual estimate is the same as the actual score. Whenever the counterfactual path fits a reliable success or failure path, the fit score places a lower or an upper bound on the plausible counterfactual estimates. And finally, whenever the counterfactual path analysis leaves more than one plausible option, I base my choice on the number of causal factors that are weaker in the counterfactual case than in the actual case—that is, that have scores empirically shown to be less conducive. As the application of these decision rules has been explained and illustrated in the three preceding chapters, let us now move directly to the results and how they can be interpreted.

Table 7.1 reports in capsule form the counterfactual path analysis for each year studied, based on the actual aggregate problem-solving scores substantiated above, as well as the counterfactual antecedents—the most plausible estimates of partial problem solving as substantiated in chapters 4 to 6.[2] The table then gives the aggregate effectiveness score that the Oslo-Potsdam formula yields for each year under study, based on the actual problem-solving scores and the corresponding counterfactual estimates.

From the table we see that the Barents Sea fisheries regime has been ineffective in balancing utilization and conservation in eight of the years studied and fully effective in four of them. Aggregate regime performance has improved markedly over time: the summarized effectiveness score during the first twelve years is 3.16, whereas the corresponding score for the last twelve years is more than twice as high, 6.84. Figure 7.3 shows the fluctuations in the regime's aggregate effectiveness scores in greater detail.

The figure shows aggregate regime effectiveness as medium or lower throughout the 1980, then high in the first half of the 1990s and, following a performance drop after 1996, again high from 2001. In the remainder of this section, we will see how these findings help illuminate the interplay of the three aspects of problem solving. Here I examine five phases of aggregate problem solving under the Barents Sea fisheries regime, drawing on the findings in chapters 4 to 6. The results from the comparative analysis in this chapter are highly compatible with those of the previous chapters except that the regime may have had a greater effect on balancing utilization and conservation during the first few years under study than is indicated in table 7.1 and figure 7.3.

A Small But Important Behavioral Success (1980–1984)
In the first half of the 1980s, the regime failed to influence any of the proven drivers of aggregate success or failure, which means that the comparative analysis cannot support a claim that the regime differed significantly. We recall from chapter 6, however, that the regime helped

Table 7.1
Aggregate Effectiveness Analysis

Actual Problem Solving		Counterfactual Problem Solving		Effectiveness Score
Year	Score	Substantiation	Estimate	
1980	0.33	No regime influence on drivers of problem solving	0.33	0
1981	0.67	No regime influence on drivers of problem solving	0.67	0
1982	0.33	No regime influence on drivers of problem solving	0.33	0
1983–84	0	Insignificant even in actual case	0	0
1985	0.33	Counterfactual path analysis narrows range to 0.67–0; option below actual score chosen since cognitional and regulatory drivers are weaker	0	0.33
1986	0.33	Counterfactual path analysis narrows range to 0.67–0; option below actual score chosen since regulatory and behavioral drivers are weaker	0	0.33
1987	0.67	Counterfactual path analysis is indeterminate; option below actual score chosen since behavioral problem solving only is weaker	0.33	0.5
1988	0.33	Counterfactual path analysis narrows range to 0.67–0; option below actual score chosen since behavioral problem solving is weaker	0	0.33
1989	0.33	Counterfactual path analysis identifies 0.33 as lowest plausible estimate	0.33	0
1990	0.67	Counterfactual path analysis is indeterminate; lowest option chosen since all three drivers are weaker than in actual case	0	0.67

Table 7.1
(continued)

Actual Problem Solving		Counterfactual Problem Solving		Effectiveness Score
Year	Score	Substantiation	Estimate	
1991	1	Counterfactual path analysis is indeterminate; 0.33 chosen since cognitional and regulatory drivers are weaker than in actual case	0.33	1
1992	0.67	Counterfactual path analysis narrows range to 0.67–0; lowest option chosen since cognitional and regulatory drivers are weaker than in actual case	0	0.67
1993	0.67	Counterfactual path analysis is indeterminate; lowest option chosen since cognitional and behavioral drivers are weaker than in actual case	0	0.67
1994–95	0.67	Counterfactual path analysis narrows range to 0.67–0; lowest option chosen since all three drivers are weaker than in actual case	0	0.67
1996	0.67	Counterfactual path analysis is indeterminate; lowest option chosen since all three drivers are weaker than in actual case	0	0.67
1997	0.33	Counterfactual path analysis narrows range to 0.67–0; option below actual score chosen since regulatory and behavioral drivers are weaker	0	0.33
1998–99	0	Insignificant even in actual case	0	0
2000	0.33	Counterfactual path analysis is indeterminate; option below actual score chosen since cognitional and behavioral drivers are weaker	0	0.33

Table 7.1
(continued)

Actual Problem Solving		Counterfactual Problem Solving		Effectiveness Score
Year	Score	Substantiation	Estimate	
2001	1	Counterfactual path analysis narrows range to 0.67–0; mid-option chosen since cognitional and behavioral drivers are weaker than in actual case	0.33	1
2002–3	1	Counterfactual path analysis identifies 0.33 as highest plausible estimate	0.33	1
2004	0.67	Counterfactual path analysis narrows range to 0.67–0; option below actual score chosen since only the cognitional driver is weaker	0.33	0.5

Note: Scores: 1 = full; 0.67 = substantial; 0.5 = medium; 0.33 = modest; 0 = insignificant. Counterfactual paths and their fit with success and failure paths are listed in appendix 5. Effectiveness scores are calculated by the Oslo-Potsdam formula.

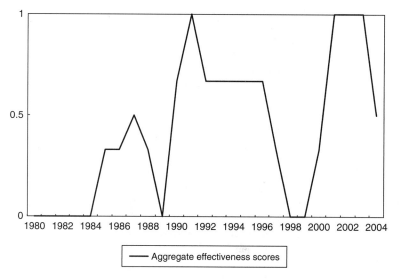

Figure 7.3
Aggregate effectiveness scores.

divert the Soviet harvesting pressure toward species other than cod in this period, when the other main regime member, Norway, was unable to control its total harvest. Such behavioral impact on one party merits closer scrutiny, not least since the level of the spawning stock in this period was dangerously low.

Stock forecasts were overly optimistic in these years, but they clearly conveyed the message to managers that the spawning stock was in a critical state. In chapter 5 we noted that Norwegian pressure for quotas in considerable excess of scientific recommendations nevertheless prevailed; and thereafter, these high total quotas were greatly overfished through practically unconstrained fishing by Norwegian coastal vessels. This low behavioral effectiveness on the part of the regime laggard at the time can be explained by the combination of readily available cod near the coast, scarce regulation of the coastal vessel fleet, and a regime-based exemption that allowed vessels using passive gear to continue harvesting even after the quota had been taken. On all three dimensions of resource management, therefore, we can conclude that the regime had little or no impact on the harvesting pressure exerted by the laggard.

However, the regime contributed significantly to the balancing of utilization and conservation aggregate because of two important features that served to contain *Soviet* harvesting pressures on cod. First, the flexibility mechanism of the Barents Sea fisheries regime has involved a mutually beneficial quota exchange, with the Soviet Union in this period purchasing large quotas for stocks found in waters under Norwegian jurisdiction, such as blue whiting and redfish, in exchange for cod. Such regulatory collaboration served both parties because those pelagic fisheries were valued relatively higher by the Soviets than by Norway. Moreover, the large Soviet trawlers had considerably greater reach than the Norwegian coastal vessels and could more readily shift from cod to other species. Second, the regime's fixed key for the initial division of the total quota allowed the Soviets to practically withdraw from the cod fisheries without fearing that Norway would thereby build a case for a bigger share of the most valuable stock in the ecosystem. Had the regime not been in place, the Soviet Union would have had strong incentives to try to match Norway's harvesting levels of cod and would have lacked access to other species more robust to its harvesting pressure.

Such behavioral effect on only one regime member is not enough to allow a firm claim as to regime significance since the behavioral leader-only model did not identify any reliable path to success or failure. It is nevertheless clear that the regime's effect on the Soviet harvesting pressure absorbed some of the detrimental effect of Norway's overfishing and can account in part—perhaps decisively—for the subsequent increase in the spawning stock from what had been dangerously low levels. In 1980, as figure 7.1 shows, the spawning stock was well below the present limit reference point associated with unknown population dynamics or stock collapse (220,000 tons; see chapter 4).

In view of the stock's vulnerability at the time, therefore, the aggregate effectiveness scores derived from the counterfactual path analysis probably underestimate the regime's contributions in the first few years of the period studied.

Cognitional Failure Constraining Success (1985–1989)

While the early 1980s show that failure on two out of three effectiveness dimensions does not rule out a somewhat positive aggregate assessment, the converse can also be true. In the second part of that decade, high scores on regulatory and behavioral effectiveness were canceled out, and more, by scientific advice in previous years that had dramatically underestimated the effects of recommended harvesting levels on stock replenishment.

Regulatory effectiveness was substantial or full in the second half of the 1980s, mostly because of the quota exchange but also because of Soviet pressures for a lower quota. The problem of keeping within the scientific advice was generally more benign than in previous years because the recommendations were higher—a tripling from 1985 to 1987. Behavioral effectiveness, too, was high, since the regime had provided the Soviet Union with the venue and the general norms needed for shaming Norway's huge passive gear overfishing, which resulted in removal of the exemption for this type of gear from 1984. The harsh shaming activity, sustained over a five-year period, and the more determinate Norwegian quota obligations led to more stringent domestic regulation of the coastal fleet being introduced earlier than would otherwise have occurred. Thus, managers heeded scientific recommendations in this period and fishers heeded the quota—two important conditions for sound resource management.

Unfortunately, these regulatory and behavioral successes were constrained from an aggregate management perspective because the high quota recommendations from 1985 were based on extremely inaccurate stock forecasts. The main cause of this drop in forecasting accuracy was the large ecosystem disturbances that occurred in connection with the return to the Barents Sea ecosystem of the Norwegian spring-spawning herring, a major stock that had crashed in the 1960s. Young herring fed on capelin larvae and juveniles, triggering a collapse of the capelin stock in 1986, and since capelin features heavily in the cod's diet, this collapse resulted in extremely low cod growth and high natural cod mortality through starvation and cannibalism. Growth and natural mortality are important parameters in the models underlying stock forecasts. When they suddenly take on highly unusual values, the substantive intricacy of forecast rises. For the second half of the 1980s, such intricacy accounts in great part for the mostly insignificant level of cognitional problem solving achieved.

The regime's aggregate effectiveness was mostly low in this period: the price to pay for the relatively high cod catches was a new drop of the spawning stock in 1987 to levels posing a high risk of stock collapse. On the other hand, this vulnerability meant that the regime effects on the Soviet harvesting pressure (by the quota exchange) and on Norway's harvesting pressure (through stricter domestic regulations) assumed particular significance. Failure in one aspect of resource management can jeopardize aggregate effectiveness, but the regulatory and behavioral contributions of the regime probably played a role in averting a full collapse of the stock.

Behavioral Failure and Missed Opportunity (1990–1996)

The regulatory urgency that followed from the near collapse of the cod stock around 1990—the situation perceived at the time was even more severe than indicated in figure 7.1, which is based on the more recent, retrospective assessment—explains part of the regulatory success of subsequent years. The regime also contributed by raising the state of knowledge, as is apparent in a series of scientific spawning stock assessments that roughly matched the previous year's forecasts. Again confirming the importance of succeeding on all three aspects of problem solving, very large quota overfishing on the part of Russian vessels during the early 1990s constrained those cognitional and regulatory achievements and prevented the spawning stock from stabilizing at the high level that had marked the 1970s.

The regime reduced Norway's harvesting pressure in the first half of the 1990s, but the real challenge to aggregate regime effectiveness came from the gradual opening of the Soviet/Russian fishing industry to the global market. By then, Russian vessels had begun to deliver steadily more of their cod catch abroad, mostly to Norway. This development had the dual effect of undermining the traditional Soviet system of quota control, based largely on the ability to cross-check reports from vessels and domestic recipient processing units, and greatly enhancing the incentives within Northwest Russia's fishing industry to exceed their cod quotas. A sharp rise in the commercial stock relative to the quota reinforced such incentives, and the result was an overfishing of the total allowable catch by as much as 50 percent in the early years of the 1990s. Indeed, in the worst year, quota overfishing equaled the difference between the ICES recommendation and its highest option, thus undermining the costly efforts by managers, and by those fishers who adhered to the rules, to stabilize the spawning stock at a high level. The exposure of such scandalous levels of quota overfishing triggered a series of initiatives to strengthen the regime's means for transparency, including the establishment of the Permanent Committee for Management and Enforcement. For a few years, the deeper collaboration among fisheries enforcement agencies in the two coastal states helped constrain quota overfishing, but the higher quotas can explain more.

Aggregate problem solving remained high throughout this phase, and the regime was important for achieving it, but the large quota overfishing cut short the long-term benefits. Behavioral failure of the magnitude experienced in the early 1990s was undoubtedly among the drivers of the reversal of fortune evident in figure 7.1: a decline of the spawning stock and, soon thereafter, of the commercial stock. The regime had failed to prevent loss of the opportunities presented by unusually high levels of the spawning stock in the early 1990s.

The Dynamics of Cognitional and Regulatory Failure (1996–2000)

The second part of the 1990s was marked by another round of widely inaccurate and overly optimistic stock assessments that generated strong expectations of high quotas. When the scientific advice grew more pessimistic, the coastal states failed to reach agreement on heeding this advice. The modest and insignificant aggregate problem-solving scores achieved from 1997 illustrate the vulnerability of any regulatory or behavioral success accompanied by cognitional failure.

Cognitional failure was caused by a new collapse of the capelin stock, partly but insufficiently counteracted by important advances in ecosystem modeling of the Barents Sea since the late 1980s. Years of intensive collaborative work among Russian and Norwegian scientists on ecosystem modeling had allowed qualitative incorporation of some ecosystem parameters in the ICES cod forecasts, but the rise in intricacy constrained its impact. Also at this time, the military authorities in Russia began to restrict the collaborative survey program in waters under Russian juris-diction. Those restrictions, which in some years affected not only Nor-wegian but also Russian research vessels, continued through the period under study and interrupted some of the time series of data that are so important in stock assessment. Although the regime made a positive dif-ference on the drivers of cognitional problem solving, that difference was too small to counter the effect of new impediments.

Insignificant regulatory effectiveness added to the poor cognitional performance. The combination of unimpressive forecasts and lack of urgency, since the spawning stock was estimated at above or near the reference, proved lethal to the prospects of reaching agreement on quotas anywhere close to the recommendation after 1997. Those prospects became even dimmer with the ICES implementation of the precaution-ary approach to scientific advice, which meant quota recommenda-tions that reflected greater safety margins than before and, when the stock fell below the reference level, catch levels low enough to allow rapid recovery.

This regulatory failure on top of the cognitional failure undermined the effect of the high behavioral effectiveness also achieved in the period. The behavioral success reflected the increasingly close collaboration between fisheries enforcement agencies in the two coastal states, but mostly that quotas were too high to constrain the fisheries significantly. Figure 7.1 shows the spawning stock again dropping below the precau-tionary reference level and approaching a dangerously low level; the regime's aggregate effectiveness dropped from high to insignificant levels in this period.

Failures, Achievements, Promises (2001–2006)

The final part of the period studied here was marked by conspicuous failures in several aspects of resource management, although with an overall improvement in catch levels and the spawning stock. A promising development appears to be under way concerning cognitional effective-ness, insofar as forecasts remained quite accurate in the last few years studied despite high substantive intricacy. Regulatory effectiveness was low through 2004, the last year allowing use of the explanatory models on cognitional and regulatory problem solving. During the last few years, however, the underlying difference between recommendation and quota had already narrowed a great deal, and the differences in 2005 and 2006 were small enough to qualify as full regulatory problem solving. The regime contributed significantly to this by developing a multiyear harvest control rule aimed at balancing the precautionary approach and the industry's need for stable quotas over time.

Behavioral effectiveness, too, dropped to an insignificant level, with a new wave of very high Russian quota overfishing that was documented from 2002 but had most plausibly begun earlier. The regime-based cooperation on monitoring and control had raised the transparency of Russian harvesting activities, but the shift of Russian landings from Norwegian to various EU ports undermined its potential. In response, the two coastal states pushed successfully for a stronger Scheme of Control and Enforcement under the broader NEAFC regime, implying greater port-state control of landings of Northeast Arctic cod and lower estimates of Russian quota overfishing after 2007.

Accordingly, these last years of the period under study have posed great challenges to the Barents Sea fisheries regime, yet the aggregate effectiveness emerges as mostly high. The multiyear harvest control rule is an important achievement, but the disconnect until recently between agreed-upon rules and Russian harvesting levels means that this regulatory advance was not a strong driver behind the improvement in the stock situation that occurred in this period. Paradoxically, the high aggregate score derives mostly from cognitional failure, which cushioned the effects of regulatory and behavioral failure: contrary to the usual pattern, the forecasts underestimated the impacts that the actual harvesting pressure would have on the spawning stock.

Summary and Implications

This chapter has focused on the aggregate effectiveness of a resource management regime—how it contributed to the social purpose of balancing of utilization and conservation. The scale developed here for measuring success in such balancing combines attention to catches and the spawning stock: a full score applies if catches as well as spawning stock are on upward slopes and the spawning stock is within the range that scientists deem optimal for maximizing long-term yield. On that scale, aggregate problem solving under the Barents Sea fisheries regime was high during the first half of the 1990s and 2000s but low throughout most of the 1980s.

This pattern has helped us examine how cognitional, regulatory, and behavioral aspects interact in producing aggregate success. Partial success scores were substantiated in the preceding chapters, except that behavioral success must be placed on the analytical level of the regime—here measured in two ways, implying high quota adherence by both regime members or by one of them. Only the more stringent version, requiring behavioral success with respect to both regime members, proved to yield a reliable path to aggregate success. It only did so, moreover, when combined with high scores on cognitional and regulatory success as well. In contrast, the combination of low regulatory problem solving with cognitional failure has been shown to yield failure reliably, at least when the cognitional failure involves underestimation of how catches will affect the spawning stock.

In the disaggregate approach to regime effectiveness, one important function of such reliable paths to actual problem solving is to support the estimation of what the levels of problem solving would be in a counterfactual no-regime situation. Combining the counterfactual partial success scores substantiated in the preceding chapters with the reliable paths to aggregate success or failure has helped narrow the range of plausible counterfactual success scores, allowing us to use the Oslo-Potsdam yardstick for measuring regime effectiveness. For this regime, aggregate effectiveness was insignificant to modest during the first part of the 1980s, but this limited regime impact was probably crucial in the early years, when the spawning stock was dangerously low. Later in that decade, and also in second half of the 1990s, good regulatory and behavioral achievements were canceled out by cognitional failure. During the first part of the 1990s, the long-term effects of cognitional and regulatory successes were undermined by behavioral failure with respect to one of the main regime members. The aggregate effectiveness that marks the regime from 2001 derived mostly from a cognitional failure that, unusually, overestimated the effects of the harvesting pressure on the spawning stock, thus canceling out regulatory and behavioral failures.

The aspects of management that have posed the severest challenges for balancing utilization and conservation have shifted over time, sometimes influenced by processes external to the regime. Examples include the abrupt ecosystem disturbances in the 1980s and 1990s, which constrained cognitional effectiveness, as well as the reorganization of the Russian fishing sector, which complicated regulatory problem solving and necessitated new measures for verifying and controlling fisher behavior. Such diversity in challenges to effective problem solving implies a corresponding diversity in the conditions for dealing successfully with them. This observation supports the basic premise that underlies the disaggregate approach to international regime effectiveness: cross-regime comparison seeking to identify the conditions that distinguish successes from failures should focus on distinctive aspects of the problem addressed by the regime in question.

Throughout the existence of the Barents Sea fisheries regime, its members have responded to new challenges by developing institutional features that support scientific survey collaboration and ecosystem modeling, reduce the economic or political costs of ambitious regulation, enhance the level of obligation to quotas, or improve the transparency of fisher behavior. In the concluding chapter 8 we look into the conditions influencing the success of such regime-based responses aiming to improve performance on the cognitional, the regulatory, and the behavioral aspects of resource management.

8

Conclusions

The aim of this book has been twofold: to develop a disaggregate approach to international regime effectiveness that can improve the balance among concerns for validity, determinacy, and generality, and to apply the approach to a specific case, the regime for managing shared fish stocks in the Barents Sea.

The first two chapters addressed international regimes generally in the sense that the concepts, theories, and methods used and explained there should apply to any international regime. Chapter 1 gave a brief overview of international regime analysis and its place in the broader study of governance. I endorsed the mainstream definition of an *effective* regime as one that contributes significantly to solving the basic problem it is intended to address. We also noted that, for many international regimes, the basic problem can be decomposed into cognitional, regulatory, and behavioral aspects—and that such decomposition offers substantial advantages for regime-effectiveness analysis. The chapter then outlined the research design of the study and pinpointed its distinctive features.

In chapter 2 I examined in greater depth some key methodological challenges in regime-effectiveness analysis—in particular, how to measure effectiveness, the need for sound counterfactual analysis, and methods for substantiating causal connections. The chapter developed a distinctive way of dealing with these challenges, using findings from the analysis of variation in problem solving to show what the level of problem solving would most plausibly have been if the regime had not existed. Causal analysis requires good models of the factors that drive or impede problem solving, so I briefly reviewed some theoretical approaches and variables identified in previous research on regime effectiveness. Central to the disaggregate approach is counterfactual path analysis, which examines the properties of drivers of and impediments to problem solving most likely without a regime—a task far more manageable than estimating the counterfactual outcome directly. Counterfactual path analysis helps substantiate the outcome estimate whenever the combination of causal properties that would apply with no regime is shown in the empirical analysis to reliably deliver either high or low scores on problem solving.

The disaggregate approach to international regime effectiveness advanced here combines such counterfactual path analysis with a yardstick for measuring effectiveness according to the difference the regime makes compared with the counterfactual no-regime situation, as well as the situation in which the problem is fully solved.

The subsequent five chapters applied this disaggregate approach to the international regime for managing shared fish stocks in the Barents Sea. In chapter 3 I described the activity system that the regime seeks to influence, as well as the national and international structures for fisheries management in the region. Each of chapters 4 to 6 applied my new approach to one of the general aspects of problem solving, demonstrating how useful a set-theoretic comparative technique, fuzzy set QCA, can be in identifying reliable paths to success or failure. Applying the same technique, I moved in chapter 7 from the parts to the whole by using the partial effectiveness assessments of preceding chapters to bring out their interaction in solving the basic problem of concern: resource management, or the balancing of utilization and conservation. That chapter summarized the empirical findings on the aggregate effectiveness of the Barents Sea fisheries regime.

This concluding chapter looks beyond the case of Barents Sea fisheries. The next section reviews briefly the experience with using the disaggregate approach, commenting on its applicability to regimes in other issue areas. Then I summarize my findings regarding the conditions that appear to influence success or failure on each aspect of the problem, examining how they relate to the results of previous studies of regime effectiveness. From those findings, the final section derives a set of implications for earth system governance.

Using the Disaggregate Approach

The approach to international regime effectiveness advanced here aims to make the analysis tractable, transparent, and readily comparable across regimes. Here we should recall two tasks that any assessment of regime effectiveness must tackle, relating to causality and adequacy. The causality task entails substantiating whether the state of the problem addressed by the regime would have been significantly different if the regime had not existed (Young 2001, 100), while the adequacy task entails evaluating any such difference according to an appropriate standard (Underdal 1992, 230). The most sophisticated way to measure regime effectiveness so far, the so-called Oslo-Potsdam formula, achieves higher validity than others do by combining the two, calculating the ratio of actual improvement to potential improvement. Assessment of both the actual and the potential improvement starts out from an estimate of a *counterfactual* state of affairs, or the level of problem solving that would pertain if the regime had not existed. Actual improvement is the distance from the counterfactual to the actual state of affairs, whereas potential improvement denotes the distance to an optimal situation (Hovi, Sprinz, and Underdal 2003; see chapter 2), which I call "full problem solving." The disaggregate approach to international regime effectiveness has helped specify and substantiate the parameters needed for assessing international regime effectiveness validly.

This section is structured by the three main features of the disaggregate approach to international regime effectiveness. Its first characteristic is decomposition of the problem addressed by the regime in a way that mirrors the main activities under it, yet applies to other regimes as well. The second feature is decomposition of the counterfactual analysis into three steps, making the analysis simpler, more transparent, and more persuasive. The third feature is decomposition of the empirical evidence by identifying distinct phases and, as appropriate, measuring regime outputs and problem developments at a level that generates a high number of observations.

Decomposing the Problem

Decomposing the problem addressed by the regime supports effectiveness assessment by making three core analytical operations more manageable: measuring problem solving, explaining it, and using findings to substantiate how problem solving would be different with no regime.

Measuring problem solving requires a yardstick that also defines the criteria for full problem solving. The approach of building and applying yardsticks that differentiate validly and determinately among cases has proved quite manageable in this study, not least because each yardstick concerns a single, clearly defined aspect of the larger phenomenon. Moreover, the partition used here links up to readily observable activities within international regimes: joint efforts to clarify the relative merits of alternative regulatory action, translate knowledge into rules, and increase adherence to rules. Such correspondence with the organization of regime activities has helped concretize the scaling of problem-solving yardsticks, including the definition of what constitutes full and insignificant levels of problem solving, as well as intermediate scale points.

Frequently, these thresholds have been specified in ways that are also applicable to other regimes, thereby inviting comparative analysis or cumulative studies. For instance, one dimension of cognitional success, salience (in the sense that expert input into decision making elucidates the policy options under consideration), varies greatly among international institutions (Mitchell, Clark, and Cash 2006). The other yardsticks of problem solving also employ "qualitative anchors" (Ragin 2000, 317) applicable well beyond the case studied. The regulatory yardstick examines the deviation from highly salient advice, the behavioral one considers the extent of noncompliance, and the aggregate yardstick asks whether the main, partly competing objectives pursued through the regime have been balanced in a way that reflects the stated intentions of regime members. Explicit and concrete yardsticks for measuring degrees of problem solving have often been missing from analyses of regime effectiveness, and my decomposition of the problem links them directly to readily observable regime activities.

The explanatory part of effectiveness analysis has also proved more tractable and valid as a result of decomposing the larger regime problem because a more discrete object of analysis narrows the range of relevant drivers and impediments. Modeling as well as empirical evaluation has become more valid because, as chapters 4 to 6 bring out, the combinations of causal factors identified as relevant in earlier studies, and found to be relevant here, are different for the three aspects. Chapter 7 showed that failure on only one of the cognitional, regulatory, or behavioral aspects of the problem greatly reduces the prospects for aggregate success. In the case studied, therefore, analyzing these aspects separately provided a richer and more nuanced explanation of the overall pattern of success and failure. Since the categories I have used for partitioning the problem apply to nearly any international regime, the findings can be compared with those from other studies of regime effectiveness, thereby supporting cumulative research, which has been relatively scarce in the field so far.

The advantages of attending separately to each aspect of the basic problem are no less apparent when we turn to the estimates of effectiveness of what problem solving would be with no regime. That is because a counterfactual estimate that involves only a narrow range of actors and activities is more likely to succeed than an estimate involving a highly complex phenomenon.

In short, decomposing the basic problem addressed by international regimes into its cognitional, regulatory, and behavioral parts makes the analytical tasks required by the Oslo-Potsdam yardstick of regime effectiveness more tractable. Partitioning the problem helps us measure success and failure using yardsticks that relate closely to observable regime activities; it supports the identification of causal drivers and impediments; and it makes the estimation of the counterfactual level of problem solving, to which we turn now, more valid.

Decomposing the Counterfactual Analysis

The most difficult parameter to determine in assessing regime effectiveness is the level of problem solving that would pertain with no regime, but the explanation of actual variation in success has proved useful. As chapter 2 showed, the difficulty stems from the lack of direct observation of the counterfactual case; the challenge is to estimate the counterfactual level of problem solving in a way that is explicit, transparent, and fully compatible with what is known about actual cases. The disaggregate way of tackling the challenge is to split the counterfactual analysis into three parts: explaining success and failure of actual cases, specifying the counterfactual causal path, and combining the two in estimating the most plausible counterfactual outcome.

The explanatory part of counterfactual analysis involves accounting for the variation in problem solving among actual observations in order to place regime-driven factors within a broader set of drivers and impediments. Earlier research on regime effectiveness has provided points of departure for building causal models, as has examination of how impediments to success for each aspect of problem solving have been tackled by the regime studied. The hypotheses inherent in my causal models were then confronted with empirical evidence.

Applying the fuzzy set QCA technique when evaluating the modeled hypotheses is not a necessary part of the disaggregate approach to regime effectiveness, but it has proved helpful. Causal analysis based on the standard comparative methods of agreement and difference is unreliable whenever more than one factor may produce an outcome, or if the effect of one factor relies on the properties of another. Such circumstances are commonly encountered by regime-effectiveness scholars. The QCA tool deals with them by clarifying whether certain configurations of properties of the modeled factors are consistently associated with either high or low scores on the outcome of interest. In chapter 2 I showed that such patterns could, if backed up by causal reasoning and other relevant evidence, support the hypothesis that the combinations in question are necessary or sufficient conditions for success or failure. The QCA technique also includes set-theoretic algebra and the reasoned introduction of simplifying assumptions to reduce such initial and complex statements in a disciplined and transparent manner.

To see how the results of this causal analysis can help in estimating counterfactual levels of problem solving, let us consider one of the empirical findings in chapter 5 concerning regulatory failure. A comparison of all cases indicated that, unless the state of the problem is perceived by the regime members as requiring urgent action, the combination of high malignancy—that is, strong incentives to violate any agreed-upon rule—and low collaboration will reliably yield behavioral rules widely deviant from salient expert advice. Regulatory collaboration refers to various joint means for enabling ambitious action, including long-term planning and cost-cutting joint implementation. Since the regional regime is the only means available for such joint planning and implementation, this finding indicates that the most plausible counterfactual problem-solving estimate in years marked by low urgency and high malignancy is regulatory failure. Thus, a general explanation for the pattern of the observed variation in problem solving, in tandem with a relatively straightforward, process-tracing-based specification of the counterfactual causal scores, helped narrow down the range of plausible counterfactual outcome estimates.

In sum, the disaggregate approach tackles the difficult and complex counterfactual question of what the no-regime level of success would be by first answering a question that is more tractable, namely, what the properties of the causal factors would be. This approach ensures high transparency with respect to the theories and evidence then used to derive the counterfactual outcome from that counterfactual antecedent. Further, it meets the criteria for sound counterfactual analysis identified in chapter 2 by producing explicit counterfactual estimates highly compatible with what is known about otherwise similar actual cases, that is, observed cases matching the counterfactual situation except that they are not under regime influence.

Decomposing the Evidence
The third main characteristic of the disaggregate approach, decomposition of the evidence, involves examining the modeled factors and outcomes over time and, with respect to behavioral problem solving, separately examining the impacts of the regime on the performance of

each of the major regime members. These moves enhance the number of observations, thereby expanding the range of analytical tools available to explain problem solving.[1]

Whereas procedures such as process tracing and structured, focused comparison do not require many observations, evaluating competing causal candidates by exerting comparative control on them usually requires more than a handful—and statistical control necessitates significantly more. I used the comparative QCA technique for all aspects of problem solving as well as in the aggregate analysis. For the behavioral aspect, with its greater number of observations available, I also used statistical inference based on rank-order correlation and multivariate linear regression. Analyzing the same material with several different techniques that yield highly compatible results, as was done in chapter 6, increases confidence in the empirical findings. Moreover, as noted in chapter 7, a simple set-theoretic operation allows us to place findings about individual regime members—or categories of members, such as leaders and laggards—on the same analytical level as those derived in the other empirical chapters involving performance by all members.

Like the disaggregation of the problem and the counterfactual analysis, decomposing the empirical evidence facilitates the operations needed for measuring regime effectiveness as the ratio of actual to potential improvement on the no-regime situation. While this study focuses on a single international regime, the disaggregate approach is applicable to more extensive analysis as well, whenever the differentiation of problem aspects is valid within a broad range of international regimes. One reason for the partition used here is precisely the recognition that activities within a wide set of international regimes, also beyond the realm of resource management, involve collaborative expert advice, norm building, and ways to enhance the impact of such norms on state and target-group action. Such generality permits comparative analysis across regimes and also supports cumulative research on regime effectiveness, to which we now turn.

Conditions Influencing International Regime Effectiveness

Two causal variables that loom large in the literature on regime effectiveness, malignancy and collaboration, emerge from this study as relevant for all aspects of problem solving, but their effects depend crucially on other conditions.[2] Other factors influence one aspect only—as the state of scientific knowledge does for regulatory success, and as obligation, transparency, and shaming do for behavioral problem solving.

This study draws on and elucidates earlier work on conditions that can promote or impede international regime effectiveness. The models of problem solving underlying my causal analysis emerged from a dialog between general propositions supported in previous studies of regime effectiveness and certain salient experiences in the history of the Barents Sea fisheries regime specifically. Some relevant examples include the blatant failures of attempts to forecast the impacts of various harvesting levels on the spawning stock, as well as fierce regulatory disputes and scandalous levels of noncompliance. The hypotheses underlying the models so derived were then confronted systematically with the available evidence, using the comparative and statistical techniques noted above.

This section relates the main findings from that confrontation of theory with evidence to previous work on international regime effectiveness. I first take up the three aspects of problem solving, beginning with the one closest to the basic problem, and then turn to their aggregation.

Behavioral Effectiveness

The behavioral problem in focus for international regimes is, as explained in chapter 1, to ensure that international rules really influence the performance of those who engage in the activities regulated by the regime. From the evidence presented in this study, we have seen that success in solving this problem can reliably be expected only when malignancy is low, and even then only if the regime has ensured high degrees of obligation *as well as* transparency. Conversely, behavioral failure seems nearly guaranteed if high malignancy is combined with low obligation, unless the regime laggard is also subjected to harsh shaming.

We recall that malignancy is about incentives to violate agreed-upon rules, and that such incentives have been high in the Barents Sea case whenever the resource has been amply available relative to the overall quota. Obligation concerns the determinacy of regime rules, which may derive either from their textual precision or from agreed-upon dispute settlement procedures, and whether the rules are legally binding. Transparency is about the ability and willingness of member states to verify target-group reports based on independent sources of information, such as on-site inspections.

The central place of malignancy on both the failure and the success paths gives firm support to an approach to behavioral effectiveness that focuses on examining the configuration of interests among the actors involved. This is the rationalist mainstream of regime analysis (see

Hasenclever, Mayer, and Rittberger 1997, 23–44; Stokke 1997), with its emphasis on incongruence between the individual interest and the social interest due to externalities or competition (Underdal 1987, 2002a; see chapter 2). If the prospective gains from violating agreed-upon regulations are sufficiently alluring, not even high scores on all the regime-based drivers of rule adherence can ensure success. In fact, even if those gains are small, they appear to override the normative pull of precise and legally binding rules frequently enough to make success unreliable unless the rules are accompanied by a compliance system that ensures behavioral transparency. While perhaps encouraging for rationalist regime scholars, this finding is rather depressing from a regime-effectiveness perspective, since material incentives to violate commitments are quite common, and overcoming them is exactly what behavioral problem solving aims to do.

Shaming is the least decisive of the factors that may prevent high malignancy from reliably delivering behavioral failure. In the case of the Barents Sea fisheries, the role of shaming has been largely indirect: whether the target of criticism has been Norway or the Soviet Union/ Russia, shaming seems to have succeeded in encouraging the laggard to take stricter domestic measures concerning regulation or compliance control, or to agree to more ambitious collaborative compliance measures.

When malignancy is low, however, my findings are more encouraging. The reliable potency of combining high obligation and good transparency under such conditions serves to support propositions deriving from earlier research concerning the normative pull of regulatory determinacy (Franck 1990; Breitmeier, Young, and Zürn 2006, 111), which is the aspect of obligation that varies in the dataset. Even under benign conditions, transparency cannot reliably deliver problem solving unless a member is strongly obliged to the rule. This is evident from Norway's consistently poor quota adherence during the first half of the 1980s, when the exemption for vessels using passive gear offered a legal loophole.

When backed up by process-tracing evidence, the high-transparency requirement for reliable success also gives empirical support to both the enforcement and the management strands of the regime-compliance literature referenced in chapter 2. The exposure of scandalous levels of rule violation in the early 1990s and 2000s, made possible through verification activities undertaken by the leader state at the time, raised the political costs of not taking compliance seriously, while also promoting steadily closer communication and more concrete collaboration among the enforcement agencies of the regime members.

Jointly, regime-driven obligation and transparency deliver behavioral success reliably if malignancy is low, and prevent high malignancy from reliably delivering failure.

Regulatory Effectiveness
The regulatory problem in focus for international regimes is to establish behavioral rules that reflect the best available knowledge on how the social purpose can be achieved. As with the behavioral aspect, the configuration of costs associated with the recommended policy is a salient factor in explaining variation in success. In this study, we have seen that political decision makers have heeded scientific recommendations reliably only when malignancy was low, and even then only if the state of knowledge was strong or if collaborative regulation was reinforced by urgency. Conversely, they have deviated greatly (and reliably) from expert advice whenever high malignancy has coexisted with low urgency, or when low urgency was combined with a weak state of knowledge and shallow regulatory collaboration.

The reliable occurrence of regulatory success among cases where there is low malignancy as well as solid knowledge can elucidate earlier findings concerning the role of expert consensus (Haas 1990) and of epistemic communities as drivers of scientific influence on political decisions (Haas 1989; Adler and Haas 1992). Through most of the years under study, consensus on the quota advice was high in the transnational network of experts who interact multilaterally through ICES and bilaterally in scientific working groups under the regime's Joint Commission on Fisheries (see chapter 3). Yet the network's persuasiveness appears to have been constrained not only by the malignancy of the policy the experts recommended but also by the state of knowledge as perceived by the managers, here measured by the reported accuracy of the most recent forecast. The process-tracing evidence indicates that the existence of a relatively integrated epistemic community has promoted regulatory problem solving, but that success has been contingent on several other factors.

The same success path also qualifies earlier findings indicating that scientific credibility (Mitchell, Clark, and Cash 2006, 316) and the conclusiveness of the evidence (Underdal 2000a, 15) are important for scientific input to influence regulatory decisions. In our dataset, that general proposition holds only under the benign condition that the recommended policy does not involve high opportunity costs for the target groups, which will usually mean that political decision makers experience little pressure to deviate from the recommendation.

Again with the proviso that malignancy must be low, the second success path brings out the importance of urgency and regime-based collaboration to decision makers' readiness to heed scientific advice. Urgency means that managers have reason to consider the state of affairs in the problem addressed by the regime as critical—here, because the spawning stock is reported to be so low as to give rise to fears of recruitment failure or even stock collapse. Regulatory collaboration is apparent in the regime mechanism for joint implementation (large-scale quota exchange), which was much used in the 1980s and lowered the costs of heeding ambitious advice, and also in the joint planning inherent in the multiyear harvest control rule agreed to in 2001.

The regulatory potency of combining urgency with cost-saving collaboration is high even among cases involving a weak state of knowledge, and that gives qualified support to findings from two strands of interest-based research. One emphasizes the effects that external shocks can have in helping states overcome deadlocks in bargaining and adopt ambitious regulations (Young 1989, 372). The other strand points to regime-based, cost-saving collaboration (Keohane 1984; Underdal 2002c, 460) and how this can induce states to take on commitments they might otherwise refuse. Again, the qualification involves malignancy: this study indicates that urgency and deep collaboration cannot deliver regulatory success reliably unless *both* are at work, and even then only if malignancy is low.

Unfortunately, both of the reliable paths to success require low malignancy. This overall finding is in line with the proposition in interest-based regime analysis that the material costs associated with a recommended policy are important points of departure for explaining adherence to scientific advice (Sebenius 1992, 361; Goldstein and Keohane 1993, 26; Underdal 2000b, 190; 2002c, 460–461).

From the perspective of regime effectiveness, the most depressing finding is that high malignancy reliably yields failure unless the state of the problem is severe enough to add urgency to the scientific input. Even the highest levels of regime-based success in obtaining credible evidence of the risks involved or in realizing cost-saving collaboration have proved unable to override the apparently lethal mix of high malignancy and low urgency.

The second failure path shows that, also under benign conditions, the same dismal outcome is almost inevitable unless at least one of the other regime-based drivers of problem solving is high. The more optimistic reading of this finding is to note the message it conveys about the importance of good, solid knowledge and cost-saving collaboration. High scores on those two regime-driven factors help not only to achieve regulatory success reliably when malignancy is low, they also help prevent low urgency from reliably delivering failure.

Cognitional Effectiveness

The cognitional problem in focus for international regimes is to build a shared, good understanding of how best to achieve the social purpose of the regime. Unlike the regulatory and behavioral aspects, cognitional problem solving has not received much attention as something that international regimes can help explain. Scholarly work has tried instead to clarify whether cognitional problem solving can be used to explain variation in regulatory problem solving—as the state of knowledge does in this study—or in overall regime effectiveness (see chapter 4). That is one reason why the model I have developed for this aspect, unlike those for regulatory and behavioral problem solving, includes two variables that cannot be expected to apply readily in areas other than environmental and resource management. The other, more important reason is that they appear to be highly relevant for explaining variation in cognitional problem solving. The factors are substantive intricacy and ecosystem modeling. Substantive intricacy refers to major shifts in those ecosystem components that affect the main resource most severely: in the Barents Sea case, especially the abundance of prey and predators. Ecosystem modeling concerns whether researchers monitor those conditions and take them into consideration in assessing how various levels of harvesting will affect the state of the stock.

This study indicates that cognitional success can be reliably expected only when substantive intricacy is low, and even then only if both cognitional collaboration and ecosystem modeling are intensive. Conversely, cognitional failure seems practically guaranteed if high intricacy is not counteracted by ecosystem modeling. Also, high malignancy seems lethal to cognitional problem solving unless counteracted by at least one of the factors under regime influence, collaboration and ecosystem modeling.

As noted, collaboration refers to joint planning or joint implementation of regime tasks, and the cognitional variety centers on scientific surveys that complement catch reports by fishers in the database underlying stock assessment work. High malignancy impedes cognitional problem solving because strong incentives to exceed regime regulations have usually implied that catch reports have been less reliable.

From the perspective of resource management, these findings offer both encouragement and a warning. It is encouraging that ecosystem modeling, which is increasingly employed under most international resource regimes, seems to make a real difference to the validity of scientific input. But even when substantive intricacy is low, such modeling seems to require reinforcement by broader scientific collaboration to enable accurate forecasting, and when intricacy is high, all that ecosystem modeling can achieve is to prevent cognitional failure from occurring consistently.

The scant attention paid so far by regime-effectiveness scholars to the role of regimes in *shaping* cognitional problem solving means that my results neither support nor qualify specific earlier findings. At a more general level, the central place of malignancy in one of the failure paths again offers support to rationalist regime analysis. On the regulatory and behavioral dimensions, the effect of collaboration has largely indicated that utilitarian considerations impinge heavily on the performance of regulators and target groups. Here, the effects of collaboration and of ecosystem modeling also reflect the greater potential for learning that derives from joining forces in highly demanding cognitional problem-solving work.

Jointly, regime-driven collaboration and ecosystem modeling reliably deliver cognitional success when substantive intricacy is low, and they prevent high intricacy as well as high malignancy from reliably delivering failure.

Aggregate Effectiveness

The basic problem in focus for an international regime stems from its socially defined purpose, whether that is to promote trade or safety at sea, to avoid dangerous changes in the climate system, or, as in the case studied in this book, to facilitate resource management. Examining the three aspects of that problem separately makes the long, complex causal chains connecting a regime and the state of the problem more tractable. However, it does not obviate a return to the larger phenomenon by aggregating the partial analyses (Yin 2003, 45). This I have done in chapter 7 by examining their interaction in solving the basic problem, specified here as balancing utilization and conservation.

The aggregate analysis indicates that success in solving that problem can be reliably achieved only if all three aspects are successfully dealt with. Conversely, aggregate failure appears guaranteed if neither cognitional nor regulatory problem solving succeeds, except in the few cases in which the effect of cognitional failure is to *exaggerate* the effects that the regulated activity has on the state of the problem.

Here I wish to highlight three implications that apply to the study of international regime effectiveness more broadly. They concern the validity of the tripartite division of the problem, the place of cognitional success in the aggregate analysis, and how the overall effectiveness of a regime often shows up as the ability to prevent difficult external conditions from reliably delivering failure—not as the ability to deliver success reliably.

First, the reliable path to aggregate success indicates that the three-part decomposition of the basic problem proposed in this book does in fact capture the essence of what states want to achieve with the regime. That essence, as shown in chapter 7, concerns the levels of catches and of the spawning stock crucial to replenishment. Success in solving all the partial problems reliably delivers aggregate success on those two main criteria.

A second observation concerns the prominence of the cognitional aspect in these findings. In most previous studies, even in areas where scientific input is salient, the emphasis has been on the regulatory and especially the behavioral aspects of problem solving (see chapters 1 and 2). The reliable path to success evident here certainly indicates that regulatory and behavioral successes are important for overall effectiveness, but it warns that the positive impact is vulnerable to poor cognitional performance. We have seen in chapter 7 that the process-tracing evidence underlines this caveat: in the second half of the 1980s and again in the second half of the 1990s, conspicuous cognitional failures canceled out the positive effects deriving from regulatory restraint and good adherence to regime rules.

The failure path underscores this point even more emphatically: high rule adherence is futile if the rules do not reflect a good understanding of the causal connections between the activity under regulation and the state of the problem. Most previous effectiveness research dealing with cognitional problem solving either has modeled it as a driver of regulatory problem solving or has narrowed in on the saliency dimension. Only a few studies, including that of Breitmeier, Young, and Zürn (2006), have paid attention to the accuracy dimension, which is the one that varies in the dataset used here: how well the causal connections between the regulated activity and the state of the problem are understood. My findings fit well with those reported by Breitmeier, Young, and Zürn (2006, 224), based on a broad comparative analysis of environmental regimes: overall effectiveness correlates positively with the growth in knowledge deriving from regime programs.

Even the few earlier studies of regime effectiveness that have included the accuracy dimension of cognitional success have not tried to identify the conditions that influence the level of accuracy. My study has clearly indicated that regime-based collaboration on scientific investigations, especially those seeking to describe the functional connections in a holistic manner, is important for cognitional success and can partly compensate for impediments deriving from malignancy or substantive intricacy. However, the underlying model was built without the advantage of earlier studies of the phenomenon and should therefore be seen as a first pass only; I noted in chapter 4 that the model explains variation in failure better than variation in success. From my findings on the centrality of cognitional problem solving in advancing aggregate success we can conclude that more research is needed to clarify how international regimes can help improve cognitional success, especially with respect to the accuracy dimension.

Finally, the aggregate analysis supports the partial effectiveness findings that a regime matters the most in situations where certain conditions that are largely outside regime influence, such as severe intricacy, low urgency, or high malignancy, would otherwise reliably lead to failure on one or several aspects of problem solving. As we see from the summary above of the partial analyses, high malignancy reliably yields failure on all aspects of resource management unless countered by one or more of the drivers of success, most of them under regime influence. The reason why failure looms whenever the resource is amply available, relative to the advice or to the quota, is that this situation implies substantial short-term opportunity costs in heeding the two. Similar comments apply regarding severe intricacy and low urgency. Under those conditions, reliable success is unlikely, and regime contributions often take the less impressive form of preventing difficult external conditions from reliably delivering failure.

In the partial effectiveness analyses in chapters 4 to 6, cases involving high scores on an impediment to success typically yielded counterfactual paths with good fit to a failure path, placing a low upper bound on the plausible range of counterfactual problem-solving estimates. Whenever actual problem solving is less than full, a lower counterfactual estimate raises the actual improvement parameter of the Oslo-Potsdam yardstick proportionally more than it raises the optimal improvement parameter, implying a higher effectiveness score. In contrast, when those nonregime conditions have been more conducive to problem solving, a good fit between the counterfactual path and the reliable success path has usually implied a high lower bound on the plausible estimates. The low or insignificant effectiveness score thus derived reflects the assessment that success would most likely also have been high in the hypothetical situation with no regime.

In the aggregate analysis, the significance of success obtained under external conditions nonconducive to problem solving shows up in two ways. First, most of the aggregate success achieved in the Barents Sea regime has occurred outside the reliable path to success—that is, in years involving failure on one or several aspects of problem solving. We noted in chapter 7 that the success path covered consistently only a quarter of the total aggregate problem-solving scores in the dataset. Second, the failure path also conveys the positive message that a high score on either the cognitional or the regulatory aspect of problem solving is enough to prevent guaranteed failure. On the whole, therefore, the aggregate success and failure paths support the evidence from the partial effectiveness analyses that regime effects on causal drivers such as collaboration, obligation, shaming, and transparency are particularly significant when the impediments to problem solving are great.

To summarize, aggregating the findings from the partial effectiveness analysis indicates that that my tripartite division of the basic problem is valid for the issue area studied here. More attention should be given in regime effectiveness to the cognitional aspect of problem solving, especially concerning the factors that influence the accuracy dimension. Finally, much of the regime's contribution to problem solving has occurred under conditions that cannot be expected to deliver success reliably. To a large extent, the regime has been effective by strengthening certain drivers of problem solving that have prevented difficult external conditions from reliably delivering failure.

Implications for Governance

Clarifying the conditions for effective resource management becomes even more valuable if we can derive practical lessons to inform subsequent governance practices. This final section builds on what we have learned about reliable pathways to success and failure and the process-tracing evidence from the Barents Sea experience to identify eight policy implications of relevance for those who create and operate institutions for international governance.

If Disagreement Blocks Problem Solving, Divert

Various diversionary tactics enshrined in the Barents Sea fisheries regime have allowed its members to conduct or support necessary problem-solving tasks without undermining their positions on auxiliary objectives—here, disputed jurisdictional issues in the region. Interstate disagreements on regulatory and enforcement competences complicate governance not only in fisheries but in other sectors as well, such as maritime transport (Molenaar 2007). Such disputes may block problem solving because of the linkage in international law between the actual exercise of authority and the strengthening of jurisdictional claims, whereby acceptance of regulatory, verification, or enforcement activities by another state implies a measure of recognition (Jennings 1963, 22–23; see chapter 3). In the part of the Barents Sea that was disputed until 2010, the diversionary move has been a system of parallel enforcement laid down in the Grey Zone Agreement, with each coastal state granting competence to board, detain, and arrest only vessels licensed by itself.

As to diversionary moves in the Fisheries Protection Zone around Svalbard, which is not formally recognized by other user states, Norway implements only nondiscriminatory measures in the zone and exercises restraint when exposing rule violations; in return, other states heed Norwegian reporting and management measures and accept inspections by the Norwegian Coast Guard. This approach involves "productive unclarity" about the legal basis for this exercise of jurisdiction, a diversionary tactic also used in Antarctic politics (Stokke and Vidas 1996b). In our case, this unclarity has allowed Norway to frame regulation and enforcement activities, and the practical acceptance of them, ultimately within its EEZ legislation, while other states may frame them through the Svalbard Treaty. Underlying the productiveness of this unclarity is the shared recognition that the total lack of such enforcement activities would jeopardize the parties' common interest in the basic problem addressed—the balancing of high catches with a stable stock replenishment.

As with the Grey Zone, the Svalbard fisheries approach involves decoupling management activities from potentially disruptive jurisdictional issues. The price of such pragmatism is somewhat less intrusive behavioral problem-solving systems in these waters.

If Other Institutions Are Better Placed, Link Up

Institutional interplay has been crucial to the effectiveness of the Barents Sea fisheries regime, which reinforces the view that governance studies gain by attending to the larger architecture or complexes of institutions cogoverning activities within broad issue areas (Biermann 2008, 287; Oberthür and Stokke 2011). The creation of the Barents Sea regional regime rested on changes in global fisheries law during the 1970s, in particular the extension of coastal state jurisdiction, which permitted a legitimate phasing out of many states that had traditionally engaged in harvesting in the region (see chapter 3). The decision to place the politically sensitive advisory function with an existing scientific institution, ICES, ensured continuity with respect to the many sources of data and the procedures for developing assessment-based recommendations, including the involvement of scientists from noncoastal states. This linkage to a broader science institution served to support cognitional as well as regulatory problem solving. The work on stock assessment and ecosystem modeling reflect the data, expertise, and scientific advances not only of the coastal states but also of the wider Northeast Atlantic fisheries research community (Gullestad 1998). In turn, this broader basis has reinforced the perception among stakeholders that the scientific advice is impartial and based on the best available knowledge.

Behavioral problem solving has also benefited from linkages to a broader institution, as is evident in the successful mobilization of the North-East Atlantic Fisheries Commission (NEAFC) for purposes of strengthening port-state controls of vessels carrying Northeast Arctic cod (Stokke 2009; also chapter 6). The rapid rise in Russian landings in European ports during the 2000s had undermined the fit between the institutional reach of the Barents Sea fisheries regime and the activity under regulation, since Russian fisheries enforcement agencies were no longer able to verify fisher reports by cross-checking them with domestic or Norwegian port-delivery data. The underlying effectiveness factor is institutional fit (Young 2008, 27). The darkest periods of the Barents Sea fisheries regime have been those when the scope of its rules or compliance structures failed to cover the activity system, as seen with the passive gear exemption, the high seas Loophole fisheries, and the Russian deliveries of cod in European ports.

We noted in chapter 1 that a similar strategy has been pursued to improve compliance with global shipping rules, within a set of regional arrangements that make use of the jurisdiction that states have over vessels voluntarily in their ports to ensure independent verification, review, and response (Molenaar 2007). In a dynamic environment, an ongoing task of governance should be to consider whether linkages to other institutions may enhance the overall capacity for problem solving.

Maintain the Saliency of Scientific Input

In close interaction with the multilateral component, ICES, the regime's bilateral science layer has been a major instrument for ensuring that scientific investigations remain salient by elucidating difficult or controversial policy issues—an important governance task (Mitchell, Clark, and Cash 2006). A rolling Joint Research Program has been developed and maintained by the leading marine research institutions of the two coastal states and approved by the Joint Commission; it is intended to coordinate fisher-independent surveys and intercalibrate equipment and methodology. Such research collaboration for forecasting accuracy became increasingly important with the drop in catch report reliability associated with the turn to international quota regulations in the mid-1970s (Halliday and Pinhorn 1996) and is evident in the reliable path to cognitional success.

The cognitional success and failure paths also indicate the value of another set of bilateral investigations for answering questions of crucial interest to decision makers: collaborative ecosystem modeling, starting out from the predator-prey relationships that impinge the most on the commercial stocks in the region (see chapter 4). In addition to such permanent or long-term endeavors, those operating the Barents Sea fisheries regimes have also established ad hoc scientific working groups to provide advice on specific matters that are controversial, such as how selectivity is affected by differences in mesh size, or that aim to facilitate the annual regulatory negotiations, as does the multiyear harvest control rule developed in the early 2000s.

While the multilateral science component of this regime ensures a measure of institutional distance between advisers and decision makers, thereby protecting the integrity of scientific advice (on such integrity, see Underdal 2000a), the bilateral component ensures a proximity that is important to its saliency.

Develop Decision Aids

The ability of those who operate the Barents Sea fisheries regime to adopt conservation and management measure that reflect scientific advice has been greatly helped by an expanding set of decision aids, the latest of which is the harvest control rule, which seeks to combine precaution and over-time quota stability (see chapter 5). The first among such aids for regulatory planning, whose impact is evident in the regulatory success and failure paths, was the set of fixed keys for allocating the shared resources agreed to during the early years of the regime. Similar keys have been developed with respect to other allocative matters, such as the share of the annual cod quotas to be set aside for noncoastal states. Their effect is to reduce the pressure to resolve difficult allocation issues by ceding on conservation.

The development of precautionary limit and target reference points is another case of such decision aids. It reflects normative developments in global fisheries law as well as a longstanding regional dialog among researchers, managers, fishers, and from the 1990s also environmental organizations, on appropriate standards for guiding management decisions (see chapter 5; also Stokke and Coffey 2004).

The rigidity of such rules may vary from case to case, since major changes in underlying conditions, such as the zonal attachment of a shared stock, may undermine their legitimacy and thereby their ability to serve as a focal point in negotiations (Schelling 1960). However, the Barents Sea experience clearly indicates that regulatory planning by means of decision aids helps keep management measures more closely within the bounds of scientific advice.

If Flexibility Can Lower Costs, Use It (Provided You Can Verify Compliance)

As with measures to mitigate greenhouse gas emissions, the costs associated with constraints on harvesting activities complicate regulatory and behavioral performance, and this is evident in the high level of malignancy that marks so many of the failure paths. Under the Barents Sea regime, the main flexibility mechanism meant to reduce such costs and thereby lessen the pressures on managers to exceed the advice and on fishers to exceed the quotas has been the transfer of fishing rights (see chapter 5). Especially during the Soviet period, such transfers allowed flexible implementation of necessary quota cuts as a result of differences between the two coastal states in their relative valuation of cod and pelagic species. This flexibility lesson may seem to counter the decision-aid argument favoring a simple allocative rule, but in fact, the two are closely connected. It was precisely the predictability provided by the fixed keys that reassured the Soviet side during the 1980s that temporarily reducing its cod catches would not jeopardize its future share of the stock (see chapter 6).

Unlike the quota transfers, whose significance waned with the incorporation of Russian fisheries into the global market economy, another flexibility mechanism has remained stable: the practice based in the Mutual Access Agreement that allows Russian vessels to take much of their quota in zones under Norwegian jurisdiction, where the fishery is better and the individual size of cod is bigger.

Similar to the joint implementation of greenhouse gas mitigation commitments (see Stokke, Hovi, and Ulfstein 2005), however, cost-saving flexibility mechanisms can work to promote resource management only if the overall compliance system can ensure that the extension of fishing rights involved is counterbalanced by corresponding reductions by the other party in other parts of the management area.

Exploit Crises

The significance of urgency in the path to regulatory success or failure demonstrates the role that crises can play as windows of opportunity for taking costly action. Achieving the institutional adaptiveness needed for responding to new challenges ranks high on the earth system governance agenda (Biermann 2008, 293). The urgency paths concern ambitious conservation measures when facing dangerously low levels of the spawning stock, but the general point of crisis-driven dynamism is evident in other regime processes as well. The scandal surrounding the exposure of massive Russian quota overfishing in the early 1990s greatly facilitated the establishment of new and dynamic collaborative elements in what had been a largely decentralized compliance system, notably with the introduction of the Permanent Committee for Management and Enforcement (see chapters 3 and 6). This body has markedly improved the flow of direct information between the fisheries enforcement agencies of the two states and expanded their knowledge about the other party's domestic compliance system. Many practical measures have followed, including an exchange of observers on each other's vessels and in ports, common conversion factors facilitating inspections, and collaborative satellite tracking. Similarly, the ability of Norway and Russia to persuade other NEAFC parties to include within that regime's Scheme of Control and Enforcement frozen fish taken outside its regulatory ambit was based on the release of shocking, solid evidence of massive quota overfishing made possible by inadequate controls in European ports (Stokke 2009).

Such unfortunate and rapid changes improve the odds for achieving potent conservation measures and for strengthening the institutional structures.

Create Soft Law If You Must, Harden It If You Can

Both the comparative analysis and the process-tracing evidence indicate that, in the Barents Sea experience, the determinacy and bindingness of obligations can contribute significantly to rule adherence (see chapters 2 and 6). This finding does not detract from the general argument that soft law is usually more flexible than hard law and can be more readily adopted and implemented by not requiring the involvement of legislatures. What it does is direct attention to the interplay between soft and hard law (Skjærseth, Stokke, and Wettestad 2006)—or more generally to the interaction of norms produced by any among a wider set of actors, including governments, industry groups, and advocacy organizations (Biermann 2008, 293), although market-based private governance has played only a modest role in fisheries management thus far. The successful shaming of Norway's coastal vessel harvesting excesses in the 1980s shows that even imprecise and nonbinding commitments can generate powerful political pressures to improve norm adherence, even when not supported by strong domestic constituencies. Norway's stricter regulation of its coastal vessel sector would have taken place later, and less forcefully, had it not been for the sustained shaming conducted by the other regime participant. Similarly, the resultant gradual removal of the passive gear exemption demonstrates the possibility of hardening a soft commitment when higher domestic implementation capacities allow this.

Hopes or fears of binding international commitments motivate those who create soft law or private norms and procedures, and attention to such interplay can enhance the performance of resource management.

Combine Enforcement and Management Logics

Enforcement tactics such as surveillance, verification, and response to rule violation are sometimes seen as adversarial and difficult to combine with a management approach that focuses on communication as means for identifying and overcoming barriers to compliance, but the Barents Sea experience suggests otherwise. The high-transparency ingredient in the reliable path to behavioral success confirms the significance of intrusive enforcement. Moreover, the process-tracing evidence indicates that shaming based on exposure of overfishing does not necessarily undermine the integrative exploration of problem-solving options among regime members. Instead, enforcement and management tactics appear to reinforce each other: in the 1990s as well as the 2000s, unilateral verification efforts by Norway were crucial for obtaining broader agreement on a less decentralized compliance system, making the Permanent

Committee a hub for management-style communication as well as for the development of stricter enforcement-style verification and control. Those two logics of compliance are complementary, not competing. Effective governance requires both.

Applicability

These governance lessons, drawn from the ups and downs in the performance of a Northeast Atlantic fisheries regime, have been phrased in general terms because they may apply more broadly. In short: Decouple complications you cannot solve. Utilize problem-solving capacities in other institutions. Create structures that permit shared knowledge building on matters of controversy or of central management importance. Develop decision aids to support predictability or to help align specific decisions and general principles. Exploit cost-saving flexibility mechanisms, but watch out for defection. Use crises to adopt stronger measures or trigger institutional adaptation. Remember the force of bindingness, determinacy, and governmental commitment when working with soft law or private norms also. And finally, build compliance systems that can release the complementary logics of enforcement and management.

The applicability of these lessons to other regimes is enhanced by the main characteristics of the disaggregate approach to international regime effectiveness advanced in this book. Lessons learned here concern the cognitional, the regulatory, and the behavioral aspects of the problem addressed by the regime, a decomposition that applies well beyond the sphere of fisheries management. The decomposition of the counterfactual analysis means that the causal factors involved in the explanatory part are drawn from a wide body of effectiveness studies involving many fields of international governance. And although the reliable paths to success or failure identified here derive from analysis of only one specific regime, the decomposition of the empirical evidence by year and actor has ensured significant variation in those general drivers of and impediments to international regime effectiveness.

Appendixes

Appendix 1: Rank-Order Validity of Oslo-Potsdam Effectiveness Scores

Although the yardstick for measuring regime effectiveness in this study—a version of the Oslo-Potsdam formula—applies mathematical subtraction and division, it does not require interval-level measurement of problem solving in order to rank cases validly. It works well also with an ordinal scale, that is, one that merely sorts observations from lower to higher values without measuring the distance between observations. The table below helps show that the rank order that derives from my yardstick is exactly the same as would have resulted on the basis of qualitative differentiation only, without assuming that the distance separating insignificant from modest problem solving is equal to the distance from modest to substantial problem solving or from substantial to full problem solving.

The Oslo-Potsdam yardstick calculates effectiveness scores by comparing the distance between an optimal state of affairs—here, full problem solving—and two reference points: the actual level of problem solving achieved with the regime in place, and the most plausible estimate of the counterfactual level of problem solving if the regime had not existed. As full problem solving implies a score of 1, variation in the effectiveness score results from the combination of actual and counterfactual problem-solving scores. Since the yardstick applies directly only to cases in which the most plausible counterfactual level of problem solving is less than full and not higher than the actual level (see chapter 2), nine such combinations are logically possible. Each is represented by a row in the table below, sorted according to the effectiveness score they yield on my yardstick, from the highest to the lowest value.

Thus, the first three rows in the table below refer to regimes that raise the level of problem solving to the highest level. In the first row, the counterfactual estimate was substantial (a score of 0.67); the actual improvement is therefore (1 – 0.67 = 0.33), which is the same as the potential improvement (also 1 – 0.67 = 0.33). Since the Oslo-Potsdam formula calculates effectiveness by the ratio of actual to potential improvement, effectiveness is full (a score of 1). In rows 2 and 3, the counterfactual levels of problem solving are lower, so the number of qualitative steps contributed by the regime is higher. Such heterogeneity among fully effective regimes does not weaken the validity of the measure since any regime that raises problem solving to the highest level merits the highest score. The alternative would be absurd: a regime facing a problem that states are capable of partly solving without the regime would be ineligible for the full effectiveness score.

The regime referred to in row 4 is inferior to those above because it fails to solve the problem fully. On the other hand, on an ordinal scale it is also clearly superior to those referred to in the rows below it. That is because those below it involve either no positive qualitative step or only one such step (from insignificant to modest or from modest to substantial), whereas the row 4 regime involves both of those steps.

That the row 5 regime is ranked above that referenced in row 6 is justified not by the number of qualitative steps it contributes—in both cases the contribution is one step only—but by a conceptual argument laid out in set-theoretic terms. As argued by Ragin (2000, 317), the midpoint of a scale is more fundamental than other thresholds since it separates cases that are more inside than outside the concept from those that are more outside than inside.

Finally, the regimes referred in rows 7 to 9 are clearly inferior to the others because they fail to raise the level of problem solving from the most plausible counterfactual level; they make no significant difference.

We may conclude that, regardless of whether problem solving is measurable at the interval level or only at the ordinal level, the four-value yardstick used in this study ranks cases validly: the same ranking would obtain if the distances between the category thresholds were different.

Table A1.1
Rank-Order Validity of Oslo-Potsdam Effectiveness Scores

	C′ PS	PS	(PS − C′ PS)/ (1 − C′ PS)	Qualitative Steps in Problem Solving
1	0.67	1	1	Substantial to full
2	0.33	1	1	Modest to substantial Substantial to full
3	0	1	1	Insignificant to modest Modest to substantial Substantial to full
4	0	0.67	0.67	Insignificant to modest Modest to substantial
5	0.33	0.67	0.5	Modest to substantial
6	0	0.33	0.33	Insignificant to modest
7	0.67	0.67	0	None
8	0.33	0.33	0	None
9	0	0	0	None

Note: **C′ PS** = counterfactual problem solving; **PS** = (actual)problem solving; **1** = full; **0.67** = substantial; **0.5** = medium; **0.33** = modest; **0** = insignificant.

Appendix 2: General Underlying Data

Table A2.1
General Underlying Data

	SSB	SSB	CSB	ADVICE	ADVICE	TAC	CTCH	CTCH	CTCH
	FRST	2008	2008	REC	HIGH	TAC	TOT	NOR	SU/RU
1980	222	108	864	390	460	390	380	232	115
1981	225	167	984	220	400	300	399	278	83
1982	377	326	751	240	434	300	364	288	40
1983	533	327	739	204	380	300	290	234	23
1984	374	251	818	150	300	220	278	231	22
1985	346	194	958	170	300	220	308	211	62
1986	393	171	1,294	388	446	400	430	232	151
1987	351	121	1,126	595	645	560	523	268	202
1988	187	203	915	340	500	451	435	223	169
1989	150	235	890	335	508	300	332	159	135
1990	259	316	963	172	312	160	212	89	75
1991	571	705	1,562	215	289	215	319	126	119
1992	1056	888	1912	257	384	356	513	168	182
1993	943	775	2,360	385	534	500	582	221	245
1994	830	615	2,155	649	750	700	771	318	292
1995	705	529	1,826	682	788	700	740	320	296
1996	832	571	1,687	746	854	700	732	319	305
1997	839	589	1,532	787	1342	850	762	358	313

1998	631	386	1,222	514	689	654	593	285	244
1999	298	293	1,101	360	494	480	485	223	210
2000	249	241	1,102	110	328	390	415	193	166
2001	300	356	1,376	263	470	395	426	188	184
2002	430	498	1,542	182	435	395	535	203	184
2003	653	548	1,609	305	425	395	552	192	182
2004	851	654	1,566	398	623	486	606	212	202
2005	701	602	1,556	453	646	485	641	208	200
2006	517	579	1,496	471	566	471	538	201	204

Note: **SSB FRST** = spawning stock biomass, Northeast Arctic cod (aged 6 years and older) (1,000 tons); assessed size at beginning of the year, given during the ICES autumn meeting; data from ICES (1978–2008). **SSB 2008** = retrospective assessment given during the ICES 2008 meeting, reported in ICES (2008a, 53). **CSB** = commercial stock biomass, Northeast Arctic cod (aged 3 years and older) (1,000 tons): data from ICES (2008b, 185). **ADVICE REC** = ICES-recommended catch level, Northeast Arctic cod (1,000 tons); data from ICES (1978–2008); figures refer to the quota year. For 1981, the ICES did not make a specific recommendation among the options; the figure given for that year is the single recommendation corresponding to the qualitative recommendation of a "considerable step towards Fmax" (ICES 1981, 222). The recommendation for 1988 was originally 530,000 tons, which is the figure used when calculating regulatory problem solving; during the spring meeting, it was adjusted downward to the figure given here (ICES 1988, 9). **ADVICE HIGH** = highest ICES option, Northeast Arctic cod (1,000 tons); explanation in chapter 4, data from ICES (1978–2008). The 1981 figure is the highest option not explicitly discouraged by the phrase "should not be considered for management" (ICES 1981, 220). **CTCH TOT** = catches, Northeast Arctic cod (1,000 tons); data on total catches from ICES (2008a, 53); data from ICES (2007b, 38). **CTCH NOR** = Norwegian catches; data from ICES (2007b, 38). **CTCH SU/RUS** = data on Soviet/Russian catches from ICES (2007b, 38) with the addition of two-thirds of the ICES-estimated unreported catches in 1990–1994 and all the ICES-estimated unreported catches in 2002–2006 (explanation in chapter 6); ICES estimates of unreported catches in ICES 2008, 37).

Appendix 3: Data on Cognitional and Behavioral Effectiveness

Table A3.1
Data Underlying the Cognitional- and the Behavioral-Effectiveness Analyses

	FORECAST			FC-DIST	CPS	CBS/-TAC	MAL-C	MAL-BN	MAL-BR	CAP	CAN2	CAN3	INTR
	FC(+2)	F(+2)O1	F(+2)O2										
1980	298	380	298	8	1	2.22	0.33	0.33	0.33	7.61			0
1981	527	630	580	−61	0.33	3.28	0.67	0.67	0.67	2.54			0
1982	425	470	420	−69	0.33	2.50	0.33	0.33	0.33	3.26			0
1983	374	415	352	−93	0	2.46	0.33	0.33	0.33	3.27			0
1984	211	235	216	−23	0.67	3.72	0.67	0.67	0.67	2.23	0.04	0	0
1985	312	330	305	−158	0	4.35	1.00	1.00	1.00	0.23	0.56	0	0.67
1986	476	477	428	−135	0	3.24	0.67	0.67	0.67	0.03	0.8	0.1	0.67
1987	900	933	840	−283	0	2.01	0.00	0.00	0.00	0.10	0.8	0.06	0.67
1988	374	394	349	−18	0.67	2.03	0.00	0.00	0.00	0.39	0.11	0.01	0.33
1989	216	238	205	69	0.33	2.97	0.67	0.67	0.67	0.87	0	0	0.33
1990	330	407	352	63	0.33	6.02	1.00	1.00	1.00	5.09	0.06	0	0
1991	398	582	502	49	0.33	7.27	1.00	1.00	1.00	3.66	0.24	0.01	0
1992	634	790	672	−3	1	5.37	1.00	1.00	1.00	2.22	0.15	0.01	0
1993	670	734	681	−27	0.67	4.72	1.00	1.00	1.00	0.17	0.45	0.07	0.67
1994	719	730	692	−26	0.67	3.08	0.67	0.67	0.67	0.12	0.63	0.2	1
1995	726	754	716	−23	0.67	2.61	0.33	0.33	0.33	0.10	0.94	0.54	1
1996	1549	1730	1527	−301	0	2.41	0.33	0.33	0.33	0.28	1.06	0.45	1
1997	715	789	706	−144	0	1.80	0.00	0.00	0.00	0.56	1.09	0.31	1

Year	FC(+2)	FC(+2)O1	FC(+2)O2	FC-DIST	CBS/TAC	CPS	MAL-C	MAL-BN	MAL-BR	CAP	CAN2	CAN3	INTR
1998	496	571	488	−106	0	1.87	0.00	0.00	0.00	1.51	0.63	0.33	1
1999	345	372	256	3	1	2.29	0.33	0.33	0.33	2.25	0.36	0.11	0.33
2000	409	456	386	18	0.67	2.83	0.67	0.67	0.67	3.11	0.26	0.07	0
2001	298	315	293	46	0.33	3.48	0.67	0.67	0.67	2.11	0.22	0.05	0
2002	418	512	435	36	0.33	3.90	1.00	1.00	1.00	0.96	0.49	0.12	0.67
2003	695	788	682	−15	0.67	4.07	1.00	1.00	1.00	0.26	0.25	0.05	0.33
2004	733	862	729	−27	0.67	3.22	0.67	0.67	0.67	0.45	0.63	0.06	0.67
2005						3.21		0.67	0.67				
2006						3.18		0.67	0.67				

Note: **FC(+2)** = forecast of the size of the spawning stock, Northeast Arctic cod (1,000 tons), at the beginning of (y + 2), given a catch level in (y + 1) corresponding the latest report (ICES 2008a); explanation in chapter 4; forecast data from ICES (1978–2008); the figure is a linear inter- or extrapolation based on the two forecasts (listed in the two columns to the right) corresponding to the options that are the closest to the catch level in (y + 1). **FC(+2)O1** = forecast of the spawning stock, Northeast Arctic cod (1,000 tons), at the beginning of (y + 2), corresponding to one of the two options (O1) that are the closest to the (y + 1) catch level; forecast data from ICES (1978–2008). **FC(+2)O2** = forecast of the spawning stock, Northeast Arctic cod (1,000 tons), at the beginning of (y + 2), corresponding to one of the two options (O2) that are the closest to the (y + 1) catch level; forecast data from ICES (1978–2008). **FC-DIST** = distance between forecast and the latest retrospective assessment of the spawning stock, Northeast Arctic cod, measured in percentage of the reassessment; data from ICES (1978–2008); a negative value denotes that the retrospective assessment is lower than the forecast. **CPS** = cognitional problem-solving scores, Northeast Arctic cod; relationship to FC(+2) explained in chapter 4. **CBS/TAC** = ratio of the commercial stock biomass to the TAC, Northeast Arctic cod; data on CBS from ICES (2008a, 53); data on TAC from JCF (1979–2005). **MAL-C** = cognitional malignancy scores, Northeast Arctic cod; relationship to CBS/TAC explained in chapter 4. **MAL-BN** = behavioral malignancy scores, Northeast Arctic cod, Norway (same as for the Soviet Union/Russia); relationship to CBS/TAC explained in chapter 6. **MAL-BR** = behavioral malignancy scores, Northeast Arctic cod, Soviet Union/Russia (same as for Norway); relationship to CBS/TAC explained in chapter 6. **CAP** = capelin availability: ratio of non-harvested capelin to the Northeast Arctic cod commercial stock; data from ICES (2006b, 88); **CAN2** = cannibalism mortality for Northeast Arctic cod aged 2; data from ICES (2006b, 161); **CAN3** = cannibalism mortality for Northeast Arctic cod aged 3; data from ICES (2006b, 161); **INTR** = intricacy scores, Northeast Arctic cod; relationship to CAP, CAN2, and CAN3 explained in chapter 4.

Appendix 4: Data on Regulatory Effectiveness

Table A4.1
Data Underlying the Regulatory-Effectiveness Analysis

	DIST-Q	RPS	CSB(-1)/REC	MAL-R	SSB(-1)	URG	FC(+1)	DIST-K	KNWL	TRNS	TR/NOQ	COL-R
1980	0	1	2.86	0.33	222	1	200		0.67	0	0	0.33
1981	36.36	0.33	3.93	0.67	225	1	244	-35	1	0	0	0.33
1982	25	0.33	4.10	0.67	377	1	221	-42	0.33	45	40	0.67
1983	47.06	0.33	3.68	0.67	533	0.67	372	11	0.33	72.5	64	0.67
1984	46.67	0.33	4.93	1.00	374	0.33	480	-23	1	40	50	0.67
1985	29.41	0.33	4.81	1.00	346	0.67	303	21	0.67	40	50	0.67
1986	3.093	0.67	2.47	0.00	393	0.67	268	14	0.67	50	31	0.67
1987	-5.88	1	2.17	0.00	351	0.67	364	12	1	70	30	0.67
1988	11.32	0.67	3.31	0.33	187	0.67	540	-261	1	32.5	18	0.67
1989	-10.4	1	2.73	0.00	150	1	249	-31	0	22	19	0.67
1990	-6.98	1	5.17	1.00	259	1	285	37	0.33	20	38	0.67
1991	0	1	4.47	0.67	571	1	342	44	0.33	10	13	0.33
1992	16.73	0.67	6.08	1.00	1056	0.33	591	54	0.33	10	7	0.33
1993	29.87	0.33	4.97	1.00	943	0	857	17	0	10	5	0.33
1994	7.858	0.67	3.64	0.67	830	0	768	10	0.67	10	3	0.33
1995	2.639	0.67	3.16	0.33	705	0	747	-3	1	12	4	0.33
1996	-6.17	1	2.45	0.00	832	0.33	697		1	8	3	0.33

Year												
1997	8.005	0.67	2.14	0.00	839	0	1,277	43	0.33	6	2	0.33
1998	27.24	0.33	2.98	0.33	631	0	811	-91	0	6	2	0.33
1999	33.33	0.33	3.42	0.33	298	0.33	576	-24	0.33	6	3	0.33
2000	254.5	0	10.02	1.00	249	1	275	-80	0	6	4	0.33
2001	50.19	0.33	4.19	0.67	300	1	286	-21	0.67	6	4	0.67
2002	117	0.33	7.57	1.00	430	1	272	-50	0	6	4	0.67
2003	29.51	0.33	5.08	1.00	653	0.67	429	31	0.33	6	4	0.67
2004	22.11	0.33	4.10	0.67	851	0.33	652	36	0.33	6	3	0.67

Note: DIST-Q = distance between the total quota (total allowable catch) and ICES recommendation on Northeast Arctic cod, measured in percentage of recommendation; data on total quota from JCF (1979–2005); data on recommendations from ICES (1979–2005). RPS = regulatory problem-solving scores, Northeast Arctic cod; relationship to Q-DIST explained in chapter 5. CSB(–1)/REC = ratio of the preceding year's commercial stock biomass to the ICES recommendation, Northeast Arctic cod; data from ICES (1978–2008). MAL-R = regulatory malignancy scores, Northeast Arctic cod; relationship to CSB(–1)/REC explained in chapter 5. SSB(–1) = the spawning stock biomass estimate of Northeast Arctic cod (1,000 tons) that the Joint Commission receives when negotiating the quota (for the subsequent year); data from ICES (1978–2006). URG = urgency, Northeast Arctic cod; relationship to SSB(–1) explained in chapter 5. TRNS = transfers of Northeast Arctic cod quotas (1,000 tons) from the Soviet Union/Russia to Norway during Joint Commission meeting; data from JCF (1979–2005). TRNS/NOQ = transfers of Northeast Arctic cod quotas from the Soviet Union/Russia to Norway during Joint Commission meeting, measured as percentage of Norway's initial quota; data from JCF (1979–2005). COL-R = regulatory collaboration scores, Northeast Arctic cod; relationship to TRNS/NOQ explained in chapter 5. FC(+1) = short-term forecast on the spawning stock of Northeast Arctic cod (1,000 tons) that the Joint Commission receives for the quota year; data from ICES (1978–2006). DIST-K = distance between the most recent forecast (F(+2) in appendix 3) for the quota year and the preceding conditional forecast (F(+1)) in appendix 3) for the quota year; data from data from ICES (1978–2006); a negative value denotes that the most recent forecast is lower than the previous. KNWL = state-of-knowledge scores, Northeast Arctic cod; relationship to K-DIST and the ad hoc procedure needed for 1980–1981 are explained in chapter 5.

Appendix 5: Actual Scores, Counterfactual Estimates, and Counterfactual Scores on Success and Failure Paths

Table A5.1
Cognitional Problem Solving

	Actual Scores					Counterfactual Estimates							
	CPS	M	I	C	E	C′ CPS	C′ M	C′ I	C′ C	C′ E	~I*C*E	M*~C*~E	I*~E
1980	1	0.33	0	0.33	0	1	0.33	0	0.33	0	0	0.33	0
1981	0.33	0.67	0	0.33	0	0.33	0.67	0	0.33	0	0	0.67	0
1982	0.33	0.33	0	0.33	0	0.33	0.33	0	0.33	0	0	0.33	0
1983	0	0.33	0	0.33	0	0	0.33	0	0.33	0	0	0.33	0
1984	0.67	0.67	0	0.67	0	0.33	0.67	0	0.33	0	0	0.67	0
1985	0	1	0.67	0.67	0	0	1	0.67	0.33	0	0	0.67	0.67
1986	0	0.67	0.67	0.67	0	0	0.67	0.67	0.33	0	0	0.67	0.67
1987	0	0	0.67	0.67	0	0	0	0.67	0.33	0	0	0	0.67
1988	0.67	0	0.33	0.67	0	0.33	0	0.33	0.33	0	0	0	0.33
1989	0.33	0.67	0.33	0.67	0	0	0.67	0.33	0.33	0	0	0.67	0.33
1990	0.33	1	0	0.67	0	0	1	0	0.33	0	0	0.67	0
1991	0.33	1	0	1	0	0	1	0	0.33	0	0	0.67	0
1992	1	1	0	1	0	0.33	1	0	0.33	0	0	0.67	0

Year													
1993	0.67	1	0.67	1	0.33	0	1	0.67	0.33	0	0	0.67	0.67
1994	0.67	0.67	1	1	0.33	0	0.67	1	0.33	0	0	0.67	1
1995	0.67	0.33	1	1	0.33	0	0.33	1	0.33	0	0	0.33	1
1996	0	0.33	1	0.67	0.33	0	0.33	1	0.33	0.33	0	0.33	1
1997	0	0	1	0.67	0.33	0	0	1	0.33	0.33	0	0	0.67
1998	0	0	1	0.67	0.33	0	0	1	0.33	0.33	0	0	0.67
1999	1	0.33	0.33	0.67	0.67	0.33	0.33	0.33	0.33	0.33	0.33	0.33	0.33
2000	0.67	0.67	0	0.67	0.67	0.33	0.67	0	0.33	0.33	0.33	0.67	0
2001	0.33	0.67	0	0.67	0.67	0.33	0.67	0	0.33	0.33	0.33	0.67	0
2002	0.33	1	0.67	0.67	0.67	0.33	1	0.67	0.33	0.33	0.33	0.67	0.67
2003	0.67	1	0.33	0.67	0.67	0.33	1	0.33	0.33	0.33	0.33	0.67	0.33
2004	0.67	0.67	0.67	0.67	0.67	0.33	0.67	0.67	0.33	0.33	0.33	0.67	0.67

Note: **CPS** = cognitional problem solving; **M** = malignancy; **I** = intricacy; **C** = collaboration; **E** = ecosystem modeling; **C′** = counterfactual; ~ = negation; * = intersection. **Numbers** are scores or estimates for causal factors or causal combinations (see in general chapter 2); **1** = full, **0.67** = substantial, **0.33** = modest, **0** = insignificant. Scores, estimates, and paths to success and failure are explained and substantiated in chapter 4.

Table A5.2
Regulatory Problem Solving

	Actual Scores					Counterfactual Estimates								
	RPS	M	U	K	C	C·RPS	C·M	C·U	C·K	C·C	~M*K	~M*U*C	M*~U	~U*~K*~C
1980	1	0.33	1	0.67	0.33	1	0.33	1	0.67	0.33	0.67	0.33	0	0
1981	0.33	0.67	1	1	0.33	0.33	0.67	1	1	0.33	0.33	0.33	0	0
1982	0.33	0.67	1	0.33	0.67	0.33	0.67	1	0.33	0.33	0.33	0.33	0	0
1983	0.33	0.67	0.67	0.33	0.67	0.33	0.67	0.67	0.33	0.33	0.33	0.33	0.33	0.33
1984	0.33	1	0.33	1	0.67	0	1	0.33	1	0.33	0	0	0.67	0
1985	0.33	1	0.67	0.67	0.67	0	1	0.67	0.67	0.33	0	0	0.33	0.33
1986	0.67	0	0.67	0.67	0.67	0.33	0	0.67	0.33	0.33	0.33	0.33	0	0.33
1987	1	0	0.67	1	0.67	1	0	0.67	1	0.33	1	0.33	0	0
1988	0.67	0.33	0.67	1	0.67	0.67	0.33	0.67	1	0.33	0.67	0.33	0.33	0
1989	1	0	1	0	0.67	0.67	0	1	0	0.33	0	0.33	0	0
1990	1	1	1	0.33	0.67	0.33	1	1	0	0.33	0	0	0	0
1991	1	0.67	1	0.33	0.33	0.67	0.67	1	0	0.33	0	0.33	0	0
1992	0.67	1	0.33	0.33	0.33	0.33	1	0.33	0	0.33	0	0	0.67	0.67

1993	0.33	1	0	0	0.33	0.33	1	0	0	0.33	0	0	1	0.67
1994	0.67	0.67	0	0.67	0.33	0.33	0.67	0	0	0.33	0	0	0.67	0.67
1995	0.67	0.33	1	0	0.33	0.33	0.33	0.33	0.33	0.33	0.33	0	0.33	0.67
1996	1	0	0.33	1	0.33	0.67	0	0.33	0	0.33	0.33	0.33	0	0.67
1997	0.67	0	0	0.33	0.33	0.33	0	0	0	0.33	0	0	0	0.67
1998	0.33	0.33	0	0	0.33	0.33	0.33	0	0	0.33	0	0	0.33	0.67
1999	0.33	0.33	0.33	0.33	0.33	0.33	0.33	0.33	0.33	0.33	0.33	0.33	0.33	0.67
2000	0	1	1	0	0.33	0	1	1	0	0.33	0	0	0	0
2001	0.33	0.67	1	0.67	0.67	0.33	0.67	1	0	0.33	0.33	0	0	0
2002	0.33	1	1	0	0.67	0	1	1	0	0.33	0	0	0	0
2003	0.33	0.67	0.67	0.33	0.67	0	1	0.67	0.33	0.33	0	0	0.33	0.33
2004	0.33	0.67	0.33	0.33	0.67	0.33	0.67	0.33	0.33	0.33	0.33	0.33	0.67	0.67

Note: **RPS** = regulatory problem-solving score; **M** = malignancy; **U** = urgency; **K** = state of knowledge; **C** = collaboration; **C'** = counterfactual; ~ = negation; * = intersection. **Numbers** are scores or estimates for causal factors or causal combinations (see in general chapter 2); **1** = full, **0.67** = substantial, **0.33** = modest, **0** = insignificant. Scores, estimates, and paths to success and failure are explained and substantiated in chapter 5.

Table A5.3
Behavioral Problem Solving, Norway

	Actual Scores					Counterfactual Estimates						
	BPS	M	O	T	S	C' BPS	C' M	C' O	C' T	C' S	~M*O*T	M*~O*~S
1980	0	0.33	0.33	0.67	0.33	0	0.33	0.33	0.67	0	0.33	0.67
1981	0	0.67	0.33	0.67	0.33	0	0.67	0.33	0.67	0	0.33	0.33
1982	0	0.33	0.33	0.67	1	0	0.33	0.33	0.67	0	0.33	0.67
1983	0.33	0.33	0.33	0.67	1	0.33	0.33	0.33	0.67	0	0.33	0.67
1984	0	0.67	0.67	0.67	1	0	0.67	0.33	0.67	0	0.33	0.33
1985	0	1	0.67	0.67	0.67	0	1	0.33	0.67	0	0	0.33
1986	0.67	0.67	0.67	0.67	0.67	0.33	0.67	0.33	0.67	0	0.33	0.33
1987	1	0	0.67	0.67	0	0.67	0	0.33	0.67	0	0.33	1
1988	1	0	0.67	0.67	0	0.67	0	0.33	0.67	0	0.33	1
1989	1	0.67	0.67	0.67	0	0.33	0.67	0.33	0.67	0	0.33	0.33
1990	1	1	0.67	0.67	0	0.33	1	0.33	0.67	0	0	0.33
1991	0.33	1	0.67	0.67	0	0	1	0.33	0.67	0	0	0.33
1992	0.67	1	0.67	0.67	0	0.33	1	0.33	0.67	0	0	0.33
1993	0.67	1	0.67	0.67	0	0.33	1	0.33	0.67	0	0	0.33

Year												
1994	0.67	0.67	0.67	0.67	0	0.33	0.67	0.33	0.67	0	0.33	0.33
1995	0.67	0.33	0.67	0.67	0	0.33	0.33	0.33	0.67	0	0.33	0.67
1996	0.67	0.33	0.67	0.67	0	0.33	0.33	0.33	0.67	0	0.33	0.67
1997	1	0	0.67	0.67	0	0.67	0	0.33	0.67	0	0.33	1
1998	1	0	1	0.67	0	0.67	0	0.33	0.67	0	0.33	1
1999	0.67	0.33	1	0.67	0	0.33	0.33	0.33	0.67	0	0.33	0.67
2000	0.67	0.67	1	0.67	0	0.33	0.67	0.33	0.67	0	0.33	0.33
2001	0.67	0.67	1	0.67	0	0.33	0.67	0.33	0.67	0	0.33	0.33
2002	0.33	1	1	0.67	0	0	1	0.33	0.67	0	0	0.33
2003	0.67	1	1	0.67	0	0.33	1	0.33	0.67	0	0	0.33
2004	1	0.67	1	0.67	0	0.33	0.67	0.33	0.67	0	0.33	0.33
2005	1	0.67	1	0.67	0.67	0.33	0.67	0.33	0.67	0	0.33	0.33
2006	1	0.67	1	0.67	0.67	0.33	0.67	0.33	0.67	0	0.33	0.33

Note: **BPS** = behavioral problem-solving score; **M** = malignancy; **O** = obligation; **T** = transparency; **S** = shaming; **C´** = counterfactual; **~** = negation; ***** = intersection. **Numbers** are scores or estimates for causal factors or causal combinations (see in general chapter 2); **1** = full, **0.67** = substantial, **0.33** = modest, **0** = insignificant. Scores, estimates, and paths to success and failure are explained and substantiated in chapter 6.

Table A5.4
Behavioral Problem Solving, Soviet Union/Russia

	Actual Scores					Counterfactual Estimates						
	BPS	M	O	T	S	C' BPS	C' M	C' O	C' T	C' S	~M*O*T	M*~O*~S
1980	1	0.33	1	0.67	0	0.67	0.33	0.33	0.67	0	0.33	0.67
1981	1	0.67	1	0.67	0	0.33	0.67	0.33	0.67	0	0.33	0.33
1982	1	0.33	1	0.67	0	0.67	0.33	0.33	0.67	0	0.33	0.67
1983	1	0.33	1	0.67	0	0.67	0.33	0.33	0.67	0	0.33	0.67
1984	1	0.67	1	0.67	0	0.33	0.67	0.33	0.67	0	0.33	0.33
1985	0.67	1	1	0.67	0	0.33	1	0.33	0.67	0	0	0.33
1986	1	0.67	1	0.67	0	0.33	0.67	0.33	0.67	0	0.33	0.33
1987	1	0	1	0.67	0	0.67	0	0.33	0.67	0	0.33	1
1988	1	0	1	0.67	0	0.67	0	0.33	0.67	0	0.33	1
1989	1	0.67	1	0.67	0	0.33	0.67	0.33	0.67	0	0.33	0.33
1990	0.33	1	1	0.67	0	0	1	0.33	0.67	0	0	0.33
1991	0	1	1	0.33	0	0	1	0.33	0.33	0	0	0.33
1992	0	1	1	0.33	0	0	1	0.33	0.33	0	0	0.33
1993	0.33	1	1	0.67	0.67	0	1	0.33	0.33	0	0	0.33

Year												
1994	1	0.67	1	0.67	0.33	0.33	0.67	0.33	0.33	0	0.33	0.33
1995	1	0.33	1	0.67	0	0.33	0.33	0.33	0.33	0	0.33	0.67
1996	1	0.33	1	0.67	0	0.33	0.33	0.33	0.33	0	0.33	0.67
1997	1	0	1	0.67	0	0.33	0	0.33	0.33	0	0.33	1
1998	1	0	1	0.67	0	0.33	0	0.33	0.33	0	0.33	1
1999	1	0.33	1	0.67	0	0.33	0.33	0.33	0.33	0	0.33	0.67
2000	1	0.67	1	0.33	0	0.33	0.67	0.33	0.33	0	0.33	0.33
2001	1	0.67	1	0.33	0.33	0	0.67	0.33	0.33	0	0.33	0.33
2002	0	1	1	0.33	0.67	0	1	0.33	0.33	0	0	0.33
2003	0	1	1	0.33	0.67	0	1	0.33	0.33	0	0	0.33
2004	0	0.67	1	0.33	0.67	0	0.67	0.33	0.33	0	0.33	0.33
2005	0	0.67	1	0.33	0.67	0	0.67	0.33	0.33	0	0.33	0.33
2006	0	0.67	1	0.33	0.67	0	0.67	0.33	0.33	0	0.33	0.33

Note: **BPS** = behavioral problem-solving score; **M** = malignancy; **O** = obligation; **T** = transparency; **S** = shaming; **C'** = counterfactual; **~** = negation; ***** = intersection. **Numbers** are scores or estimates for causal factors or causal combinations (see in general chapter 2): **1** = full, **0.67** = substantial, **0.33** = modest, **0** = insignificant. Scores, estimates, and paths to success and failure are explained and substantiated in chapter 6.

Table A5.5
Aggregate Problem Solving

	Actual Scores				Counterfactual Estimates					
	APS	CPS	RPS	BPSA	C' APS	C' CPS	C' RPS	C' BPSA	CRB	~C*~R
1980	0.33	1	1	0	0.33	1	1	0	0	1
1981	0.67	1	0.33	0	0.67	1	0.33	0	0	1
1982	0.33	0.33	0.33	0	0.33	0.33	0.33	0	0	0.33
1983	0	0.33	0.33	0.33	0	0.33	0.33	0.33	0.33	0.33
1984	0	0	0.33	0	0	0	0	0	0	0.33
1985	0.33	0.67	0.33	0	0	0.33	0	0	0	0.67
1986	0.33	0	0.67	0.67	0	0	0.33	0.33	0	0.67
1987	0.67	0	1	1	0.33	0	1	0.67	0	1
1988	0.33	0	0.67	1	0	0	0.67	0.67	0	0.67
1989	0.33	0.67	1	1	0.33	0.33	0.67	0.33	0.33	1
1990	0.67	0.33	1	0.33	0	0	0.33	0	0	1
1991	1	0.33	1	0	0.33	0	0.67	0	0	1
1992	0.67	0.33	0.67	0	0	0	0.33	0	0	0.67

1993	0.67	1	0.33	0.33	0.33	0.33	0	1
1994	0.67	0.67	0.67	0.67	0	0.33	0.33	0.67
1995	0.67	0.67	0.67	0.67	0	0.33	0.33	0.67
1996	0.67	0.67	1	0.67	0	0.67	0.33	1
1997	0.33	0	0.33	1	0	0.33	0.33	0.67
1998	0	0	0.33	1	0	0.33	0.33	0.33
1999	0	0	0.33	0.67	0	0.33	0.33	0.33
2000	0.33	1	0	0.67	0.33	0	0.33	1
2001	1	0.67	0.33	0.67	0.33	0.33	0	0.67
2002	1	0.33	0.33	0	0.33	0	0	0.33
2003	1	0.33	0.33	0	0.33	0	0	0.33
2004	0.67	0.67	0.33	0	0.33	0.33	0	0.67

Note: **APS** = aggregate problem solving; **CPS** = cognitional problem solving; **RPS** = regulatory problem solving; **BPSA** = behavioral problem solving (all members); C´ = counterfactual; ~ = negation; * = intersection. **Numbers** are scores or estimates for causal factors or causal combinations (see in general chapter 2); **1** = full, **0.67** = substantial, **0.33** = modest, **0** = insignificant. Scores, estimates, and paths to success and failure are explained and substantiated in chapter 7. The cognitional series are shifted forward by one year; see note 1 in chapter 7.

Notes

Chapter 1

1. On international regime effectiveness, see in particular Andresen and Wettestad (1995, 2004), Bernauer (1995), Breitmeier, Young, and Zürn (2006), Brown Weiss and Jacobson (1998), Haas, Keohane, and Levy (1993), Hovi, Sprinz, and Underdal (2003), Miles et al. (2002), Mitchell (1994, 2002, 2008), Sprinz and Helm (1999), Stokke and Vidas (1996c), Underdal (1992, 2002a, 2002b, 2002c, 2008), Underdal and Young (2004), Victor, Raustiala, and Skolnikoff (1998a), and Young (1992, 1999a, 1999b, 2001, 2003).

2. Entry in Mayhew (2010).

3. "Post-Westphalian" refers to the peace treaty concluded between the Holy Roman Emperor and the King of France and their respective allies at Münster, Westphalia, on October 24, 1648. It consolidated a process long under way (Churchill and Lowe 1999, 4) toward acceptance of the principle of independent, territorially defined states—as opposed to family dynasties and imperial relations based on personal allegiances—as the central actors in the creation and operation of rules on war, peace, trade, and other issues involving interactions over large geographic areas.

4. Young (1986, 105–108) provides an in-depth, critical discussion of Krasner's definition.

5. On thin and thick concepts and theories, see Coppedge (1999).

6. Young's (1986, 106) criticism of Krasner's definition as "conceptually thin" reflects a different usage of "thickness" that highlights explicit connections to larger systems of ideas that can support it—in Galtung's (1969, 464) terms, "validity from above." In contrast, Kratochwil and Ruggie (1986) advocate explicit connection to a specific system of ideas they find relevant but missing in most regime research, namely, sociological analysis, which highlights the connections between norms, practice, and the meanings actors ascribe to behavior.

7. For other recent conceptual discussions of regime interplay, see Gehring and Oberthür (2008), Oberthür and Gehring (2006b), Leebron (2002), and Young (1996, 2002). Systematic and comparative inquiries into regime interplay are provided by Young and colleagues (2008, on biosafety), Oberthür and Gehring (2006a,

on environmental and trade regimes at the EU and broader international levels), and Stokke (2001a, on international fisheries regimes).

8. For an overview of early contributions on institutional consequences, see, for instance, Sabine and Thorson (1973). Underdal (2004, 2008) and Mitchell (2008) provide recent reviews of approaches and performances in the regime-effectiveness research.

9. The 1991 paper has been published in a revised form as Young and Levy (1999); see in particular pp. 4–5.

10. See, for instance, the entries "resource management" and "resource alloca-tion" in Mayhew (2010).

11. Case studies of regime effectiveness have been reported by Haas, Keohane, and Levy (1993), Stokke and Vidas (1996c), Victor, Raustiala, and Skolnikoff (1998a), Brown Weiss and Jacobson (1998), Young (1999), and Miles et al. (2002). Only the last of those projects also uses statistical techniques.

12. On "good-neighborly relations" as a regime objective, see Framework Agree-ment, Preamble (1975). On the coastal states' concern with their competing sovereignty claims, see chapter 3 in this book.

13. The references section in this book includes separate subsections for liter-ature, treaties, Joint Commission protocols, ICES documents, and news media.

14. In 2008 the ICES Advisory Committee on Fisheries Management was merged with two other advisory committees to form the ICES Advisory Committee.

15. Reports to the Storting are issued by the ministry in question, usually in the Norwegian language. *Stortingsforhandlinger* (records of debates in the Storting) are published in Norwegian by the Storting.

16. On the international management of Barents Sea fisheries, see in particular Aasjord and Hønneland (2008), Churchill (1993, 1999), Churchill and Ulfstein (1992), Gullestad (1998), Hoel (1994), Hønneland (1998, 2000, 2003, 2004, 2005a, 2005b, 2006, 2012), Hønneland and Nilsen (2001), Jørgensen (1999, 2009), Jørgensen (2004), Kotov (1994), Matishov et al. (2004), Nikitina and Pearse (1992), Pedersen (2008a, 2008b), Sagdahl (1992), Stokke (1992, 2001a, 2001d, 2009, 2010), Stokke, Anderson, and Mirovitskaya (1999), and Stokke and Hoel (1991).

17. See ICES (2006a); the Russian figure does not rise significantly even if we add to the official landings (as the Norwegian authorities suggest is appropriate) most of the unreported catches estimated for the Barents Sea in the early 1990s and after 2001 (see chapter 6).

18. See the preface to this book. While these inputs have been important for the quality control they provide, I am of course alone responsible for the argument and evaluation in all parts of the present study.

Chapter 2

1. This requirement combines several of Tetlock and Belkin's (1996a, 19–31) criteria: "co-tenability," or consistency among a counterfactual's "connecting

principles," which are statements that must be true about the actual world if the counterfactual is to hold; as well as consistency with well-established historical facts, statistical generalizations, and causal accounts. Distinguishing among these four may be useful for some purposes, but it could be argued that the last three criteria simply flesh out differing aspects of cotenability.

2. In July 1944, major Western allies of the United States met in Bretton Woods, New Hampshire, to establish the political basis for three major postwar economic institutions: the General Agreement on Tariffs and Trade (which came to form the basis for the World Trade Organization), the World Bank, and the International Monetary Fund; see, for instance, Spero (1990).

3. This is true in particular of Haas, Keohane, and Levy (1993), Stokke and Vidas (1996c), and Young (1999). On the concepts of mechanism underlying studies of regime effectiveness, see Hovi (2004).

4. According to Bunge (1997, 415), a concrete system is "a bundle of real things held together by some bonds or forces, behaving as a unit in some respect and (except for the universe as a whole) embedded in some environment"; he lists three variants—natural, social, and technical. George and Bennett's (2005, 135–137) definition of a mechanism is very close to that of Bunge.

5. Allison's (1969, 711) famous phrase also invokes mechanisms at the level of individuals, including maximization of utility.

6. Elster (1998, 47–48) distances himself from his earlier (1983, 23) association of "mechanism" with microreductive explanation and highlights instead lower levels of determinacy as the crucial feature, along with fine-grained account—on the argument that different mechanisms may be at work at the same time.

7. I directed the Antarctic project and participated in the project that produced Young (1999b).

8. For this reason, Mill ([1853] 1904, 256–258) also terms the indirect method "the joint method of agreement and difference."

9. Italics in the original; I have reversed the order of the two parts of this sentence.

10. The number of observations within each cell may form the basis for weighting such partial effects to derive aggregate scores (Hellevik 1988, 14–18).

11. Italics in the original. Specifically, Miles and associates (2002) combine qualitative case study analysis with logical comparison, correlation analysis, and logistical regression.

12. The exception is a case where the score on one or several causal conditions is ambiguous, corresponding to a fuzzy set score of 0.5 (Ragin 2000, 186). Such cases belong equally much (or little) to the ideal-type corners that correspond to full and insignificant scores on the causal factor or combination, but with the four value categories in this study, ambiguous coding is not an option.

13. An ordinal scale orders observations from lower to higher values; an interval scale also measures the distance, in some relevant metric, between observations.

14. Ragin and Sonnett (2006) use the same criteria to determine whether the counterfactual cases needed for deriving a more general solution are "easy" or "difficult."

15. Helm and Sprinz (2000) do not consider this possibility.

16. For details, see appendix 1.

17. To be meaningful, certain nonessential QCA operations, such as estimation of "fuzzy adjustment"—a procedure that mimics the use of confidence intervals in statistical analysis (Ragin 2000, 247–248)—require measurement at interval level. However, the most important QCA measures, consistency and coverage, are also meaningful at ordinal level, although they work better at interval level (see above).

Chapter 3

1. Average prices of cod paid to the fishers are published by the Norwegian Fishermen's Sales Organization, which has a monopoly on firsthand sales in northwestern and northern Norway. In 2008, the average price was 15.5 Norwegian kroner per kilo and the U.S. dollar had an average exchange value of 5.64.

2. Murmansk oblast, with Murmansk as the biggest city, is today a federal subject of the Russian Federation and part of the Northwestern Federal District.

3. On the drawing of baselines, see the Law of the Sea Convention, Articles 5–8.

4. In late 1991, Russia became the legal successor to the Soviet Union with respect to the treaties that underlie the Barents Sea fisheries regime.

5. The official English translation of the Framework Agreement uses the term "Mixed Commission," but "Joint Commission" has become the common rendering in government sources.

6. Head of Advisory Services Hans Lassen, ICES Secretariat, personal communication, 26 May 2007.

7. According to the parties, this 50/50 split of the cod quota for the first season under joint regulation, 1977, "does not prejudice future quota allocation" (JCF 1976a, item 10), but they have never deviated from it since that time (see chapter 1).

8. Head of Section Einar Ellingsen of the Norwegian Fisheries Directorate, personal communication, 22 November 2005; see also Ulvatn et al. (2006). However, since 1992 the Norwegian Coast Guard may request information from the Russian enforcement agencies as to what *species* each vessel is licensed to take (Hønneland 1998, 63).

9. Norway, Regulations on a Fisheries Protection Zone at Svalbard (1977).

10. Norway, Act on the Economic Zone (1976); Norway, Svalbard Act (1925).

11. Norway, Regulations on a Fisheries Protection Zone at Svalbard (1977), Article 2; my translation. The general prohibition against nonlicensed fishing by foreigners in the EEZ is found in Norway, Act on the Economic Zone (1976), Article 4.

12. For instance, Ministry of Foreign Affairs spokesman Per Paust, referred to in *Nordlys* (2 August 1986, 5), and more recently (2004) Commander of the Coast Guard Geir Osen, cited in Pedersen (2008a, 917).

13. Norway-Greenland Agreement. On the linkage to Greenland fishing in the Fisheries Protection Zone, see the statements by Odd G. Skagestad of the Norwegian Ministry of Foreign Affairs to *Nordlys* (25 June 1991, 30); see also *Nordlys* (26 September 1991, 23).

Chapter 4

1. The corresponding biological reference point in ICES advice is F_{max}, with "F" referring to fishing mortality (the relative quantity of fish dying from being caught); the exploitation pattern concerns the distribution of the fishing mortality rate over the age groups of the stock. A second reference point used by ICES and other advisory bodies is F_0, which is lower than F_{max} but is associated with higher catch per unit effort (ICES 1990a, 54).

2. More recently, ICES (2003, 12) has adjusted the precautionary reference point to 460,000 tons; see also the robustness discussion below.

3. Assessments of herring, then in a process of recovery from a major collapse in the 1960s, were overly pessimistic in the period (Nakken 1998, 33).

4. In most years, options are relatively close, so any difference between a linear and a curvilinear adaptation would be insignificant.

5. The assessment data must be converged over a three-year period to obtain significantly higher reliability than in the first year (Nakken 1998, 33; also Godø 2003, 129). Thus, the 2004 forecast concerns the spawning stock in 2006, and the ICES (2008a) report is the first reassessment that is clearly more reliable than the initial assessment.

6. Using absolute values permits ready comparison of optimistic and pessimistic forecasts.

7. Norway, Ministry of Fisheries (2003–2004, 52–53). In the Grey Zone, reports were to be delivered to the state that has licensed the vessel (see chapter 2).

8. Former director of PINRO Georgy Luka confirmed considerable staff cuts in this period (personal communication, 29 July 1992).

9. Research Director Arvid Hylen, IMR, personal communication, 28 July 1993, and Research Director Åsmund Bjordal, IMR, personal communication, 7 October 2002. Annual grants for this purpose from the Ministry of Foreign Affairs were in the range of U.S. $300,000–400,000.

10. Steinar Olsen of the IMR, personal communication, 26 April 1995; Research Director Åsmund Bjordal, personal communication, 7 October 2002.

11. See JCF (1991, annex 5) on ocean currents and JCF (1992, annex 5) on sorting grids, initially to protect cod in the shrimp fishery, later for protection of juveniles during cod trawling.

12. Director-General Kåre Bryn of the Norwegian Ministry of Foreign Affairs, quoted in *NTBTekst* (29 October 1997).

13. See JCF (1998, items 5.1 and 14; 1999, items 5.1 and 14; 2000, item 14; 2001, item 13; 2002, items 5.1 and 12). In 2002, Norway reciprocated, denying Russian research vessels access to Norway's EEZ (JCF 2002, item 13).

14. The interpretation that the Russian naval authorities have triggered these denials of access has also been expressed by Norwegian Ministry of Foreign Affairs spokesperson Ingvar Havnen, quoted in *Fiskeribladet* (7 August 1997, 2), and by Kåre Bryn of the same ministry, quoted in *NTBTekst* (29 October 1997).

15. Research Director Åsmund Bjordal, IMR, personal communication, 7 October 2002.

16. Capelin is a short-lived species that dies after spawning. A relatively large part of the stock is therefore harvested prior to spawning.

17. As appendix 3 shows, purely distributional considerations (the steepness and category-size criteria; see chapter 1) would indicate a threshold for high capelin availability at a ratio of 1, but the observation that the only intermediate case—1998, with a ratio of 1.5—is a year with high cannibalism mortality even among three-year-olds provides a qualitative anchor for placing it above that level. Below I examine the robustness of findings to variation in this threshold.

18. See annex 5 in JCF (1991, 1992); on follow-up activities, see JCF (1993, annex 5).

Chapter 5

1. Below I examine the robustness of findings to variation in the procedure for measuring the state of knowledge over time; that robustness is high.

2. Two mid-term revisions of the recommendation occurred in the period under study, in 1988 and in 1992; see ICES (1989, 8; 1993, 8). The 1988 revision induced the coastal states to reduce that year's quota (*Aftenposten*, 29 June 1988, 3). In both cases, our comparative analysis here uses the first regular advice and quota decision for the year in question as the basis for measuring malignancy and problem solving, because those are the observations most comparable to the others.

3. During the first four years, some additional transfers occurred later in the season, as the Soviet authorities calculated that their fishers would not be taking the full remainder of the quota (Norway, Ministry of Fisheries 1982; 1983; 1984; 1985; 1986). The transfer figures used here do not include those additional transfers since they cannot have influenced the quota negotiations.

4. More recently, ICES (2003, 12) has adjusted the precautionary reference point to 460,000 tons; see also the robustness discussion below.

5. See appendix 5, table A5.2. The theoretically more potent paths represented in the dataset and failing the reliability criterion are those with full scores on all factors (1985, 2001), those with full scores on all factors except collaboration (1981), and those with full scores on all factors except urgency (1984).

6. Consistency scores are 1 for the first term, 0.91 for the second, 1 for the third, 0.90 for the fourth, and 0.91 for the fifth term.

7. This finding is sensitive to the coding of knowledge, however (see the robustness analysis above).

8. This particular finding is sensitive to the coding of malignancy and problem solving.

Chapter 6

1. Unlike in chapters 4 and 5, the outcome and all explanatory factors allow specification without reference to the ICES retrospective analyses of its annual spawning stock assessments. The retrospective assessment is more reliable than the first assessments only after converging data over three years, so the information needed for coding variables that use the retrospective assessments (in this study, cognitional problem solving and the state of knowledge) is available for a period that is two years shorter than that for other variables.

2. Norwegian Minister of Fisheries Jan Henry T. Olsen, cited in *NTBTekst* (29 April 1993). The remainder was ascribed to third-country vessels whose quota compliance was also Russia's responsibility since they were fishing on Russian licenses in its EEZ or in the Grey Zone.

3. The Norwegian Commissioner, Gunnar Kjønnøy, quoted in *NTBTekst* (19 November 1992).

4. Eivind Bolle, cited in Stortinget (8 April 1981, 3017); my translation.

5. At first glance, an additional category combining full scores on malignancy, obligation, and shaming with insignificant transparency would also qualify as a reliable failure path with this alternative coding procedure, but the low consistency of the theoretically more potent superset that also includes cases without shaming removes that path.

6. Thus, chance would yield such correlation in no more than five out of a 100 trials.

7. Bivariate and multiple correlations among the causal factors are moderate and far from the level that would indicate multicollinearity; significant bivariate interfactor correlations range from –0.28 to 0.12 (the conventional threshold for worry is 0.8) and the coefficients of determination when regressing each causal factor against all others range from 0.08 to 0.28 and would have to approach 1 to cause worry (Lewis-Beck 1980, 60).

8. Increasing variance could indicate heteroskedasticity, which, like auto-correlation, invalidates significance tests but does not bias the coefficients (Lewis-Beck 1980, 28). Outliers exceed the plus/minus 2 band.

9. Similarly, Spearman's rank-order coefficient in table 6.1 drops to –0.05 and is no longer statistically significant.

10. The fisheries minister explicitly related the considerably stricter time regulations introduced in 1981 to Soviet pressure on the Joint Commission; see Eivind Bolle to the Storting (Stortinget, 8 April 1981, 3017).

11. Representative Per Aas (Christian Democratic Party) in a query to the minister (Stortinget, April 1981, 315).

12. In 1989, the Friends of the Earth Norway applied for, but failed to obtain, observer status at the Joint Commission meeting (Hønneland 2006, 43).

Chapter 7

1. The cognitional success series is shifted forward one year since each data point refers to the year of the forecast, which is one year prior to the quota year. For the sole year uncovered by the cognitional success findings in chapter 4 (1980, which reflects cognitional success in 1979), I assign a full cognitional success score, since that year's forecast (ICES 1979, 26–27) deviated from the level indicated by the more recent assessment by only 4 percent.

2. Appendix 5, table A5.5 gives those antecedents and their fit with the success or failure paths for aggregate problem solving.

Chapter 8

1. A further effect is reduce the complexity of the counterfactual situation, thereby further concretizing and simplifying the estimation of the most plausible range of counterfactual problem-solving scores.

2. Collaboration is not modeled directly when explaining the variation in behavioral problem solving. It enters indirectly, since variations in the transparency surrounding Soviet and Russian harvesting activities depend on regime-based compliance collaboration (see chapters 2 and 6).

References

Literature

Aasjord, Bente. 2001. Norsk-russisk rulett i Barentshavet? *Internasjonal Politikk* 59 (3): 303–332.

Aasjord, Bente, and Geir Hønneland. 2008. Hvem kan telle "den fisk under vann"? Kunnskapsstrid i russisk havforskning. *Nordisk Øst-Forum* 22 (3–4): 289–312.

Abbott, Kenneth W., Robert O. Keohane, Andrew Moravcsik, Anne-Marie Slaughter, and Duncan Snidal. 2000. The Concept of Legalization. *International Organization* 54 (3): 401–419.

Abbott, Kenneth, and Duncan Snidal. 2000. Hard and Soft Law in International Governance. *International Organization* 54 (3): 421–456.

Adler, Emanuel, and Peter M. Haas. 1992. Conclusion: Epistemic Communities, World Order, and the Creation of a Reflective Research Program. *International Organization* 46 (1): 367–390.

Aggarwal, Vinod K. 1983. The Unraveling of the Multi-Fiber Arrangement, 1981: An Examination of International Regime Change. *International Organization* 37 (4): 617–645.

Aglen, Asgeir, Konstantin Drevetnyak, and Konstantin Sokolov. 2004. Cod in the Barents Sea (Northeast Arctic Cod): A Review of the Biology and History of the Fishery and Its Management. In *Management Strategies for Commercial Marine Species in Northern Ecosystems*, Proceedings of the 10th Norwegian-Russian Symposium, Bergen, August 2003, ed. Å. Bjordal, H. Gjøsæter, and S. Mehl, 27–39. IMR/PINRO Joint Report Series 1. Murmansk: Institute of Marine Research.

Albin, Cecilia. 1995. Rethinking Justice and Fairness: The Case of Acid Rain Emission Reductions. *Review of International Studies* 21 (2): 119–143.

Allison, Graham. 1969. Conceptual Models and the Cuban Missile Crisis. *American Political Science Review* 63 (3): 689–718.

Andresen, Steinar. 1992. International Verification in Practice: A Brief Account of Experiences from Relevant International Cooperative Measures. In *Achieving*

Environmental Goals: The Concept and Practice of Environmental Performance Review, ed. Erik Lykke, 101–118. London: Belhaven Press.

Andresen, Steinar, Tora Skodvin, Arild Underdal, and Jørgen Wettestad. 2000. *Science and Politics in International Environmental Regimes*. Manchester: Manchester University Press.

Andresen, Steinar, and Jørgen Wettestad. 1995. International Problem-solving Effectiveness: The Oslo Project Story So Far. *International Environmental Affairs* 7 (2): 127–149.

Andresen, Steinar, and Jørgen Wettestad. 2004. Case Studies of the Effectiveness of International Environmental Regimes. In *Regime Consequences: Methodological Challenges and Research Strategies*, ed. Arild Underdal and Oran R. Young, 49–69. Dordrecht: Kluwer Academic.

Baldwin, David A. 1993. Neoliberalism, Neorealism, and World Politics. In *Neorealism and Neoliberalism: The Contemporary Debate*, ed. David A. Baldwin, 3–25. New York: Columbia University Press.

Balton, David A. 1996. Strengthening the Law of the Sea: The New Agreement on Straddling Fish Stocks and Highly Migratory Fish Stocks. *Ocean Development and International Law* 27 (1/2): 125–152.

Bennett, Andrew. 2004. Case Study Methods: Design, Use, and Comparative Advantages. In *Models, Numbers and Cases: Methods for Studying International Relations*, ed. Detlef F. Sprinz and Yael Wolinsky-Nahmias, 19–55. Ann Arbor: University of Michigan Press.

Bernauer, Thomas. 1995. The Effect of International Environmental Institutions: How We Might Learn More. *International Organization* 49 (2): 351–377.

Biermann, Frank. 2008. Earth System Governance: A Research Agenda. In *Institutions and Environmental Change: Principal Findings, Applications, and Research Frontiers*, ed. Oran R. Young, Leslie A. King, and Heike Schroeder, 277–301. Cambridge, MA: MIT Press.

Bodansky, Daniel. 1999. The Legitimacy of International Governance: A Coming Challenge for International Environmental Law? *American Journal of International Law* 93 (3): 596–624.

Bogstad, B., T. Bulgakova, K. Drevetnyak, A. Filin, K. H. Hauge, Y. Kovalev, Y. Lepesevich, et al. 2005. *Report of the Basic Document Working Group (BDWG) to The Joint Norwegian–Russian Fisheries Commission, October 2005, on Harvest Control Rules for Management of Fisheries on Cod and Haddock— and Optimal Long Term Optimal Harvest in the Barents Sea Ecosystem.* http://regjeringen.no/upload/kilde/fkd/prm/2005/0085/ddd/pdfv/262877 -vedlegg_11_bdwg-2005_final.pdf.

Bogstad, Bjarte, and Harald Gjøsæter. 2001. Predation by Cod (Gadus Morhua) on Capelin (Mallotus Villosus) in the Barents Sea: Implications for Capelin Stock Assessment. *Fisheries Research* 53 (2): 197–209.

Borgström, Georg. 1968. *Revolusjon i verdens fiskerier*. Oslo: Gyldendal.

Breitmeier, Helmut, Oran R. Young, and Michael Zürn. 2006. *Analyzing International Environmental Regimes: From Case Study to Database*. Cambridge, MA: MIT Press.

Brown Weiss, Edith, and Harold K. Jacobson, eds. 1998. *Engaging Countries: Strengthening Compliance with Environmental Accords.* Cambridge, MA: MIT Press.

Bunge, Mario. 1997. Mechanism and Explanation. *Philosophy of the Social Sciences* 27 (4): 410–465.

Burke, William T. 1989. Fishing in the Bering Sea Donut: Straddling Stocks and the New International Law of Fisheries. *Ecology Law Quarterly* 16 (1): 285–310.

Burke, William T. 1994. *The New International Law of Fisheries: UNCLOS 1982 and Beyond.* Oxford: Clarendon Press.

Caddy, John. 1997. Checks and Balances in the Management of Marine Fish Stocks: Organizational Requirements for a Limit Reference Point Approach. *Fisheries Research* 30 (1–2): 1–15.

Cashore, Benjamin, Graeme Auld, and Deanna Newsom. 2004. *Governing through Markets: Forest Certification and the Emergence of Non-State Authority.* New Haven, CT: Yale University Press.

Castberg, Rune. 1992. *Næringsstruktur og utenriksøkonomi i Murmansk fylke.* FNI Report 2/1992. Lysaker: Fridtjof Nansen Institute.

Chayes, Abram, and Antonia Handler Chayes. 1995. *The New Sovereignty: Compliance with Treaties in International Regulatory Regimes.* Cambridge, MA: Harvard University Press.

Christensen, Pål, and Abraham Hallenstvedt. 2005. *I kamp om havets verdier: Norges Fiskarlags historie.* Trondheim: Norges Fiskarlag.

Churchill, Robin R. 1993. Fisheries Issues in Maritime Boundary Delimitation. *Marine Policy* 17:44–57.

Churchill, Robin R. 1999. The Barents Sea Loophole Agreement: A "Coastal State" Solution to a Straddling Stock Problem. *International Journal of Marine and Coastal Law* 14 (4): 467–490.

Churchill, Robin R., and Alan V. Lowe. 1999. *The Law of the Sea.* Manchester: Manchester University Press.

Churchill, Robin R., and Geir Ulfstein. 1992. *Marine Management in Disputed Areas: The Case of the Barents Sea.* London: Routledge.

Clark, William C., Josee van Eijndhoven, and Jill Jäger, eds. 2001. *Learning to Manage Global Environmental Risks: A Functional Analysis of Social Respones to Climate Change, Ozone Depletion, and Acid Rain.* Vol. 2. Cambridge, MA: MIT Press.

Clark, William C., Ronald B. Mitchell, and David W. Cash. 2006. Evaluating the Influence of Global Environmental Assessments. In *Global Environmental Assessments: Information and Influence,* ed. Ronald B. Mitchell, William C. Clark, David W. Cash, and Nancy M. Dickson, 1–28. Cambridge, MA: MIT Press.

Coppedge, Michael. 1999. Thickening Thin Concepts and Theories: Combining Large N and Small in Comparative Politics. *Comparative Politics* 31 (4): 465–476.

Cutler, A. Claire, Virginia Haufler, and Tony Porter, eds. 1999. *Private Authority and International Affairs*. Albany, NY: SUNY Press.

de La Fayette, L. A. 2001. The Marine Environmental Protection Committee: The Conjunction of the Law of the Sea and International Environmental Law. *International Journal of Marine and Coastal Law* 16 (2): 155–238.

de La Fayette, L. A. 2008. Oceans Governance in the Arctic. *International Journal of Marine and Coastal Law* 23 (3): 531–566.

Devanney, Jack. 2006. *The Tankship Tromedy: The Impending Disasters in Tankers*. Tavernier, FL: CTX Press.

Downs, George W., David M. Rocke, and Peter N. Barsoom. 1996. Is the Good News about Compliance Good News about Cooperation? *International Organization* 50 (3): 379–406.

Easton, David. 1965. *A Systems Analysis of Political Life*. New York: John Wiley.

Eckstein, Harry. 1975. Case Study and Theory in Political Science. In *Handbook of Political Science*. Vol. 7, *Strategies of Inquiry*, ed. Fred I. Greenstein and Nelson W. Polsby, 79–137. Reading, MA: Addison-Wesley.

Elster, Jon. 1978. *Logic and Society: Contradictions and Possible Worlds*. Chichester: John Wiley.

Elster, Jon. 1983. *Explaining Technical Change: A Case Study in the Philosophy of Science*. Cambridge: Cambridge University Press.

Elster, Jon. 1998. A Plea for Mechanisms. In *Social Mechanisms: An Analytical Approach to Social Theory*, ed. Peter Hedström and Richard Swedberg, 45–73. Cambridge: Cambridge University Press.

Fearon, James D. 1991. Counterfactual and Hypothesis Testing in Political Science. *World Politics* 43:169–195.

Filin, A. A., B. Bogstad, H. Gjøsæter, V. A. Ivshin, J. E. Stiansen, O. V. Titov, A. G. Trofimov, and S. Tjelmeland. 2008. Ecosystem Information Potential for Improvement of Advice for Sustainable Fisheries. In *Joint PINRO/IMR Report on the State of the Barents Sea Ecosystem in 2007, with Expected Situation and Considerations for Management*, ed. J.E. Stiansen and A.A. Filin, 133–145. IMR–PINRO Joint Report Series 1/2008. Bergen, Norway: Institute of Marine Research.

Food and Agriculture Organization. 2009. *The State of World Fisheries and Aquaculture 2008*. Rome: Food and Agriculture Organization of the United Nations.

Franck, Thomas M. 1990. *The Power of Legitimacy among Nations*. New York: Oxford University Press.

Franck, Thomas M. 1995. *Fairness in International Law and Institutions*. Oxford: Clarendon Press.

Galtung, Johan. 1969. *Theory and Methods of Social Research*. Oslo: Universitetsforlaget.

Gautier, Donald L., Kenneth J. Bird, Ronald R. Charpentier, Arthur Grantz, David W. Houseknecht, Timothy R. Klett, Thomas E. Moore, et al. 2009. Assessment of Undiscovered Oil and Gas in the Arctic. *Science* 342 (5931): 1175–1179.

Gehring, Thomas. 2011. The Institutional Complex of Trade and Environment: Toward an Interlocking Structure and a Division of Labor. In *Managing Institutional Complexity: Regime Interplay and Global Environmental Change*, ed. Sebastian Oberthür and Olav Schram Stokke. Cambridge, MA: MIT Press.

Gehring, Thomas, and Sebastian Oberthür. 2008. Interplay: Exploring Institutional Interaction. In *Institutions and Environmental Change: Principal Findings, Applications, and Research Frontiers*, ed. Oran R. Young, Leslie A. King, and Heike Schroeder, 187–223. Cambridge, MA: MIT Press.

George, Alexander L. 1979. Case Studies and Theory Development: The Method of Structured, Focused Comparison. In *Diplomacy: New Approaches in History, Theory, and Policy*, ed. Paul Gordon Lauren, 43–68. New York: Free Press.

George, Alexander L., and Andrew Bennett. 2005. *Case Studies and Theory Development in the Social Sciences*. Cambridge, MA: MIT Press.

George, Alexander L., and Timothy J. McKeown. 1985. Case Studies and Theories of Organizational Decision Making. In *Advances in Information Processing in Organizations*. Vol. 2, ed. Robert Coulam and Richard Smith, 21–58. Greenwich, CT: JAI Press.

Godø, Olav Rune. 2003. Fluctuation in Stock Properties of North-East Arctic Cod Related to Long-Term Environmental Changes. *Fish and Fisheries* 4 (2): 121–137.

Goldstein, Judith, and Robert O. Keohane. 1993. Ideas and Foreign Policy: An Analytical Framework. In *Ideas and Foreign Policy: Beliefs, Institutions, and Political Change*, ed. Judith Goldstein and Robert O. Keohane, 3–30. Ithaca, NY: Cornell University Press.

Goldthorpe, John H. 1997. Current Issues in Comparative Macrosociology: A Debate on Methodological Issues. *Comparative Social Research* 16:1–26.

Gorbachev, Mikhail. 1987. Tale i Murmansk, 1. oktober 1987 (Speech in Murmansk, October 1, 1987). In Russian. Norwegian translation by the USSR Embassy in Oslo, on file with author. English text available at Foreign Broadcast Information Service (FBIS)-SOV-87-191, 2 October).

Grieco, Joseph M. 1988. Anarchy and the Limits of Cooperation: A Realist Critique of the Newest Liberal Institutionalism. *International Organization* 42 (3): 485–508.

Guba, Egon G., and Yvonna S. Lincoln. 1989. *Fourth Generation Evaluation*. Newbury Park, CA: Sage.

Gulbrandsen, Lars H. 2009. The Emergence and Effectiveness of the Marine Stewardship Council. *Marine Policy* 33 (4): 654–660.

Gullestad, Petter. 1998. The Scope for Research in Practical Fishery Management. *Fisheries Research* 37 (1): 251–258.

Haas, Ernst B. 1964. *Beyond the Nation-State: Functionalism and International Organization*. Stanford, CA: Stanford University Press.

Haas, Ernst B. 1970. The Study of Regional Integration: Reflections on the Joy and Anguish of Pretheorizing. *International Organization* 24 (4): 607–646.

Haas, Ernst B. 1990. *When Knowledge Is Power: Three Models of Change in International Organizations.* Berkeley, CA: University of California Press.

Haas, Peter M. 1989. Do Regimes Matter? Epistemic Communities and Mediterranean Pollution Control. *International Organization* 43 (3): 377–405.

Haas, Peter M. 1992. Banning Chlorofluorocarbons: Epistemic Community Efforts to Protect Stratospheric Ozone. *International Organization* 46 (1): 187–224.

Haas, Peter M. 2002. UN Conferences and Constructivist Governance of the Environment. *Global Governance* 8:73–91.

Haas, Peter M., Robert O. Keohane, and Marc A. Levy, eds. 1993. *Institutions for the Earth: Sources of Effective International Environmental Protection.* Cambridge, MA: MIT Press.

Halliday, R. G., and A. T. Pinhorn. 1996. North Atlantic Fishery Management Systems: A Comparison of Management Methods and Resource Trends. *Journal of Northwest Atlantic Fishery Science* 20 (Special Issue).

Hardin, Garrett. 1968. The Tragedy of the Commons. *Science* 162 (3859): 1243–1248.

Hasenclever, Andreas, Peter Mayer, and Volker Rittberger. 1997. *Theories of International Regimes.* Cambridge: Cambridge University Press.

Hellevik, Ottar. 1988. *Introduction to Causal Analysis: Exploring Survey Data by Crosstabulation.* Oslo: Scandinavian University Press.

Hellevik, Ottar. *Introduction to Causal Analysis: Exploring Survey Data by Crosstabulation.* Oslo: Scandinavian University Press.

Helm, Carsten, and Detlef F. Sprinz. 2000. Measuring the Effectiveness of International Environmental Regimes. *Journal of Conflict Resolution* 44 (5): 630–652.

Hersoug, Bjørn. 1992. Norsk fiskerinæring: Landanalyse. In *Fiskerinæringens hovedtrekk: Landanalyser av Danmark, Færøyene, Grønland, Island og Norge,* ed. Bjørn Hersoug, 231–287. Nord-REFO Report No. 30. Copenhagen: Nord-REFO.

Hilborn, Ray, Jean-Jacques Maguire, Ana M. Parma, and Andrew A. Rosenberg. 2001. The Precautionary Approach and Risk Management: Can They Increase the Probability of Successes in Fishery Management? *Canadian Journal of Fisheries and Aquatic Sciences* 58 (1): 99–107.

Hoel, Alf Håkon. 1994. The Barents Sea: Fisheries Resources for Europe and Russia. In *The Barents Region: Cooperation in Arctic Europe,* ed. Olav Schram Stokke and Ola Tunander, 115–130. London: Sage.

Holden, M. J., and D. F. S. Raitt. 1974. *Manual of Fisheries Science, Part 2: Methods of Resource Investigation and Their Application.* Rome: Food and Agriculture Organization of the United Nations.

Hønneland, Geir B. 1998. Autonomy and Regionalisation in the Fisheries Management of Northwestern Russia. *Marine Policy* 22 (1): 57–66.

Hønneland, Geir. 2000. *Coercive and Discursive Compliance Mechanisms in the Management of Natural Resources: A Case Study from the Barents Sea.* Dordrecht: Kluwer Academic.

Hønneland, Geir. 2003. East Meets West: Environmental Discourse in the European Arctic. *Journal of Environmental Policy and Planning* 5 (2): 181–199.

Hønneland, Geir. 2004. *Russian Fisheries Management: The Precautionary Approach in Theory and Practice.* Leiden: Martinus Nijhoff.

Hønneland, Geir. 2005a. Fisheries Management in Post-Soviet Russia: Legislation, Principles, and Structure. *Ocean Development and International Law* 36 (2): 179–194.

Hønneland, Geir. 2005b. Towards a Precautionary Fisheries Management in Russia? *Ocean and Coastal Management* 48 (7–8): 619–631.

Hønneland, Geir. 2006. *Kvotekamp og kyststatssolidaritet: Norsk-russisk fiskeriforvaltning gjennom 30 år.* Bergen: Fagbokforlaget.

Hønneland, Geir. 2012. *Making Fishery Agreements Work: Post-Agreement Bargaining in the Barents Sea Fisheries.* Cheltenham, UK, and Northampton, MA: Edward Elgar.

Hønneland, G., and Frode Nilssen. 2001. Quota Allocation in Russia's Northern Fishery Basin: Principles and Practice. *Ocean and Coastal Management* 44 (7–8): 471–488.

Hovi, Jon. 2004. Causal Mechanisms and the Study of International Environmental Regimes. In *Regime Consequences: Methodological Challenges and Research Strategies*, ed. Arild Underdal and Oran R. Young, 71–86. Dordrecht: Kluwer Academic.

Hovi, Jon, Detlef F. Sprinz, and Arild Underdal. 2003. Regime Effectiveness and the Oslo-Potsdam Solution: A Rejoinder to Oran Young. *Global Environmental Politics* 3 (3): 105–107.

Hovi, Jon, Olav Schram Stokke, and Geir Ulfstein. 2005. Introduction and Main Findings. In *Implementing the Climate Regime: International Compliance*, ed. Olav Schram Stokke, Jon Hovi, and Geir Ulfstein, 1–14. London: Earthscan.

Hveem, Helge. 1970. "Blame" as International Behavior: A Contribution to Interstate Interaction Theory. *Journal of Peace Research* 7 (1): 49–67.

Jacobson, Harold K., and David A. Kay. 1983a. A Framework for Analysis. In *Environmental Protection: The International Dimension*, ed. David A. Kay and Harold K. Jacobson, 1–22. Totowa, NJ: Allanheld, Osmun.

Jacobson, Harold K., and David A. Kay. 1983b. Conclusions and Policy. In *Environmental Protection: The International Dimension*, ed. David A. Kay and Harold K. Jacobson, 310–332. Totowa, NJ: Allanheld, Osmun.

Jacobson, Harold K., and Edith Brown Weiss. 1998a. A Framework for Analysis. In *Engaging Countries: Strengthening Compliance with Environmental Accords,* ed. Edith Brown Weiss and Harold K. Jacobson, 1–18. Cambridge, MA: MIT Press.

Jacobson, Harold K., and Edith Brown Weiss. 1998b. Assessing the Record and Designing Strategies to Engage Countries. In *Engaging Countries: Strengthening Compliance with Environmental Accords*, ed. Edith Brown Weiss and Harold K. Jacobson, 511–554. Cambridge, MA: MIT Press.

Jennings, Robert Yewdall. 1963. *The Acquisition of Territory in International Law*. Manchester: Manchester University Press.

Jentoft, Svein, Bonnie J. McCay, and Douglas C. Wilson. 1998. Social Theory and Fisheries Co-Management. *Marine Policy* 22 (4–5): 423–436.

Jørgensen, Anne-Kristin. 1999. *Norsk og russisk fiskerikontroll i Barentshavet— en sammenlikning med hensyn til effektivitet*. Master's thesis, University of Oslo.

Jørgensen, Anne-Kristin. 2009. Recent Developments in the Russian Fisheries Sector. In *Russia and the North*, ed. Elana Wilson Rowe, 87–106. Ottawa: University of Ottawa Press.

Jørgensen, Jørgen Holten. 2004. Svalbard: russiske persepsjoner og politikkutforming. *Internasjonal Politikk* 62 (2): 177–197.

Joyner, Christopher C. 2001. On the Borderline? Canadian Activism in the Grand Banks. In *Governing High Seas Fisheries: The Interplay of Global and Regional Regimes*, ed. Olav Schram Stokke, 207–333. Oxford: Oxford University Press.

Joyner, Christopher C., and Zachary Tyler. 2000. Marine Conservation versus International Free Trade: Reconciling Dolphins with Tuna and Sea Turtles with Shrimp. *Ocean Development and International Law* 31 (1–2): 127–150.

Kay, David A., and Harold K. Jacobson, eds. 1983. *Environmental Protection: The International Dimension*. Totowa, NJ: Allanheld, Osmun. Published under the auspices of the American Society for International Law.

Keltner, Dacher, and Brenda N. Buswell. 1997. Embarrassment: Its Distinct Form and Appeasement Functions. *Psychological Bulletin* 122 (3): 250–270.

Keohane, Robert O. 1984. *After Hegemony: Cooperation and Discord in the World Political Economy*. Princeton, NJ: Princeton University Press.

Keohane, Robert O. 1986. Theory of World Politics: Structural Realism and Beyond. In *Neo-Realism and its Critics*, ed. Robert O. Keohane, 158–203. New York: Columbia University Press.

Keohane, Robert O. 1989. Neoliberal Institutionalism: A Perspective on World Politics. In *International Institutions and State Power: Essays in International Relations Theory*, ed. Robert O. Keohane, 1–20. Boulder, CO: Westview Press.

Keohane, Robert O. 1993. The Analysis of International Regimes: Toward A European-American Research Programme. In *Regime Theory and International Relations*, ed. V. Rittberger, with P. Mayer, 23–48. Oxford: Clarendon Press.

Keohane, Robert O., Peter M. Haas, and Marc A. Levy. 1993. The Effectiveness of International Environmental Institutions. In *Institutions for the Earth: Sources of Effective International Environmental Protection*, ed. Peter M. Haas, Marc A. Levy, and Robert O. Keohane, 3–26. Cambridge, MA: MIT Press.

Keohane, Robert O., and Lisa L. Martin. 2003. Institutional Theory as a Research Programme. In *Progress in International Relations Theory: Appraising the Field*, ed. Colin Elman and Miriam Fendius Elman, 71–107. Cambridge, MA: MIT Press.

Keohane, Robert O., and Joseph S. Nye, Jr. 1975. International Interdepence and Integration. In *Handbook of Political Science*. Vol. 8, ed. Fred I. Greenstein and Nelson W. Polsby, 363–401. Reading, MA: Addison-Wesley.

Keohane, Robert O., and Joseph S. Nye, Jr. 1977. *Power and Interdependence: World Politics in Transition*. Boston: Little, Brown.

Keohane, Robert O., and Joseph S. Nye, Jr. 1987. Power and Interdependence Revisited. *International Organization* 41 (4): 724–753.

King, Gary, Robert O. Keohane, and Sidney Verba. 1994. *Designing Social Inquiry: Scientific Inference in Qualitative Research*. Princeton, NJ: Princeton University Press.

King, Gary, Robert O. Keohane, and Sidney Verba. 1995. The Importance of Research Design in Political Science. *American Political Science Review* 89 (2): 475–481.

Kock, Karl-Hermann. 1992. *Antarctic Fish and Fisheries*. Cambridge: Cambridge University Press.

Kotov, Vladimir. 1994. Implementation and Effectiveness of International Environmental Regimes during the Process of Economic Transformation in Russia. Working Paper No. 123, International Institute for Applied Systems Analysis, Laxenburg.

Krasner, Stephen D. 1982. Structural Causes and Regime Consequences: Regimes as Intervening Variables. *International Organization* 36 (2): 185–206.

Krasner, Stephen D., ed. 1983. *International Regimes*. Ithaca, NY: Cornell University Press.

Kratochwil, Friedrich. 1993. Contract and Regimes: Do Issue Specificity and Variations of Formality Matter? In *Regime Theory and International Relations*, ed. Volker Rittberger, with Peter Mayer, 73–93. Oxford: Clarendon Press.

Kratochwil, Friedrich, and John G. Ruggie. 1986. International Organization: A State of the Art on an Art of the State. *International Organization* 40 (4): 753–775.

Leebron, David W. 2002. Linkages. *American Journal of International Law* 96 (1): 5–27.

Levy, Marc A. 1993. European Acid Rain: The Power of Tote-Board Diplomacy. In *Institutions for the Earth: Sources of Effective International Environmental Protection*, ed. Peter M. Haas, Marc A. Levy, and Robert O. Keohane, 75–132. Cambridge, MA: MIT Press.

Levy, Marc A., Robert O. Keohane, and Peter M. Haas. 1993. Improving the Effectiveness of International Environmental Institutions. In *Institutions for the Earth: Sources of Effective International Environmental Protection*, ed. Peter M. Haas, Marc A. Levy, and Robert O. Keohane, 397–426. Cambridge, MA: MIT Press.

Levy, Marc A., Gail Osherenko, and Oran R. Young. 1991. The Effectiveness of International Regimes: A Design for Large-Scale Collaborative Research. Hanover, NH: Dartmouth College, Hanover, NH. Mimeo.

Levy, Marc A., Oran R. Young, and Michael Zürn. 1995. The Study of International Regimes. *European Journal of International Relations* 1 (3): 267–330.

Lewis-Beck. Michael S. 1980. *Applied Regression: An Introduction.* Beverly Hills, CA: Sage.

Lindberg, Leon N. 1970. Political Integration as a Multidimensional Phenomenon Requiring Multivariate Measurement. *International Organization* 24 (4): 649–731.

Lipset, Seymour Martin. 1983. *Political Man: The Social Basis of Politics.* London: Heinemann.

Litfin, Karen. 1994. *Ozone Discourses: Science and Politics in Global Environmental Cooperation.* New York: Columbia University Press.

Little, Daniel. 1995. Causal Explanation in the Social Sciences. *Southern Journal of Philosophy* 34 (S1): 31–56.

Loreti, Christopher P., Scot A. Foster, and Jane E. Obbagy. 2001. *An Overview of Greenhouse Gas Emissions Verification Issues.* Arlington, VA: Pew Center on Global Climate Change.

Marks, Gary, Liesbet Hooghe, and Kermit Blank. 1996. European Integration from the 1980s: State Centric vs. Multi-level Governance. *Journal of Common Market Studies* 34 (3): 341–378.

Matishov, G., N. Golubeva, G. Titova, A. Sydnes, and B. Voegele. 2004. Barents Sea: Global International Water Assessments (GIWA) Regional Assessment 11 (UNEP). University of Kalmar, Kalmar, Sweden.

Mayhew, Susan. 2010. *A Dictionary of Geography.* Oxford: Oxford University Press.

McDonald, Helen, Solveig Glomsrød, and Ilmo Mäenpää. 2006. Arctic Economy within the Arctic Nations. In *The Economy of the North*, ed. Solveig Glomsrød and Iulie Aslaksen, 41–64. Oslo: Statistics Norway.

Mearsheimer, John J. 1995. The False Promise of International Institutions. *International Security* 19 (3): 5–49.

Miles, Edward L. 2002a. Sea Dumping of Low-Level Radioactive Waste, 1964 to 1982. In *Environmental Regime Effectiveness: Confronting Theory with Evidence,* Edward L. Miles, Arild Underdal, Steinar Andresen, Jørgen Wettestad, Jon Birger Skjærseth, and Elaine M. Carlin, 87–116. Cambridge, MA: MIT Press.

Miles, Edward L. 2002b. The Management of Tuna Fisheries in the West Central and Southwest Pacific. In *Environmental Regime Effectiveness: Confronting Theory with Evidence,* Edward L. Miles, Arild Underdal, Steinar Andresen, Jørgen Wettestad, Jon Birger Skjærseth, and Elaine M. Carlin, 117–148. Cambridge, MA: MIT Press.

Miles, Edward L., Arild Underdal, Steinar Andresen, Jørgen Wettestad, Jon Birger Skjærseth, and Elaine M. Carlin. 2002. *Environmental Regime Effectiveness: Confronting Theory with Evidence.* Cambridge, MA: MIT Press.

Miles, Matthew B., and A. Michael Huberman. 1994. *Qualitative Data Analysis: An Expanded Source-Book*. Thousand Oaks, CA: Sage.

Mill, John Stuart. (1853) 1904. *A System of Logic: Ratiocinative and Inductive. Being a Connected View of the Principles of Evidence and the Methods of Scientific Investigation*. London: Longmans.

Mitchell, Ronald B. 1994. *Intentional Oil Pollution at Sea: Environmental Policy and Treaty Compliance*. Cambridge, MA: MIT Press.

Mitchell, Ronald B. 1998. Sources of Transparency: Information Systems in International Regimes. *International Studies Quarterly* 42 (1): 109–130.

Mitchell, Ronald B. 2002. A Quantitative Approach to Evaluating International Environmental Regimes. *Global Environmental Politics* 2 (4): 58–83.

Mitchell, Ronald B. 2008. Evaluating the Performance of Environmental Institutions: What to Evaluate and How to Evaluate It? In *Institutions and Environmental Change: Principal Findings, Applications, and Research Frontiers*, ed. Oran R. Young, Leslie A. King, and Heike Schroeder, 79–114. Cambridge, MA: MIT Press.

Mitchell, Ronald B., William C. Clark, and David W. Cash. 2006. Information and Influence. In *Global Environmental Assessments: Information and Influence*, ed. Ronald B. Mitchell, William C. Clark, David W. Cash, and Nancy M. Dickson, 307–338. Cambridge, MA: MIT Press.

Mitchell, Ronald, Moira L. McConnell, Alexei Roginko, and Ann Barrett. 1999. International Vessel-Source Oil Pollution. In *The Effectiveness of International Environmental Regimes: Causal Connections and Behavioral Mechanisms*, ed. Oran R. Young, 33–90. Cambridge, MA: MIT Press.

Molenaar, E. J. 2007. Port State Jurisdiction: Towards Comprehensive, Mandatory and Global Coverage. *Ocean Development and International Law* 38 (1–2): 225–257.

Nakken, Odd. 1998. Past, Present and Future Exploration and Management of Marine Resources in the Barents Sea and Adjacent Areas. *Fisheries Research* 37 (1–3): 23–36.

Nikitina, Elena N., and Peter H. Pearse. 1992. Conservation of Marine Resources in the Former Soviet Union: An Environmental Perspective. *Ocean Development and International Law* 23 (4): 369–382.

Nilssen, Frode, and Geir Hønneland. 2001. Institutional Change and the Problems of Restructuring the Russian Fishing Industry. *Post-Communist Economies* 13 (3): 313–330.

North-East Atlantic Fisheries Commission. 2006. *Scheme of Control and Enforcement (adopted 2006, with subsequent amendments)*. London: North-East Atlantic Fisheries Commission.

Norway. 1925. Svalbard Act (Lov om Svalbard, 17 July 1925). Available at http://lovdata.no.

Norway. 1976. Act on the Economic Zone (Lov om Norges økonomiske sone, 17 December 1976). http://lovdata.no.

Norway. 1977. Regulations on a Fisheries Protection Zone at Svalbard (Forskrift om fiskevernsone ved Svalbard, 3 June 1977). http://lovdata.no (accessed 18 October 2011).

Norway, Directorate of Fisheries. 2008. *Statusrapport for 2008: Russisk uttak av nordøst-arktisk torsk og hyse.* Bergen: Directorate of Fisheries.

Norway, Ministry of Fisheries. 1982. Kvoteregulering av utenlandsk fiske i Norges økonomiske sone i 1982. *Notat*, August 1, 1982. Oslo Ministry of Fisheries.

Norway, Ministry of Fisheries. 1983. Kvoteregulering av utenlandsk fiske i Norges økonomiske sone i 1983. *Notat*, September 5, 1983. Oslo Ministry of Fisheries.

Norway, Ministry of Fisheries. 1984. Kvoteregulering av utenlandsk fiske i Norges økonomiske sone i 1984. *Notat*, August 1984. Oslo Ministry of Fisheries.

Norway, Ministry of Fisheries. 1985. Kvoteregulering av utenlandsk fiske i Norges økonomiske sone i 1985. *Notat*, March 15, 1985. Oslo Ministry of Fisheries.

Norway, Ministry of Fisheries. 1986. Kvoteregulering av utenlandsk fiske i Norges økonomiske sone i 1986. *Notat*, February 6, 1986. Oslo Ministry of Fisheries.

Norway, Ministry of Fisheries. 2002–2003. *St.meld. 20 (2002–03). Strukturtiltak i kystfiskeflåten.* Oslo: Ministry of Fisheries.

Norway, Ministry of Fisheries. 2003–2004. *St.meld. 45 (2003–04). Om dei fiskeriavtalene Noreg har inngått med andre land for 2004 og fisket etter avtalane i 2002 og 2003.* Oslo: Ministry of Fisheries.

Norway, Ministry of Fisheries. 2007–2008. *St.meld. 34 (2007–08). Om dei fiskeriavtalene Noreg har inngått med andre land for 2008 og fisket etter avtalane i 2006 og 2007.* Oslo: Ministry of Fisheries.

Norway, Ministry of Fisheries. 2008–2009. *St.meld. 45 (2008–09). Om dei fiskeriavtalene Noreg har inngått med andre land for 2009 og fisket etter avtalane i 2007 og 2008.* Oslo: Ministry of Fisheries.

Norway, Office of the Auditor General. 2007. *Riksrevisjonens undersøkelse av forvaltningen og kontrollen av fiskeressursene i Barentshavet og Norskehavet— en parallell revisjon mellom norsk or russisk riksrevisjon.* Dokument nr. 3-serien. Oslo: Office of the Auditor General.

Norwegian Coast Guard. *Årsrapport Kystvaktskvadron Nord 2002.* Sortland: Norwegian Coast Guard, Squadron North.

Norwegian Coast Guard. 2004. *Årsrapport Kystvaktskvadron Nord 2004.* Sortland: Norwegian Coast Guard, Squadron North.

Nye, Joseph S. 1970. Comparing Common Markets: A Revised Neo-Functionalist Model. *International Organization* 24 (4): 796–835.

Oberthür, Sebastian, and Thomas Gehring. 2006a. Conceptual Foundations of Institutional Interaction. In *Institutional Interaction in Global Environmental*

Governance: Synergy and Conflict among International and EU Policies, ed. Sebastian Oberthür and Thomas Gehring, 19–51. Cambridge, MA: MIT Press.

Oberthür, Sebastian, and Thomas Gehring, eds. 2006b. *Institutional Interaction in Global Environmental Governance: Synergy and Conflict among International and EU Policies*. Cambridge, MA: MIT Press.

Oberthür, Sebastian and Olav Schram Stokke, eds. 2011. *Managing Institutional Complexity: Regime Interplay and Global Environmental Change*. Cambridge MA: MIT Press.

Olson, Mancur. 1971. *The Logic of Collective Action: Public Goods and the Theory of Groups*. Cambridge, MA: Harvard University Press.

Orrego Vicuña, Francesco. 1989. The Effectiveness of the Decision-Making Machinery of CCAMLR: An Assessment. In *The Antarctic Treaty System in World Politics*, ed. Arnfinn Jørgensen-Dahl and Willy Østreng, 25–43. London: Macmillan.

Ostrom, Elinor. 1990. *Governing the Commons: The Evolution of Institutions for Collective Action*. Cambridge: Cambridge University Press.

Ostrom, Elinor, Joanna Burger, Christopher B. Field, Richard B. Norgaard, and David Policansky. 1999. Revisiting the Commons: Local Lessons, Global Challenges. *Science* 284 (5412): 278–282.

Oude Elferink, Alex G. 1994. *The Law of Maritime Boundary Delimitation: A Case Study of the Russian Federation*. Dordrecht: Martinus Nijhoff.

Parson, Edward A. 2003. *Protecting the Ozone Layer: Science, Strategy, and Negotiation in the Shaping of a Global Environmental Regime*. Oxford: Oxford University Press.

Pedersen, Torbjørn. 2008a. The Constrained Politics of the Svalbard Offshore Area. *Marine Policy* 32 (6): 913–919.

Pedersen, Torbjørn. 2008b. The Dynamics of Svalbard Diplomacy. *Diplomacy and Statecraft* 19 (2): 236–262.

Pennington, Michael, and Tore Strømme. 1998. Surveys as a Research Tool for Managing Dynamic Stocks. *Fisheries Research* 37 (1–3): 97–106.

Permanent Committee for Management and Enforcement of the Joint Commission on Fisheries. *See* Protocols from sessions of the JFC.

Peterson, M. J. 1993. International Fisheries Management. In *Institutions for the Earth*, ed. Peter M. Haas, Robert O. Keohane, and Marc A. Levy, 249–305. Cambridge, MA: MIT Press.

PINRO 1982. Memorandum av Vitenskapelig Polarinstitutt for Havfiskeri og oseanografi /PINRO/ om tilstand av den arktiske nord-östlige torskebestand og tiltak til fiskeregulering. Attached to Soviet Union, Note of 22 April 1982 from the Government of the Union of the Socialist Soviet Republics to the Government of the Kingdom of Norway. On file with author.

Potter, William C. 1980. Issue Area and Foreign Policy Analysis. *International Organization* 34 (3): 405–428.

Puchala, Donald J. 1970. International Transactions and Regional Integration. *International Organization* 24 (4): 732–763.

Ragin, Charles C. 1987. *The Comparative Method: Moving Beyond Qualitative and Quantitative Strategies.* Berkeley: University of California Press.

Ragin, Charles C. 1994. *Constructing Social Research: The Unity and Diversity of Method.* Thousands Oaks, CA: Pine Forge Press.

Ragin, Charles C. 2000. *Fuzzy-set Social Science.* Chicago: University of Chicago Press.

Ragin, Charles C. 2006. Set Relations in Social Research: Evaluating their Consistency and Coverage. *Political Analysis* 14 (3): 291–310.

Ragin, Charles C. 2008. *Redesigning Social Inquiry: Set Relations in Social Research.* Chicago.: University of Chicago Press.

Ragin, Charles, and John Sonnett. 2006. Between Complexity and Parsimony: Limited Diversity, Counterfactual Cases, and Comparative Analysis. In *Vergleichen in der Politikwissenschaft*, ed. Sabine Kropp and Michael Minkenberg, 180–197. Wiesbaden: VS Verlag für Sozialwissenschaften.

Rochester, J. Martin. 1986. The Rise and Fall of International Organizations as a Field of Study. *International Organization* 40 (4): 777–813.

Rosenau, James N. 1995. Governance in the Twenty-First Century. *Global Governance* 1:13–43.

Ruggie, John Gerard. 1975. International Responses to Technology: Concepts and Trends. *International Organization* 29 (3): 557–583.

Ruggie, John Gerard. 1992. Multilateralism: The Anatomy of an Institution. *International Organization* 46 (3): 561–598.

Russia. 2007. Rapport om resultatene av ekspertanalysen "Effektiviteten av utnyttelsen av kvoter på akvatiske biologiske ressurser tildelt for 2004–2005 til Den russiske føderasjon og Kongeriket Norge i samsvar med Den blandede russisk-norske fiskerikommisjonens bestemmelser." Published (in Norwegian) in Norway, Office of the Auditor General, 2007. Riksrevisjonens undersøkelse av forvaltningen og kontrollen av fiskeressursene i Barentshavet og Norskehavet— en parallell revisjon mellom norsk og russisk riksrevisjon, 203–238. Oslo: Office of the Auditor General, Doc. 3:2.

Russia. 2008. Governmental decree No. 136. 3 March 2008. *O pravitelstvennoy kommissii po voprosam razvitiya rybokhozyaystvennogo kompleksa* (On the government commission for questions concerning the development of the fisheries complex).

Sabine, George H., and Thomas L. Thorson. 1973. *A History of Political Theory.* Hinsdale, IL: Dryden Press.

Sagdahl, Bjørn. 1992. *Ressursforvaltning og legitimitetsproblemer: En studie av styringsproblemer ved forvaltning av norsk-arktisk torsk.* Report No. 15. Bodø: Nordlandsforskning.

Sand, Peter H. 1991. Lessons Learned in Global Environmental Governance. *Environmental Affairs Law Review* 18 (2): 213–277.

Sartori, Giovanni. 1991. Comparing and Miscomparing. *Journal of Theoretical Politics* 3 (3): 243–257.

Schelling, Thomas C. 1960. *The Strategy of Conflict.* Cambridge, MA: Harvard University Press.

Schoenbaum, Thomas J. 1997. International Trade and Protection of the Environment: The Continuing Search for Reconciliation. *American Journal of International Law* 91 (2): 268–313.

Schwach, Vera. 2000. *Havet, fisken, og vitenskapen: Fra fiskeriundersøkelser til Havforskningsinstitutt.* Bergen: Institute of Marine Research.

Sebenius, James K. 1992. Challenging Conventional Explanations of International Cooperation: Negotiation Analysis and the Case of Epistemic Communities. *International Organization* 46 (1): 323–365.

Sen, Sevaly. 1997. The Evolution of High-Seas Fisheries Management in the North-East Atlantic. *Ocean and Coastal Management* 35 (2): 85–100.

Serebryakov, Valery, and Per Solemdal. 1993. Russland og Norge i samarbeid om utforskningen av nordområdene. *Fiskets Gang* 79:39–44.

Skjærseth, Jon Birger. 2002. Towards the End of Dumping in the North Sea: The Case of the Oslo Commission. In *Environmental Regime Effectiveness: Confronting Theory with Evidence,* Edward L. Miles, Arild Underdal, Steinar Andresen, Jørgen Wettestad, Jon Birger Skjærseth, and Elaine M. Carlin, 65–85. Cambridge, MA: MIT Press.

Skjærseth, Jon Birger, Olav Schram Stokke, and Jørgen Wettestad. 2006. Soft Law, Hard Law, and Effective Implementation of International Environmental Norms. *Global Environmental Politics* 6 (3): 104–120.

Smith, Roger K. 1987. Explaining the Non-Proliferation Regime: Anomalies for Contemporary International Relations Theory. *International Organization* 41 (2): 253–281.

Snidal, Duncan. 1985. The Limits of Hegemonic Stability Theory. *International Organization* 39 (4): 579–614.

Spero, Joan Edelman. 1990. *The Politics of International Economic Relations.* London: Unwin Hyman.

Sprinz, Detlef F., and Carsten Helm. 1999. The Effect of Global Environmental Regimes: A Measurement Concept. *International Political Science Review* 20 (4): 359–369.

Statistics Norway. 2008. *Statistical Yearbook of Norway 2008.* Oslo: Statistics Norway.

Stinchcombe, Arthur. 1991. The Conditions of Fruitfulness of Theorizing about Mechanisms in Social Science. *Philosophy of the Social Sciences* 21 (3): 367–388.

Stokke, Olav Schram. 1990. The Northern Environment: Is Cooperation Coming? *Annals of the American Academy of Political and Social Science* 512 (1): 58–69.

Stokke, Olav Schram. 1992. Towards a Regional Fisheries Industry? *International Challenges* 12 (4): 81–86.

Stokke, Olav Schram. 1996. The Effectiveness of CCAMLR. In *Governing the Antarctic: The Effectiveness and Legitimacy of the Antarctic Treaty System*, ed. Olav Schram Stokke and Davor Vidas, 120–151. Cambridge: Cambridge University Press.

Stokke, Olav Schram. 1997. Regimes as Governance Systems. In *Global Governance: Drawing Insights from the Environmental Experience*, ed. Oran R. Young, 27–63. Cambridge, MA: MIT Press.

Stokke, Olav Schram. 1998. Nuclear Dumping in Arctic Seas: Russian Implementation of the London Convention. In *The Implementation and Effectiveness of International Environmental Commitments: Theory and Practice*, ed. David G. Victor, Kal Raustiala, and Eugene B. Skolnikoff, 475–517. Cambridge, MA: MIT Press.

Stokke, Olav Schram. 2000. Managing Straddling Stocks: The Interplay of Global and Regional Regimes. *Ocean and Coastal Management* 43 (2–3): 205–234.

Stokke, Olav Schram, ed. 2001a. *Governing High Seas Fisheries: The Interplay of Global and Regional Regimes*. Oxford: Oxford University Press.

Stokke, Olav Schram. 2001b. *The Interplay of International Regimes: Putting Effectiveness Theory to Work*. FNI Report 10/2001. Lysaker: Fridtjof Nansen Institute.

Stokke, Olav Schram. 2001c. Introduction. In *Governing High Seas Fisheries: The Interplay of Global and Regional Regimes*, ed. Olav Schram Stokke, 1–19. Oxford: Oxford University Press.

Stokke, Olav Schram. 2001d. Managing Fisheries in the Barents Sea Loophole: Interplay with the UN Fish Stocks Agreement. *Ocean Development and International Law* 32 (3): 241–262.

Stokke, Olav Schram. 2004a. Boolean Analysis, Mechanisms, and the Study of Regime Effectiveness. In *Regime Consequences: Methodological Challenges and Research Strategies*, ed. Arild Underdal and Oran R. Young, 87–119. Dordrecht: Kluwer Academic.

Stokke, Olav Schram. 2004b. Trade Measures and Climate Compliance: Institutional Interplay between WTO and the Marrakesh Accords. *International Environmental Agreement: Politics, Law and Economics* 4 (4): 339–357.

Stokke, Olav Schram. 2007a. Examining the Consequences of Arctic Institutions. In *International Cooperation and Arctic Governance: Regime Effectiveness and Northern Region Building*, ed. Olav Schram Stokke and Geir Hønneland, 12–26. London: Routledge.

Stokke, Olav Schram. 2007b. A Legal Regime for the Arctic? Interplay with the Law of the Sea Convention. *Marine Policy* 31 (4): 402–408.

Stokke, Olav Schram. 2007c. Qualitative Comparative Analysis, Shaming, and International Regime Effectiveness. *Journal of Business Research* 60 (5): 501–511.

Stokke, Olav Schram. 2009. Trade Measures and the Combat of IUU Fishing: Institutional Interplay and Effective Governance in the Northeast Atlantic. *Marine Policy* 33 (2): 339–349.

Stokke, Olav Schram. 2010. Barents Sea Fisheries: The IUU Struggle. *Arctic Review of Law and Politics* 2 (2): 207–224.

Stokke, Olav Schram, Lee G. Anderson, and Natalia Mirovitskaya. 1999. The Barents Sea Fisheries. In *The Effectiveness of International Environmental Regimes: Causal Connections and Behavioral Mechanisms*, ed. Oran R. Young, 91–154. Cambridge, MA: MIT Press.

Stokke, Olav Schram, and Clare Coffey. 2004. Precaution, ICES and the Common Fisheries Policy: A Study of Regime Interplay. *Marine Policy* 28 (2): 117–126.

Stokke, Olav Schram, and Alf Håkon Hoel. 1991. Splitting the Gains: Political Economy of the Barents Sea Fisheries. *Cooperation and Conflict* 26 (2): 49–65.

Stokke, Olav Schram, and Geir Hønneland, eds. 2007. *International Cooperation and Arctic Governance: Regime Effectiveness and Northern Region Building*. London: Routledge.

Stokke, Olav Schram, Jon Hovi, and Geir Ulfstein, eds. 2005. *Implementing the Climate Regime: International Compliance*. London: Earthscan.

Stokke, Olav Schram, and Øystein B. Thommessen, eds. 2003. *Yearbook of International Co-operation on Environment and Development 2003/2004*. London: Earthscan.

Stokke, Olav Schram, and Ola Tunander, eds. 1994. *The Barents Region: Cooperation in Arctic Europe*. London: Sage.

Stokke, Olav Schram, and Davor Vidas. 1996a. The Effectiveness and Legitimacy of International Regimes. In *Governing the Antarctic: The Effectiveness and Legitimacy of the Antarctic Treaty System*, ed. Olav Schram Stokke and Davor Vidas, 13–31. Cambridge: Cambridge University Press.

Stokke, Olav Schram, and Davor Vidas. 1996b. Conclusions. In *Governing the Antarctic: The Effectiveness and Legitimacy of the Antarctic Treaty System*, ed. Olav Schram Stokke and Davor Vidas, 432–456. Cambridge: Cambridge University Press.

Stokke, Olav Schram, and Davor Vidas, eds. 1996c. *Governing the Antarctic: The Effectiveness and Legitimacy of the Antarctic Treaty System*. Cambridge: Cambridge University Press.

Stortinget. 1977–1978. *Innst. S. 190 (1977–1978)*. Standing Committee on Foreign Affairs and the Constitution. Oslo: Storting.

Stortinget. 1978. *St.f.* (Deliberations in the Storting). March 9, 1978. *Stortingstidende* 1978: 2179–2220. Oslo: Storting.

Stortinget. 1981. *St.f.* (Deliberations in the Storting). April 4, 1981. *Stortingstidende* 1981: 3016–3018. Oslo: Storting.

Strange, Susan. 1982. Cave! hic dragones: A Critique of Regime Analysis. *International Organization* 36 (2): 479–497.

Tamnes, Rolf. 1997. *Norsk utenrikspolitkks historie: Oljealder 1965–1995*. Oslo: Universitetsforlaget.

Tan, Alan Khee-Jin. 2006. *Vessel-Source Marine Pollution: The Law and Politics of International Regulation*. Cambridge: Cambridge University Press.

Tetlock, Philip E., and Aaron Belkin. 1996a. Counterfactual Thought Experiments in World Politics: Logical, Methodological, and Psychological Perspectives. In

Counterfactual Thought Experiments in World Politics: Logical, Methodological, and Psychological Perspectives, ed. Philip E.

Tetlock and Aaron Belkin, 1–38. Princeton, NJ: Princeton University Press.

Tetlock, Philip E., and Aaron Belkin. 1996b. *Counterfactual Thought Experiments in World Politics: Logical, Methodological, and Psychological Perspectives.* Princeton, NJ: Princeton University Press.

Thór, Jón Th. 1995. *British Trawlers and Iceland 1919–1976.* Publications of the Department of Economic History of the University of Gothenburg No. 69. Gothenburg: University of Gothenburg.

Thürer, Daniel. 2000. Soft Law. In *Encyclopedia of Public International Law 4*, ed. Rudolf Bernhardt, 452–460. Amsterdam: Elsevier.

Tjelmeland, S., and B. Bogstad. 1998. MULTSPEC: A Review of a Multispecies Modelling Project for the Barents Sea. *Fisheries Research* 37 (1–3): 127–142.

Ulfstein, Geir. 1995. *The Svalbard Treaty: From Terra Nullius to Norwegian Sovereignty.* Oslo: Scandinavian University Press.

Ulvatn, Sigbjørn, Tor Glistrup, Asgeir Aglen, and Bjarte Bogstad. 2006. Overfiske i Barentshavet. In *Havets ressurser og miljø*, 169–173. Bergen: Institute of Marine Research.

Underdal, Arild. 1980. *The Politics of International Fisheries Management: The Case of the Northeast Atlantic.* Oslo: Universitetsforlaget.

Underdal, Arild. 1987. International Cooperation: Transforming "Needs" into "Deeds.". *Journal of Peace Research* 24 (2): 167–183.

Underdal, Arild. 1989. The Politics of Science in International Resource Management: A Summary. In *International Resource Management: The Role of Science and Politics*, ed. Steinar Andresen and Willy Østreng, 253–268. London: Belhaven Press.

Underdal, Arild. 1992. The Concept of Regime "Effectiveness." *Cooperation and Conflict* 27 (3): 227–240.

Underdal, Arild. 2000a. Science and Politics: The Anatomy of an Uneasy Partnership. In *Science and Politics in International Environmental Regimes: Between Integrity and Involvement*, ed. Steinar Andresen, Tora Skodvin, Arild Underdal, and Jørgen Wettestad, 1–21. Manchester: Manchester University Press.

Underdal, Arild. 2000b. Comparative Conclusions. In *Science and Politics in International Environmental Regimes: Between Integrity and Involvement*, ed. Steinar Andresen, Tora Skodvin, Arild Underdal, and Jørgen Wettestad, 181–201. Manchester: Manchester University Press.

Underdal, Arild. 2002a. One Question, Two Answers. In *Environmental Regime Effectiveness: Confronting Theory with Evidence*, ed. Edward L. Miles, Arild Underdal, Steinar Andresen, Jørgen Wettestad, Jon Birger Skjærseth, and Elaine M. Carlin, 3–45. Cambridge, MA: MIT Press.

Underdal, Arild. 2002b. Methods of Analysis. In *Environmental Regime Effectiveness: Confronting Theory with Evidence*, ed. Edward L. Miles, Arild Underdal, Steinar Andresen, Jørgen Wettestad, Jon Birger Skjærseth, and Elaine M. Carlin, 47–59. Cambridge, MA: MIT Press.

Underdal, Arild. 2002c. Conclusions: Patterns of Regime Effectiveness. In *Environmental Regime Effectiveness: Confronting Theory with Evidence*, ed. Edward L. Miles, Arild Underdal, Steinar Andresen, Jørgen Wettestad, Jon Birger Skjærseth, and Elaine M. Carlin, 433–465. Cambridge, MA: MIT Press.

Underdal, Arild. 2004. Methodological Challenges in the Study of Regime Effectiveness. In *Regime Consequences: Methodological Challenges and Research Strategies*, ed. Arild Underdal and Oran R. Young, 27–48. Dordrecht: Kluwer Academic.

Underdal, Arild. 2008. Determining the Causal Significance of Institutions: Accomplishments and Challenges. In *Institutions and Environmental Change: Principal Findings, Applications, and Research Frontiers*, ed. Oran R. Young, Leslie A. King, and Heike Schroeder, 49–78. Cambridge, MA: MIT Press.

Underdal, Arild, and Oran R. Young, eds. 2004. *Regime Consequences: Methodological Challenges and Research Strategies*. Dordrecht: Kluwer Academic.

U.S. Congress. 1871. *Act of February 9, 1871, Sess. III, Res. 22, 16 Stat. 593–94. Joint Resolution for the Protection and Preservation of the Food Fishes of the Coast of the United States.*

Victor, David G., Kal Raustiala, and Eugene B. Skolnikoff. 1998a. Introduction and Overview. In *The Implementation and Effectiveness of International Environmental Commitments: Theory and Practice*, ed. David G. Victor, Kal Raustiala, and Eugene B. Skolnikoff, 1–46. Cambridge, MA: MIT Press.

Victor, David G., Kal Raustiala, and Eugene B. Skolnikoff, eds. 1998b. *The Implementation and Effectiveness of International Environmental Commitments: Theory and Practice*. Cambridge, MA: MIT Press.

Walford, Lionel A. 1958. *The Living Resources of the Sea: Opportunities for Research and Expansion*. New York: Ronald Press.

Walsh, Virginia M. 2004. *Global Institutions and Social Knowledge*. Cambridge, MA: MIT Press.

Waltz, Kenneth N. 1979. *Theory of International Relations*. Reading, MA: Addison-Wesley.

Warbrick, Colin, Dominic McGoldrick, and David H. Anderson. 1996. The Straddling Stocks Agreement of 1995: An Initial Assessment. *International and Comparative Law Quarterly* 45 (2): 463–475.

Weale, Albert. 1992. Implementation Failure: A Suitable Case for Review? In *Achieving Environmental Goals. The Concept and Practice of Environmental Performance Review*, ed. E. Lykke, 43–66. London: Belhaven Press.

Weber, Steven. 1996. Counterfactuals, Past and Future. In *Counterfactual Thought Experiments in World Politics: Logical, Methodological, and Psychological Perspectives*, ed. Philip E. Tetlock and Aaron Belkin, 268–288. Princeton, NJ: Princeton University Press.

Wettestad, Jørgen. 2002a. *Clearing the Air: European Advances in Tackling Acid Rain and Atmospheric Pollution*. Aldershot: Ashgate.

Wettestad, Jørgen. 2002b. The Vienna Convention and Montreal Protocol on Ozone-Layer Depletion. In *Environmental Regime Effectiveness: Confronting Theory with Evidence*, Edward L. Miles, Arild Underdal, Steinar Andresen,

Jørgen Wettestad, Jon Birger Skjærseth, and Elaine M. Carlin, 149–170. Cambridge, MA: MIT Press.

Wettestad, Jørgen. 2005. Enhancing Climate Compliance: What are the Lessons to Learn from Environmental Regimes and the EU? In *Implementing the Climate Regime: International Compliance*, ed. O. S. Stokke, J. Hovi, and G. Ulfstein, 209–232. London: Earthscan.

Wolfke, Karol. 1993. *Custom in Present International Law*. Dordrecht: Martinus Nijhoff.

Yin, Robert K. 2003. *Case Study Research. Design and Methods*. London: Sage.

Young, Oran R. 1980. International Regimes: Problems of Concept Formation. *World Politics* 32 (3): 331–356.

Young, Oran R. 1982. Regime Dynamics: The Rise and Fall of International Regimes. *International Organization* 36 (2): 277–297.

Young, Oran R. 1986. International Regimes: Toward a New Theory of Institutions. *World Politics* 39 (1): 104–122.

Young, Oran R. 1989. *International Cooperation: Building Regimes for Natural Resources and the Environment*. Ithaca, NY: Cornell University Press.

Young, Oran R. 1991. *Report on the "Regime Summit" held at Dartmouth College*. Hanover, NH: Institute of Arctic Studies.

Young, Oran R. 1992. The Effectiveness of International Institutions: Hard Cases and Critical Variables. In *Governance without Government: Order and Change in World Politics*, ed. James N. Rosenau and Ernst-Otto Czempiel, 160–194. Cambridge: Cambridge University Press.

Young, Oran R. 1994. *International Governance: Protecting the Environment in a Stateless Society*. Ithaca, NY: Cornell University Press.

Young, Oran R. 1996. Institutional Linkages in International Society: Polar Perspectives. *Global Governance* 2 (1): 1–24.

Young, Oran R. 1999a. Regime Effectiveness: Taking Stock. In *The Effectiveness of International Regimes: Causal Connections and Behavioral Mechanisms*, ed. Oran R. Young, 249–279. Cambridge, MA: MIT Press.

Young, Oran R., ed. 1999b. *The Effectiveness of International Environmental Regimes: Causal Connections and Behavioral Mechanisms*. Cambridge, MA: MIT Press.

Young, Oran R. 2001. Inferences and Indices: Evaluating the Effectiveness of International Environmental Regimes. *Global Environmental Politics* 1 (1): 99–121.

Young, Oran R. 2002. *The Institutional Dimensions of Environmental Change: Fit, Interplay, and Scale*. Cambridge, MA: MIT Press.

Young, Oran R. 2003. Determining Regime Effectiveness: A Commentary on the Oslo-Potsdam Solution. *Global Environmental Politics* 3 (3): 97–104.

Young, Oran R. 2008. Introduction. In *Institutions and Environmental Change: Principal Findings, Applications, and Research Frontiers*, ed. Oran R. Young, Leslie A. King, and Heike Schroeder, 1–45. Cambridge, MA: MIT Press.

Young, Oran R., W. Bradnee Chambers, Joy A. Kim, and Claudia ten Have, eds., 2008. *Institutional Interplay: The Case of Biosafety and Trade.* Tokyo: United Nations University.

Young, Oran R., and Marc A. Levy (with Gail Osherenko). 1999. The Effectiveness of International Environmental Regimes. In *The Effectiveness of International Environmental Regimes: Causal Connections and Behavioral Mechanisms,* ed. Oran R. Young, 1–32. Cambridge, MA: MIT Press.

Young, Oran R., Leslie A. King, and Heike Schroeder, eds. 2008. *Institutions and Environmental Change: Principal Findings, Applications, and Research Frontiers,* 277–301. Cambridge, MA: MIT Press.

International Treaties

General Note on Availability: Treaties published in the *United Nations Treaty Series* are available at http://treaties.un.org; treaties to which Norway is a party are published in the series *Overenskomster med fremmede makter*, published by the Norwegian Ministry of Foreign Affairs, and are in most cases available at http://lovdata.no/traktater/index.html.

Convention on Long-Range Transported Air Pollution. Geneva, November 13, 1979; entry into force March 6, 1983. *United Nations Treaty Series* 1302: 217.

Convention on the Continental Shelf. Geneva, April 29, 1958; entry into force June 10, 1964. *United Nations Treaty Series* 499: 311.

Convention on the High Seas. Geneva, April 29, 1958; entry into force September 30, 1962. *United Nations Treaty Series* 450: 11.

European Economic Area Agreement (Agreement on the European Economic Area). Oporto, May 2, 1992; entry into force January 1, 1994. *Overenskomster med fremmede makter* 1994: 2. Oslo: Ministry of Foreign Affairs.

FAO Agreement on Port State Measures. Rome, November 22, 2009; not in force. http://fao.org.

Fish Stocks Agreement (Agreement for the Implementation of the Provisions of the United Nations Convention on the Law of the Sea of 10 December 1982 relating to the Conservation and Management of Straddling Fish Stocks and Highly Migratory Fish Stock). *United Nations Treaty Series* 2167: 3.

Framework Agreement (Avtale mellom Norge og Sovjetunionen om samarbeid innen fiskerinæringen). Moscow, April 11, 1975; entry into force the same day. *Overenskomster med fremmede makter* 1975: 546. Oslo: Ministry of Foreign Affairs. English translation: Norway and Union of Soviet Socialist Republics Agreement on Co-Operation in the Fishing Industry. *United Nations Treaty Series* 983: 8.

Framework Convention on Climate Change (United Nations Framework Convention on Climate Change). New York, May 9, 1992; entry into force March 21, 1994. *United Nations Treaty Series* 1771: 107.

Grey Zone Agreement (Avtale mellom Norge og Sovjetunionen om en midlertidig praktisk ordning for fisket i et tilstøtende område i Barentshavet). Oslo, January

11, 1978; provisional entry into force the same day; entry into force April 27, 1978. *Overenskomster med fremmede makter* 1978: 436.

High Seas Living Resources Convention (Convention on Fishing and Conservation of the Living Resources of the High Seas). Geneva, April 29, 1958; entry into force March 20, 1966. *United Nations Treaty Series* 559: 285.

Kyoto Protocol (Kyoto Protocol to the United Nations Framework Convention on Climate Change). Kyoto, December 10, 1997; entry into force February 16, 2005. *United Nations, Treaty Series* 2303: 148.

Law of the Sea Convention (United Nations Convention on the Law of the Sea). Montego Bay, December 10, 1982; entry into force November 16, 1994. *United Nations Treaty Series* 1833: 3.

Loophole Agreement (Agreement between the Government of Iceland, the Government of Norway and the Government of the Russian Federation concerning Certain Aspects of Co-operation in the Area of Fisheries). St. Petersburg, May 15, 1999; entry into force the same day. *Overenskomster med fremmede makter* 1999: 838.

Mutual Access Agreement. English translation: Union of Soviet Socialist Republics and Norway Agreement Concerning Mutual Relations in the Field of Fisheries. *United Nations Treaty Series* 1157: 147.

NEAFC Convention (Convention on Future Multilateral Co-operation in North-East Atlantic Fisheries). London, November 18, 1980; entry into force March 17, 1982. *United Nations Treaty Series* 1285: 129.

Norway-Greenland Agreement (Avtale mellom Norge og Grønland/Danmark om gjensidige fiskeriforbindelser). Copenhagen, June 9, 1992; entry into force March 4, 1994; provisionally implemented September 24, 1991 (prior to formal adoption) in accordance with Article 9. *Overenskomster med fremmede makter* (1994), 1500.

Norway-Russia Maritime Delimitation Agreement (Treaty between the Kingdom of Norway and the Russian Federation concerning Maritime Delimitation and Cooperation in the Barents Sea and the Arctic Ocean). Murmansk, September 15, 2010; not in force.

Svalbard Treaty (Treaty between Norway, the United States of America, Denmark, France, Italy, Japan, the Netherlands, Great Britain and Ireland and the British Overseas Dominions and Sweden concerning Spitsbergen). Paris, February 9, 1920, entry into force August 14, 1925. *Overenskomster med fremmede makter* (1925): 551.

Vienna Convention on the Law of Treaties. Vienna, August 22, 1969; entry into force January 27, 1980. *United Nations Treaty Series* 1155: 654.

Protocols from Sessions of the Joint Norwegian-Soviet Commission on Fisheries/Joint Norwegian-Russian Commission on Fisheries

General Note on Availability: Protocols from the Joint Commission sessions are on file with the author and available from the Norwegian Ministry of Fisheries and Coastal Affairs. Protocols from the 23rd through the 28th session are published in annexes to the annual *Report to the Storting/White Paper (St.meld.)* by the Ministry of Fisheries and Coastal Affairs concerning fisheries agreements with foreign states, respectively St.meld. 49 (1994–95), St.meld. 48 (1995–96), St.meld. 11 (1997–98), St.meld. 47 (1997–98), St.meld. 49 (1998–99), St.meld. 44 (1999–2000).

JCF. 1976a. Protokoll fra den 1. sesjon i Den blandede norsk-sovjetiske fiskerikommisjon.

JCF. 1976b. Protokoll fra den 2. sesjon i Den blandede norsk-sovjetiske fiskerikommisjon.

JCF. 1979. Protokoll fra den 8. sesjon i Den blandede norsk-sovjetiske fiskerikommisjon.

JCF. 1981. Protokoll fra den 10. sesjon i Den blandede norsk-sovjetiske fiskerikommisjon.

JCF. 1982. Protokoll fra den 11. sesjon i Den blandede norsk-sovjetiske fiskerikommisjon.

JCF. 1983. Protokoll fra den 12. sesjon i Den blandede norsk-sovjetiske fiskerikommisjon (annex 3 contains revised Rules of Procedure).

JCF. 1984. Protokoll fra den 13. sesjon i Den blandede norsk-sovjetiske fiskerikommisjon.

JCF. 1985. Protokoll fra den 14. sesjon i Den blandede norsk-sovjetiske fiskerikommisjon.

JCF. 1990. Protokoll fra den 19. sesjon i Den blandede norsk-sovjetiske fiskerikommisjon.

JCF. 1991. Protokoll fra den 20. sesjon i Den blandede norsk-sovjetiske fiskerikommisjon.

JCF. 1992. Protokoll fra den 21. sesjon i Den blandede norsk-russiske fiskerikommisjon.

JCF. 1993. Protokoll fra den 22. sesjon i Den blandede norsk-russiske fiskerikommisjon.

JCF. 1994. Protokoll fra den 23. sesjon i Den blandede norsk-russiske fiskerikommisjon.

JCF. 1995. Protokoll fra den 24. sesjon i Den blandede norsk-russiske fiskerikommisjon.

JCF. 1996. Protokoll fra den 25. sesjon i Den blandede norsk-russiske fiskerikommisjon.

JCF. 1997. Protokoll fra den 26. sesjon i Den blandede norsk-russiske fiskerikommisjon.

JCF. 1998. Protokoll fra den 27. sesjon i Den blandede norsk-russiske fiskerikommisjon.

JCF. 1999. Protokoll fra den 28. sesjon i Den blandede norsk-russiske fiskerikommisjon.

JCF. 2000. Protokoll fra den 29. sesjon i Den blandede norsk-russiske fiskerikommisjon.

JCF. 2001. Protokoll fra den 30. sesjon i Den blandede norsk-russiske fiskerikommisjon.

JCF. 2002. Protokoll fra den 31. sesjon i Den blandede norsk-russiske fiskerikommisjon

JCF. 2004. Protokoll fra den 33. sesjon i Den blandede norsk-russiske fiskerikommisjon.

JCF. 2005. Protokoll fra den 34. sesjon i Den blandede norsk-russiske fiskerikommisjon.

JCF. 2008. Protokoll fra den 37. sesjon i Den blandede norsk-russiske fiskerikommisjon.

JCF. 2009. Protokoll fra den 38. sesjon i Den blandede norsk-russiske fiskerikommisjon.

PCME (Permanent Committee of Regulation and Control). 2000. Protokoll. Møte i Det permanente utvalg for forvaltnings- og kontrollspørsmål på fiskerisektoren, Henningsvær 16.–20. oktober 2000. Annex to JCF 2000.

PCME (Permanent Committee of Regulation and Control). 2001. Protokoll. Møte i Det permanente utvalg for forvaltnings- og kontrollspørsmål på fiskerisektoren, Murmansk 2.–8. oktober 2001. Annex to JCF 2001.

ICES Documents

General Note on Availability: ICES documents are published by the International Council for the Exploration of the Sea, Copenhagen. Many of them are available at http://ices.dk.

ICES. 1965. Herring Committee and Distant Northern Seas Committee. *Conference and Meeting Documents* 161.

ICES. 1979. Reports of the ICES Advisory Committee on Fisheries Management, 1978. *Cooperative Research Report* 85.

ICES. 1980. Reports of the ICES Advisory Committee on Fisheries Management, 1979. *Cooperative Research Report* 93.

ICES. 1981. Reports of the ICES Advisory Committee on Fisheries Management, 1980. *Cooperative Research Report* 102.

ICES. 1982. Reports of the ICES Advisory Committee on Fisheries Management, 1981. *Cooperative Research Report* 114.

ICES. 1983. Reports of the ICES Advisory Committee on Fisheries Management, 1982. *Cooperative Research Report* 119.

ICES. 1988. Reports of the ICES Advisory Committee on Fisheries Management, 1987. *Cooperative Research Report* 153.

ICES. 1989. Reports of the ICES Advisory Committee on Fisheries Management, 1988. *Cooperative Research Report* 161.

ICES. 1990a. Report of the Seventh Dialogue Meeting. *Cooperative Research Report* 171.

ICES. 1990b. Reports of the ICES Advisory Committee on Fisheries Management, 1989, Part 1. *Cooperative Research Report* 168.

ICES. 1993. Reports of the ICES Advisory Committee on Fisheries Management, 1992, Part 1. *Cooperative Research Report* 193.

ICES. 1994. Reports of the ICES Advisory Committee on Fisheries Management, 1993, Part 1. *Cooperative Research Report* 196.

ICES. 1996. Reports of the ICES Advisory Committee on Fisheries Management, 1995, Part 1. *Cooperative Research Report* 214.

ICES. 1997. Report of the ICES Advisory Committee on Fisheries Management, 1996, Part 1. *Cooperative Research Report* 221.

ICES. 1998. Report of the ICES Advisory Committee on Fisheries Management, 1997, Part 1. *Cooperative Research Report* 223.

ICES. 1999. Report of the ICES Advisory Committee on Fisheries Management, 1998, Part 1. *Cooperative Research Report* 229.

ICES. 2000. Report of the ICES Advisory Committee on Fisheries Management, 1999, Part 1. *Cooperative Research Report* 236.

ICES. 2001. Report of the ICES Advisory Committee on Fisheries Management, 2000, Part 1. *Cooperative Research Report* 242.

ICES. 2003. Report of the ICES Advisory Committee on Fisheries Management, 2003, Part 1. *Cooperative Research Report* 261.

ICES. 2004. Report of the ICES Advisory Committee on Fisheries Management and the ICES Advisory Committee on Ecosystems, 2004. *ICES Advice 2004*, Book 2, Part 1.

ICES. 2005. Report of the ICES Advisory Committee on Fisheries Management, Advisory Committee on the Marine Environment and Advisory Committee on Ecosystems, 2005. *ICES Advice 2005*, Book 3.

ICES. 2006a. Report of the ICES Advisory Committee on Fisheries Management, Advisory Committee on the Marine Environment and Advisory Committee on Ecosystems, 2006. *ICES Advice 2006*, Book 3.

ICES. 2006b. Arctic Fisheries Working Group Report 2006.

ICES. 2007. Report of the ICES Advisory Committee on Fisheries Management, Advisory Committee on the Marine Environment and Advisory Committee on Ecosystems, 2007. *ICES Advice 2007*, Book 3.

ICES. 2008a. Report of the ICES Advisory Committee on Fisheries Management, Advisory Committee on the Marine Environment and Advisory Committee on Ecosystems, 2006. *ICES Advice 2008*, Book 3.

ICES. 2008b. Arctic Fisheries Working Group Report 2008.

ICES. 2010. Arctic Fisheries Working Group Report 2010.

News Media

General Note on Availability: Archived articles from major Norwegian news media are available through http://retriever-info.com/no. In the list below, this concerns *Aftenposten*, *Nordlys*, and *NTBTekst*.

Aftenposten (daily newspaper), Oslo. http://aftenposten.no.

Fishing News International (monthly newspaper), London.

Fiskaren (biweekly newspaper), Bergen; now merged with *Fiskeribladet*. http://FiskeribladetFiskaren.no.

Fiskeribladet (bi-weekly newspaper), Harstad; now merged with *Fiskaren*. http://FiskeribladetFiskaren.no.

Nordlys (Tromsø daily newspaper). http://nordlys.no.

NTBTekst (Norwegian News Agency). http://ntb.no.

RIA Novosti (Moscow News Agency). http://rian.ru.

Index